Liberal Thought in Argentina, 1837–1940

Liberal Thought in

Argentina, 1837–1940

Edited and with an

Introduction by

NATALIO R. BOTANA

AND **EZEQUIEL GALLO**

Translated from the Spanish

by IAN BARNETT

LIBERTY FUND

Indianapolis

This book is published by Liberty Fund, Inc., a foundation established to encourage study of the ideal of a society of free and responsible individuals.

The cuneiform inscription that serves as our logo and as the design motif for our endpapers is the earliest-known written appearance of the word "freedom" (*amagi*), or "liberty." It is taken from a clay document written about 2300 B.C. in the Sumerian city-state of Lagash.

Translations, introduction, editorial additions, and index © 2013 by Liberty Fund, Inc.

Cover image: Detail from *Los Constituyentes de 1853,* by Antonio Alice in 1935 (5.50 × 3.60 m.). Photo by Luciano Gonzalez Perlender; reproduction authorized by Congreso de la Nación Argentina.

Library of Congress Cataloging-in-Publication Data
Liberal thought in Argentina, 1837–1940 / edited and with an introduction by Natalio R. Botana and Ezequiel Gallo; translated from the Spanish by Ian Barnett.
     pages   cm
     Includes bibliographical references and index.
     ISBN 978-0-86597-851-5 (hardcover: alk. paper)
     ISBN 978-0-86597-852-2 (pbk.: alk. paper)
     1. Liberalism—Argentina—History.   2. Republicanism—Argentina—History.
3. Political culture—Argentina.   4. Argentina—Politics and government—1817–1860.
5. Argentina—Politics and government—1860-1910.   6. Argentina—Politics and government—1910-1943.   I. Botana, Natalio R., editor of compilation.   II. Gallo, Ezequiel, editor of compilation.
  JC574.2.A7L53 2013
  320.510982′09034—dc23   2013009394

LIBERTY FUND, INC.
8335 Allison Pointe Trail, Suite 300
Indianapolis, Indiana 46250-1684

Contents

CHAPTER 4

Liberalism in Government and in Opposition (1880–1910) / 277

Introduction

Tulio Halperín Donghi wrote in "Liberalism in a Country Born Liberal" that liberal ideas have had undeniable importance in Argentina since its independence.[1] The origin of the liberal tradition is thus an integral part of the origin of the country, a trait common to the Spanish American nations that came into being during the turbulent period after the fall of the Spanish Empire in America.

By 1810, the writings of such figures representative of liberal thought in the River Plate as Manuel Belgrano, Juan Hipólito Vieytes, and Mariano Moreno already provided precedents. Once the independentist movement was under way, these writers were joined by the likes of Gregorio Funes, Bernardo de Monteagudo, Bernardino Rivadavia, and Valentín Gómez.

Two main features stand out in this set of ideas: first, the combination of classical liberalism in connection with agriculture, trade, and industry, on the one hand, and republicanism after the principle of monarchic legitimacy, on the other, waned in the space of a few years; second, repeated efforts between 1810 and 1830 to translate these ideas into a stable institutional framework and a constitution respected by the armed factions failed. The result was a political system of quasi-independent provinces that formed a primitive confederation without a representative congress that was dominated by the dictatorial regime of Juan Manuel de Rosas. In the province of Buenos Aires, Rosas reserved for himself the management of foreign affairs and tax control of Argentina's only overseas port.

Over this twenty-year period, the liberal opposition to Rosas — most

---

1. T. Halperín Donghi, "Argentina: Liberalism in a Country Born Liberal," in J. Love and N. Jacobsen, eds., *Guiding the Invisible Hand: Economic Liberalism and the State in Latin American History* (New York: Praeger, 1988). The Chronology at the end of this volume gives important dates.

of its proponents in exile—developed a political philosophy that culminated, between 1853 and 1860, in the approval of a constitution. That constitution, with a succession of reforms, has remained in effect to the present day. Liberal principles from U.S. and European traditions have played a key part in it.

The Constitution marks an important political and intellectual divide in Argentina, and for that reason we have decided to open this anthology of texts at that precise moment. This compilation presents texts, organized chronologically, in five chapters that reflect the stages of the rise, heyday, and decline of liberalism in Argentina.

I. LIBERALISM DURING THE DICTATORSHIP OF ROSAS (1837–1850)

In 1847, Juan Bautista Alberdi published *La República Argentina, 37 años después de su Revolución de Mayo* (The Argentine Republic 37 years after the May Revolution) in Chile.[2] In it, Alberdi developed a strategy for the institutional development of liberal thought in Argentina. This strategy may perhaps be summarized in James Madison's judgment in Federalist No. 51 (1788): "In framing a government which is to be administered by men over men, the great difficulty lies in this: you must first enable the government to control the governed; and in the next place oblige it to control itself."

Alberdi's analysis in this essay takes account of the fact that the revolution for independence in Argentina immediately turned into a civil war between two irreconcilable camps. Alberdi believed that neither freedom nor the civilization deriving from it could emerge from war. Consequently if the historical process gave rise to a de facto power—the dictatorship of Rosas—that could later be limited by a constitution.

In Alberdi's view, Rosas' power in those years was imposed in response to external aggression and domestic conflict. This perhaps utopian idea referred to the ancient philosopher's dream of the tyrant's passion being restrained by reason. Rosas the dictator emerges from this text as a figure representative of colonial tradition and a symbol of power obtained exclusively by force, while Alberdi presented himself as emblematic of the constitution and of individual liberties. Power with-

---

2. For a brief account of Alberdi's career and those of other thinkers and politicians featured in this volume, see Short Biographies at the end of this volume.

out a constitution was tyranny, while a constitution without power, as revealed by Alberdi's review of thirty-seven years of Argentine history, was synonymous with anarchy.

This approach reveals a connection between the intentions of the actors and their unforeseeable consequences that resembles many of the theoretical assumptions of the Scottish Enlightenment: for example, the fact that the idea of unity advocated by the centralist faction was imposed by Rosas' federal faction, which defended the opposing project of decentralization. Both parties had contributed to the outcome that power, without which political society and civil freedom are impossible, was to emerge from the war fully formed.

With these reflections Alberdi began to lay the foundation for an analysis both philosophical and historical which, according to the lessons provided by Montesquieu in *De l'esprit des lois* (1748), had to take into account the particular features of nations, their habits, and their customs.

Such a theoretical view had precedents in the writings of several of Alberdi's contemporaries, including his teacher, Esteban Echeverría, and Domingo Faustino Sarmiento. Echeverría was a romantic poet and political writer who assimilated the ideas that originated in France and Italy (not yet consolidated as a nation) in the 1830s and were presented, with the force of a creed, mainly through four authors: Giuseppe Mazzini, Alexis de Tocqueville, Félicité de Lamennais, and François Guizot.

In 1837, as Rosas began to tighten his iron grip on freedom of opinion, a literary salon was organized in Buenos Aires under the influence of the Mazzini-inspired organization Young Europe:[3] the Asociación de la Joven Generación Argentina (Association of the Young Argentine Generation). Echeverría authored its *Palabras simbólicas* (Symbolic words).

This text uses Tocqueville's idea expounded in the first part of *De la démocratie en Amérique* (1835) as a preamble to a disquisition on the concepts of association, progress, fraternity, equality, liberty, Christianity, and democracy. Echeverría adopted Tocqueville's principle that equality in the modern world is both providential and unavoidable. The function of liberty consists in limiting this force, which is in many respects blind

---

3. A political association founded by Giuseppe Mazzini (1805–1872) and other European exiles in Berne, Switzerland, with the object of unifying the republican movements (Young Germany, Young Italy, Young Poland). It operated only from 1834 to 1836.

and given to establishing new forms of despotism. In this sense, Eche-verría saw the Rosist system, built as it was on state-controlled universal male suffrage, as a Creole version of the Bonapartism in which the process begun by the French Revolution culminated.

Given this point of departure, the effort of "the new generation," as Echeverría called it, should be oriented toward the formation of a democratic regime based on an interpretation of the role of Christianity that flowed from Lamennais' thinking in *De la religion considerée dans ses rapports avec l'ordre politique et social* (1826). This way of conceiving liberal Catholicism in France distinguished the religious from the political sphere and guaranteed freedom of worship. Christianity was for Echeverría a force capable of inbuing civil society with the values of fraternity without the clericalism typical of the Hispanic world.

Acting together, liberty, equality, and fraternity should culminate in the establishment of a political regime founded on a limited concept of sovereignty, or "sovereignty of reason," according to the theory put forward by Guizot in several of his books, especially *Du gouvernement représentatif et de l'état actuel de la France* (1816). In accordance with the sovereignty of reason, democracy entailed the broadest individual and civil freedom, but political freedom was to be exercised only by the sensible, rational part of society. Democracy for Echeverría was not therefore synonymous with the absolute despotism of the masses and the majority. The most ignorant and indigent group of the population had to be prevented from exercising their right to vote. This principle of universal application of civil liberties with a restricted application of political liberties would endure in Argentina long after Echeverría.

Shortly after Echeverría published his *Palabras simbólicas,* Domingo Faustino Sarmiento began his work as a journalist and educator from his exile in Chile. In 1845, after publishing several texts on grammar and pedagogy, Sarmiento serialized the work that would make him famous in the pages of a newspaper. He entitled the work *Civilización y barbarie: Vida de Juan Facundo Quiroga* (Civilization and barbarism: The life of Juan Facundo Quiroga) and presented himself as an emulator of Tocqueville. Rather than being the biography of one of Argentina's more representative caudillos, however, *Civilización y barbarie* is a powerful and convincing sociological, cultural, and political re-creation of Argentina at the time.

The title of the work posits a dualist interpretation of society that, according to French eclectic philosophy as expounded among others by Victor Cousin (*Cours de l'histoire de la philosophie moderne,* 1829) and François Guizot (*Histoire générale de la civilisation en Europe,* 1828), must find its resolution in a transcendent synthesis. Civilization and barbarism are two opposite worlds—the Argentine cities and the hostile countryside surrounding them—that intertwine and, following the rhythm of revolution and war, create new realities. The appeal of this point of view lay not so much in Sarmiento's ability to transfer the romantic myth of barbarism to the Argentine plains, but in his revelation of the presence of caudillos contesting the established society of urban patricians. Revolution thus awakened a previously unknown history.

Sarmiento's account of the revolution breaks down into two stages. The first arises in the cities that inherit the colonial order; the second buries these attempts at civilization and sets rural society in motion. The men of the independence and the first legislators belong to the pioneering phase, and caudillos such as Quiroga to the second phase. Both will be destroyed by the urban tyranny that Rosas establishes in Buenos Aires.

Civilización y barbarie, having taken readers on a tour of Argentina's geography, customs, peoples, and social and political processes at its formative period, ends with a paradox: Rosas is indeed merely repeating the old story of despotism motivated by reciprocal terror. But this despotism, while practicing vice, unwittingly creates the opportunity to restore some virtue.

With the Rosas regime overthrown, Argentina will be ripe for a transforming liberal policy. Barbarous society can be transmuted into civil society through education, immigration, the distribution of agricultural property, and foreign capital investment: this was Sarmiento's program in *Civilización y barbarie.*

It was a program left incomplete, perhaps due to a lack of appropriate models. Also in 1845, Sarmiento embarked on a trip through Europe, Africa, and America commissioned by the Chilean government to study those countries' education systems and immigration policies. Sarmiento collected his observations, written in letter form, in two volumes that were published between 1849 and 1851 under the title *Viajes por Europa, África y América, 1845-1847* (Travels in Europe, Africa, and America, 1845-1847). The letters assemble his critical judgments on the politics and society of France, Spain, Italy, Switzerland, and Prussia. Sarmiento could not abide the battered legitimacy of regimes unable to find a positive solution to the conflict between tradition and modernity that opened up toward the end of the eighteenth century.

Although it was in many ways exemplary, Sarmiento criticized European culture for its inequality. He was unhappy with this spectacle until he arrived in the United States. Like Tocqueville before him (in the two volumes of *De la démocratie en Amérique,* published in 1835 and 1840), and alongside James Fenimore Cooper (*The American Democrat,* 1838) and George Bancroft (*History of the United States, from the Discovery of the American Continent,* 1838), the American experience opened Sarmiento's eyes to a possible future capable of combining liberty and equality with science and education.

In the United States he saw a society on the move, a representative republic whose popular base was getting broader, that reproduced, in spite of the blemish of slavery, the founding covenant of the New England Pilgrim fathers. These contractual forms were anchored in politics and society. They re-created a civic and private associationism; cleared virgin territories; built towns with churches, newspapers, and schools; and organized businesses that fueled a consumer society. Steamships, railroads, and a market network traversed the nation; advertisements transmitted images of products to the furthest territories in which the Native American populations had been brought to bay or annihilated; and this whole process was crowned by public schools that provided popular instruction.

In the United States, Sarmiento discovered a culture of pioneers and educators such as Horace Mann[4] in which the theoretical principles of knowledge were destroying the rigidity of an aristocratic society and distributing practical rationality, inventions, and technology. Above all, that "*disparate*" (folly), as he termed it, was propounding a convergence of the republic as a form of government and democracy as a form of society. Sarmiento introduced the liberal outlook of the United States to Argentina in opposition to the European liberal tradition, which—

---

4. Horace Mann (1796–1859), American education reformer, representative, and later senator for Massachusetts; on the creation of the Massachusetts Board of Education he was appointed secretary. He became a friend of Sarmiento on the latter's visit to the United States. His wife, Mary Peabody Mann, published a partial translation of Sarmiento's *Facundo.*

with certain exceptions—had predominated since the beginnings of Independence.

II. THE FRAMEWORK OF THE NATIONAL CONSTITUTION (1852–1860)

When Alberdi wrote *La República Argentina 37 años después de su Revolución de Mayo,* he did not foresee that five years later an uprising starting in Entre Ríos Province with the backing of the Brazilian Empire would topple Rosas once and for all. The insurrection, led by Justo José de Urquiza, was waged in the name of the constitution that the country needed after four decades of war and dictatorship.

Alberdi published two works between 1852 and 1855 that display a tension between two liberal visions of society: *Bases y puntos de partida para la organización política de la República Argentina* (Bases and starting points for the political organization of the Argentine Republic) and *Sistema económico y rentístico de la Confederación Argentina según su Constitución de 1853* (The economic and revenue system of the Argentine Confederation according to its Constitution of 1853). Against the backdrop of conflicts surrounding the Constituent Congress summoned by Urquiza, Alberdi formulated a theory in which the idea of a society based on immigration, railroads, and industry coexisted with the order born of the spontaneous exercise of individual freedom.

In these two works Alberdi struck up a dialogue between the liberal schools of thought arising out of the tradition of Saint-Simon in France (for example, Michel Chevalier in his *Lettres sur l'Amérique du Nord avec une carte des États-Unis d'Amérique,* 1836) and the classical liberalism of Adam Smith (*An Inquiry into the Nature and Causes of the Wealth of Nations,* 1776) followed up by Jean-Baptiste Say (*Cours complet d'économie politique,* 1828–1829). If, on the one hand, the protagonist of Alberdian society is the individual without obstacles or impediments, the exclusive subject of freedom, the other side of this abstract definition is the European immigrant who brings to Argentina in his knapsack the living matter of industrial civilization, the working practices, and the practical education grounded in his experience.

It is no simple task to accurately gauge the primacy of one view or the other. But reducing the nuances to a pattern, the *Bases* can be seen as a eulogy to mores as creators of liberty, and the *Sistema* as a eulogy to liberty as creator of mores. Along the lines of Montesquieu, Alberdi wanted to renew, in the far south of America, a special relationship between individual freedom and the customs that offer this human faculty firm ground on which to settle.

But the *Bases* and the *Sistema* were also written to enable Argentina to procure a republican constitution and an economic regime suited to its purposes. This principle of legitimacy was effectively the only way to achieve the ends of European civilization in America. The constitution brought together all that was permanent and necessary (the rule of law, rights and guarantees, the form of government) with an explicit program of civilization. The constitution thus stood for both authority and progress. Although it was addressed to the Republic's inhabitants, for whom the constitution guaranteed the exercise of freedom, *Bases* based these principles on the fertility of the new civilization of immigrants.

Thus conceived, the program aimed not just to transplant populations, but to establish the free action of labor, capital, and property in Argentina. In his *Sistema,* Alberdi adduced that the true reformer had nothing to do with a ruler determined on enacting particular laws, creating monopolies, or satisfying the interests of some inhabitants at the expense of others. He conceived of the constitution as a supreme law that, in order to promote liberty, repealed the mass of laws and regulations constituting past servitude. The reforms he proposed translated an ideal that found repugnant both the privileges of colonial mercantilism and the will of a government that becomes a banker or entrepreneur of industry and communication.

All this called for an overhaul of the federal treasury. Nationalizing the custom house, eliminating the provincial customs offices, became necessary conditions for the development of the state's revenue system. Given such an assumption, the main fiscal resource came from indirect taxation in the form of customs duties on imports, provided these taxes were legislated by a spartan government motivated by the prudent use of public credit.

In order to prosper and gain legitimacy, this ambitious plan had to be based on religious tolerance and a historic pact that, thanks to a mixed formula of government, would reconcile the warring centralist and federal factions. Alberdi was a steadfast defender of the Catholic religion in the liberal manner of Montesquieu and Tocqueville. He believed the dilemma was inevitable: either Argentina practiced intolerant Catholicism and remained a backward, sparsely populated territory, or it became a prosperous, religiously tolerant nation. Hence, religion was a springboard for the social order as an indirect means to political organization.

Alberdi believed that religious beliefs ought to curb the passions, coinciding, in this case, with the work ethic of the industrial order and with the education given by the example of a life more civilized than that prevailing in Argentina. This kind of spontaneous education, produced by transplanting the most advanced foreign populations, should not be confused with the kind of public instruction that the likes of Sarmiento advocated with an enthusiasm from which he never wavered during his long life. Alberdi accordingly adopted an idea of education through customs and good habits that had to fend off a misunderstood concept of popular instruction based on military hero worship.

Liberators such as José de San Martín and Simón Bolívar, rural caudillos, and warmongering presidents belonged, in Alberdi's mind, to a colonial legacy that spawned violence, charlatanism, and idleness. Tired of orators and rhetoricians, lawyers and theologians, Alberdi dreamed of a society regenerated by engineers, geologists, and naturalists trained in the applied sciences.

The keystone of Alberdi's new policy was the national Constitution, conceived, in his words, as the legal and historical expression of a "possible republic." This proposal was original because it took into account the historical background of the civil war between the centralist and federal factions, and at the same time recognized and valued the dominance of the executive power in Spanish American political culture.

On the first point, Alberdi advanced a theory of federalism different from the one that prevailed in the United States. In the latter experience, the states preceded the organization of the federal union at the Philadelphia Convention in 1787. In Argentina, on the other hand, colonial unity, which survived in the early years of independence, preceded disintegration in several provinces as an effect of the civil wars. For Alberdi, federalism was therefore a concession the legislator had to make when faced with the historical impossibility of establishing a centralist constitution, as several failed attempts demonstrated.

Faced with this reality, Alberdi proposed a transaction between the opposing forces of unity and federation that would extract the best from each and combine them in a mixed formula. Hence, it was necessary to take stock of the two forces' funds of power. The centralist tradition had its source in the colonial political order and had later gained prestige thanks to the collective sacrifice in the Wars of Independence, to the Argentine flag, to shared glories. The word *Argentina* derived from this tradition, seen as a symbol of a common sovereignty, as yet implicit but attractive nevertheless.

Diametrically opposed to what *federalism* meant in the United States, the federal tradition in Argentina was a result of the breakup of the old united territory; the interregnum of isolation; the diversity of the soil, climate, and production; the legacy of municipal governments that dated back to the cabildos; the exercise of power in the provinces during three decades of autonomy; and the enormous and costly distances in a space that lacked roads, canals, and transport. These traditions had engendered political and social habits that had to be merged in order to satisfy both provincial liberties and the prerogatives of the entire nation.

All things considered, this interpretation of federalism was favorable to the national government and to a centralization that — besides historical analyses of the country — had three main sources: the one responding to the federalist side of the U.S. Constitution, as illustrated by Alexander Hamilton in *The Federalist Papers* and Joseph Story in *Commentaries on the Constitution of the United States* (1833); the one deriving from other centralist interpretations of federalism such as those of the constitutionalist Pellegrino Rossi in his classes of constitutional law at the University of Paris (1835–1837); and, finally, the precedent of the Chilean constitution Alberdi experienced while in exile during the 1840s and early 1850s.

The constitutional stability of Chile as against the unstable authoritarianism he saw in Argentina, the distinction between civil liberties common to all inhabitants and political liberties restricted to a small core of citizens, inspired in Alberdi a strong conception of a republican presidential system with monarchic overtones embodied in the predominant figure of the national executive power and of the president holding that office. As Alberdi used to say, the executive must be given all possible power, but only under the rule of a constitution. This tension between liberal ideals about limited power and the risk of presidential hegemony entailed by the centralist traditions pervades these works by Alberdi.

The first part of the Constitution of the Argentine nation, approved by the General Constituent Congress on May 1, 1853, and amended in 1860 and 1866, reveals these tensions. Although he was not directly involved in this congress, the draft constitution Alberdi appended to the edition of the *Bases* and the role of his colleague and friend Juan María

Gutiérrez in the editorial committee for the final text of the Constitution both suggest Alberdi's decisive influence, though it was by no means the only one, especially after the amendment of 1860, which by its additions brought the text closer to the model of the U.S. Constitution.

In any case, a review of the articles making up the first part of the Constitution at the time allows us to specify its main features in greater detail, both in terms of the goals of progress it stipulates and of the institutional means at its disposal. For one thing, the preamble differs from that of the U.S. Constitution in its invocation to God and its offer of the constitutional guarantees "to all men of the world who wish to dwell on Argentine soil." This universal incitement to immigration is specified in Article 25, by which the federal government must promote European immigration, and Article 20, which bestows full civil rights on foreigners without them having to adopt citizenship or pay any extraordinary compulsory contributions.

These aims are guaranteed by a classical liberal repertoire of individual rights and by a representative government, mentioned specifically in Articles 14, 15, 16, 17, 18, 19, 22, 29, and 32. Nevertheless, two instruments to consolidate national power are explicitly legislated in Article 6, through which the federal government intervenes in the territory of the provinces to defend republican government and repel external invasions or seditious acts, and in Article 23, which gives the federal government the power to declare a state of siege in any portion of the territory affected by internal unrest or external attack. With this precaution the Constitution structurally incorporated the adoption of extraordinary measures that both Alberdi and Sarmiento had observed with approval in Chilean constitutional practices.

With these favorable omens Argentina entered a long period that might be described as the heyday of liberalism.

III. LIBERALISM IN A NEW NATION (1853–1880)

The 1853 Constitution opened a new phase in Argentina's institutional development. Some earlier problems persisted, however, the most serious being the confrontation between the Argentine Confederation and the state of Buenos Aires. This conflict came to an end in 1862, when the federal government began to establish its supremacy. Certain local conflicts continued in the following years, but the process of institutionalization now under way continued advancing with significant landmarks such as the 1860 constitutional reform; the creation of the Supreme Court of Justice of the nation; and the enacting of the Civil, Commercial, and Criminal codes. This was a time when ideas of liberal origin were highly influential. The contribution of President Bartolomé Mitre (1862–1868) in the formulation and dissemination of these ideas was considerable and significant. Even before taking office, Mitre had outlined a doctrine as governor of Buenos Aires Province that persisted throughout subsequent decades. In 1857, indeed, he proposed continuing a tariff policy protecting wheat cultivation in Buenos Aires while noting its provisional nature in an initial statement of commitment to the principles of free trade. Strictly speaking, this position resurfaced at the national level in 1876, after which time the protection of wheat was shelved as a result of the massive influx of Argentine wheat in international markets.

Other authors later repeated the thesis Mitre defended in 1857, which was none other than that postulated by the German historical school of "infant industry," whereby certain productive activities must be protected in their initial stages and only afterward allowed to compete freely. The protection's temporary nature was always stressed, and it was accompanied, as in Mitre's case, with a statement about the superiority of free trade. Carlos Pellegrini, one of the best-known defenders of the infant industry school, expressed this seemingly paradoxical situation in the Argentine Senate: "We want protection in order to arrive at free trade" (1899).

Mitre clearly stated his adherence to classical liberal principles in three later documents. In the first of these he gave an original analysis of Argentine development up to that time, pointing out that the country was the only one in Latin America that did not owe its wealth to either minerals or tropical produce. In his view, the Río de la Plata had made a meager living from the work of its inhabitants, hampered by the trade monopoly foisted on it by Spain. It was the abolition of this monopoly that encouraged the inhabitants' labor and was therefore the very basis of the region's material development. The work was thus a full-blown eulogy to the role of commercial exchange.

The second document, the "Discurso de Chivilcoy" (Chivilcoy speech), is as original as the first. In it, Mitre criticized politicians who set agriculture above livestock breeding and considered the latter a primitive activity. It was stock breeding, Mitre claimed, that had been responsible for populating Argentine territory and had at the same time laid the foundation for the subsequent development of agriculture. Mitre accordingly stressed the complementary nature of the two activities. He also strongly emphasized the creativity of countrymen and farmhands, which "teaches practical lessons to the wise and the powerful." On this point Mitre advanced an analysis on popular knowledge that has been in vogue in recent times (see, for example, Michael Polanyi, *Personal Knowledge: Toward a Post-Critical Philosophy,* 1958).

Mitre's third document deals with a subject that pervaded Argentine literature in subsequent decades, namely, the importance of immigration in the settlement and development of Argentine territory. Mitre rejected projects that sought to promote what he called "artificial immigration" and came out clearly in favor of a spontaneous free flow. Interestingly, in an age of belief in the superiority of immigration from Northern Europe, Mitre emphasized the contributions made in various fields by inhabitants of Italian extraction.

Liberal positions were sometimes accompanied by notions bound up with the construction of the new national state. This situation introduced a degree of conceptual tension to which Bartolomé Mitre's thinking was not immune. This was apparent in his article "Gobiernos Empresarios" (Governments as business managers) about the role of the state in certain activities. Basing his position on Chevalier's above-mentioned studies on the United States, Mitre supported state participation in certain activities such as the development of communications. Mitre's article was refuted in an article by José Hernández, author of the Argentine classic *Martín Fierro.* Hernández defended a rigid anti-state position, even in the development of communications, one of the exceptions ("roads") accepted by Adam Smith.

An influential text at the time was Nicolás Avellaneda's study of the 1865 public land laws. Avellaneda, later president of the Republic (1874–1880), was heavily influenced by what he interpreted as the experience of the United States in this area. For Avellaneda, any legislation had to clearly state the principle of private property in the distribution of public lands, and he therefore rejected the idea of leasing them. A reading of the text and the discussions of the day gives the impression that what Avellaneda rejected was the method of emphyteusis practiced since the days of Rivadavia in the early 1820s.[5] He viewed any system that did not directly grant private property as conspiring against attracting immigrants to populate the new lands.

Education, both primary and secondary, was a recurring concern throughout this period. Leandro N. Alem referred to this issue in his speech in the parliamentary discussion about the role of the state in the development of education. Alem expressed hostility to the central power's interference in education, which in his view should be in the hands "of the district, the township, the neighborhood, and even individual initiative." Alem cited the experience of the United States and stressed the success of the localized system there. It is interesting that in this and other cases of the period, the U.S. experience dominated political debates. Alem's address expresses a concern that would become a permanent feature of his thinking, namely, that interference by public authorities would negatively affect citizens' activity and creativity. He exhorted citizens to participate. "What will become of higher education if the central government is not responsible for it! . . . But, by God, I would and do say in turn, work a little, stir yourselves . . . rise up like important figures in order to exert the influence you are entitled to in the political movement of the country, without relying on external inspiration!"

Toward the end of this period, Domingo Faustino Sarmiento published an article in the bold and aggressive tones typical of his writings. In this work, Sarmiento rejected the idea of the social contract as developed by J. J. Rousseau (*Du contrat social ou principes du droit politique,* 1762) and Thomas Paine (*Rights of Man,* 1791). He illustrated the critique with a description of the disastrous effects this principle had had on the French Revolution: "The revolution, to render equality, fraternity, and freedom the universal law, led to the empire of a fortunate soldier, and the free people knew no other law than the military discipline of armies, nor any equality other than that of one man attaining the rank of marshal for every 100,000 who died in the battlefields." While Sarmiento did not quote Tocqueville (*L'Ancien Régime et la Révolution,* 1857) or Edmund Burke (*Reflections on the Revolution in France,* 1791), the influence of both thinkers, especially the latter, is clear.

---

5. Emphyteusis was a system through which the state granted private individuals who paid a levy the long-term exploitation of lands that had been the property of the Crown.

Sarmiento's analysis pointed to what he considered the right path to follow—the one taken in England, where a gradual evolutionary process that kept in mind earlier traditions had achieved far sounder institutional results than those achieved in France. Sarmiento's preferred model did not refer just to the British experience, but also took in and valued developments in the United States of America.

The concern reflected by Sarmiento's remarks on the social contract and the French and British experiences was of course meant for local ears: for those preparing for a war that threatened institutional stability in the name of the right to rebellion based on the existence of a "previous contract." In a way, the text can be read as a bid to consolidate Argentina's institutional development, which was in its infancy.

IV. LIBERALISM IN GOVERNMENT AND IN OPPOSITION (1880–1910)

The 1880s opened with two works significantly influenced by Benjamin Constant's classic speech of 1819 about ancient and modern liberty (*La liberté des anciens comparée à celle des modernes,* 1819). In the first, by Leandro N. Alem, this influence operated through the writings of another Frenchman, Édouard Laboulaye (*Le Parti liberal: son programme et son avenir,* 1861). The second, by Juan Bautista Alberdi, showed the impact of Constant via the historian Fustel de Coulanges (*La cité antique,* 1864). Adam Smith ("the king of economists," according to Alberdi) and Herbert Spencer (*Essays Intellectual, Moral and Physical,* 1861) were also major influences.

Alem's speech was intended to voice opposition to the plan to federalize the city of Buenos Aires, a measure that in his view would seriously damage the federal system of the Constitution and leave "the fate of the Federal Argentine Republic . . . to the will and passions of the head of the national executive." The text is possibly one of the more influential in Alem's long opposition to the central power.

Alem felt that this increase in the power of central government authority threatened the initiative and vigor of the citizenry. The remedy he suggested was expressed in orthodox classical liberal terms: "Govern as little as possible, for the less external government man has, the more freedom advances, the more he governs himself, and the more his initiative strengthens and his activity develops."

Alberdi reached similar conclusions in his work, albeit with other aims: "The omnipotence of the Fatherland inevitably becomes the omnipotence of the government in which it is embodied. This is not only the negation of liberty, but also of social progress, for it suppresses private initiative in the work of such progress." Alberdi also claimed that the "patriotic" enthusiasm typical of the "freedom of the ancients" necessarily leads to war and not "to freedom, which is fueled by peace."

Alberdi felt that this attitude lay at the root of some of the problems besetting South America. The great heroes of the continent (San Martín, Bolívar, Pueyrredón, etc.) had taken the notions of homeland and freedom from Spain, and were thus undoubtedly "champions of freedom," but in the sense of the homeland's independence from Spain, not its freedom from state interference. In the United States, in contrast, the notion of independence was tied to the idea of individual freedom inherited from Great Britain.

Shortly afterward, however, in 1881, Alberdi published *La República Argentina consolidada con Buenos Aires como capital,* in which he returned to positions that were at odds with the teachings of his earlier piece. In this later work he effectively celebrated the consolidation of the national executive, which he considered an essential factor in the construction of Argentine nationality. This tradition became established in the following decades, leading to liberalism of a conservative kind that was perhaps most emphatically expressed by Julio A. Roca, who ruled Argentina from 1880 to 1886. This period saw a series of centralizing measures that tended to transfer sovereignty from the provincial states to the national government. These measures affected the army, the currency, and the recently incorporated new territories, and promoted a moderate protectionism influenced by the German school that was dubbed "rational" by its exponents. The transfers of sovereignty also affected the Catholic Church: a law passed in 1884 placed primary education within the sphere of the national government, and shortly after that, in 1887, the Civil Registry Office was created.

The controversy over public elementary education produced positions rooted in a dubious liberalism. Pedro Goyena defended the continuation of religious education in elementary school, while Delfín Gallo, a deputy for the ruling party, justified the official measure. Among other things Gallo cited the need to create a favorable environment for immigrants of different religious backgrounds, but also to establish the supremacy of the national Congress over and above the will of the "popes." The ideology prevalent in the 1880s, however, abounded with liberal turns of phrase. Roca himself expressed his intention in 1883 to contribute to the creation of "a nation open to all currents of the spirit without castes, with no religious or social concerns, no tyrannies or Commune . . . consecrating every freedom and every right of man." In 1889, at a conference of the Pan-American Union, Foreign Affairs Minister Roque Sáenz Peña voiced this spirit in no uncertain terms. Sáenz Peña successfully opposed U.S. plans to create a continental customs union, which he saw as a threat to the Argentine government's liberal policy on immigration ("the immigrant is our friend"). He favored keeping the customhouses open and recommended a return to Gournay's old motto: "*Laissez faire, laissez passer.*"

Opposition to the governments of the day lay mainly in the hands of two political forces: the Unión Cívica (Civic Union), founded in 1890, and the Unión Cívica Radical (Radical Civic Union), founded in 1891 and headed by Leandro N. Alem, who set about the task with ideas from both classical liberalism and civic republicanism. He voiced the liberal view in a speech in the Argentine Senate in which he pointed out that Macaulay's contention in his *Critical and Historical Essays* (1843–1844) about England's Glorious Revolution as compared to the French Revolution could also be applied to his party's position. For Alem, who had led a rebellion against the established government, the revolution had been in defense of the rights and freedoms established by the national Constitution. He argued that the movement he led was conservative in nature because it defended established institutions. He combined this attitude with John Locke's view that when an authority exceeds the legitimate limits of its power, it endorses the right to rebellion (*Two Treatises of Government,* 1699).

From this point on, Alem's position began to lean toward civic republicanism, an attitude expressed in the provincial uprisings he led in 1893. During this period, which ended tragically with his suicide in 1896, the Radical leader's attitudes continued to be heavily influenced by distinctly liberal ideas. In 1891, for example, as president of the Unión Cívica, he strongly criticized the existence of official banks ("the union of bank and rifle"), which he saw as another expression of the "damned centralizing tendency."

Under Alem's leadership, the party he founded was perhaps the fullest expression of classical liberalism in terms of the central place this body of ideas conferred on the limitation of power. Francisco Barroetaveña, one of Alem's collaborators, expressed this view in his opposition in 1894 to a bill to make Spanish compulsory in primary education. Barroetaveña viewed this measure as a crime against the increasing numbers of immigrants of different nationalities who were settling in Argentine territory. Using the writings of Laboulaye (*L'état et ses limites*, 1863) and John Stuart Mill (*Considerations on Representative Government*, 1865) in his exposition, he warned of the dangers of setting the precedent of language unity, as the next thing would be to call for "religious unity, racial unity, other centralist unities, which in addition to conspiring against the Constitution and the freedoms it guarantees, would conspire against the prosperity and civilization of the Republic."

In 1894, the Radical Party newspaper, *El Argentino,* embarked on a long-drawn-out controversy with the pro-government *La Tribuna* about protection and free trade. *La Tribuna* stood for moderate "rational protection," while *El Argentino* took a line more favorable to free trade. Barroetaveña defended this position in the Chamber of Deputies when he requested a reduction in the customs tariffs in force, arguing that free trade had promoted "astonishing development" without any protection for cattle breeding and agriculture—development that should not be checked by a protectionist policy.

The echoes of the position taken by Alem and his followers were still being heard after the Radical leader's death. In 1904 one of Alem's old disciples, Pedro Coronado, outlined related ideas in Parliament on the occasion of the debate on the Residence Act, an instrument empowering the president of the Republic to expel anarchist immigrants involved in acts of "sedition," without a judge's intervention. Coronado objected to the unconstitutional powers bestowed on the president and referred in his argument to what William Pitt the Younger had stated in what he called the Bible of the English Constitution: "I shall tell what is done with a child entering school for the first time. The teacher approaches him and says: 'Every man's home is his castle.' The child asks: 'Is it surrounded by a moat or ramparts?' 'No,' replies the teacher, 'The wind may blow through it, the rain may penetrate it, but not the King.' How different from what happens in our country!"

Liberal ideas also influenced some of the positions of the newly created Socialist Party (1896). Its founder, Juan B. Justo, steadfastly championed two principles cherished by liberal economists: free trade and the gold standard. Regarding the latter, Justo criticized Eteocle Lorini's defense of the 1899 Currency Conversion Act (in Lorini's *La Repubblica Argentina e i suoi maggiore probleme de economia e di finanza,* 1902–4) and his emphasis on the positive advantages that inconvertibility had had for Argentine economic development. Justo viewed the Italian's position as unacceptable from both a scientific and a social point of view, in the latter case, because inconvertibility had always played a negative role in the Argentine worker's standard of living. Justo and the socialists of the day believed that only the gold standard was capable of ensuring wage stability.

The last contribution in this period was José Nicolás Matienzo's analysis of the federal representative government of the Argentine Republic. Matienzo, a member of Alem's Radical Party, had different views on some of Argentina's institutional troubles. Some of these woes, such as electoral fraud and corruption, he viewed as to a large extent being a consequence of the effect of the constitutional reform of 1860 in strengthening the power wielded by the provincial governors. Unlike Alem, Matienzo saw the solution to what he considered serious political problems in a decrease of the power of governors and a proportionally incremental presence of central government. He felt that the right path had been taken not by the United States but by Canada, where any power not delegated to the provinces was allocated to the federal government. This position allowed Matienzo to go on defending the continued existence of the federal system, which he saw as deeply rooted in Argentine national history. In his harsh critique of the political system of the day, Matienzo still managed to praise some achievements of the period beginning in 1880: "Institutional deficiencies have not prevented the Argentine Republic from progressing in terms of population, wealth, culture, and civil liberties, more so than any other Latin American country."

V. LIBERALISM ON THE DEFENSIVE (1912–1940)

The period between 1912 and 1940 saw a gradual decline of liberalism in Argentina that extended into later periods not dealt with here. Yet there was no shortage of voices promoting the defense of liberal ideals via different political schools ranging from reformist conservatism through radicalism to socialism. Several aspects merit highlighting: political liberalism, which sought, via a new electoral law and reforms to the national Constitution, to improve electoral practices; the fight against protectionist tendencies; the defense of contracts as voluntary agreements not subject to specific legislation; the evolutionist view of society as a creator of civilized values; and the condemnation of totalitarian dictatorship in its various guises.

The electoral reforms of 1912 rounded off the process that began after the events of 1890. At the beginning of the last century, Congress discussed the electoral law advocated by Joaquín V. González, President Julio A. Roca's interior minister. Once passed, the law lasted just two years. In line with the experience of Great Britain and the United States, Roca and González proposed a single member district regime to elect national deputies and electors for president. The climate of the times — the Centenary of Independence — favored reforms designed to purge the voting proceedings of fraud and venality.

The bill backed by President Roque Sáenz Peña and Interior Minister Indalecio Gómez a decade later was more successful — so successful that the most popular opposition party, the Unión Cívica Radical, returned to the electoral fray and was victorious in the 1916 presidential elections. The central idea of these reforms was to complement the vigorous exercise of civil liberties, already visible nationwide, with the no less vigorous and transparent exercise of political freedom. In other words, social, demographic, and educational progress had to be matched by political progress based on honest, competitive elections.

These were not, of course, the only reasons for the conflicts arising in the political and social spheres. Faced by such difficulties, the therapy to rehabilitate politics in Argentina was to make the male vote compulsory. If, in 1902, Joaquín V. González defended the voluntary secret ballot, Roque Sáenz Peña persuaded Congress in 1912 to approve the compulsory secret ballot linked to a system of preference distribution called the "incomplete list." Compulsory male suffrage was thus a master stroke incorporated in a centralizing, volitionary plan with the general recruitment of native and naturalized eighteen-year-olds fit to vote.

The implementation of this electoral legislation coincided with the impact of the First World War on the international economies and markets. This upheaval, the origin of the subsequent totalitarian regimes, triggered a wave of protectionism worldwide. Paradoxically, one of the most vigorous and consistent of the antiprotectionist liberal positions was put forward in Argentina by Juan B. Justo, who founded the Socialist Party in 1896. Justo's antiprotectionist policy was added, in the Socialist Party program, to the protection of the currency's value against inflationary monetary emission and the preaching of free cooperation among voluntary associations.

This program was intended to increase workers' wages, or at least to shore up their buying power against the threat of "inept businessmen," as Justo called them, setting up monopolies sheltered by the high tariffs of customs protectionism. In light of these debates, it is possible to see a liberal moment in the Argentine socialism of the time similar to those seen in other schools of thought such as conservatism, republicanism, and radicalism.

The 1922 ruling by the Argentine Supreme Court of Justice that a law approved by the national Congress authorizing the regulation of urban leases was constitutional marked the beginning of the end of liberal ideas in Argentina. The ruling revealed a substantive change in the doctrine previously upheld by the Supreme Court in matters relating to economic and commercial activity. Although endorsed by most of the Supreme Court, however, the ruling received a dissenting vote from the Court's president, Antonio Bermejo, who based his position primarily on the ideas of Juan Bautista Alberdi and emphasized the fact that the decision was a significant departure from the liberal premises of the national Constitution. Bermejo warned that "if the faculty of public powers to fix rents is accepted . . . it would be necessary to accept also the power of fixing the price of labor and of all things that are the object of trade among men." The episode was short-lived, and the law was abandoned a year later when the causes that had prompted it disappeared. Its importance was not, however, negligible for the evolution of ideas.

Another liberal moment worthy of consideration came during the presidency of Unión Cívica Radical leader Marcelo T. de Alvear on the occasion of the bill his interior minister, José N. Matienzo, introduced to the Congress to declare the need for partial reform of the Constitution. The Committee of Constitutional Affairs of the Senate, where the bill was sent, did not even consider it, revealing the scant attention merited by such liberal reformism in the 1920s.

The reforms proposed, which followed recent precedents in the United States, included the direct election of senators. The presence in this bill of an evolutionist criterion in constitutional matters also merits attention. Both Alvear and Matienzo shared the idea that the fundamental law should gradually be improved by amendments warranted by experience. These criteria did not thrive in Argentina in subsequent decades, and evolutionism and gradual limited reforms were the main victims.

Similar problems became evident on the fiscal front. The bill President Alvear introduced to Congress in 1924, this time jointly signed with his finance minister, Víctor M. Molina, exemplifies the fiscal anarchy that had emerged in Argentina as a result of the superimposition of national and provincial taxes. In the earlier view of Adam Smith, summarized by Alberdi in his *Sistema,* the liberal temper of tax legislation had to draw inspiration from the criteria of simplicity and taxpayers' perception of them.

The reality reflected by this bill is quite different. It rather refers to a crowded, mazelike fiscal regime in which consumer goods are taxed simultaneously by the federal government and the provinces. Leaving aside the rather involved remedies proposed by this legislation, it is important to stress the trend already prevailing in the 1920s, a trend that would become more pronounced in later years. This description of the tax system in Argentina also shows the difficulties inherent in the federal regime where tax collection was concerned, and the need, acknowledged in Article 4 of the bill, to compensate provinces levying internal taxes on general consumer goods in Argentina with proportional cuts in the relevant customs duty.

During the 1930s, liberal ideas were overshadowed by opposite schools of thought. This was the case with the totalitarian ideas that emerged in the Hispanic world (Spain and Portugal) and later, more forcefully and aggressively, in Mussolini's Italy and Hitler's Germany. Likewise, the Russian Revolution spawned a clearly more antiliberal left than the one that found expression in the social democratic parties of the Second International. In the democratic world, the economic crisis of 1929 contributed to the emergence of solutions that, like the New Deal, relied to a great extent on state intervention. Argentina's experience in those years was similar, and the liberal response to all these challenges was weak. One exception was Emilio Coni, a prestigious and influential economic historian and professor in the Faculty of Economics at the University of Buenos Aires, who published a letter explaining to the "Martians" what was happening on our planet. In this early contribution from

1933, Coni warned of the uncontrollable advance of interventionist ideas in the field of economics.

Possibly the most original contribution, however, is José Nicolás Matienzo's lecture titled "La civilización es obra del pueblo y no de los gobernantes" (Civilization is the work of the people, not of the rulers). In this work Matienzo adhered explicitly to the evolutionary ideas of Adam Smith and Herbert Spencer (*First Principles*, 1862, and *The Factors of Organic Evolution*, 1887), and made public his debt to the ideas of Alberdi. Matienzo's thesis was suggested to him "by unfair criticisms that, during the dictatorship that has just elapsed, have frequently been made regarding the ability of the people to manage their own life." Alluding to the de facto government of General Uriburu (1930–1932), Matienzo warned of the rise of right-wing totalitarian ideas at that time associated with the regimes of Primo de Rivera and Benito Mussolini. Matienzo rounded off his analysis in classic liberal style by asserting that "civilization is the work of private initiative among the members of the people, not of the official action of government agents."

The 1930s were thus not as generous in the production of liberal ideas as previous decades had been, with one notable exception at the end of the period. In July 1940, Marcelo T. de Alvear, a former president of the Republic and head of the main opposition party, the Unión Cívica Radical, delivered a lecture at the British Chamber of Commerce. German troops were at the time winning victory after victory in Europe, and the USA was still neutral. Under such difficult circumstances, Alvear expressed his explicit support for the countries threatened by the Nazi offensive. His speech drew on the example of Great Britain, which he held up as a model of political civilization based on democratic and liberal principles, a tradition the Argentine Republic ought to join.

CONCLUSIONS

This introduction has examined the extended period when liberal ideas had a significant bearing on Argentine political and social thinking. From the moment Hipólito Vieytes alluded to the "sublime Adam Smith" in Letter Twelve of his *Semanario de Agricultura, Industria y Comercio*, a weekly periodical, this trend garnered influences from the different schools that characterized the liberal tradition in the world.

In Argentina, liberalist ideas were embedded in a milieu marked by the changing fortunes of the new nation's institutional development. It is important to review some of these specific features. First, the vast majority of those who expressed this kind of thinking were politicians rather than academics, and this sometimes affected the quality and consistency of their arguments. Second, the exposition of liberal ideas took place during the debates involved in building the key institutions of the Argentine nation. As we saw in connection with James Madison, this entailed one of the peculiar difficulties of liberal thought, namely, how to seek limits to power while at the same time generating and organizing it. This difficulty surfaced especially over the creation of a strong central power, which sometimes bore only a passing resemblance to the teachings of liberal thought. And last, these principles were imported from various European and U.S. schools and therefore had to be adapted to the realities and exigencies of the local environment.

For all these restrictions, liberal ideas made headway in Argentina, and—especially from the mid-nineteenth century onward—they played a vital role in the new country's growth and consolidation. This contribution was expressed in the different fields of national endeavor, producing works and contributions of unquestionable analytical value.

As in many other parts of the world, the influence of liberal ideas began to wane in the 1930s. This decline is apparent in the decreasing quantity and originality of the contributions from the dwindling group of institutional players who still subscribed to this school of thought.

Argentine liberalism, however, has been left with a rich heritage of principles that also became a reality at the social and institutional levels. Aside from the intellectual works collected in this volume, perhaps the most permanent contribution of this body of ideas has been the promotion of an open and plural society with high social mobility.

NOTE TO THE READER
Original footnotes in this edition are identified with "[A.N.]"; those of the current editors are identified with "[E.N.]."

Natalio R. Botana and Ezequiel Gallo are both Emeritus Professors at Torcuato Di Tella University in Buenos Aires, Argentina.

1

Liberalism during the Dictatorship of Rosas
(1837–1850)

JUAN BAUTISTA ALBERDI

The Argentine Republic, Thirty-seven Years after the May Revolution (1847)

> Toutes les aristocraties, anglaise, russe, allemande, n'ont besoin que de montrer une chose en témoignage contre la France: — Les tableaux qu'elle fait d'elle-même par la main de ses grands écrivains, amis la plupart du peuple et partisans du progrès. . . .
>
> Nul peuple ne résisterait à une telle épreuve. Cette manie singulière de se dénigrer soi-même, d'étaler ses plaies, et comme d'aller chercher la honte, serait mortelle à la longue.
> — J. Michelet[1]

Today more than ever, anyone who was born in the beautiful country between the Andes mountain range and the River Plate has the right to cry out with pride, "I am an Argentine."

On the foreign soil on which I reside, not as a political exile, having left my home country legally, of my own free choice, just as an Englishman or a Frenchman can reside outside his country as it suits him; in the lovely country that receives me as a guest and provides so many pleasures to foreigners, without offending its flag, I lovingly kiss the Argentine colors and take pride in seeing them prouder and more honorable than ever before.

The truth be told to the discredit of none: the colors of the River

---

Original title: "La República Argentina, 37 años después de su Revolución de Mayo." Source: Juan Bautista Alberdi, *Obras completas de Juan Bautista Alberdi* [Complete works of Juan Bautista Alberdi], vol. 3 (Buenos Aires: La Tribuna nacional, 1886).

1. Jules Michelet (1798–1874). Quotation is from his *Le peuple* (1846): "All aristocracies, be they English, Russian, German, need show only one thing as witness against France: The pictures she makes of herself by the hand of her great writers, most of them friends of the people and advocates of progress. . . . No people could resist such a test. That strange obsession of self-denigration, of displaying its wounds, would in time be lethal." [E.N.]

Plate have known neither defeat nor defection. In the hands of Rosas[2] or Lavalle,[3] when they have not sponsored victory, they have presided over liberty. If they have ever fallen into the dust, it has been against their own; at war with their own family, never at the feet of the foreigner.

Save your tears, then, those generously sobbing over our misfortunes. In spite of them, no people on this part of the continent is entitled to feel pity for us.

In its life as a nation, the Argentine Republic does not have one man, one deed, one defeat, one victory, one success, one loss to be ashamed of. All reproaches, save that of villainy. Our right comes from the blood that runs in our veins. It is Castilian blood. It is the blood of El Cid, the blood of Pelagius.[4]

Full of patriotic warmth, and possessed of that impartiality that comes from the pure sentiment of one's own nationalism, I wish to embrace them all and enclose them in a painting. Blinded sometimes by partisan spirit, I have said things that might have flattered the ear of zealous rivals: may they hear me now with less flattering words. Will there be no excuses for the selfishness of my local patriotism, when partiality in favor of one's own land is everyone's right?

Besides this I am led by a serious idea, namely, the need of every man in my country to reflect today on where our national family now stands: what political means do we, its sons, possess; what are our duties; what needs and desires are the order of the day of the famous Argentine Republic?

It would not be strange for someone to find this pamphlet Argentine, as I shall write it in blue-and-white ink.

If I say that the Argentine Republic is prosperous in the midst of upheaval, I recognize a fact that everyone can sense: and if I add that it has the means to be more prosperous than all, I am writing no paradox.

---

2. Juan Manuel de Rosas (1793–1877), governor of the province of Buenos Aires (1829–1832, 1835–1852) and leader of the Argentine Confederation, ruled as a dictator until defeated by Justo José de Urquiza in the Battle of Caseros (1852). [E.N.]

3. Juan Lavalle (1797–1841), Argentine general, fought in the Wars of Independence; during the civil wars he led the army of the Unitarios against Rosas but was defeated. [E.N.]

4. Spanish Pelayo, first king of Asturias (d. 737); he defeated the Moors in the Battle of Covadonga (722). [E.N.]

There can be no man alive who would deny that it is in a respectable state and has nothing to be ashamed of. Why not say it once and for all with our heads held high? The Argentine Republic has moved foreign sensibilities with the images of its civil war. It has seemed barbarous, cruel. But it has never been the butt of anyone's ridicule. And misfortune that does not reach the point of mockery is far from being the ultimate misfortune.

At all times, the Argentine Republic has appeared at the forefront of the movement of this America. For right and for wrong, its power to take the initiative is the same: when it does not imitate its liberators, it mimics its tyrants.

In the revolution, Moreno's[5] plan encompassed our continent.

In the war, San Martín[6] showed Bolívar the road to Ayacucho.[7]

Rivadavia[8] gave the Americas his plan of progressive improvements and innovations. What statesman before him put on the order of the day the question of roads, canals, banks, public education, staging posts, religious freedom, abolition of privileges, religious and military reform, colonization, trade and shipping treaties, administrative and political centralization, organization of the representative system, electoral system, customs, taxation, rural laws, useful associations, European imports of unheard-of industries? The sum of decrees from his day is a perfect administrative code, just as the decrees of Rosas contain the catechism of the art of subjugating despotically and teaching obeisance with blood.

Twenty years from now, many states of the Americas will deem themselves advanced because they will be doing what Buenos Aires did thirty years ago: and forty years will elapse before they have their own Rosas. I say their Rosas, because they will have him. Not in vain is he today called

5. Mariano Moreno (1778–1811), lawyer and journalist, secretary of the Primera Junta (first governing body, installed May 25, 1810). [E.N.]

6. José de San Martín (1778–1850), Argentine general, liberator of Argentina, Chile, and Peru. [E.N.]

7. Simón Bolívar (1783–1830), leader of the independence movement in northern South America. His army, led by Antonio José de Sucre, gained a decisive victory over the Spanish Royalist forces in the Battle of Ayacucho in Peru (1824). [E.N.]

8. Bernardino Rivadavia (1780–1845), president of Argentina 1826–1827, advocated a strong centralist government but was obliged to resign due to opposition from the Federal Party. [E.N.]

Man of the Americas. He truly is, for he is a political type who will be seen around America as a logical product of that which produced him in Buenos Aires and which exists in sister states. In all places the orange tree, when it gets to a certain age, gives oranges. Where there are Spanish republics, formed from former colonies, there will be dictators once development reaches a certain level.

They should not be upset by this idea. This means that they will advance as much as the Argentine Republic has advanced today, regardless of the means. Rosas is at once a sickness and a cure: America says this of Buenos Aires, and I repeat it as true of the future America.

This is not a malignant and vengeful omen of a desired evil. Although I oppose Rosas, as a party man, I have said that I write this with Argentine colors.

Rosas is not a simple tyrant in my eyes. If in his hand there is a bloody rod of iron, I also see on his head the rosette of Belgrano.[9] I am not so blinded by love of my party as not to recognize what Rosas is, in certain respects.

I know, for example, that Simón Bolívar did not occupy the world so much with his name as the current governor of Buenos Aires does.

I know that the name of Washington is worshipped in the world but is no better known than that of Rosas.

The United States, despite its fame, does not today have a public figure held in higher esteem than General Rosas.—The people speak of him from one end of America to the other, although he has not done as much as Christopher Columbus. He is as well known in Europe as a man in the public eye in England or France. And there is no place in the world where his name is not known, because there is no place outside the reach of the English or French press, which for the last ten years have repeated his name day after day. What orator, what celebrated writer of the nineteenth century has not named him, has not spoken of him on many occasions? Guizot, Thiers, O'Connell, Lamartine, Palmerston, Aberdeen.[10] What celebrated parliamentarian of this era has not

9. Manuel Belgrano (1770–1820), lawyer, journalist, and military leader; creator of the Argentine flag, member of the Primera Junta. [E.N.]

10. François Guizot (1787–1874), French politician and historian, a supporter of constitutional monarchy, was influential during the July Monarchy (1830–1848). Adolphe Thiers (1797–1877), French statesman and historian. Daniel O'Connell (1775–1847),

mentioned him, speaking to the face of Europe. Shortly he will be a romantic hero: the stage is set for a young genius, remembering what Chateaubriand, Byron,[11] and Lamartine gained from their journeys, to set sail across the Atlantic, in search of an immense and virginal territory ripe for poetry, offered by the most beautiful country, the most esteemed and the most abundant in remarkable traits of the New World.

Byron, who once thought of visiting Venezuela and was so eager to cross the line of the equinox, would have been attracted to the banks of the immense River Plate, if the man who could have offered the most colors through his life and character to the pictures from his diabolical and sublime brush had lived in his day. Byron was the predestined poet of Rosas, the poet of *The Corsair, The Pirate, Mazeppa,* and *Marino Faliero.* It would be fitting if the hero, like the singer, were defined as *angel or demon,* as Lamartine called the author of *Childe Harold.*

It would be necessary not to be an Argentine to be unaware of the truth of these facts, and be proud of them, without getting involved in examining the legitimacy of the right with which they cede in honor of the Argentine Republic. It is enough to see that glory is independent sometimes of justice, of usefulness, and even of good common sense.

So I will say in all sincerity something I consider consistent with what I have expressed here:—if Rosas' rights to Argentine nationality were lost, I would contribute with no small sacrifice to bringing about their rescue. It is easier for me to declare than to explain the motive, because it pleases me to think that Rosas belongs to the River Plate.

But, when speaking thus someone names Rosas, he speaks of an Argentine general, he speaks of a man of the Plate, or rather he speaks of the Argentine Republic. To speak of the esteem in which Rosas is held is to speak of the esteem in which Rosas' country is held. Rosas is not an entity that can be conceived in abstract terms without relation to the people he governs. Like all notable men, the extraordinary de-

---

Irish political leader who campaigned for the Emancipation Act. Alphonse de Lamartine (1790–1869), French poet, writer, and politician. Henry Temple, Viscount Palmerston (1784–1865), British statesman, twice prime minister of Great Britain. George Hamilton-Gordon, earl of Aberdeen (1784–1860), Scottish politician, prime minister of Great Britain 1852–1855. [E.N.]

11. François-René de Chateaubriand (1768–1848), French romantic writer and politician. George Gordon, Lord Byron (1788–1824), English romantic poet. [E.N.]

velopment of his character presupposes that of the society to which he belongs. Rosas and the Argentine Republic are two entities implicated in each other. He is what he is because he is Argentine: his elevation implies that of his country; the spirit of his will, the firmness of his nature, the power of his intelligence are not traits of his own, but traits of the people, which he reflects in his person. The idea of a Bolivian or Ecuadorian Rosas is absurd. Only the Plate could today produce a man who has done what Rosas has done. A strong man always implies many others of the same spirit around him. With an army of sheep, a lion at its head would be taken prisoner by a single hunter.

Suppress Buenos Aires, and its masses and its innumerable able men, and you will have no Rosas.

The leadership of the Argentine Republic is attributed to him alone. What a great error! He is reasonable enough to listen when he appears to be leading; like his country, he is very capable of ordering when he seems to obey.

Rosas is no Peter the Great.[12] The greatness of Argentina is older than he. Rosas is forty years later than Liniers;[13] thirty years later than Moreno, Belgrano, San Martín; twenty years later than Rivadavia. Under his leadership, Buenos Aires sent a haughty *no* to the allied English and French. In 1807 it did more than that, without having Rosas at its head. In its streets, it tore apart fifteen thousand soldiers of the flower of the British armies, and snatched the one hundred standards that today adorn its temples.

In 1810, without Rosas at its head, it cast to the ground the crown that Christopher Columbus led to the New World.

On July 9, 1816, the Argentine Republic wrote the golden page of its independence, and the name of Rosas is not at the foot of that document.

In that same year, the Argentine armies climbed with cannons and

---

12. Peter the Great (1672–1725), tsar and emperor of Russia, modernized his country and transformed it into an important European power. [E.N.]

13. Santiago de Liniers (1753–1810), French military officer in the service of Spain, defeated the English forces that invaded Buenos Aires in 1806 and 1807; viceroy from 1806 to 1809; took the side of the Royalists in 1810 and was executed by the revolutionaries. [E.N.]

cavalry mountains twice as high as those of Mont-Cenis and St. Bernard, to help Chile to do what had been achieved on the other side. But it was not Rosas who signed the victorious bulletins from Chacabuco and Maypo,[14] but the Argentine José de San Martín.

All the glory of Rosas, to the square of four and multiplied ten times by itself, does not form a trophy comparable in esteem with Pizarro's[15] standard, obtained by San Martín in his campaign in Peru in 1821.

This is not to diminish Rosas' merit. This is to increase the merit of the Argentine Republic. This is to say that it is not Rosas who has taught it to be brave and heroic.

From this there follows a very logical and natural conclusion, namely, that as soon as Rosas ceases to be at the head of the Argentine Republic, another man as notable as he with other scenes as memorable as his will be attracting the world's attention to the Republic, which from the first days of this century has never ceased to be esteemed for its men and for its deeds.

But today, are Rosas and his party perhaps the only things that Argentina has to offer that are extraordinary and worthy of admiration?

That would be to see a half-truth, not the whole truth.

No one is great unless measured against other great men. There is much praise for Rosas' heroic perseverance. But does not the perseverance of his action imply the perseverance of the resistance that he seeks to snuff out? If the persistence with which Rosas has pursued his enemies for the last twenty years shows that interest in a never-changing will, no less admirable is the invariable tenacity with which they have reacted to his power in the same space of time.

It is not my intention here to strike a comparative parallel of the merits of the two parties into which the Argentine Republic is divided. Halves of my country, equally loved, one and the other, I want the heroism that lies in both of them to be seen. In both can be observed the characters of a great political party. South America has not seen in the

14. San Martín's army defeated the Spanish forces in both the Battle of Chacabuco (1817) and the Battle of Maipú (Maypo, 1818), thus completing the liberation of Chile. [E.N.]

15. Francisco Pizarro (1478–1541), Spanish conqueror of Peru, defeated the Inca Empire. [E.N.]

history of its civil wars two parties more tenacious in their action, more committed to their dominant idea, better organized, more loyal to their flag, clearer in their aims, more logical and consistent in their progress.

These qualities do not hold as much importance in the Unitario Party[16] because it has not been embodied in a single man. It has not had that man because oppositions never have him, for they declare and organize themselves into militias in the heart of the popular masses: it has had infinite heads instead of one, and that is why its action has been divided and disturbed, which has made its results sterile.

But is not the consistency of Rosas and his men as admirable as the consistency of those men who at home and abroad and everywhere have fought for the past twenty years, braving with the fortitude of heroes all the setbacks and sufferings of foreign life, never yielding, never deserting their flag, never changing sides under cover of those weak amalgams celebrated in the name of parliamentary law?

There have been mutual reproaches, sometimes deserved, though usually unfair. The antagonist having to fight with undisciplined masses, with makeshift soldiers, chiefs, arrangements, and resources, has been the object of unpleasant accusations. But what opposition has not included excesses of this kind? Did not the holy war of independence from Spain have innumerable such traits that the glow of success and justice have left in silence? Can one not hear even today secret murmurings against the great names of San Martín and Bolívar, Carrera and O'Higgins,[17] Monteagudo[18] and La Mar,[19] for unnoticed acts which in the labyrinth of a great war were practiced by the masses under their command?

Reveal, let us see, justly or not, some act of cowardice, some behavior of dissolute indignity that stains the life of Rivadavia, Agüero, Pico, Al-

---

16. The Unitario Party advocated a centralist form of government. In this translation the name of the party and of its members (the Unitarios) have been left in their original form.

17. José Miguel Carreras (1785–1821) and Bernardo O'Higgins (1778–1842) were leaders of the war for independence in Chile. [E.N.]

18. Bernardo de Monteagudo (1789–1825), Argentine revolutionary, lawyer, and politician, was active in Argentina, Chile, and Peru with San Martín and Bolívar. [E.N.]

19. José de La Mar (1778–1830), president of Peru 1822–1823 and 1827–1829, participated in the war of independence. [E.N.]

sina, Varela, Lavalle, Las Heras, Olavarria, Suárez,[20] and so many others enrolled as chiefs in the noble ranks of the Unitario Party!

This praise is not a feature of that routine declamation of the parties. It is the just vindication of one-half of the Argentine Republic.

Both sides accuse each other of faults and offenses. Perhaps they have these faults, perhaps they committed such offenses, and the first of them is having taken up arms to tear each other apart. But once they have gone to war — the last aberration of passion and fervor — should it seem strange that they should then incur other offenses? To what else could the fever of a bloody contest lead, in which are at stake honor, political faith, and the interest for a cause considered that of the homeland itself?

The Federal Party made use of tyranny: the Unitario Party made use of alliances with foreign powers. Both did wrong. But why have those who have looked on this alliance as a crime of treason forgotten that the crime of tyranny is no less a crime? There are, then, two offenses that account for each other. I say offenses, and not crimes, because it is absurd to claim that the Argentine parties have been criminal in the abuse of their means.

Rosas has people who understand his perspective because he is the victor. The Unitarios have not, because they have been defeated. Thus is the world in its judgment. They call Lavalle a traitor because he died defeated in Jujuy. If he had entered Buenos Aires victorious, they would have called him *libertador*. If O'Higgins or San Martín had been defeated at Maypo, captured and hanged the next day in the square in Santiago; if the same had happened to the September revolutionaries and the domination of the Spanish had subsisted until today, those great men of the highest rank would be forgotten as obscure rebels worthy of the gallows, where they would atone for their *treason*.

Passion, in its language of lies and hyperbole, has been able to give the name of *treason* only to the simple military alliance that the Unitarios made with the forces of England and France.

Treason is a crime, but there is no crime when there is no intention to do evil. It is, then, something more than hasty procedure; it is an act of imbecility to presume that men of sincerity, of fervor, of patriotism such as Lavalle, Suárez, Olavarría, etc., could have harbored the intention of dishonoring the colors that they had defended since childhood

20. All leaders of the Unitario Party. [E.N.]

in a hundred glorious, honorable combats, risking their lives to foreign bullets! If other men had done it, without the precedents of those men, the sophism would be less manifest. But to accuse of treason to their country those who created and founded the homeland with their swords and their blood! Lavalle, Paz, Rodríguez, who had no fortune but their glorious trophies obtained in the war of South American independence, must have had the intention to fight so that after their triumph they would hand over to a foreign power the homeland, its independence, its insignia, and even their personal honor and freedom! The tyrants have worn out the meaning of the word *treason* in their abuse of it, to the extent that it is rare that anytime, especially in young and warring countries, it is applied justly. But when it is used against the Unitarios of the Argentine Republic, one commits something more than a common error: one commits, as I have said, an act of inexcusable imbecility. Tiberius, the dark and bloody Tiberius, once saw the crime of treason even in a poem, in an indiscreet and confidential word, in a tear, in a smile, in the most insignificant things.[21] Dionysius the *tyrant* condemned to death a man who dreamed he had murdered him. Alter a little the meaning of the word *treason,* said Montesquieu, and a legal government will become an arbitrary one.

"A grave reproach," says Chateaubriand, "will be tied to the memory of Bonaparte. Toward the end of his reign his yoke became so heavy that the hostile feelings toward the foreigner softened; and an invasion, today a painful memory, took on at the time it occurred, the air of a campaign of freedom. . . . The Lafayettes, the Lanjuinais, the Camilo Jordans, the Ducis, the Lemerciers, the Cheniers, the Benjamin Constants, standing erect among the impetuous crowd, dared to spurn the victory and protest against the tyranny" . . . "Let us abstain, then, from saying that those who are led by fate to fight against a power that belongs to their country must be villains: in all times and countries, from the Greeks to our day, all opinions have backed the forces that could ensure them victory. One day it will be read in our *Memoirs* the ideas of M. de Malesherbes on the emigration. We do not know in France a single party that has not had men on foreign soil, merging with enemies and marching against France. Benjamin Constant, Bernadotte's aide-de-camp, served

---

21. Tacitus, *Annals,* books 6 and 11. [A.N.]

in the allied army that entered Paris, and Carrel was caught, arms in hand, in the Spanish ranks."[22]

It is needless to say that Lafayette, Chénier, Constant,[23] Carrel are names that all the parties in France take pride in counting among their celebrated men. From where does this way of seeing them arise, in spite of those actions, which a sophist would dub *treason?* From the universal conviction that their intentions in executing them were entirely French and patriotic; and that only a totally exceptional situation could have placed them in the position of seeking the good of the country by means of such a course.

The Unitarios of Buenos Aires have done less than Constant, Carrel,[24] and Lafayette in France: they have never marched against anything that could be said to be their country. They have marched with their flag, with their cockade, with their chiefs, along their path, toward their separate and particular ends; after demanding and obtaining solemn written statements, protecting the honor and integrity of the Republic, against all pernicious eyes of the foreigner. It was impossible to use this delicate means of reaction with more discretion, reserve, and prudence than they did. The documents that prove it are well known, as is the justification born from its results.

Other high and noble intentions also explain the conduct of the Argentines who in 1840 joined the French forces to attack the power of General Rosas. That coalition had more farsighted intentions than a simple change of governor in Buenos Aires.—I will mention them with the same sincerity and frankness with which they were manifested then. They may be erroneous: that depends on each man's way of thinking. But deceit was never in play at their conception. They belonged gen-

---

22. *Congress of Verona,* by Chateaubriand, chaps. 31 and 37. In support of what this historian says, it suffices to remember the glorious English Revolution, instigated and supported by a Dutch fleet and thirteen thousand bayonets. [A.N.]

23. Gilbert du Motier, marquis de Lafayette (1757–1834), French military officer, fought in the American Revolutionary War and was an influential liberal politician in France. André Chénier (1762–1794), French poet executed during the Terror of the French Revolution. Benjamin Constant (1767–1830), French writer and politician of liberal ideas. [E.N.]

24. Armand Carrel (1800–1836), French republican politician and journalist. [E.N.]

erally to the young men of the opposing party; and they owed them to their political studies at school. To suspect that treason could have mixed with them is to suppose that there were people foolish enough to initiate public law students in the mysteries of that dark diplomacy, which according to some, seeks to change the political principle of government in the Americas.

The transcendent idea of the young defenders of that alliance was to introduce, reconciling it with the perfect nationality of the country, the influence of the civilizing action of Europe by honorable means admitted by the law of nations, in order to establish a feasible political order in the Americas, in which the most advanced and liberal ideas would be supported by a majority of the enlightened population, developed under the influence of laws and institutions that protected such a trend. They wanted, in short, to find a formula that would solve the problem of the establishment of political freedom in the Americas, a problem still unsolved, since the solution does not lie in those written constitutions, which are inadequate and impracticable, and whose only use is frequently to encourage the hypocrisy of freedom, at odds with genuine freedom. Is there anyone unaware that South America, ever since the proclamation of unlimited democracy, is in a false position? That the order practiced until now is transitory because it is inadequate, and that it is necessary to bring things to more normal and genuine bases? Can anyone who sincerely ponders on what our current constitutions are fail to understand the importance and difficulty of this matter and the profound need to deal with it?

So: those young men tackling this question, which concerns the very life of this part of the New World, thought that while the numerical advantage of the ignorant, proletarian multitude prevailed, clothed in the revolution of popular sovereignty, freedom would always be replaced by the despotic military regime of just one man. And that the only means to ensure the preponderance of the enlightened minorities of these countries was to enlarge it with ties and connections with civilized influences from abroad, UNDER CONDITIONS COMPATIBLE WITH AMERICAN INDEPENDENCE AND DEMOCRACY, IRREVOCABLY PROCLAIMED BY THE REVOLUTION.

Absurd or wise, this was the thought of those who in that period supported the alliance with European forces to subjugate the party of the plebeian multitude captained and organized militarily by General Rosas. The supporters of those ideas maintained them publicly and openly in the press, with the candor and disinterest inherent in the character of youth.

That question is so grave, affecting in such a way the political existence of the new states of America, so uncertain and dark, and so few steps have been taken toward its solution, that one would have to be very backward in experience and good political sense to qualify one or another attempted solution as strange. That point has attracted the attention of all men who have given serious thought to the political fate of the New World, and errors of thinking therein have been committed by Bolívar, San Martín, Monteagudo, Rivadavia, Alvear, Gómez,[25] and other men no less esteemed for their merit and American patriotism. A thousand others will err behind them in solving this problem, and they will not be the lower or less distinguished heads, since the only ones for whom the question is already solved are the demagogues who deceive the multitude and the limited spirits who deceive themselves.

If, then, the Argentine parties have fallen into error in the adoption of their means, it has not been due to vice nor to cowardice of the spirit, but to passion that, while still noble and pure in its intentions, is almost always blind to the use of its means, and the lack of experience that the new states of this continent suffer from as regards the path along which they must take their steps in public life.

No, the Argentine Republic is not a depraved country, as is supposed by those who judge it by the precepts she has given herself in the delirium of revolutionary fever. It is her political parties who have defamed her abroad, mutually exaggerating their faults in the heat of the fight and implying others as a vulgar means of attack and destruction. To judge the Argentine Republic by what her parties at arms write in the press is to judge France by the lugubrious portraits made by the impatient misanthropy of some of her great writers who, living in the perfection of the future, see in the present only vices, disorder, iniquity, and lies.

25. Carlos María de Alvear (1789–1852), Argentine general, statesman, and diplomat; supreme director of the United Provinces of the River Plate in 1815. Valentín Gómez (1774–1839), Argentine priest and politician, rector of the University of Buenos Aires. [E.N.]

Every party has taken care to hide or disfigure the advantages and merits of its rival. According to the Rosas press, the more educated half of the Argentine Republic is equal to the southern hordes of Pehuenches and Pampas.[26] It is made up of *savage* Unitarios (as if to say the *progressive savages,* union being the most advanced term, the highest ideal of political science). The Unitarios, for their part, have often seen in their rivals the Carib Indians of the Orinoco. When one day they share the peaceful embrace in which the most enflamed struggles end, how different will be the picture of the Argentine Republic painted by the sons of both camps.

What noble confessions will not be heard sometime from the mouths of the frenetic Federales! And the Unitarios, with what pleasure will they not see men of honor and great hearts come out from beneath that frightful mask under which their rivals today disguise themselves, giving way to the tyrannical demands of the situation!

In the meantime, it is not necessary to make felons of the writers who involuntarily damage the country, damaging themselves also, even though Michelet says that it diminishes their luster in the eyes of the foreigner. The representative peoples must live today like the Roman who wanted to dwell in a glass house to show off the transparency of his private life. It is necessary to live a life of truth and show it to the world as it is, with its faults and its merits. To right the wrong it is necessary to say it out loud: society and power are deaf: for them to hear, one must speak with the trumpet of the press and from the rostrum. But it is impossible to raise one's voice at home without the neighbor hearing. There is nothing else for it than to take shelter under the comforting axiom that says—I am a man and I consider myself alien to nothing. If some peoples have no errors to lament, it is because they have not begun to live. The great nations have left their stains behind. The backward peoples have them in their future. In the people, as in the man, disease is an abnormal and transitory state: our country is nearing the end of its maladies.

One hears also that the Argentine Republic suffers a general backwardness as a consequence of its long and bloody war. This error, generally accepted outside its frontiers, also comes from the same causes as the

---

26. Indian tribes of the Argentine plains. [E.N.]

other. Doubtless war is less fecund in certain advances than peace: but it brings with it certain others that are peculiar to war, and the Argentine parties have obtained them with an effectiveness equal to the intensity of their suffering.

The Argentine Republic has more experience than all her brethren of the south, for the simple reason that she has suffered more than any other. She has traveled a road that the others are about to begin.

As she is closer to Europe, she has received sooner the influx of her progressive ideas, which were put into practice by the revolution of May 1810, and sooner than all others she reaped the good and bad fruits of her development: being for this reason at all times, *future* for the states further from the trans-Atlantic spring of American progress, which constitutes the past of the states of the Plate. Thus, even in what today is taken as a signal of backwardness in the neighboring republic, it is more advanced than those who claim to be exempt from these setbacks, because they have not yet begun to experience them.

A noteworthy fact, a part of the definitive organization of the Argentine Republic has prospered through her wars, receiving important services even from her adversaries. That fact is the centralization of national power. Rivadavia proclaimed the idea of unity: Rosas has achieved it. Among Federales and Unitarios, the Republic has been centralized, which means that the issue is only about voices that merely harbor the high spirits of young peoples; and which ultimately, both one and the other, have served their homeland, promoting its national unity. The Unitarios have lost, but *unity* has triumphed. The Federales have conquered, but *federation* has succumbed. The fact is that from the heart of this war of names, power has emerged fully formed, without which society is unachievable and freedom itself impossible.

Power implies the habit of obedience as the basis of its firm existence. That habit has put down roots in both parties. Within the country, Rosas has taught his supporters and his enemies to obey; outside the country, his absent enemies, without the right to govern, have spent their lives in obedience, and one way or another, both have reached the same goal.

In this regard, no country of South America has more powerful means of inner order than the Argentine Republic.

There is no country in the Americas that brings together greater practical knowledge of the Spanish American states than that Republic, because it is the country that has had the greatest number of capable men scattered outside its territory, and living regularly inserted in the acts of public life of the states where they reside. The day when those men return to their country and meet at deliberative assemblies, what useful applications, comparative terms, practical knowledge, and curious allusions will they bring from their memories of their past lives abroad!

If men learn and gain with their travels, what won't happen to the people? It can be said that one-half of the Argentine Republic has been traveling in the world for ten or twenty years. Made up especially of young men, who are the homeland of tomorrow, when they return to their native soil after a life wandering, they will come in possession of foreign languages, legislation, industries, habits, which are then ties of brotherhood with the other peoples of the world. And how many, as well as knowledge, will bring capital to the national wealth! The Argentine Republic will not gain less if it leaves some of its sons scattered around the world, connected forever to foreign countries, because those very sons will extend the source of attachment to the country that gave them the life that they pass on to their children.

The Argentine Republic had the arrogance of youth. Half of its inhabitants have become modest, suffering from the despotism that commands without right to reply: and the other half, carrying out the instructive existence of the foreigner.

The plebeian masses, elevated into power, have softened their ferocity in that atmosphere of culture that the others left behind, to descend in search of the warmth of the soul, which in morals as in geology is greater the further one descends. This transitory change of roles must have been advantageous for the general progress of the country. One learns to govern by obeying; and vice versa.

While the Republic has not advanced in glory, it has done so at least in fame and renown; and on this point it owes such results to the two parties in equal measure. While Rosas deserved admiration for having repelled the foreign powers, his enemies have merited no less for having moved those powers to their advantage. The first party in the Americas to have repelled the states of Europe is that of Rosas; and the first to have been capable of moving them to take an active part in supporting them is the Unitario Party. The Argentine Republic is, then, the South American state that has most strongly made its action felt in its relations with the great powers of Europe.

The affairs of the Plate have for many years attracted the attention of the French Chambers and the English Parliament.

The Times of London—the world's leading newspaper—has concerned itself with Rosas five hundred times, no matter in what regard. The *Revue des Deux Mondes, Le Constitutionnel, La Presse, Le Journal des Debats,* and all the political newspapers of Paris have for the last eight years shown as much interest in the Plate as in any other European state.

The greatest orators of this century have brought their fervor into play one hundred times when dealing with the River Plate, and they are familiar with its affairs.

Argentine gold is the first to have been used by any state of the Americas to pay foreign writers, in Europe and on this continent, to write favorably and systematically about Rosas.

There is no press better known in all of South America than that of Buenos Aires, and in the neighboring states unlimited numbers of newspapers have existed destined to live in thrall to the affairs of the River Plate, in favor of either one party or the other. Those foreign newspapers, when not Unitarios, have been Rosistas, but always Argentine. Dealing with something from the neighboring country, they have paid tribute to it with courtesy and respect. *Le gouvernement espagnol se fait journaliste,*[27] as Girardin once said: for a long time now, that of Buenos Aires has become *Gaceta, British Packet,* and *Archivo Americano.*

All this is all the more likely to flatter the Argentine Republic, all the more so given that it is the smallest state of all Hispanic America by population, with the exception of the Republic of Uruguay. It is difficult to find a smaller and more boisterous family in the world than the Argentine family. It would be rightly called a loud-mouthed charlatan if it were not the Spanish American state that has produced the most numerous and extraordinary things. It is the only one in which an entire respectable European army has been overcome without a single man escaping, nor a single standard. It is the only one where the reaction against the Spanish government was not defeated, not even for a single day, after the day it started, May 25, 1810. It is the only one to have defeated the empire of Brazil, beating it in battles and taking from it a whole fleet, an infinity of flags, and forcing it to relinquish, by means

27. "The Spanish government becomes a journalist." Émile de Girardin (1806–1881), French journalist. [E.N.]

of glorious treaties, rights that it expected to hold onto all its life. It is the only one that possesses the standard of the Spanish conquest on this continent, the country that today receives greater spontaneous signals of something more than respect and consideration from the American states that surround it; the only one that in its recent wars, within and without, has aroused the amazement of all, for its constancy, its heroism, its ability, and its strength, whether this is judged in the person of one party or another.

In thinking of all this, any Argentine, wherever he is in the world, may see the light of May shine, with no regret for belonging to the nation of his birth.

However, all this is not enough. All this does not satisfy the true fate of the Argentine Republic. All this is extraordinary, lucid, surprising. But the Argentine Republic, in order to be a happy people in itself, has a need for more modest, useful, and real cases than all that brilliance of military triumphs and intelligent splendor. She has dazzled the world with the precociousness of her ideas. She has martial glories that peoples who have lived ten times more than she do not possess. She has so many flags taken in victorious combat that she could decorate her forehead with a turban made up of all the colors of the rainbow, or fly a flag as high as the Colonne de Vendôme, and more radiant than the bronze of Austerlitz.—What is the use of this, without other advantages, which, the poor thing, are still necessary in such number?

She has already done more than enough for fame; and very little for happiness.

She possesses immense glories; but, alas! She does not have a single liberty. *May they be eternal,* thank heavens, *the laurels that she succeeded in winning,* as she swore not to live without them. But remember that the first words of her revolutionary genesis were those three that form together a holy code and a sublime verse, saying: *liberty, liberty, liberty.*

Fortunately, she knows already, at the cost of blood and tears, that the enjoyment of that benefit is subject to difficult and gradual conditions that it is necessary to fulfill. Thus, if in the early days she was eager for liberty, today she will be happy with a more than moderate liberty.

In her first songs of victory she forgot a word less resonant than that of *liberty,* but which represents a counterweight that helps liberty to stay on her feet: *order.*

One order, one rule, one law: this is the supreme need of her political situation.

She needs this because she does not have it.

She can possess it because she has the necessary means.

There is no law that rules the inner government of the Argentine Republic and the exercise of private guarantees. This is the most public fact that that country may offer.

It does not have a political constitution, and in this is the only exception on the whole continent.

There is no question now as to whether it should be centralist or federal. If it is federal, so be it, but let there be a law that regulates that federation; let there be a federal constitution. Although the written charter or constitution is not the law or the pact, nevertheless, she proves it, she fixes it and keeps it invariable. The written word is a need of order and harmony. The stability of any important contract is guaranteed in writing: what contract could be more important than the great constitutional contract?

Nor is there a question as to whether it should be liberal. Let it be despotic, let it be tyrannical, if it wishes, that law; but let there be a law. That at least is progress, that tyranny is practiced by law instead of by the will of one man. The worst of despotism is not its harshness but its inconsequence. The written law is as immutable as faith.

To say that the Argentine Republic is not capable of governing itself under a constitution, even if it is despotic or monarchical, is to imply that the Argentine Republic is not in the same league as any of the states of South America, but below them all; it is to imply that she is less capable than Bolivia, than Ecuador, than Paraguay, which good or bad possess a written constitution that is passably observed.

This is absurd.

The Argentine Republic has more means of organization than any other state of South America. What it needs is to coordinate these means.

Which of them possesses the most real, effective, and recognized power? He who claims *to have the power,* to have the foundation stone of the political edifice.

That power needs a law because it does not have it. It is objected, that with it the fact of its existence would be impossible. — In such a case, make it as despotic as one wishes; but give it a law. Without that law of internal subordination, the Argentine Republic may have a beautiful exterior, but it will be nothing within but a tomb of the living. Otherwise it is better to be Argentine from afar, to receive the honorable reflection of the glory without feeling the hero's feet on one's shoulders.

What state of South America possesses a respectively higher number of enlightened inhabitants willing to occupy themselves with industry and work, as a result of the tiredness and weariness of the previous disturbances?

There are those who see a germ of disorder in the return of the émigrés. But that is to fear the conduct of the sinner precisely because he emerges from education. Emigration is the richest school for teaching: Chateaubriand, Lafayette, Mme. Staël, King Louis Philippe[28] are illustrious disciples educated by her. Argentine emigration is the instrument prepared to serve the organization of the country, perhaps in the hands of Rosas himself. His current men are soldiers because up until now they have done nothing but fight: for peace, people of industry are needed; and Argentina's emigrants have had to cultivate this in order to survive abroad.

What today is emigration was the most skilled portion of the country, as it was the richest; it was the most educated, as it asked for institutions and understood them. If it is agreed that Chile, Brazil, Uruguay, where they have mainly resided, are countries that have much good in terms of examples, one must admit that the emigrants who have settled there have had to learn, at least to lead a quiet and busy life.

How could they leave and take dangerous habits with them? He who is less willing to emigrate is he who has emigrated once before. One does not emigrate twice in life. The first is enough to make one circumspect.

Moreover, have not those émigrés, almost all of whom were young when they left, grown in age, in habits of restfulness, in experience? It is indubitably so. But one makes the mistake of supposing them still as restless, fervent, demanding, zealous, with all the qualities they had when they left the country.

In this regard, what happens in Buenos Aires is reproduced in all the provinces. — In all of them there are today abundant materials of order: as they have all suffered, in all of them the spirit of moderation and tol-

28. Germaine de Staël (1766-1817), French novelist and essayist. Louis-Philippe d'Orléans (1773-1850), king of France 1830-1848; his reign is known as the July Monarchy. [E.N.]

erance has taken root. The longing to change things radically has already disappeared. Many influences have been accepted that before were rejected, and in which today normal things are seen that it is necessary to have if one is to establish order and power.

Those who before were repelled with the dictate of *caciques* are today accepted in the bosom of society in which they have made themselves worthy, acquiring more educated habits, more civilized sentiments. Those chiefs, once coarse and rustic, have cultivated their spirit and character in the school of leadership, where many times inferior men are ennobled and enlightened. To govern ten years is to take a course in politics and administration. Each of those men is today one of the means to reach in the interior a stable and advantageous arrangement.

There is no one better than Rosas himself and the circle of important men who surround him to lead the country to the execution of a general arrangement at this time.

What has Rosas done thus far to the advantage of the country, speaking impartially and in good faith? — Nothing: — A great noise, and a great accumulation of power. That is to say, he has laid the foundations of something that does not yet exist and is about to be created. Making noise and accumulating power for the sole pleasure of appearances and authority is frivolous and puerile. These things are obtained in order to operate other real things of genuine importance to the country. Napoleon triumphed in Jena, in Marengo, in Austerlitz, in order to be emperor and to enact the five codes, found the university, the École Normale, and other establishments, by which he endures longer in the memory of the world than by the laurel wreath and the bronze.

Rosas has not yet done anything useful for his country; until now he has been making preparations. He has more power than anyone to do good: just as steam drives the progress of industry, so his arm could propel Argentine progress.

So far he is not a great man: he is only an extraordinary man. Only he who does great things of durable and evident use to the nation deserves the title of great. To obtain fame one need only do surprising things, no matter how extravagant and sterile they are. If Rosas were to disappear today, what would remain that had been created by his hand? What could rouse the sincere gratitude of his homeland? Having temporarily repelled the claims of England and France?

That may have a vain splendor, but it does not amount to a real benefit, because the repelled pretensions do not compromise an interest in any way grave for the Argentine republic.

Having created power? Not even this. Power is not that useful institution, suitable for freedom itself, when it is not an institution organized on invariable bases. Until now, it is an accident: it is the mortal person of Rosas.

It is inconceivable that neither he nor his circle concern themselves with this question, nor work so that the terrible things done until now give at least some fruit of benefit that could justify those things in the eyes of posterity, whose first ranks are only one step from those men!

What are they waiting for, then, to make a start on their work?

The establishment of a general peace, they respond.

This is an error! Peace can come only via the path of law. The constitution is the most powerful means of pacification of internal order. The dictatorship is a constant provocation to fight: it is sarcasm, it is an insult to those who obey it without reservations, without limits. The dictatorship is anarchy formed and converted into a permanent institution. Chile owes its peace to its constitution, and there is no durable peace in the world that does not originate in an explicit agreement that ensures the balance of all public and personal interests.

The reputation of Rosas is so incomplete, it is so exposed to turning into smoke and nothingness. There is so much ambiguity in the value of his titles, so much contrast in the colors under which it is offered, that even those who out of blindness, envy, or some bad sentiment praise his glory when they judge the conduct of his foreign policy, turn mute and consider themselves beaten when the picture is turned over and they are shown the domestic situation.

On this point there is no worthwhile sophism or deception. There is no written constitution in the Argentine Republic; there are no individual, fundamental laws that could take its place. The exercise of the laws that did exist in Argentina has been suspended, while General Rosas is the indefinite trustee *of the sum of political power.*

This is a fact. Here there is no calumny, fervor, or partisan spirit. I acknowledge, I accept all that General Rosas may wish to claim of himself as noble and worthy of respect. But he is a dictator. He is a leader invested with despotic and arbitrary powers whose exercise recognizes no counterweight. This is a fact. It matters little that he uses a power conferred legally. This does not detract from the fact that he is a dictator: the fact is the same, even if the origin is different.

To live in Buenos Aires is to live under the regime of the military dictatorship. One may praise all one likes the moderation of that power: it may at best be a noble dictatorship. In the times in which we live, the ideas have reached a point at which there is more appetite for stingy constitutions than generous dictatorships.

To live under despotism, even if it is legal, is a real misfortune.

This misfortune weighs on the noble and glorious Argentine Republic.

This misfortune has come to be unnecessary and sterile.

Such is the state of the question of its political and social life: the Argentine Republic is the first in glories, the first in fame, the first in power, the first in culture, the first in means to be happy; and the most unfortunate of all, in spite of that.

But her misfortune is not one of destitution. She is unfortunate in the manner of those opulent families, who amid outer pomp and luster, cry out under domestic despotism and discontent.

Forty years ago, afflicted by a less brilliant oppression, Argentina had the fortune to shake it off, and the fruits of her victorious courage were the laurels of her May Revolution.

She has gone on to make greater efforts to rid herself of the adversary who shelters in her entrails: but she has achieved nothing, for between foreign despotism and national despotism there is a difference in favor of the latter, of the magical influence that adds to any cause, the flag of the people. How could you destroy a power that has the astuteness to shelter behind national glory and raise in its battlements the beloved colors of the homeland? What would you do in the presence of such a happy strategy? Invincible by the vanity of the country itself, there is no other way than to capitulate to it, if it has enough honor to lay down in good faith his arbitrary weapons in the religious hands of the Law.

Rosas kneeling, by a spontaneous movement of his will, before the altars of the law is a picture that leaves behind in glory the lion of Castile, submissive at the feet of the Republic crowned in laurels.

But if the picture is more beautiful, it is also less plausible; as it sometimes takes less to defeat a monarchy of three centuries than to crush a proud aberration of personal self-love.

In short: who, if not Rosas, who has gained such unexpected triumphs, is fit to obtain the no less unexpected triumph over himself?

The problem is difficult, though; and it is no small difficulty.

But whatever the solution may be, there is one thing that is true by any reckoning: and it is that the Argentine Republic has before it its most beautiful period of good fortune and prosperity. The rising sun that is seen on her coat of arms is a historic symbol of her destiny: for her, all is future, future greatness and outstanding hope.

Valparaíso, May 25, 1847

2

ESTEBAN ECHEVERRÍA
Symbolic Words (1837) (Excerpts)

I

1. ASSOCIATION

Society is a fact embossed on the pages of history, and the necessary condition instilled in man by Providence for the free exercise and full development of his faculties in making the universe his own. Society is the vast theater where his power grows, where his intelligence is nourished, and where the fruits of his tireless activity appear in quick succession.

Without association there can be no progress; or rather, association is the necessary condition of all civilization and progress.

To work for the spirit of association to spread and be shared among all classes is to set about the great task of progress and civilization for our country.

There can be no true association except among equals. Inequality engenders hatred and passions that suffocate fraternity and weaken social bonds.

To extend the orbit of association and at the same time strengthen and increase it, it is necessary to even out social individualities, or make an effort to attain equality.

In order for association to broadly match its purposes, it is necessary to organize and form it in such a way that social interests and individual interests do not clash or damage each other, or combine the two elements: the social element and the individual, the country and the independence of the citizen. In the alliance and harmony of these two principles lies the whole question of social science.

Original title: "Palabras simbólicas." Source: *Obras completas de D. Esteban Echeverría* [Complete Works of Esteban Echeverría], critical edition by Juan María Gutiérrez (Buenos Aires: C. Casaralle, impr. y libreria de Mayo, 1870–1874), vol. 4 (originally published in 1838).

The rights of man and the right to association are equally legitimate.

Politics must concentrate its labors toward ensuring for each citizen his liberty and individuality through association.

Society must protect the individual independence of all of its members, as all individualities are obliged to join forces for the good of the country.

Society must not absorb the citizen or demand the absolute sacrifice of his individuality. Nor does social interest allow the exclusive predominance of individual interests, because society would then dissolve, as its members would not be joined to each other by a common bond.

The will of a people or of a majority cannot establish laws that undermine individual rights, because there is no absolute authority whatsoever on Earth, because none is an infallible organ of supreme justice, and because above human laws there is the law of conscience and reason.

No legitimate authority rules but in the name of law, justice, and truth: it is up to the national will, the true public conscience, to interpret and decide finally what is just, true, and obligatory: herein lies the domain of positive law. But beyond that law, and in a higher sphere, there exist the rights of man, which as the basis and essential condition of social order overrule and prevail over the positive law.

No majority, party, or assembly has the right to establish a law that attacks natural laws and the principles that preserve society, or that puts the security, freedom, and lives of all men at the mercy of the whim of one man.

Any people that commits this act is foolish, or at least stupid, because it uses a right that it does not possess, because it sells what is not its own to sell, the freedom of others; as it cannot do this, it sells itself, enslaving itself when it is free under the laws of God and nature.

The will of a people could never sanction as just what is essentially unjust.

To plead the national interest as an excuse for the violation of these rights is to introduce Machiavellianism and effectively subject men to the disastrous rule of force and arbitrariness. The welfare of the people does not stem from anything but the religious and inviolable respect for the rights of each and every one of its members.

In order to be able to exercise certain rights over its members, society owes them all justice, equal protection, and laws that guarantee their person, their property, and their freedom. It is obliged to shield them from every injustice or violence: to keep their reciprocal passions at bay, so that they will not harm themselves; to provide them with the means to work without any hindrance whatsoever, for their own well-being, without damaging that of others; to place each man under the safeguard of *all* so that he may peacefully enjoy what he possesses or has acquired through his labor, his industry, or his talents.

The social power that does not do this; that divides instead of fraternizing; that sows distrust and ill will; that stokes the partisan spirit, the spirit of vengeance; that fosters perfidy, espionage, and betrayal, and seeks to convert society into a swarm of informers, executioners, and victims, is an iniquitous, immoral, and abominable power.

The institution of government is useful, moral, and necessary only if it seeks to ensure for each citizen his essential rights and above all his freedom.

The perfection of the association is proportionate to the freedom of each and every person. To achieve this it is necessary to preach fraternity, generosity, mutual sacrifice among the members of the same family. It is necessary to work so that individual forces, instead of isolating themselves and concentrating on their own selfishness, come together simultaneously and collectively for a single goal: the progress and growth of the nation.

The predominance of the individual has led us to perdition. Selfish passions have sown anarchy in the soil of freedom and sterilized its fruits: this has led to the loosening of social ties; here selfishness is contained in all hearts and shows its deformed and menacing face everywhere; these hearts do not beat to the sound of the same words or at the sight of the same symbols; minds are not linked by a common belief in the homeland, in equality, in fraternity and liberty.

How to revive this disintegrating society?

How to make the sociable element of the human heart predominate and save the country and civilization? The remedy exists only in the spirit of association.

Association, progress, liberty, equality, fraternity, correlative terms of the great social and humanitarian synthesis; divine symbols of the successful future of all peoples and of humanity.

Freedom can be realized only by means of equality, and equality without the assistance of association or coming together of all individual forces toward a single, undefined object; *continuous* progress, a fundamental formula of nineteenth-century philosophy.

That social organization offering greater guarantees for the development of equality and liberty and giving more scope to the free and harmonious exercise of human faculties would be the more perfect; that government more analogous with our customs and our social condition would be the better one.

The road to freedom is equality; equality and freedom are the principles that engender democracy.

Democracy is therefore the regime that suits us and the only one that is feasible for us.

It is our mission to prepare the elements to organize and form the seed of democracy that exists in our society.

The Association of the Young Argentine Generation represents the future of the Argentine nation in its provisional organization: its mission is essentially organic. It seeks to spread its spirit and doctrine; to extend the circle of its progressive tendencies; to foster enthusiasm for the great national association by unifying opinion and concentrating it in the homeland and in the principles of equality, liberty, and fraternity of all men.

It will work to reconcile and harmonize the citizen and the homeland, the individual and the association; and in preparing the elements of the organization of the Argentine nationality based on the democratic principle.

In its final form it will seek to bring together the two fundamental ideas of the period: *homeland* and *humanity,* and make the progressive movement of the nation march alongside the progressive movement of the great humanitarian association.

II

2. PROGRESS

"Humanity is like a man who lives forever in constant progress."[1] With one foot in the present and another reaching out into the future,

---

1. Pascal. [A.N.] Echeverría's attribution of this quotation to the French philosopher and mathematician Blaise Pascal (1623–1662) is doubtful. [E.N.]

humanity marches indefatigably, as if impelled by God's spirit, in search of the Eden promised to her hopes.

The heavens, the Earth, the animals, mankind, the whole universe has a life that is developed and manifests itself in time through a series of continuous generations: this law of development is called the *law of progress.*

Just like man, organic beings, and nature, peoples are also in possession of a life of their own, whose continuous development constitutes their progress, because life is nothing more in all creation than the incessant exercise of activity.

All human associations exist because of progress and for progress, and civilization itself is nothing more than the indelible testimony of humanitarian progress.

All of man's and society's endeavors are directed toward procuring the well-being they crave.

The well-being of a people is related to and is born from their progress.

"To live by the law of one's being is well-being. Only through the free and harmonious exercise of all their faculties can men and peoples attain the most extensive application of this law."[2]

A people that does not work to improve its condition is a people that does not obey the law of its being.

The revolution for us is progress. America, believing that it could improve its condition, emancipated itself from Spain; since then it has entered the path of progress.

To progress is to become civilized, or to guide the action of all one's strength to achieving well-being, or in other words, the realization of the *law of one's being.*

Europe is the center of the civilization of centuries and of humanitarian progress.

America must therefore study the progressive movement of European intelligence; but without being blindly tied to its influences. Free

---

2. Young Europe. [A.N.] A political association founded by Giuseppe Mazzini (1805–1872) and other European exiles in Berne, Switzerland, with the object of unifying the republican movements (Young Germany, Young Italy, and Young Poland); it was operated from 1834 to 1836. The quotations are taken from its manifesto. [E.N.]

inquiry and choice are the right and criteria of an enlightened reason. It must appropriate all that can contribute to the fulfillment of its needs; it must walk with the torch of the human spirit if it is to know itself and light up its path.

Every people has its own life and intelligence. "From the development and exercise of this its special mission is born, which participates fully in the general mission of humanity. This mission builds nationality. Nationality is sacred."[3]

A people that enslaves its intelligence to the intelligence of another people is stupid and sacrilegious.

A people that stands still and does not progress has no mission whatsoever, and will never manage to form its nationality.

When American intelligence has reached the level of European intelligence, the sun of its complete emancipation shall shine.

III

3. FRATERNITY — 4. EQUALITY — 5. LIBERTY

"Human fraternity is mutual love, or that generous disposition that makes man inclined to do unto others what he would have done unto him."[4]

Christ made it divine with his blood, and the prophets sanctified it with their martyrdom.

But man then was weak because he lived for himself and only with himself. Humanity or *the concord of the human family,* coming together for the same end, *did not exist.*

The tyrants and the selfish easily snuffed out the divine light of the word of the Redeemer with their deadly breath, and set father against son, brother against brother, family against family, in order to rule.

Blinded and confined in his *ego,* man thought it just to sacrifice the well-being of others to his passions, and peoples and men warred and tore each other apart like wild animals.

"By the law of God and mankind all men are brothers. Any act of selfishness is an attack on human fraternity."[5]

Selfishness is the death of the soul. The selfish man does not feel love,

---

3. Young Europe. [A.N.]

4. Young Europe. [A.N.]

5. Young Europe. [A.N.]

or charity, or friendliness toward his brothers. All his acts are for the satisfaction of *ego;* all his thoughts and actions revolve around his *ego;* and duty, honor, and justice are empty, meaningless words for his depraved spirit.

Selfishness becomes deified and makes its heart the center of the universe. All tyrants are selfishness embodied.

It is the duty of all men who know their mission to fight it hand-to-hand until it is annihilated.

Fraternity is the golden chain that must link all pure and truly patriotic hearts; without this there is no strength, no union, no homeland.

Any act, any word that seeks to loosen this tie is an attack on the homeland and on humanity.

Let us forget the errors of our forefathers; man is fallible. Let us fairly take stock of their deeds and let us see what we would have done under the same circumstances. What we are and what we shall be in the future, we owe to them. Let us open up the sanctuary of our hearts to those who truly served the homeland and sacrificed themselves for it.

The selfish and the evil shall get their due; the judgment of posterity awaits them. The motto of the new generation shall be fraternity.

"Under the law of God and of mankind, all men are equal."[6]

For equality to become a reality it is necessary for men to be imbued with their rights and obligations unto each other.

Equality amounts to those rights and duties being equally admitted and declared by all, and no one being able to avoid the action of the law that establishes them, each man being equally entitled to their enjoyment in proportion to his intelligence and labor. *All privilege is an attack on equality.*

There is no equality where the wealthy class takes precedence and has more privileges than others.

Where a certain class monopolizes the public future.

Where influence and power paralyze the action of the law for some and strengthen it for others.

Where only the parties, not the nation, are sovereign.

Where taxation is not shared equally and in proportion to the assets and industry of each man.

6. Young Europe. [A.N.]

Where the poorer class suffers alone the harshest social burdens, such as military service, etc.

Where the last henchman of power can violate the security of the liberty of the citizen with impunity.

Where rewards and jobs are not given on fact-based merit.

Where each public employee is a mandarin to whom the citizen must bow.

Where public employees are servile agents of power, not paid by and dependent on the nation.

Where the parties grant titles and rewards at their whim.

Where talent and integrity have no merit, but abject stupidity and adulation do.

Any privilege granted to a civil, military, or religious corporation, academy, or university, any exceptional or special law, is also an attack on equality.

Society, or the power that represents it, owes all its members equal protection, security, and liberty; if it is granted to some and not to others, there is inequality and tyranny.

Social power is not moral, nor does it fulfill its ends if it does not protect the weak, the poor, and the needy; that is, if it does not put to use the means that society has put in its hands to bring about equality.

Equality is related to the enlightenment and the well-being of citizens.

Enlightening the masses on their true rights and obligations, educating them in order to make them capable of exercising their citizenship and instilling in them the dignity of free men, protecting them and stimulating them to work and be industrious, giving them the means to acquire well-being and independence: this is how we raise them to a position of equality.

The only *hierarchy* that must exist in a democratic society is that which originates in nature and is as invariable and necessary as nature itself.

Money can never be a qualification if it is not in the hands of the pure, the charitable, and the virtuous. A stupid and villainous soul, a depraved and selfish heart, might be favored by fortune; but neither the gold nor the incense of the lowest commoner will ever instill in them what nature has *denied them: republican capacity and virtues.*

God, supreme intelligence, wanted man to stand out for his reason and intelligence so that he would rule over all creation and overcome all other creatures.

Intelligence, virtue, capacity, proven merit; these are the only hierarchies of man's natural and divine origin.

Society acknowledges only merit attested for in deeds. Society asks of the general, covered in titles and medals: what useful victory have you brought for your country? Of the leader and the affluent it asks: what relief have you brought to the poverty and needs of the people? Of the individual: for what deeds have you merited the respect and consideration of your fellow citizens and humanity? And of all of us, in short: under what circumstances have you proven yourselves to be capable, virtuous, and patriotic?

He who has no answer to these questions, and yet manifests pretensions and seeks supremacy, is a fool who deserves only our pity and contempt.

The problem with social equality lies in this principle: "To each man according to his capacity; to each man according to his deeds."[7]

"Under the law of God and of humanity all men are free."

"Freedom is the right that every man has to use his faculties without any hindrance whatsoever in the pursuit of his well-being, and to choose the means that might help him achieve his goal."[8]

The free exercise of individual faculties must not cause injury or violence to the rights of others. Do not unto others what you would not have done unto yourself; human liberty has no other limits.

There is no liberty where man cannot change his abode as he pleases.

Where he is not permitted to enjoy the fruits of his industry and his labor.

Where he must sacrifice his time and his assets to power.

Where he can be harassed and insulted by the thugs of an arbitrary power.

Where without having broken the law, without prior judgment or

---

7. Saint-Simon. [A.N.] Claude Henri de Rouvroy, comte de Saint-Simon (1760–1825), French philosopher and economist; his socialist ideas had a great influence on materialistic and utopic ideologies during the nineteenth century. [E.N.]

8. Young Europe. [A.N.]

due process whatsoever, he can be incarcerated or deprived of the use of his physical or intellectual faculties.

Where his right to speak or publish his opinions is limited.

Where a religion or form of worship is imposed on him that differs from that which his conscience judges to be true.

Where he can be arbitrarily disturbed in his home, torn from the bosom of his family, and banished beyond his homeland.

Where his security, his life, and his assets are at the mercy of a leader's whim.

Where he is obliged to bear arms without absolute need and without this being required by the common good.

Where obstacles and conditions are placed on the exercise of any industry whatsoever, such as printing, etc.

IV

6. GOD, THE CENTER AND PERIPHERY OF OUR
RELIGIOUS BELIEF; CHRISTIANITY; ITS LAW

The natural religion is that imperious instinct that leads man to pay homage to his Creator.[9]

Man's relationships with God are, like those of son to father, of a moral nature. As God is the pure source of our life and our faculties, of our hopes and joys, in exchange for those assets we give him the only offering that can please him, the homage of our hearts.

But natural religion has not been enough for man because, lacking as it is in certainty, life, and sanction, it has not satisfied the needs of his conscience; and it has been necessary for positive religions that base their authority on historic facts to come and proclaim the laws that must rule those intimate relations between man and his Creator.

The best of all positive religions is Christianity, because it is nothing more than the revelation of the moral instincts of humanity.

The Gospel is the law of God because it is the moral law of conscience

---

9. In several paragraphs, this one especially, there are some critical opinions provoked by the exceptional situation in which our country found itself; their intention will be clear to readers of the River Plate. However, let there be a warning, because if these opinions are considered in *abstract,* they may appear erroneous or contradictory to readers unfamiliar with our affairs. [A.N.]

and of reason. Christianity brought to the world fraternity, equality, and liberty, and redeemed the human race by restoring its rights. Christianity is in its essence a civilizing and progressive force.

The world was immersed in darkness and the word of Christ illuminated it, and out of chaos grew a world. Mankind was a corpse, and it received life and resurrection with his spirit.

The Gospel is the law of love, and as the Apostle James says, the perfect law, which is the law of liberty. Christianity must be the religion of democracies.

Examine everything and choose what is good, says the Gospel; and thus it has proclaimed the independence of reason and of the freedom of conscience, because freedom lies mainly in the right to examine and to choose.

All religions imply worship. Worship is the visible part or the outer manifestation of religion, just as the word is the necessary element of thought.

Religion is a tacit pact between God and the human conscience; it forms a spiritual bond that joins the creature with its Maker. Man should therefore direct his thoughts to God as he sees fit. God is the only judge of the actions of his conscience, and no earthly authority may appropriate that divine prerogative, and will never be able to do so, because conscience is free.

If freedom of conscience is suppressed, the voice and the hands shall exercise, automatically, one might say, the practices of worship; but the heart will deny it and will guard freedom in its inviolable sanctuary.

If freedom of conscience is the individual's right, then freedom of worship is a right of religious communities.

If freedom of conscience is recognized, it would be contradictory not to then recognize freedom of worship, which is nothing more than the immediate application of the former.

The profession of beliefs and of worship will be free only when no obstacle whatsoever is placed in preaching the doctrine of the former, or on the practice of the latter, and when the individuals of any religious communion have the same civil and political rights as other citizens.

Religious society is independent of civil society; the former directs its hope to another world, the latter concentrates it here on Earth; the mission of the former is spiritual, that of the latter temporal. The tyrants have forged chains from religion for man, whence the impure alliance of power and the altar has come forth.

It is not the government's responsibility to regulate beliefs, placing itself between God and the human conscience: but to protect the principles that preserve society and safeguard social morals.

If any religion or worship were to publicly or directly, in deed or writing, offend social morals and disturb order, it will be the duty of the government to take action to suppress its excesses.

The government's jurisdiction in terms of religion should limit itself to ensuring that they do not offend each other or sow social discord.

The state, as a political body, cannot have a religion, because as it is not an individual person it lacks its own conscience.

The dogma of the dominant religion is also unjust and an attack on equality because it pronounces social excommunication on those who do not profess its creed, and deprives them of their natural rights without exempting them from social burdens.

The principle of freedom of conscience could never be reconciled with the dogma of the state religion.

If freedom of conscience is recognized, no religion may be declared dominant, or sponsored by the state; all religions must be respected and protected equally, as long as their morals are pure and their worship does not infringe on social order.

The word *tolerance,* in terms of religion and worship, indicates only the absence of liberty and contains an insult to the rights of mankind. What is inhibited or evil is tolerated; a right is recognized and proclaimed. The human spirit is a free essence; freedom is an indestructible element of its nature and a gift from God.

The priest is the minister of worship; the priesthood is a public burden. The mission of the priest is to *moralize,* to preach brotherhood— charity, that is, the law of peace and love, the law of God.

The priest who stirs up passions and provokes vengeance from the pulpit of the Holy Spirit is impious and sacrilegious.

Love your neighbor as yourself; love your enemies, says Christ; this is the word of the priest.

The priest must preach tolerance, not persecution of indifference and impiety. Force makes hypocrites, not believers, and ignites fanaticism and war.

"How will they have faith in the word of the priest if he himself does

SYMBOLIC WORDS (1837) : 39

not obey the law?" He who says, 'I know him,' but disobeys his commandments is a liar, and the truth is not in him."[10]

"We do not demand blind obedience, says Saint Paul; we teach, we prove, we persuade: *Fides suadenda non imperanda,* reiterates Saint Bernard."[11]

The mission of the priest is exclusively spiritual, because in mixing mundane passions and interests he compromises and blemishes the sanctity of his ministry and brings upon himself scorn and hatred in place of love and veneration.

The vicars and ministers of Christ must not take any temporal employment or authority whatsoever; *Regnum meum non est de hoc mundo,* our divine master said, and he showed thus the limits of the Church's authority.

The clergy, as members of the state, are under its jurisdiction and cannot form a privileged body distinct from society. Like all other citizens, they must be bound by the same burdens and obligations, the same civil and penal laws, and the same authorities. All men are equal; only merit and virtue can engender supremacy.[12] . . .

X

12. ORGANIZATION OF THE FATHERLAND
ON DEMOCRATIC FOUNDATIONS

Equality and liberty are the two central axes, or rather, the two poles of the world of democracy.

Democracy arises from a necessary fact, namely, the equality of the classes, and marches steadily toward the conquest of the broadest kingdom of liberty, of *individual, civil, and political freedom.*

10. Saint John, Ep. IX, chap. 2. [A.N.]

The author's citation is incorrect. Only the second part of the quotation is from 1 John 2:4. The English translation is taken from the Revised Standard Version of the Bible. [E.N.]

11. The reference to Saint Paul is doubtful. Bernard of Clairvaux's maxim is "Fides suadenda non imponenda" (By persuasion, not by imposition, are men won to faith) (Sermon 66). [E.N.]

12. We have not been able or wanted to touch on all the points that the religious question covers: we have been content to indicate the most essential ones for now that involve the state of our society. [A.N.]

Democracy is not a form of government, but the very essence of all republican governments, or instituted by all for the good of the community or the society.

Democracy is the rule of liberty based on the equality of the classes.

All modern political associations seek to establish the equality of the classes, and it can be assured, in observing the progressive movement of the European and American nations, "that the gradual development of equality of conditions is a providential fact; it has the principal characteristics of one: it is universal, it is lasting, it escapes every day from human power; all events, like all men, serve its development."[13]

Democracy is the government of the majorities or the uniform *consent* of the reason of all men, working for the creation of the law and to decide supremely over all that interests society.

That general and uniform consent constitutes the *sovereignty of the people.*

The sovereignty of the people is unlimited in all that belongs to society, in politics, in philosophy, in religion; but the people are not sovereign as regards the individual, his conscience, his property, his life, and his liberty.

Association has been established for the good of all men; it is the common foundation of all individual interests or the animated symbol of the strength and intelligence of each one.

The goal of society is to organize democracy and ensure to each and every one of its members *the broadest and most free enjoyment of their natural rights; the broadest and freest exercise of their faculties.*

Therefore the sovereign people or the majority cannot violate those individual rights, limit the exercise of those faculties, which are at once the origin, the bond, the condition, and the goal of society.

From the moment it violates them, the pact is broken, society dis-

13. Tocqueville. [A.N.] Alexis de Tocqueville (1805–1859), French political writer and historian, is best known for his work *De la démocratie en Amérique.* The English translation of the quotation is taken from the introduction to *Democracy in America: Historical-Critical Edition of De la démocratie en Amérique,* ed. Eduardo Nolla, translated from the French by James T. Schleifer, a bilingual French-English edition, vol. 1 (Indianapolis: Liberty Fund, 2010). See http://oll.libertyfund.org/index.php?option=com _frontpage&Itemid=149. [E.N.]

solves, and each man shall be the absolute owner of his will and his actions and derive his right from his strength.

It follows from here that the limit of collective reason is the *right;* and the limit of individual reason, the *sovereignty of the reason of the people.*

The rights of man come before the rights of society. The individual under God's law and the law of mankind is the sole owner of his life, his property, his conscience, and his liberty: his life is a gift from God; his property, the sweat of his brow; his conscience, the eye of his soul and the intimate judge of his actions; his freedom, the necessary condition for the development of the faculties that God has given him so that he might live happily, the very essence of his life, as life without freedom is death.

The right of the association is therefore circumscribed by the orbit of individual rights.

The sovereign, the people, the majority dictate the social and positive law with the goal of strengthening and enacting the primeval law, the natural law of the individual. So it is that, far from denying man part of his freedom and rights when he enters society, he has, on the contrary, come together with the others and formed the association in order to ensure and extend them.

If the positive law of the sovereign follows natural law, that right is legitimate and all must obey it, on pain of punishment as offenders; if it violates it, it is illegitimate and tyrannical and no one is obliged to obey it.

The individual's right to resist the tyrannical decisions of the sovereign people or of the majority is therefore legitimate, as is the right to repel force with force, and to kill the thief or murderer who attacks our property or our lives, as this is born from the very conditions of the social pact.

The sovereignty of the people is unlimited as long as it respects the right of man: first principle.

The sovereignty of the people is absolute as long as reason is its norm: second principle.

Only collective reason is sovereign, not the collective will. The will is blind, whimsical, irrational; the will wants, reason examines, weighs, and decides.

It therefore follows that the sovereignty of the people may reside only in the *reason of the people,* and that only the sensible and rational part of the social community is summoned to exercise it.

The ignorant part remains under the protection and safeguard of the law dictated by the uniform consent of the rational people.

Democracy, then, is not the absolute despotism of the masses, nor of the majorities; it is the rule of reason.

Sovereignty is the greatest and most solemn act of reason of a free people. How can those who do not know of its importance take part in this act? Those who through their lack of enlightenment are incapable of discerning right from wrong in terms of public affairs? Those who, ignorant as they are of what best suits them, have no opinion of their own and are therefore exposed to yield to the suggestions of the malicious? Those who through their imprudent vote might compromise the liberty of the country and the existence of society? I say, how could the blind see, the crippled walk, the mute speak; that is, how could he who has neither capacity nor independence take part in sovereign acts?

Another condition for the exercise of sovereignty is industry. The idler, the vagabond, he who has no trade, cannot be part of the sovereign, because he is not tied by any interest whatsoever to society and will easily give his vote for gold or threats.

He whose well-being depends on the will of another and enjoys no personal independence cannot be entitled to sovereignty, as he would hardly sacrifice his interests for the independence of his reason.

The tutelage of the ignorant, of the vagabond, of he who does not have personal independence, is therefore necessary. The law does not prevent them from exercising sovereign rights per se, only as long as they remain minors; it does not divest them of these but imposes a condition for possessing them; the condition of emancipating themselves.

But the people, the masses, do not always have the means in their hands to gain their emancipation. Society or the *government* that represents it must put it within their reach.

It should foster industry, destroy the fiscal laws that hinder its development, not overburden it with taxation but leave it to exercise its activity freely and austerely.

It should spread enlightenment throughout society and hold out a beneficent hand to the poor and the destitute. It should seek to raise the proletarian class to the level of the other classes, emancipating first its body in order to then emancipate its reason.

To emancipate the ignorant masses and open for them the road to sovereignty it is necessary to educate them. The masses have only their instincts; they are more sensitive than rational; they want the good, but they do not know where to find it; they wish to be free, but they do not know the path to freedom.

Education for the masses must be systematized.

By giving them morals, religion will make fertile in their hearts the seeds of good habits. Elementary education will put them in a position to attain greater enlightenment and one day grasp the rights and duties imposed on them by citizenship.[14]

The ignorant masses, however, while temporarily deprived of the exercise of the rights of sovereignty or political liberty, fully enjoy their individual liberty; like all members of society, their natural rights are inviolable; in addition, civil liberty protects them, as it does everyone; the same civil, penal, and constitutional law, dictated by the sovereign, protects their lives, their property, their conscience, and their liberty; it brings them to court when they commit a crime, condemning them or absolving them.

They cannot participate in the creation of the law that forms the rights and duties of the associate members as long as they remain under tutelage or in minority of age, but that same law gives them the means to emancipate themselves and keeps them in the meantime under its protection and defense.

Democracy works to even out conditions and make the classes equal.

Class equality includes individual liberty, civil liberty, and political liberty. When all members of the association are in full and absolute possession of these liberties and jointly exercise sovereignty, democracy shall have been definitively constituted on the indestructible basis of class equality; this is the third principle.

We have unraveled the spirit of democracy and set out the limits of the sovereignty of the people. Let us now examine how the sovereign acts, or in other words, what apparent or visible form it imposes on its decisions, and how it organizes the government of democracy.

For the creation of a law, the sovereign delegates its powers, reserv-

14. The Association shall at an opportune time present a complete plan of popular education, and shall propose adequate means for bringing it into effect. [A.N.]

ing the power to enact the law. The delegate represents the sovereign's interests and reason.

The legislator exercises a limited and temporary sovereignty; his norm is reason.

The legislator issues the organic law and formulates therein the rights and duties of the citizen and the conditions of the pact of association.

It divides social authority into three great powers, of whom it draws the limits and attributes that constitute the symbolic unity of democratic sovereignty.

The legislative power represents the reason of the people, the judiciary its justice, and the executive its action and will; the first creates the law, the second applies it, and the third executes it; the first votes on expenditure and taxation and the immediate organ of the desires and needs of the people; the second is the organ of social justice, manifested in the laws; the third is the tireless administrator and agent of social interests.

These three powers are truly independent; but far from isolating themselves and condemning themselves to immobility, offering mutual resistance to maintain a certain illusory balance, they will proceed harmoniously, via different routes, to the single goal of social progress. Their strength shall be the sum of the three joint forces, their wills shall unite in a single will; just as reason, sentiment, and will constitute the moral unit of the individual, the three powers shall form the unity that shall lead to democracy, or the legitimate organ of sovereignty, intended to pass judgment without appeal on all matters that interest society.

The conditions of the pact are written; the cornerstone of the social edifice has been laid; the government is organized and driven by the spirit of the fundamental law. The legislator presents it to the people; the people approve it, if it is the living symbol of their reason.

The work of the constituent legislator is done.

If the organic law is not the expression of public reason proclaimed by its legitimate representatives, if they have not spoken in this law of the interests and opinions of their constituents, if they have not succeeded in interpreting their thoughts; or in other words, if the legislators, ignoring their mission and the vital demands of the people they represent, have become miserable plagiarists and copied, from here and there, articles from other countries' constitutions, instead of writing one with living roots in the popular conscience, their work shall be an aborted monster, a lifeless body, an ephemeral law without action that could never be sanctioned by public judgment.

The legislator will have betrayed the trust of his constituents; he will be an imbecile.

If on the contrary the work of the legislator fully satisfies public reason, his work is great, his creation sublime, and resembles the work of God.

Then neither the people, nor the legislator, nor any social authority whatsoever will be able to raise its sacrilegious hand in that sanctuary where the supreme and inviolable law is written in divine letters; the law of laws, which each and every man has acknowledged, proclaimed, and sworn before God and man to respect.

Sovereignty, it can be said, has been embodied in that law, the reason and consent of the people is there; order, justice, and liberty are there; therein lies the safeguard of democracy.

This law could be revised, improved in time, and adapted to the progress of public reason by an assembly elected ad hoc by the sovereign; but until such time comes which the law itself indicates, its power is omnipotent; its will dominates all wills; its reason rules over all reason.

No majority, no party, no assembly may break this law, on pain of being usurpatory and tyrannical.

That law is the touchstone for all other laws; its light illuminates them, and all thoughts and actions of the social body and of the constituted powers are born from it and converge at its center. It is their driving force and around it gravitate, like heavenly bodies around the sun, all the partial forces that make up the world of democracy.

With democracy thus constituted, the sovereignty of the people arises from that point and starts to exercise its unceasing and unlimited action, but always circling in the orbit that the organic law traces; its right does not go beyond this.

Through its representatives, it makes and reverses laws, innovating every day, taking its activity everywhere and imposing an incessant movement, a progressive transformation to the social machine.

Each act of its will is a new creation; each decision of its reason is progress.

Politics, religion, philosophy, art, industry; it examines everything, develops it, puts it to the supreme vote, and enacts it; the voice of the people is the voice of God.

From this we can deduce that if the people have no enlightenment or

morality; that if the seeds of a constitution are not, so to speak, disseminated in their customs, in their sentiments, in their memories, in their
traditions, the work of organizing it is unrealizable; that the legislator is
not called upon to create an organic law, or to adapt that of other countries to his, but to know the instincts, needs, interests, all that forms the
intellectual, moral, and physical life of the people he represents, and
proclaim them and formulate them in a law; and that legislators must
only be those who combine the highest capacity and noblest virtue with
the most complete knowledge of the spirit and demands of the nation.

From here it also arises that if the legislator is conscious of his duty,
before examining which form of government would be preferable, he
must find out whether the people are in a fit condition to be ruled by
a constitution, and if this is the case offer them not the best and most
perfect constitution in theory, but that which is best adapted to their
condition.

"I have given the Athenians not the best laws," said Solon,[15] "but those
which they are in a fit state to receive."

From this it can be inferred that when public reason is not ripe, the
constituent legislator has no mission whatsoever, and as he cannot be
conscious of his dignity, or of the importance of the role he represents,
he is part of a farce that he himself does not understand, and passes or
copies laws with the same ease as he would the briefs of his legal practice
or the accounts of his business.

From this, in short, we can deduce the need to prepare the legislator
before entrusting to him the work of a constitution.

The legislator will not be prepared if the people are not. How can the
legislator do the right thing if the people are ignorant of what is good?
If they do not appreciate the advantages of liberty? If they prefer inertia
over activity? Their habits over innovations? What they know and can
touch over what they do not know and view from afar?

For this reason, to prepare the people and the legislator it is vital to
draw up first the subject of the law, that is, to spread the ideas that should be
embodied in the legislators and realized in the laws, making them circulate, giving them popularity, incorporating them into the public spirit.

It is necessary, in a word, to enlighten the reason of the *people* and

15. Athenian statesman and lawmaker (ca. 638 B.C.-558 B.C.). Quotation taken from
Plutarch, *Solon,* 15, 1. [E.N.]

that of the *legislator* on political questions before proceeding to *constitute* the nation.

Only on this condition will we achieve what we all earnestly desire, that a *future legislator* or a national representation may appear capable of understanding and remediating the ills that beset society, of satisfying its desires and laying the foundation of an unshakeable and permanent social order.

As long as the public spirit is not sufficiently mature, the *constitutions* will do no more than fuel anarchy and foster in all spirits the scorn of all law, of all justice, and of the most sacred principles.

As democracy is the *government of the people* by itself, it requires the constant action of all of man's faculties and cannot be made firm without the assistance of enlightenment and morality.

Democracy, arising from the principle of class equality, seeks to take root in the ideas, customs, and sentiments of the people and elaborates its laws and institutions so that they might extend and strengthen its predominance.

All the efforts of our governments and legislators must be directed toward fulfilling the aims of democracy.

The Association of the Young Argentine Generation believes that the seed of democracy exists in our society; its mission is to preach, to spread its spirit, and to devote the action of its faculties so that one day democracy will be established in the Republic.

It knows that many obstacles will be placed in its path by certain aristocratic remnants, certain retrograde traditions and laws, the lack of enlightenment and of morality.

The Association knows that the work of organizing democracy is not done in a day; that constitutions are not improvised; that liberty can be based only on the foundations of enlightenment and customs; that a society is not enlightened and moralized at a single stroke; that the reason of a people aspiring to be free can ripen only with time; but, having faith in the future and believing that the high aims of the revolution were not only to bring down the former social order, but also to rebuild a new order, will work with the full extent of its faculties so that the generations to come, reaping the fruit of its labor, may have in their hands better elements than us to organize and constitute Argentine society on the unshakeable foundation of equality and democratic liberty.

DOMINGO FAUSTINO SARMIENTO

3

Civilization and Barbarism: The Life of Juan Facundo Quiroga:[1] Introduction to the 1845 Edition

Je demande à l'historien l'amour de l'humanité ou de la liberté; sa justice impartiale ne doit pas être impassive. Il faut, au contraire, qu'il souhaite, qu'il espère, qu'il souffre, ou soit heureux de ce qu'il raconte.— Villemain, *Cours de littérature*[2]

I will evoke you, dread shadow of Facundo, so that, shaking off the bloodstained dust that covers your ashes, you may rise up to explain the secret life and internal convulsions tearing at the innards of a noble people! You hold the secret: reveal it to us! Ten years after your tragic death, the man of the cities and the gaucho of the Argentine plains, when taking different trails through the desert, would say: "No, he is not dead! He is still alive! He will return!"

True! Facundo is not dead; he is alive in the popular traditions, in the politics and revolutions of Argentina; in Rosas, his heir, his complement: his soul has passed into this other, more finished, more perfect mold; and what was in him merely instinct, beginning, tendency, became in Rosas system, effect, and end. Rustic, colonial, barbaric nature changed in this metamorphosis into art, system, and regular policy capable of presenting itself to the face of the world as the way of being

Original title: *Civilización y barbarie: Vida de Juan Facundo Quiroga:* Introducción a la edición de 1845. Source: *Facundo,* critical edition by Alberto Palcos (Buenos Aires: Universidad Nacional de la Plata, 1938).

1. Juan Facundo Quiroga (1788–1835), Argentine caudillo, governor of La Rioja Province, and one of the more important leaders of the Federal Party. He was murdered at Barranca Yaco, in Córdoba Province. [E.N.]

2. Abel-François Villemain, French literary writer (1790–1870). The quotation is taken from his *Cours de littérature française* (1828–1829): "I ask the historian to love humanity or liberty; his impartial justice must not be dispassionate. On the contrary, he must desire, hope, suffer, or be happy about what he narrates." [E.N.]

of a people embodied in one man who has aspired to take on the airs of a genius dominating events, men, and things.

Facundo, provincial, barbaric, courageous, bold, was replaced by Rosas,[3] the son of cultured Buenos Aires, without being so himself; by Rosas, false, cold-hearted, calculating mind, who does evil without passion and slowly organizes despotism with all the intelligence of a Machiavelli. A tyrant without rival today on Earth, why do his enemies want to deny him the title of *Great,* which his courtiers lavish on him? Yes, great and very great he is, to the glory and shame of his homeland, for if he has found thousands of degraded beings to yoke themselves to his wagon and haul it over corpses, there are also thousands of generous souls who, in fifteen years of bloody combat, have not given up hope of vanquishing the monster presented to us by the enigma of the political organization of the Republic. A day will finally come when they will solve it; and the Argentine Sphinx, half cowardly woman, half blood-thirsty tiger, shall die at their feet, giving the Thebes of the Plate the elevated rank that is its due among the nations of the New World.

It is necessary, however, to untie this knot that the sword has been unable to cut, to study thoroughly the twists and turns of the threads that form it, and search in our national precedents, in the physiognomy of our soil, in our popular customs and traditions, the places where they are attached.

The Argentine Republic is today the region of Hispanic America that, in its outward expression, has drawn the preferential attention of the European nations, which on no few occasions have found themselves embroiled in its disturbances, or drawn, as if by a maelstrom, toward the center where such conflicting elements swirl. France was on the point of giving in to this attraction and, not without great efforts of rowing and sailing, not without losing the rudder, managed to steer away and remain at a distance. Its most skilled politicians have been unable to understand anything their eyes have seen when casting a hasty glance over the American power challenging that great nation. On seeing the burning lavas that churn, boil, crash, and roar in this great hub of internecine struggle, those who hold themselves to be best informed have said: "It is an insignificant volcano, without a name, one of many that appear in America: soon it will be extinguished"; and they have turned their gaze

3. See Alberdi, "The Argentine Republic," note 2, in this volume. [E.N.]

elsewhere, satisfied at having provided a solution as easy as it is exact to the social phenomena they have seen only superficially as a group. South America in general, and especially the Argentine Republic, has lacked a Tocqueville who, equipped beforehand with the knowledge of social theories, like the scientific traveler with barometer, octant, and compass, would come to penetrate into the interior of our political life, as into a vast field not yet explored or described by science, and reveal to Europe, to France, so eager for new phases in the life of the different portions of humanity, this new way of life, which has no known, clearly marked precedent. The mystery of the obstinate struggle tearing the Republic to shreds would then have been explained; the conflicting, unconquerable elements that collide would have been classified distinctly: the configuration of the land and the habits that this engenders; the Spanish traditions and the iniquitous, plebeian national consciousness left by the Inquisition and Hispanic absolutism; the influence of the opposing ideas that have disrupted the political world; indigenous barbarism; European civilization; the democracy enshrined by the revolution of 1810; equality, whose dogma has penetrated to the lowest layers of society, all these would have been allocated their part. This study, which we are not yet in a state to conduct due to our lack of philosophical and historical instruction, conducted by competent observers, would have revealed to the astonished eyes of Europe a new world in politics, a naïve, frank, and primitive struggle between the latest progress of the human spirit and the rudiments of savage life, between populous cities and shady forests. The problem of Spain would then have become clearer, that straggler behind Europe which, cast between the Mediterranean and the ocean, between the Middle Ages and the nineteenth century, joined to cultured Europe by a broad isthmus and separated from barbaric Africa by a narrow strait, is teetering between two opposing forces, now rising up on the scales of the free peoples, now falling on those of despotism; now unholy, now fanatical; now a declared constitutionalist, now an imprudent despot; sometimes cursing its broken chains, now folding its arms and crying out for the yoke to be imposed upon it, which appears to be its condition and its mode of existence. What! The problem of European Spain could not be resolved by a minute examination of American Spain, as the ideas and morality of the parents are traced through the education and habits of the children? What! Does it mean nothing for history and philosophy this eternal struggle of the Hispanic American peoples, that supine dearth of political and industrial ability that has them worried and twisting and turning with no fixed north, no precise object, no knowing why they cannot find a day of rest, nor what enemy hand tosses and pushes them into the fatal whirlwind that drags them, against their will and without being able to evade its evil influence? Was it not worth knowing why in Paraguay, a land cleared by the *wise* hand of the Jesuits, a *wise man* educated in the classrooms of the ancient University of Córdoba turns a new page in the history of the aberrations of the human spirit, encloses a people within the bounds of its primitive forests, and, erasing the paths that lead to this hidden China, conceals and hides its prey for thirty years in the depths of the American continent, without letting it utter a single cry, until, dead from old age and the still fatigue of standing motionless trampling on a submissive people, it may in the end say, in a weary and barely intelligible voice to those who roam his environs: I am still alive!, but how I have suffered! *quantum mutatus ab illo!*[4] What a transformation Paraguay has suffered; what bruises and sores the yoke has left on its neck, which put up no resistance! Does the spectacle of the Argentine Republic deserve study, which, after twenty years of internal convulsion, of experiments with organization of all kinds, produces, in the end, from the depths of its bowels, from the depths of its heart, the same Doctor Francia[5] in the person of Rosas, but greater, more self-possessed, and more hostile, if that is possible, to the ideas, customs, and civilization of the peoples of Europe? Is not the same rancor against the foreign element discovered in him, the same idea of government authority, the same insolence to challenge the disapproval of the world, and in addition, his wild originality, his coldly fierce nature, and his obstinate will, even to the sacrifice of the fatherland, as in Saguntum and Numantia;[6] to the abjuration of the future and the rank

4. "How changed from what he once was!" (Virgil, *Aeneid,* ii, 274). [E.N.]

5. José Gaspar Rodríguez de Francia (1766–1840), commonly known as Doctor Francia, was a Paraguayan leader of the independence movement who ruled Paraguay as "Perpetual Dictator" from 1816 until his death. [E.N.]

6. Celtiberian towns in what is now Spain. Their citizens decided to commit suicide and burn their town rather than fall into the hands of their enemies. Saguntum was taken by Hannibal in 219 B.C., and Numantia was razed by the Romans in 133 B.C. [E.N.]

of a cultured nation, like the Spain of Philip II and Torquemada?[7] Is this an accidental whim, a mechanical deviation caused by the appearance on the scene of a powerful genius; just as the planets leave their regular orbits, attracted by the approach of another, yet without quite escaping the attraction of their center of rotation, which then resumes its preponderance and brings them back into their regular course? M. Guizot[8] has said from the French rostrum: "There are two parties in America: the European party and the American party; the latter is the stronger"; and when alerted to the fact that 108 Frenchmen have taken up arms in Montevideo and have joined their futures, their lives, and their welfare to the triumph of the civilized European party, he merely adds: "The French are most meddlesome, and compromise their nation with other governments." God be praised! M. Guizot, the historian of European *civilization,* who has determined the new elements that modified Roman civilization, and has penetrated into the tangled labyrinth of the Middle Ages to show how the French nation has been the crucible in which the modern spirit has been elaborated, mixed, and recast; M. Guizot, minister of the king of France, as the only solution to this expression of deep sympathy between the French and the enemies of Rosas just says: "The French are most meddlesome!" The other American peoples who, indifferent and impassive, look on this struggle and these alliances of an Argentine party with any European element lending its support, filled with indignation in their turn, exclaim: "These Argentines are very friendly with the Europeans!" And the tyrant of the Argentine Republic takes it upon himself officiously to finish their sentence, adding, "Traitors to the American cause!" True! they all say; traitors!, that is the word. True! we say; traitors to the barbarian, absolutist, Spanish, American cause! Have you not seen the word *savage* fluttering over our heads?

There's the rub: to be or not to be savage. Is not Rosas, according to this, an isolated incident, an aberration, a monstrosity? Or is he, on the contrary, a social manifestation; is he a formula for the way of being of a people? Why do you insist on fighting him, then, if he is inevitable, necessary, natural, and logical? My Lord! Why do you fight him! . . . Because a venture is arduous, is it therefore absurd? Because the evil prin-

7. Philip II was king of Spain from 1556 to 1598. Tomás de Torquemada (1420–1498), a Dominican friar, was Inquisitor General of Spain from 1482 to 1492. [E.N.]

8. See Alberdi, "The Argentine Republic," note 10, in this volume. [E.N.]

ciple triumphs, should the field be abandoned with resignation? Are civilization and freedom weak in the world today because Italy groans under the weight of every despotism, because Poland wanders the face of the Earth begging a loaf of bread and a little freedom? Why do you fight him! ... Are we not alive, those of us who, after so many disasters, still survive; or have we lost our awareness of what is right and of our homeland's future because we have lost a few battles? What! are ideas also left among the remains of the fighting? Are we able to do something different than what we do, precisely as Rosas cannot stop being what he is? Is there nothing providential in these struggles of the people? Was victory ever awarded to him who does not persevere? Indeed, are we to abandon one of the most privileged soils of America to the ravages of barbarism and have a hundred navigable rivers abandoned to the water-birds that are in calm possession and wander them *ab initio?*

Are we voluntarily to close the door on European immigration, which knocks repeatedly on it to people our deserts, and make us, in the shadow of our flag, a people as innumerable as the sands on the shore? Are we to leave aside, illusory and vain, the dreams of development, power, and glory with which we have been lulled since childhood, the forecasts that are enviously directed at us by those in Europe who study the needs of humanity? After Europe, is there any uninhabited Christian world that can be civilized other than America? Are there in America many peoples who are, like the Argentine people, called on to receive the European population that overflows like liquid in a glass? Do you not ultimately want us to invoke science and industry to our assistance, to call to them with all our might to come and sit in our midst, the one free from any obstacle to thought, the other safe from all violence and all coercion? Oh! This future is not so easily relinquished! It is not relinquished because an army of twenty thousand men guards the gateway to the fatherland: soldiers die in combat, desert, or switch flags. It is not relinquished because fortune has favored a tyrant for long and heavy years: fortune is blind, and the day she does not happen to find her favorite amid the dense smoke and suffocating dust of combat, farewell tyrant! farewell tyranny! It is not relinquished because all the brutal and ignorant colonial traditions have accomplished more, in a time of irrationality, in the mind of the unskilled masses: political upheavals also bring experience and light, and it is a law of humanity that new interests, fertile ideas, and progress will ultimately triumph over antiquated traditions, ignorant habits, and stagnant concerns. It is not relinquished because there are thousands of guileless men in a people, who take good for evil, selfish men who profit from it, indifferent men who see it but take no interest, timid men who do not dare to fight it, corrupt men, in short, who unknowingly deliver themselves to it out of an inclination to evil, out of depravity: there has always been all this in every people, and never has evil definitively triumphed. It is not relinquished because the other American peoples cannot lend us their aid, because governments see from afar only the glint of organized power and cannot distinguish in the humble and desolate darkness of revolutions the great elements that are struggling to develop; because the so-called liberal opposition abjures its principles, imposes silence on its conscience, and, to squash an importunate insect underfoot, stamps the noble sole the insect was attached to. It is not relinquished because the peoples en masse turn their backs on us on account of our miseries and our greatnesses being too far away from their sight to affect them. No! a future so immense, a mission so lofty, is not relinquished because of such a series of contradictions and difficulties: difficulties are vanquished, contradictions end by dint of contradiction!

From Chile, we cannot give anything to *those who persevere* in the struggle under all the hardships of privations and with the exterminating blade, which, like the sword of Damocles, hangs above their heads at all times. Nothing! save ideas, consolations, encouragement; no weapon is allowed the combatants save the one that the *free press* of Chile supplies to all free men. The press! The press! Here then, tyrant, is the enemy you suffocated among us. Here then is the golden fleece we try to conquer. Here then is how the press of France, England, Brazil, Montevideo, Chile, and Corrientes will disturb your sleep amid your victims' sepulchral silence; here then is the fact that you have felt compelled to steal the gift of tongues in order to palliate evil, a gift given only to preach goodness. Here then is the fact that you stoop to justify yourself and go among all the European and American peoples begging a venal, fratricidal pen, so that, by means of the press, it will defend him who has put it in chains! Why do you not allow in your homeland the discussion you keep up in all other peoples? For what, then, so many thousands of victims sacrificed by the dagger; for what so many battles, if, after all, you were to end up in the peaceful discussion of the press?

He who has read the foregoing pages may think it is my intention to paint an impassioned picture of the acts of barbarism that have dishonored the name of Don Juan Manuel de Rosas. Let them be reassured, those who nurture any such fear. The last page of this immoral biography has not yet been written; the measure is not yet full; the days of its hero have not yet been counted. Moreover, the passions he arouses in his enemies are still too rancorous for themselves to put faith in their impartiality or their justice. It is with another character that I must occupy myself: Facundo Quiroga is the caudillo whose deeds I wish to record on paper.

For ten years now the Earth has covered his ashes, and very cruel and poisoned would seem the calumny that went to dig the graves in search of victims. Who fired the *official* bullet that halted his career? Did it come from Buenos Aires or Córdoba? History will explain this mystery. Yet Facundo Quiroga is the most naïve type of character from the Argentine Republic's civil war; he is the most American figure presented by the revolution. Facundo Quiroga links and connects together all the elements of disorder that, even before his appearance, were stirring separately in each province; he transforms a local war into a national, Argentine war, and triumphantly presents, after ten years' work, devastation, and fighting, the result that only he who assassinated him was able to exploit.

I believe I will explain the Argentine revolution through the biography of Juan Facundo Quiroga, for I believe that he adequately explains one of the tendencies, one of the two different sides that vie within that unique society.

I have therefore evoked my memories and completed them by searching for details provided by men who knew him in his childhood, who were his supporters or his enemies, who have witnessed with their own eyes some events, heard about others, and had exact knowledge of a particular period or situation. I still hope for more details than I have, which are already plentiful. If a few inaccuracies have escaped me, I beg those who spot them to inform me of them; for in Facundo Quiroga I do not see simply a caudillo, but an expression of Argentine life, as colonization and the special characteristics of the land have made it, to which I feel the need to devote some serious attention, for without this, the life and deeds of Facundo Quiroga are vulgarities that did not deserve to enter the domain of history, save episodically. But Facundo, in relation to the physiognomy of the grandly savage nature that prevails in the vast extent of the Argentine Republic; Facundo, the faithful expression of the way of being of a people, of their concerns and instincts; Facundo, in short, being what he was not by an accident of character but by inescapable precedents beyond his will, is the most singular, most notable historical character that can be presented to the contemplation of men who understand that a caudillo at the head of a large social movement is no more than the mirror in which the beliefs, needs, concerns, and habits of a nation are reflected, in colossal dimensions, at a given time in its history. Alexander is the image, the reflection of warlike, literary, political, and artistic Greece; of skeptical, philosophical, and enterprising Greece, pouring across Asia to extend the sphere of its civilizing action.

That is why we need to pause over the details of the inner life of the Argentine people, to understand its ideal, its personification.

Without these precedents, nobody will understand Facundo Quiroga, as no one, in my view, has yet understood the immortal Bolívar[9] on account of the incompetence of the biographers who have traced the picture of his life. In the *Enciclopedia nueva* I have read a brilliant work on General Bolívar that does that American caudillo all the justice he deserves for his talents and his genius; but in that biography, as in all the others that have been written about him, I saw the European general, the marshals of the empire, a less colossal Napoleon; but I did not see the American caudillo, the head of an uprising of the masses; I see a pale imitation of Europe, and nothing that reveals America to me.

Colombia has plains, pastoral life, pure, barbarous, American life, and from there the great Bolívar set out; from that mud he built his glorious edifice. How is it, then, that his biography likens him to any European general in his illustrious garb? It is because the classic European concerns of the writer distort the hero, removing his poncho in order to present him from day one in tails, exactly as the lithographers of Buenos Aires have painted Facundo in a frock coat, believing his jacket, which he never took off, inappropriate. Well: they have made a general, but Facundo disappears. They can study Bolívar's war in France in that of the Chouans: Bolívar is a Charette[10] of broader dimensions. Had the

9. See Alberdi, "The Argentine Republic," note 7, in this volume. [E.N.]

10. Chouans is the name given to the royalist peasants who revolted against the French Revolution in the last decade of the eighteenth century. François de Charette (1763–1796) was one of their leaders. [E.N.]

Spaniards penetrated into the Argentine Republic in 1811, our Bolívar would perhaps have been Artigas,[11] had this caudillo been so lavishly endowed by nature and education.

The treatment of the history of Bolívar by the European and American writers is more suitable for San Martín[12] and others of his kind. San Martín was not a popular caudillo; he was really a general. He had been educated in Europe and came to America, where the government was a revolutionary one, and he could easily form the European army, discipline it, and wage regular battles according to the rules of science. His expedition on Chile is truly a conquest, like that of Italy by Napoleon. But had San Martín been obliged to be at the head of Montoneras,[13] to be defeated here, to go then and muster a group of plainsmen from somewhere, they would have hanged him at his second try.

Bolívar's drama consists, then, of other elements besides those we know about today: it is necessary to place the American scenery and costumes first in order to subsequently show the character. Bolívar is, still today, a tale wrought on true information: Bolívar, the real Bolívar, is not yet known to the world, and it is very likely that, when they translate him into his native language, he shall appear more surprising and greater still.

Reasons of this sort have moved me to divide this hastily written work into two parts: one in which I map out the terrain, the landscape, the theater on which the scene is to be performed; the other in which the character appears, with his costume, his ideas, his system of action; in such a way that the former will be already revealing the latter, without need for comment or explanation.

11. José Gervasio Artigas (1764–1850), Uruguayan leader considered the "father of Uruguayan independence." [E.N.]

12. See Alberdi, "The Argentine Republic," note 6, in this volume. [E.N.]

13. Bands of gauchos, followers of the federal caudillos, during the civil wars in Argentina. [E.N.]

4

DOMINGO FAUSTINO SARMIENTO
The United States (1847) (Excerpt)

November 12, 1847

To Don Valentín Alsina.

I leave the United States, my esteemed friend, in that state of excitement caused by the spectacle of a new drama, full of incidents, with no plan or unity, bristling with crimes that shed a sinister light on acts of heroism and abnegation, amid fabulous splendors of decorations that mimic age-old forests, flowery meadows, perilous mountains, or human abodes in whose peaceful space reign virtue and innocence. I wish to tell you I leave in a sad mood, pensive, satisfied, and enthralled with half of my illusions shattered or wilted, while other illusions struggle with reason to adorn once again that imaginary prospect in which we always confine ideas about objects we have not seen, in the same way that we lend a face and a tone of voice to the friend known only by letter. The United States is something without precedent, a kind of folly shocking at first sight, and frustrating expectations by fighting against received wisdom, and yet this inconceivable folly is great and noble, at times sublime, always temperate; and it appears with such shows of permanence and organic strength that ridicule would slide off its surface like an impotent bullet off the hard scales of an alligator. That social body is not a deformed being, a monster of some known species, but a new kind of animal produced by political creation, strange like those megatheria whose bones can still be found on the surface of the land. So that, to learn to contemplate it, it is first necessary to educate one's own judgment, concealing its apparent organic failings, in order to appreciate it in its own nature, at the risk of, once the earlier surprise fades, becoming enthusiastic about

Original title: "Estados Unidos." Source: *Viajes por Europa, África y América: 1845–1847* [Travels in Europe, Africa, and America: 1845–1847], in *Obras Completas de Domingo Faustino Sarmiento* [Complete works of Domingo Faustino Sarmiento], vol. 5 (Buenos Aires, Luz del Día, 1949).

it, finding it beautiful, and proclaiming a new standard of human things, as romanticism did so as to have its monstrosities forgiven when casting down the old idol of Roman-French poetics.

My good friend, you and I have been educated under the iron rod of the grandest of tyrants, combating him unceasingly in the name of law, of justice, in the name of the republic. In short, implementing the conclusions reached by human conscience and intelligence, you and I, like many others, have found pride and encouragement on seeing the halo of light that illuminates the north in the midst of the massive night that hangs over South America. Finally, we have told each other so as to toughen ourselves against present evils: the republic exists, strong and invincible; there is a light; the day of justice, equality, law will come; the light will radiate toward us when the south reflects the north. And in truth, the republic exists! But it happens that in contemplating it up close, we find that many of its features do not match the abstract idea we had of it. In North America the ugliest ulcers of the human species have disappeared while at the same time others, already healed even among the European peoples, appear and turn cancerous here, as new diseases become manifest for which no remedy is yet known or even sought. Thus, our republic, liberty and strength, intelligence and beauty; that republic of our dreams when the misguided tyrant should fall, and whose organization we argued frankly about among ourselves in exile, and under the harsh goading of the needs of that time; that republic, my dear friend, is a desideratum still possible on Earth, if there is a God who guides slow human destinies for good, if justice is a sentiment inherent in our nature, its organic law and the purpose of its long preparation.

If I did not fear, then, that the quotation might give the wrong idea, I would say in giving account of my impressions of the United States, the words that Voltaire puts into the mouth of Brutus:

Et je cherche ici Rome, et ne la trouve plus![1]

Just as in Rome or in Venice there once existed a patrician government, here there exists democracy; the republic, the public thing, will come later. Our consolation, however, lies in the idea that these demo-

---

1. "And I look for Rome here, and cannot find it!" (Voltaire, *La mort de César* [1736], act II, scene 1). [E.N.]

crats are today those who are the closest on Earth to finding the key to the political solution that Christian populations search for in the dark, stumbling on the monarchy as in Europe, or checked by brutal despotism as in our own poor country.

Do not expect me to give you an orderly description of the United States, although I have visited all its great cities and crossed or followed the borders of twenty-one of its richest states. I mean to follow another path. At the level of civilization that the noblest part of the human species has reached, for a nation to be eminently powerful, or capable of being so, territorial conditions are required that nothing can permanently replace. If God were to entrust me with the formation of a great republic, our republic *à nous,* for example, I would not accept such a serious assignment, except on condition that he give me at least these foundations: space without known limits so that one day two million inhabitants might idle there; broad exposure to the seas, coasts riddled with gulfs and bays; a diversified surface but without causing difficulties for railroads and canals, which must cross the country in all directions; and as I will never consent to going without the railroads, there must be so much coal and iron that in the year of grace, 4751, mines will be still working as on the first day. The extreme abundance of timber for construction would be the only obstacle that I would bear for the easy clearing of the land; I would personally take responsibility for giving an appropriate direction to navigable rivers, which must crisscross the country in all directions, turn into lakes where the perspective required it, flow into all the seas, join together all climes, so that the production of the poles would go in a straight line to the tropics and vice versa. Then for my future aims I would request an abundance everywhere of marble, granite, porphyry, and other quarried stones, without which nations cannot imprint on the forgetful land the eternal traces of its footprints.

"A land of Cockaigne!" a Frenchman might say. "The Barataria isle!" a Spaniard would offer.[2] "Fools!" This is the United States, just as God has made it, and I would swear that in creating this piece of the world, he knew very well that by the nineteenth century the castoffs of his poor humanity, elsewhere trampled on, enslaved, or starving so that the privileged few might idle, should come together here, develop without

2. From medieval Europe, imaginary lands of plenty. The "Insula Barataria" appears in Cervantes's *Don Quixote.* [E.N.]

hindrance, grow, and by their example avenge the human species for so many centuries of tutelage by the powerful, and suffering. Why did the Romans not discover this land, eminently adequate for the industry that they did not exercise, for the peaceful invasion of the colonist, so lavish in well-being for the individual? Why was it that the Anglo-Saxon race stumbled across this piece of the world that fit in so well with its industrial instincts, and why did the Spanish race get as its share South America, where there were silver and gold mines, and meek and servile Indians, which was just the thing for their laziness as masters, their backwardness and industrial ineptitude? Is there not order and premeditation in all these things? Is there not Providence? Oh, friend, God is the easiest solution to all these difficulties.

I forgot to ask for my republic, and I do so here so that it may go on record, to be given neighboring populations of Spanish stock, such as Mexico, and there on the horizon, Cuba, an isthmus, etc.

I am not the first to be surprised by this in the nature of the United States. A fellow traveler wrote to one of his friends from Europe:

> I have no knowledge of any place where God has exceeded himself as here. He was undoubtedly in a very good mood when he sketched those degrees of 0° and 6° of longitude, east and west of Washington. This is beautiful and fluently drawn. Every river is six miles wide, every lake at least four hundred in circumference; everywhere immense forests of trees in perfect harmony with the landscape. Not a single arid hill or island; vegetation everywhere, like up in the Pyrenees.

As for the general ordering of this country, I shall give you a few brief notions. Imagine a square space of land measuring two and a half million square miles, bathed by diverse seas toward the south, east, and west. To the north a river, its source a chain of lakes as capacious as the Caspian Sea, functioning as a border and providing the country with a line of navigation from its inland depths to the coasts of the Atlantic. And as the mouth of the St. Lawrence, which is that boundary river, falls outside the limits of the United States, level with Montreal, Lake Champlain heads south no broader than a river, until almost touching the source of the Hudson, connecting by this waterway the emporium of New York with the lakes and upper and lower Canada.

As the square we have drawn is just a little smaller than Europe, it

theoretically needed an inner artery where life could circulate and penetrate. To meet this requisite, from the proximity of Lake Erie, the Mississippi flows south, the most abundant river on Earth, navigable over
fifteen hundred consecutive miles, incorporating the waters of the Ohio,
the Arkansas, the Illinois, the Missouri, the Tennessee, the Awash [sic],
and many others, which from east and west, alternatively bring on their
murky waves the products of the remotest plantations down to the Gulf
of Mexico. For this is remarkable about the distribution of the waters
of North America: they flow together into an immense receptacle and
march east together in the St. Lawrence, while others head south, clus-
tering in the Mississippi, with only the Hudson, the Potomac, and the
Susquehanna left apart from those two great river basins.

The Yankees would have seemed mere novices had they not completed the well-known plan of Providence with canals, so that goods
from Canada might have a waterway indifferently to New York or New
Orleans, covering a line of inland navigation greater than the distance
between America and Europe. Furthermore, as an American state must
live necessarily from the exports of its raw materials, its cereals and furs,
it should preferentially face the Atlantic; and its primary need is that
from all points its transport routes converge and come together at the
mouths and orifices of that immense octopus, whose simple structure
offers only intestinal tube and mouths. But imagine that the larval state
has to pass through diverse transformations before entering the family
of the more perfect animals, endowed with diverse systems, such as
blood, nervous, digestive, etc., then life becomes more complicated, and
the animal no longer exists for the mouth, but the mouth for the animal.
As internal life becomes more complicated it demands secretory vessels,
where food is better prepared; which amounts to saying, because the
allegory is becoming tiresome, that with the excess of population and
the development of wealth, a national industry is born, and the state,
without diminishing its movement of exports and imports, acquires at
last an internal life that it needs to satisfy by itself and for itself. China
in Asia, Germany and France in Europe, are examples of this domestic life, which fuels powerful industries and a greater accumulation of
wealth. When the time comes for the United States, it is conceivable
that the coastal cities will not be the only centers of wealth, as to shorten
distances there will be new industrial poles in the center of the country
that will spread and irradiate the products of national labor to the outer

edges. Now, search on a map of the United States for a suitable point for this internal secretion, combining also conditions of viability and abundance of elements of manufacture, steel, timber, coal, etc. If you do not find it soon, I shall show you. From the interior of Pennsylvania, the rivers Ohio, Alleghany, and Monongahela come together to run into the Mississippi, the great artery that distributes and fulfills internal movement as we have seen.

At the confluence of these rivers is situated Pittsburgh, which is connected via artificial canals and railroads to Baltimore in Chesapeake Bay, Philadelphia, New York, and Boston to the north. By turning over a little the earth on which Pittsburgh is built, a layer of coal is found, covering around fourteen thousand square miles, that is, a space slightly smaller than the whole of England. Throughout the adjacent country and on the banks of the rivers, the owners can open a mine entrance under their homes in order to extract this substance to feed the factories; and in Marietta we alighted from our steamer, crossed two streets of the city, and without further ado entered a mine of bitumen coal that was being extracted from a hill by hand, carried in wheelbarrows, and poured immediately onto the deck of ships that dock on the riverbanks to receive it. From there, in convoys of shapeless rafts that, without sails or oars, abandon themselves to the river current, the coal goes to New Orleans, to compete profitably with the timber that is felled in the nearby forests, the price of which depends on the daily wage of the woodcutter. So much for coal; while regarding iron, it is found in equal abundance everywhere, and thanks to these enviable advantages of position, Pittsburgh today arises amid the forests of America, wrapped in a dense cloak of thick, stinking smoke, earning it already the name of the Yankee Birmingham, and it will be a future London because of its multitude of factories and its cotton, which arrives from New Orleans to be dyed and woven there, with mechanisms that are almost always ahead of European advances in terms of perfection. To give some idea of what Pittsburgh could be, I shall remind you that at the end of the last century, the adjacent territory was in the hands of the savages: in 1800 it already had forty-five thousand inhabitants; and by 1845 it had reached a population of two million.

As the population of the United States is advancing toward the Pacific at a rate of seven hundred miles per year, a more inland industrial center will later become necessary. To this end, in the area where the Missouri, which runs over twelve hundred miles, joins the Mississippi, not far from the point where, on the opposite bank the Ohio flows into it, a coal deposit has been placed which, from what has been found so far, extends over an area of some sixty thousand square miles!

I do not mean to make Providence an accomplice of all of North America's usurpations, nor of its bad example that in a more or less remote period might attract, politically unite, or annex, as they say, Canada, Mexico, etc. Then the union of free men will begin at the North Pole, to end, due to lack of land, at the Isthmus of Panama. . . .

By then the lakes will be in the center of this giant union, and by then too the state of Michigan, surrounded like a peninsula by the lake of the same name, the Huron, the St. Clair, and the tip of Lake Erie, will profitably use the enormous coal deposits contained at its center. In the meantime, and because of that infallible instinct with which the Yankee sniffs out places fertile in riches, on the banks of the latter of those freshwater seas, along this strip of land, the city of Buffalo has begun to appear, a city that was never even a village, and had last year thirty thousand inhabitants, and today must have fifty thousand, given the extent of Yankee progress. A railroad that runs through five degrees of longitude from Albany without any pretense whatsoever, spills every day into its streets a flood of men who come from Europe and sail up the Hudson to pick out, among the forests in between, a piece of land on which to settle a new family, like those races of Shem and Japheth, who departed from ancient Babel to share among themselves the unpopulated land. There is an equal confusion of tongues among those who arrive, although the land soon enforces on them its own, and like water smoothing down the jagged edges of different stones to form pebbles as if they were a family of brothers, thus, gathering together, mixing among themselves these floods of fragments of ancient societies, a new one is formed, the youngest and most daring republic of the world. Oh, what tangible truth lies in the moral mysteries of our race; what close, inevitable relations are shown by physical things! The liberty that has emigrated to the north gives the man who arrives there the wings to fly; streams of men roll through primeval forests, and the word travels silently over their heads on threads of iron, to encourage far away that invasion of man on the soil that was reserved for him; of the aged and expert spirit on the matter that is still uncultivated, and waiting *ab initio* for him to give it shape. Franklin, as you know, was the first to take in hand the frightful lightning bolt and explain it to an astonished world. Working from Franklin's discovery (I speak in the practical sense of the lightning rod, which he gave to mankind), Volta, Oersted, Alexander, Ampère, Arago had written and tried much on the electric telegraph, when Morse, a North American, performed his tests with the aid of the thirty thousand dollars[3] supplied by the United States Congress. Is it not outstanding that the United States should have taken the glory of having invented the lightning rod and sulfuric ether to save mankind from two great evils, and provided planetary swiftness to the movements of man, with Fulton's application of steam and Morse's electric telegraph? In France I left behind telegraph lines of this type at the trial stage, from Rouen to Paris, from Paris to Lille, and this at the service of the government. In the United States by the time of my departure there was a circle beginning at New York, connecting Washington, Baltimore, Philadelphia, and returning to New York, over 455 miles; another ring that links New York to New Haven, Hartford, Springfield, Boston, and back to New York, over 452 miles; a line to Albany that begins from the center itself, 150 miles, with one branch extending from there to Buffalo, 250 miles, another to Rochester, 252 miles, and another to Montreal, 205 miles.

The stagecoach network that delivers mail all across the Union every day covers 142,295 miles, and there are 853 miles of artificial canals. The United States has 3,600 miles of seashore, and 1,200 miles border the lakes. New York is the port for inland river, canal, and lake navigation measuring 3,000 miles; New Orleans is the port to a further 20,000 miles of such navigation, subdivided into navigable rivers, and which when joined with the Mississippi, the lakes, and the St. Lawrence, produce the most astonishing line of inland river circumnavigation.

Nature had already provided the great features of the territory of the Union; but without the profound knowledge of public wealth that North Americans possess, the work would have remained incomplete. From Philadelphia to St. Louis, the distance from Buenos Aires to Mendoza, the country is crossed by a great national road, because in this direction the country is not suited to canals, as the gradients of the waters are in-

3. Wherever Sarmiento wrote "pesos" we have translated the word as "dollars," as that seems to be what he meant. For other currency denominations that appear, see note 5, below. [E.N.]

clined to the south and to the east. But from Lake Erie there descends a navigable canal joining the Ohio between Cincinnati and Pittsburgh, bringing with negligible freight costs the products of the extreme north of Lake Superior and Canada down to New Orleans. From the eastern end of Lake Erie another canal begins which, linked via a branch canal to Lake Ontario, flows at Troy into the Hudson and connects Chicago, fourteen degrees to the west, by water to New York and Quebec. Beginning at Pittsburgh, a canal skirts the Allegheny Mountains and connects Philadelphia on the Atlantic with New Orleans on the Gulf of Mexico, tracing a route across the continent of more than a thousand leagues. It would be pointless to concern ourselves with the railroad lines, which in part complete the lines of the lakes, or run across them, providing every state, city, and village with inexpensive, fast, daily, easy transport, affordable to all, appropriate for all goods. Tocqueville has said that the railroads reduced transport costs by a quarter of their earlier price. Canals have nearly abolished freightage, as it is hardly noticeable; and yet, such is the wealth of products transported, that these public works produce millions for the treasury in annual revenue.

From the general appearance of the country, or of its organization concerning the distribution of means of action placed by God and used and completed by man, I shall move straight to the village, center of political life, just as the family is the center of domestic life. The United States is there in the village with all its features, something that cannot be said of any other nation. The French or Chilean village is the negation of France or Chile, and nobody would wish to accept its customs, its dress, or its ideas as the manifestation of national civilization. The North American village is the whole state, in its local government, press, schools, banks, municipality, census, spirit, and appearance. From the heart of a primeval forest the stagecoach or the wagons roll out into a small cleared space, in the center of which ten or twelve houses stand. These are brick-built, constructed with the help of machines, giving their sides the smoothness of mathematical figures, mortar joining them in slender, straight lines. Said houses are built to two stories and covered with painted wooden roofs. Doors and windows are painted white, held and closed by patent locks; and green shutters brighten and vary the regular distribution of the houses. I mention these details because they alone suffice to characterize a people and inspire a number of thoughts. The first to come to me on witnessing this ostentation of wealth and well-being is the one provided by a comparison of the productive strengths of nations. Chile, for example, and what applies to Chile can be applied to Spanish America as a whole, has one and a half million inhabitants. What proportion is there between the houses, those that merit the name, and the families who inhabit them? In the United States all men live in houses such as those that I have described above, surrounded by all the most advanced instruments of civilization, save for the pioneers who still live in the forests and those travelers who lodge in immense hotels. From here there arises an economic phenomenon that I shall note in brief. Suppose that twenty million North Americans inhabit one million houses. How much capital is invested in satisfying this single need? Manufacturers of everything from bricks to machinery have made colossal fortunes with their products; patent lock factories sell their wares in numbers one hundred times greater than anywhere else in the world, at the service of a lesser number of men. The cast-iron stoves used in homes in every village would suffice to give movement and occupation to the factories of London; and the value of the houses inhabited by North Americans in these villages, which I will not term poorer for it is not appropriate, would be equal to the territorial and real estate wealth of any of our countries.

The kitchen, more or less spacious, depending on the number of family members, consists of an inexpensive cast-iron range with a complete service of pots and cooking utensils, all the work of some factory engaged in this business. In an inside area are stored plows, invented by a Frenchman, and the most powerful farming implement known to man: its plowshare cuts a furrow half a yard wide; a movable blade cuts through the weeds, and the slightest effort from the farmhand prevents it from hitting the trunk of a tree. Its light wooden body is always painted red, and the harnesses of the horses that draw it are the craft of a saddler, always polished and with yellow buckles and brass fittings to adjust them. The axes of the house are also of the best and most advanced construction known; for the ax is the elephant's trunk of the Yankee, his toothpick and his finger, like the knife is to us, or the jack-knife to the Spaniard. A four-wheeled cart, the wheels as light as the legs of a cockroach, always varnished and polished as if straight from the factory, with shining, complete harnesses, better than those of the *fiacres* of Paris, allow the locals to travel. One machine is used to thresh the corn; another to clean the wheat; and each agricultural or domestic task calls for the inventive talent of the craftsman. The land adjacent to the house, used as a vegetable garden, is separated from the street or public way by a wooden fence, painted entirely in white most artistically. Bear in mind that I am describing a poor village with barely twelve houses, still surrounded by uncleared forests and separated by hundreds of leagues from the great cities. My village also has many public establishments, a brewery, a bakery, several taverns or cheap eateries, all with signs in gold letters perfectly rendered by some sign maker. This is a capital point. The signs in the United States are throughout the Union a work of art, and the most unequivocal display of the country's progress. I have been amused in Spain and all over South America, examining what signs there are, written with stunted, hunchbacked letters and showing with their spelling errors the supine ignorance of the artisan or amateur who drew them.

The North American is a classical man of letters when it comes to signs, and a crooked or coarse lettering, or a spelling mistake, would leave any shopkeeper with a deserted counter. There must be at least two hotels in the village for the lodging of travelers, a printing press for a diminutive newspaper, a bank, and a chapel. The post office receives every day the newspapers of the surrounding area, or from the larger cities, to which the villagers have subscribed; and letters, parcels, and travelers come and go daily, as the transport of mail, even to the most distant destinations, is in four-wheeled vehicles with accommodation for the passengers. The streets, which fan out as the population grows, are like the streets of large cities, thirty yards wide, including sidewalks six yards wide on either side, shaded by lines of trees which of course have been planted there. The center of the street is, while there are no means to cobble it, a swamp in which all the swine of the village root, swine that have such an exalted place in the domestic economy that their products throughout the Union are equal in importance to wheat.

And as it is a rule that the nest is an indication of the bird, I will say some words about the villagers. Those who are saloon owners, shopkeepers, or of some other sedentary profession wear an everyday suit made up of the following garments: shiny boots, trousers and tailcoat of black cloth, a satin vest, also black, grosgrain tie, a small cloth cap; and, hanging from a black cord, a golden trinket in the form of a pencil or a key. At the end of this cord and firmly immersed in the pocket is the most curious piece of the Yankee suit. If you wish to study the transformations that the pocket watch has passed through from its invention up to the present day, ask the hour of any Yankee you may meet. You shall see fossil watches, behemoth watches, ghost watches, vermin's den watches, three-story watches, puffed out, with a drawbridge and secret staircase, whereby one might descend with a flashlight to wind them up. The model of Dulcamara's watch in *The Elixir of Love*[4] emigrated with the first Puritans, and its descendants enjoy the right to citizenship and are enlisted in the fearful Nativist Party, professing doctrines of the most exalted *Americanism*. Every ship that arrives from Europe carries hundreds of these immigrants, which are sold to the highest bidder in New York, Boston, New Orleans, and Baltimore, from the price of twelve reals[5] and upward, supplying this national popular demand for watches. The Yankee has a billfold in his pocket, and when going to bed, he lightly marks out symbols that indicate the path marked out for his actions for the following day. Believe me, there is no exaggeration in this common distribution of civilized means in villages as in cities, and in men of all classes. I take at random the tiniest villages, whose description I have at hand. Bennington contains a village hall, a church, two academies (schools), a bank, and around three hundred inhabitants.

Norwich, on the right bank of the Connecticut, has several churches, a bank, and seven hundred inhabitants.

Haverhill has a village hall, a bank, a church, an academy, and seventy houses, etc.

Westward, where civilization decreases, and in the Far West, where it is almost nonexistent due to the sparseness of the population in the countryside, the appearance indubitably changes, comfort is reduced to the bare necessities, and the houses are log cabins, built in twenty-four hours, logs placed one on top of the other and crossed over on the corners by means of slots; but even in these remote plantations, there is a perfect equality of appearance in the population, in their attire, in their manners, and even in their intelligence; the shopkeeper, the doctor, the sheriff, the farmer, all have the same appearance. The farmer is the head of a household, the owner of two hundred or two thousand acres of land,

4. Dr. Dulcamara is an itinerant quack in Gaetano Donizetti's comic opera *L'elisir d'amore* (The elixir of love). [E.N.]

5. An old Spanish coin. It is difficult to establish an equivalence in dollars. Sarmiento's use of currency denominations is not quite consistent. [E.N.]

as the case may be. His plowing instruments, his engines, are the same; that is, the best known to man. And if there happens to be a religious meeting in the neighborhood, from the depths of the forests, descending from the mountains, spilling out onto the roads, farmers will be seen on horseback in large numbers, with their trousers and black tailcoats, and the little girls in their dresses of the freshest and most graceful materials. Aboard a steamer on a long journey, I occasionally had the opportunity to approach a well-dressed man noticeable for his courteous ease of manners. One morning, as we approached a city, to my surprise I saw him take from his cabin a drum, tune it, and start to play the call, inviting the young men of that place to join in. He was a drummer! At times the chain of his watch fell onto the drumhead and momentarily hampered the set of sticks. There is, then, absolute equality in customs and forms. The degrees of civilization or wealth are not expressed as among us by special attire. There is no jacket or poncho, but a dress common to all and even a shared roughness of manner that keeps up the appearance of equality in education.

But even this is not the most characteristic part of these people: it is their ability for appropriating, sharing, popularizing, conserving, and perfecting all uses, instruments, procedures, and assistance that the most advanced civilization has placed in the hands of men. In this, the United States is unique in the world. There is no insurmountable routine delaying for centuries the adoption of a known improvement; there is, on the contrary, a predisposition to adopt everything. An advertisement in a newspaper about a modification to a plow, for example, is transcribed within a day by all the periodicals of the Union. The following day it is being talked about at all the plantations, and ironsmiths and manufacturers have attempted at the same time, in two hundred places in the Union, the construction of the model, and have the new machines on sale. Within a year it has been put into practice throughout the Union. You would have to wait a century for such a thing in Spain, France, or our America.

The Salvá dictionary,[6] for that of the [Spanish] Royal Academy cannot be relied upon today, defines the word *civilization* as "that degree of culture that populations and persons acquire when they pass from natural coarseness to delicacy, elegance, and gentleness of voices and customs

---

6. Vicente Salvá (1786–1849), *Nuevo diccionario de la lengua castellana*, 1846. [E.N.]

befitting educated people." I would call this civility; as neither affected voices nor extremely delicate customs represent moral and physical perfection, nor the forces that civilized man develops to subject nature to his use.

After the villages of the United States, the traveler's attention is caught by the roads that connect them, whether dirt roads, paved roads, railroads, or navigable rivers. If God were to suddenly call the world to account, he would catch two-thirds of the North American population marching, like ants, which comes to the same thing that I have written about their buildings; for with everyone traveling, no enterprise is impossible or unproductive, in terms of viability. One hundred and twenty leagues of railroad from Albany to Buffalo are traversed in twenty-four hours for twelve dollars; and for fifteen, including four sumptuous and succulent daily meals, two thousand two hundred miles of sailing by steamer in ten days from Cincinnati to New Orleans, along the Ohio and the Mississippi Rivers. The steamer and the railroad train cross through primeval forests, among the dark and solitary branches of which the pensive traveler fears the appearance of the last vestige of the savage tribes, who no more than ten years ago called these places the hunting grounds of their forefathers.

The great number of passengers means low ticket prices; and the low ticket prices encourage those who have no precise reason for traveling to do so. The Yankee leaves his home to breathe a little air, to have an outing; he takes a round trip of fifty leagues by steamer or train, and then goes back to his business. When the canny eye of industry spots a potential railroad route, an association clears the space sufficiently to indicate where the track should go; the lines of the future railroad are made from the felled trees, placing thin strips of iron on top of them. The train sets out tentatively at first, finding its balance, dropping down here, now rising over this perilous track; passengers pour in from everywhere, and with the produce that they leave the real railroad is built, never safe, so as not to make it costly, which does not greatly increase the number of accidents. The train is always comfortable, spacious, and if the seats are not as soft as the first-class ones in France, they are not as stupidly hard as second-class seats in England; for in the United States, as there is only one class in society, which is made up by *man,* there are not three or even four classes of passenger cars, as in Europe. But where North American luxury and grandeur stand out without rival on this planet is in the steamers of the northern rivers. Those steamers that sail in the Mediterranean would resemble nutshells or sewers compared with them! They are floating palaces, three stories high, with balconies and decks for strolling. The gold glitters in the capitals and architraves of the thousand columns that, as on the *Isaac Newton,* flank immense halls capable of accommodating the Senate and the Chamber of Deputies. Artistically suspended damask drapes conceal cabins for five hundred passengers, colossal dining rooms with endless burnished mahogany tables, and china and silver dinner service for a thousand diners. This ship can hold two thousand passengers; it has 750 beds, 200 separate rooms; it measures 341 feet in length, 85 in width, and carries a load of up to 1,450 tons.

The steamer *Hendrick* measures 341 feet long and 72 feet wide; it has 150 separate rooms, 600 cabins with feather mattresses, providing general accommodation for two thousand passengers, all for one dollar, covering a distance of 144 miles. An inhabitant of New York goes to Troy or Albany by night; the following morning he is speaking to his correspondent, and by the evening he is back in New York to engage in his business, having made a one-hundred-league journey in the space of ten or twelve business hours. The South American recently disembarked from Europe, where he has been enraptured in admiration of the progress of industry and the power of man, may wonder in astonishment on seeing such colossal American constructions, such ease of locomotion, whether Europe really is at the forefront of the civilized world. I have seen French, English, and Sardinian sailors express their astonishment quite candidly on finding themselves so small, so far behind this gigantic people.

There is in those ships of the Hudson a *sancta sanctorum,* a space into which the profane eye does not enter, a mysterious dwelling whose delights one can at most suspect from the gusts of perfumes that waft out when the door is momentarily opened. The North Americans have created customs without example or precedent on Earth. *The single woman,* or the *man of female gender,* is free as a butterfly until such time comes to wrap herself in the domestic cocoon to fulfill her social functions through marriage. Before such time, she travels alone, wanders the streets of the cities, and has love affairs, chaste and at the same time uninhibited, in the public eye, under the indifferent eye of her parents. She receives visits from persons who have not introduced themselves

to her family, and at two in the morning returns home from a dance accompanied by whomever she has exclusively waltzed or polkaed with
all night. Her good puritan parents sometimes joke with her about said
person, of whose affection they have learned by word of mouth, and the
crafty woman contents herself with defeating such conjecture, denying
the evidence.

After two or three years of flirting—a North American verb—dances,
walks, journeys, and coquetry, the girl in question quite casually over
lunch asks her parents if they know a tall, blond young man, an engineer
by profession, who often comes to see her, from time to time, every day.
They have been waiting for this introduction for a year. The outcome is
that a marriage is agreed upon in the family, of which the parents are informed the prior evening, and which they already knew about thanks to
all the gossips in the neighborhood. The wedding once performed, the
bride and groom then take the next railroad train and flaunt their happiness in forests, towns, cities, and hotels. In railroad coaches one always
sees these charming young couples in their early twenties, embracing,
resting on the chest of the other, and giving each other such expressive
caresses that they edify all bystanders, making even the most obstinate
bachelor determine to marry immediately. The promotion of marriage
could not be done in more suggestive terms than this open-air display of
matrimonial rapture. Due to this the Yankee never makes it to the age of
twenty-five without having a numerous family; and I can find no other
explanation for the astonishing propagation of the species on that fortunate soil. In 1790 the population was around four million; 1800, five million; 1810, seven million; 1820, nine million; 1830, twelve million; 1840,
seventeen million; by 1850, there will be twenty-three million. Immigration influences these figures, but in limited proportions. The immigrant is not a prolific animal, until he has been influenced by the Yankee.

Returning, then, to the thousands of couples who go around en-
livening and invigorating the atmosphere with their gentle springtime
breezes, the steamers of the Hudson and other classic rivers have specially prepared apartments for them. This chamber is called the bridal
chamber. Enameled tinted glass lends the soft colors of the rainbow to
the gentle light of the room; rose-colored lamps burn by night; and
night and day the perfume of flowers, the scented waters, and the aro-
mas from burners whet the thirst for pleasure consuming the chosen
dwellers. The factories of Paris are yet to produce damasks or muslins

costly enough to wrap the veritable Saturnalia of the bridal chamber in their loose pleats and under low golden ceilings. After seeing Niagara Falls, bathing in the thermal baths of Saratoga, having seen one hundred cities and covered one thousand leagues of the country, the bride and groom return, fifteen days later, exhausted, amazed, and contented, to live the saintly boredom of domestic life. The woman has forever bidden farewell to the world, the pleasures of which she enjoyed for so long with such liberty; to the fresh green forests, witnesses to her loves; to the waterfall, the roads, and the rivers. From now on, the closed domestic asylum is her perpetual penitentiary; the roast beef her eternal accuser; the swarm of blond, bubbly children her continuous torment; and an uncivil husband, although good-natured, sweating by day and snoring by night, her accomplice and her phantom. I believe those itinerant loves in which American *flirtation* ends produce the mania for traveling that distinguishes the Yankee, who it can be said is a born traveler. The frenzy for travel grows in frightful proportions year on year. The produce of all the public works, railroads, bridges, and canals of different states in 1844, compared with those of 1843, showed an increase of four million dollars; which caused an increase in one year alone of eighty million in the value of such works, giving a return of 5 percent. The Yankee knows the distances between cities by heart, and on seeing a city, from the passenger cars or steamers, there is a general movement of hands thrusting into pockets, unfolding the topographic map of the surroundings and pointing out with a finger the place in question. In ten years, a single New York shop has sold one and a half million atlases and maps for popular use. I am sure that in Paris there is not a single shop having made a like issue to supply the whole world. Every state has its geological chart showing the composition of its soil and its explorable elements; each county has a topographic chart in ten different editions of all sizes and at a variety of prices. No sooner had the first cannon shot been fired on the Mexican border than the Union was inundated with millions of maps of Mexico, on which the Yankee traces army movements, gives battle, advances, takes the capital, and stays there until fresh news comes on the telegraph showing him the real position of the armies, to make them march again, with one finger on the map and through conjectures and calculations, placing it *in less than an hour* in Mexico City. The Mexicans might learn from them to their advantage about the country they obliviously inhabit.

But let us continue with the description of the appearance of the roads. In the lakes and in other rivers of greater length than the Hudson, the steamers dock at certain places along the banks to renew their provision of firewood, an operation performed in less time than the changing of mules at Spanish staging posts, or for passengers to alight or board. From the heart of an ancient forest and along almost impassable paths, one sees a family of ladies in ball gowns, accompanied by gentlemen dressed in their timeless black tailcoats, sometimes a topcoat as a variant, or at most an elderly man with a puritan-style velvet overcoat; long white hair to the shoulders, in the style of Franklin, and a round hat with low crown. The carriage that carries them is of the same build and as neatly varnished as those that travel the streets of Washington. The horses with shining harnesses are of English stock, having lost none of their svelte beauty or Arabian form in emigrating to the New World; because the North American, far from barbarizing the elements given to him by European civilization, as we did when we settled as colonists, works to make them more perfect and take them to a further stage. The sight of this uniform decency, and of that general well-being, while satisfying the heart of those who take pleasure in contemplating a part of the human species, possessing the enjoyment and advantages of association in equal proportions among them, ultimately tires the eye with its monotonous uniformity; the portrait is sullied at times by the appearance of a farmhand with untidy clothes, a faded and dirty frock coat, or ragged tailcoat, reminding the traveler of Spanish and South American beggars, with their unpleasant appearance. The view is not beautified, for example, by the novelesque attire of the Neapolitan countryside; the lofty feather hat of the female water sellers of Venice; the mantilla of Seville's *manolas;* nor by the gold-embroidered apparel of the Jewish women of Algiers or Oran. France herself, who despotically decrees the fashion for all peoples, entertains the traveler with the coifs of her country women, invariable and characteristic in each province, and which in the area around Bordeaux go so far as to take the terrifying height of two-thirds of a yard above the head, like those ornamental combs formed from the shell of a whole Galápagos turtle that the ladies of Buenos Aires once wore with pride; this analogy along with Chilean sheepskin saddle blankets and spurs has made me suspect that the spirit of the province, of the village, is everywhere fertile with unwieldy things.

A country girl from the United States can be recognized only by her rosy cheeks, her round, chubby face, and the candid, *bewildered* smile that distinguishes her from city folk. Aside from this and their somewhat worse taste and less ease for wearing cashmeres or shawls, North American women all belong to the same class, with a variety of features that generally honor the human species.

On this journey which with you, my good friend, I have been taking all over the United States, whether strolling on the galleries or on the deck of the steamers, or preferring the more sedentary vehicle of the railways, we must finally arrive, I will not say at the gates of a city, a European phrase that indicates the walls that imprison them, but at the quay, whence with three hundred other passengers we shall go to *billet ourselves* in one of the magnificent hotels, which have four-horse carriages and smart domestics awaiting us at the door, unless we wish to proceed on foot with our traveling bags under our arm. As the steamer on which I sailed down the Mississippi drew closer, turning around one of those semicircular curves traced by that calm but immense mass of water, the dome of St. Charles was pointed out to us on the horizon, towering over tiered masses of forests tinged by the autumn, at the base of which there spread out in lines of emerald green the extensive sugar plantations, a consoling indication, after seven hundred leagues of water and forest, of the proximity of New Orleans; and although the appearance of the neighboring landscape does not favor the comparison, the sight of that distant dome brought to my memory that of St. Peter's in Rome, which can be seen from all points of the horizon, as if it alone existed there; standing as colossal from twenty leagues away, as one would not believe when contemplating it up close. At last I was to see in the United States a basilica in the classical architectural style and in dimensions befitting religious worship. Someone asked us if we had a hotel in which to lodge, indicating the St. Charles as the most suitable. From the dome, he added, you will have at sunrise the vastest panorama of the city, the river, the lake, and the surrounding countryside. The St. Charles, which lifted its proud head above the surrounding hills and forests, the St. Charles that brought reminiscences of St. Peter's in Rome, was nothing more than an inn!

Here is a kingly people who build palaces in order to rest their heads one night beneath their vaults; this is man worshipped as man, and the artistic wonders used, lavished, to glorify the popular masses. Nero had his Domus Aurea; the Romans plebeians had merely their catacombs for shelter.

Our admiration did not diminish in the slightest on approaching the foot of the superb palace that has been the envy of many European princes, and to which in the United States, with the exception of the Capitol in Washington, no civil or religious monument is superior in dimensions and good taste. Over the granite foundation, intended for wine cellars and storerooms, is built a white marble base on which rise twelve fluted columns of a composite order; six of these advance over the general plan, supporting a handsome pediment. The frontage of the walls, which on both sides continue the façade, contain four levels of floors between the height corresponding to that between the base and the architrave of the columns, yet with the windows preserving architectonic proportions. Under the portico formed by the pediment is the Jove-like statue of Washington guarding the entrance, which leads to a spacious rotunda, paved in marble, matching the great dome that sits above it. In this spacious enclosure there are tables overflowing with collections of periodicals from all over the Union and Europe from the last fortnight.

The accounts offices of the hotel are found at the front; grand staircases twist into the air above like bronze serpents, ascending in all directions to the upper rooms and up to the dome itself, surrounded by a gallery of Corinthian columns where the monument ends. A profuse and ordered crowd of servants are ready to obey the traveler's slightest whim, and a fireplace that might contain a ton of coal entertains and comforts him in winter; meanwhile his name is registered in the great book, always open for this purpose, and his rooms indicated so that his luggage might be carried there. Powerful gas illumination distributes streams of sunlight from a thousand spouts spread out inside the building. To the left there extends toward the back of the construction the dining room, surrounded by columns, illuminated by colossal bronze chandeliers. It is wide enough to contain three mahogany tables running parallel along the room, over a distance of a little less than half a block. Seven hundred diners gather around these tables in the winter, the season of greatest activity and people in New Orleans. The inside of the building matches in luxury its colossal exterior. My travel companion, filled with social ideas of a superior order, had shown himself, in previous conversations, almost indifferent as to the advantages of one or another system of government. But after walking the internal passageways leading to hundreds of rooms decorated with every kind of luxury that the diverse condition of the guests might demand, and which, according to him, extended over fabulous distances, he told me, "I have been converted, by the intercession of Saint Charles; now I believe in the republic, I believe in democracy, I believe in everything; I forgive the puritans, even the one who ate raw tomato sauce with the tip of his knife and before the soup. However, all must be forgiven to the people who raise monuments to the dining room, and crown the kitchen with a dome such as this!"

The St. Charles, despite being the St. Peter of hotels, is nevertheless neither the most spacious nor the best built of the popular palaces, although its construction cost some $700,000. Every great city of the United States is proud to possess two or three huge hotels, which battle it out to be the height of luxury and comfort, offering minimal prices to the people. The Astor Hotel in New York is a majestic granite construction that fills with its great mass one side of Washington Square; and in none of the temples that abound in that city have greater sums been invested. Having visited the United States and seen the results attained there spontaneously, a disquieting thought came upon me, namely, that to find out if a machine, an invention, or a social doctrine is useful and applicable to future development, it needs to be tested on the touchstone of its spontaneous application by the Yankees. Today, hotels play a crucial role in the domestic life of nations. The sedentary peoples, such as Spain and her descendants, do not need hotels, the home is sufficient for them; in active towns, with modern life, with a future, the hotel is more important than any other public building. One hundred years ago the hotel was barely known in Paris, and unknown throughout the rest of Europe. Forty years ago Fourier based his social theory about living quarters on the phalanstery, or the hotel, capable of accommodating two thousand persons, providing them with comforts that the family isolated in the domestic home cannot obtain. The proof that Fourier[7] was not wrong lies in the North American hotel, which, following the simple impulse of convenience, has now taken on a monumental form and dimensions barely less than phalansterian. The Christian churches,

7. Charles Fourier (1772–1837), French philosopher and utopian socialist, and founder of the "École societaire."

subdivided into sects in the United States, from the cathedrals that they were before, have become mere chapels.

The spires of the temple grow lower as beliefs subdivide, while the hotel inherits the dome of the ancient tabernacle and takes on the shape of the thermal baths of the emperors, where the importance of the individual has reached the height of North American democracy. Religious architecture continues to dry out and fade, while popular architecture is improvised in the United States, forms, dimensions, and regulations that will ultimately be particular to the country. The American bank is a construction as solid as an iron safe, with an Ionic facade, or otherwise Egyptian. Why do the Yankees choose two such solid orders to enclose the iron safe? Above all American monuments there stands a lightning rod; and it is now customary in architecture to place at the summit of the domes, as a pinnacle, the statue of Franklin, holding the lightning rod. So we already have a Mercury, entrusted with guarding the domestic shelter, or a Saint Barbara patron saint for lightning! If the Americans have not created, then, a style of architecture, they will have at least some national applications, character and form suggested by political and social institutions, as has happened in all styles of architecture bequeathed to us by ancient times. A strange confusion reigns today in Europe about the application of fine arts. The reinstating and restoring of gothic cathedrals has followed the so-called romantic literature movement. The Pantheon created by the French Republic has been left aimless, as if awaiting better times to fulfill its goal. The temple of glory built by Napoleon, the most Greek, most Olympic construction ever before seen by Romans or the French, is today the temple of La Madeleine, with a pleasant and placid architecture that seems to mock the tears of the repentant Loreta of Jerusalem; and the images of the Virgin and the saints have gone to mingle in the museums, to stand shoulder to shoulder with the statues of pagan gods or the nudes of profane painting in Rome, London, Dresden, or Florence. In the United States the outer forms are appropriated for objects of worship, if you'll pardon the expression. The bank is Ionic, the hotel is sometimes Corinthian and always monumental, and the inventor of the lightning rod now has his elevated place and his architectural role, and even the pine cone of Roman architecture has been prolonged, to transform it into the image of the corncob, the symbol of American agriculture.

As for the inner layout of the grand hotel, there is nothing more normal than the order common to all these establishments. At the entrance is a portico, containing the administration offices. There is a registry book in which the arriving guest enters his name, and in the margin of which the receptionist adds the number 560, or 227, which is the number of the room allocated to him; the room's bell rings there, like all those of the establishment, lined up in neat rows at the same office. In the lobby are affixed all the posters of the city, for the benefit of the traveler: theater plays, meetings, the sermon of the day, steamer departures, the railway schedule, etc. In an adjoining room is the reading room, containing the main newspapers of the Union and the latest editions from Europe. A smoking room, and four or five drawing or reception rooms, make up in these parts the public amenities of the establishment. Thermal baths are available at all hours to guests. The ladies also have their reception and meeting rooms, decorated in style and luxury. Two or three pianos are also included in the possessions of these establishments.

At half past seven in the morning the unbearable vibration of the Chinese gong, reverberating throughout the corridors, notifies the inhabitants that it is time to rise. At eight there is a new and prolonged noise to announce that breakfast is served. The multitude of guests, rushing from each of the corridors, heads for the entrance to the immense refectory. Here life among these people begins to show, who are as serious when they laugh as when they eat. Where all men are equal down to the last individual of the society, there is no protection for the weak, for the same reason that there are no hierarchies to separate the powerful. Woe betide the women in this solemn act of popular sovereignty, if the provisional regulations of the hotel did not come to their assistance!

Article 1—Nobody may sit at the common table until the ladies, with their consorts, or relatives, have taken their places at the head and the adjoining sides of the table.

Art. 2—The public is asked to refrain from smoking or chewing tobacco at table.

Art. 3—At the chime of the bell, men must sit at the remaining seats.

With these provisions well understood, the gastronomic public lines up behind their places, with both hands placed on the backs of the chairs, looking left and right for the servant who is to ring the much-awaited bell. Said servant takes the chiming instrument in his hand, and

the double line becomes visibly moved; at the slightest indicative movement of the bell, the bodies ripple like ears of wheat in the lightest of
breezes. The bell is raised as about to be chimed, and a controlled release
of noisily shuffling chairs accompanies, nay, precedes the shrill tinkling
of shaken copper, and instantaneously an artillery fire of clinking plates,
knives, and forks continues for five minutes, and from the tempestuous
noise spreading through the air one can hear from half a league away
that the meal has been served in the hotel. It is impossible to follow
with the naked eye the developments occurring there in that hullabaloo,
notwithstanding the activity and skill of fifty or one hundred domestics, who try to bring a certain rhythmic order to uncovering dishes, or
pouring tea or coffee. The North American has two minutes allocated
for luncheon, five for dinner, ten for smoking or chewing tobacco, and
all free moments for having a look at the newspaper you are reading, the
only newspaper of interest as the other is already seized by him.

Breakfast, lunch at eleven, dinner, and tea are the four mandatory
meals for these ever-changing communities, without any rule hindering
serving breakfast at five in the morning for those who have to depart on
a morning steamer or train, nor is there ever lacking a meal served for
those who arrive, regardless of the hour of day or night. And yet, what
incongruence! What incest! And what promiscuity in the foods! The
pur sang Yankee eats all foods, desserts, and fruits from the same plate,
one at a time or all together. We have seen a man from the Far West, a
region of doubtful location, like the Ophir of the Phoenicians, begin
his meal with fresh tomato sauce, taken in enormous quantities, alone
and with the tip of his knife. Sweet potatoes with vinegar! We were
frozen with horror, and my fellow traveler was gastronomically indig-
nant to see these abominations: "And no fire pours from heaven!"—he
cried out—"the sins of Sodom and Gomorrah must have been lesser
than those committed at every step by these puritans!"

In the reading rooms, four or five gadflies will lean heavily on your
shoulders to read the same bit of tiny print you are reading. If you go
down a staircase or wish to pass through a door, uncrowded though it
may be, he who follows will push you if you lean on something. If you
are quietly smoking your cigar, a passer-by will remove it from your
mouth to light his own, and if you are not ready to receive it, he will
take the trouble personally to shove it back in your mouth. If you have
a book in your hands, as soon as you close it slightly to look elsewhere,

your neighbor will take possession of it to read two chapters at one go. If the buttons of your overcoat are embossed with the heads of deer, horses, or boars, whoever notices this will come to examine them one by one, making your person turn from right to left, from left to right, to better inspect this walking museum. Finally, if you wear a full beard in the countries of the north, indicating that you are French or Polish, with every step you will find yourself surrounded by a circle of men who will contemplate you with childlike curiosity, calling over their friends or acquaintances so that they may be gratified in person by this curious novelty.

It is understood that you may also take these liberties as everybody else does, without anyone raising a complaint or it seeming disagreeable to anybody. But where the national spirit and instinct shine through in their true light is in the Yankee attitudes in society. These merit some explanation. In a people such as this, that advances its frontiers one hundred leagues a year, where a state is improvised in six months, that travels from one end of the Union to the other in a matter of hours, and emigrates to Oregon, feet must be held in such high esteem, as those who think feel for the mind, and those who sing for their chests. In North America you shall see evidence at every step of the religious worship that the nation pays to those noble and dignified instruments of wealth, namely, one's feet. While conversing with any Yankee of good breeding, he will raise his foot to knee height, take off his shoe in order to massage his foot and hear the complaints that the toes might make about such excessive service. Four individuals seated around a marble table will unfailingly place their eight feet upon it, unless they can find a seat upholstered in velvet, for the Yankee prefers its softness to marble. In the Freemont Hotel in Boston, I have seen seven Yankee dandies in friendly discussion, seated as follows: two with their feet upon the table; one with his on the cushion of an adjacent chair; another with his leg flung over the arm of his own chair; another with both heels resting on the edge of the cushion of his own chair, so as to prop his chin between his knees; another hugging, or wrapping his legs round the back of his chair, in the same way that we might rest an arm. This position, impossible for the other peoples of the world, I have tried without success, and I recommend it to you in order to administer cramp as punishment for any given indiscretion; another man, if I have not listed the seven already, was seated in some other absurd posture. I do not recall whether

I have seen any North Americans sitting on the back of the chair with their feet on the cushion: what I am sure of is that I have never seen one pride himself on the courtesy of sitting in a natural position. Sprawling down is the height of elegance, and connoisseurs in the matter reserve this mark of good taste for when there are ladies present, or when a Locofoco[8] hears a Whig speech. The secretary of the Chilean legation, on arriving in Washington, needed to speak to a deputy. He went to the Capitol, informed himself as to his seat during the session, and finally reached the point where Mr. N was snoring deeply, sprawling in his seat with his legs stretched out on the seat of his neighbor. It was necessary to wake him up, and when informed as to the matter, he settled himself on the other side, no doubt waiting for the interminable discourse of some orator of an opposing opinion to conclude. The Americans profess the admirable and conciliatory principle that politics and religion should be discussed only with those who are of the same persuasion or opinion. This system is based on an extensive knowledge of human nature. The Yankee orator endeavors to confirm his own people in their beliefs, rather than persuading the opposition, who sleep through his speech or think about their own business. The conclusion of all this is that the Yankees are the most uncivil little animals under the sun to wear tailcoats and topcoats. This has been declared by judges as capable as Captain Marryat, Miss Trollope,[9] and other travelers; although it is true that if in France and England the colliers, lumberjacks, and innkeepers were to sit at the same table as the artists, deputies, bankers, and landowners, as occurs in the United States, the Europeans might form a different opinion about their own culture. In the cultured countries, good manners have a natural limit. The English lord is uncivil in his pride and scorn for his inferiors, while the masses are uncivil in their brutality and ignorance. In the United States, civilization is exerted over such a large number that refinement occurs more slowly, the influence of the uncouth mob reacting on the individual, forcing him to adopt the habits of the majority, and creating in the end a kind of national taste that turns into pride and concern. Europeans mock these crude habits, which are

8. Member of a radical faction of the Democratic Party in the 1830s. [E.N.]

9. Captain Frederick Marryat (1792–1848), English navy officer, wrote *Diary in America* (1839); Mrs. Frances Trollope (1779–1863), English writer, published *Domestic Manners of the Americans* in 1832. [E.N.]

more apparent than real, and the Yankees with their spirit of contradiction persist in them, and seek to place them under the aegis of American liberty and spirit. Without favoring these habits, or endeavoring to excuse them, having toured the foremost nations of the Christian world I am convinced that the North Americans are the only cultured people to exist on Earth, the latest result to be achieved by modern civilization.

The vast majority of Americans wear watches, while in France less than one-tenth of the population does so. The vast majority of Americans wear tailcoats and all the other complementary garments, clean and of a good quality. In France, the nankeen blouse is worn by four-fifths of the population.

All Americans use iron closed-top ranges, Durand plows, and carriages. They dwell in comfortable, clean homes. The day worker earns a duro[10] a day. They have railroads, artificial canals, and navigable rivers, in greater number and covering greater distances than all of Europe together. The comparative statistic of the railroads was as follows: In 1845: England, 1,800 miles; Germany, 1,339; France, 560; United States, 4,000; which is equivalent to 86 miles in England for every million inhabitants, 16 in France, and 222 in the United States. Their electric telegraph lines are today, the only ones in the world, at the disposal of the people, who can in a fraction of time send notices and orders from one end of the Union to the other.

The only people in the world that reads en masse and uses writing for all their needs, where two thousand periodicals satisfy public curiosity, is that of the United States, where education and well-being are spread everywhere and within reach of those who wish to obtain it. Is there anywhere on Earth with such equality? France, with thirty-six million individuals the oldest civilized nation in the world, has 270,000 registered voters, the only people who by law are not declared beasts as the rest are not acknowledged as having sufficient reason to govern themselves.

In the United States every man, by virtue of being a man, is entitled to have judgment and will in political affairs, and indeed he does. Meanwhile, France has a king, four hundred thousand soldiers, fortifications in Paris that have cost two billion francs, while the people starve to death. North Americans live without government, and their permanent

---

10. A *duro* is the equivalent of five Spanish pesetas. [E.N.]

army amounts to only nine thousand men, it being necessary to make a journey to specific places in order to see the equipment and appearance of the North American soldiers; for there are families and villages of the Union that have never set eyes on them. Europeans and even South Americans fault the Yankees with many character vices. As far as I am concerned, I look with reverence upon these defects, and put them down to the human species, the century, inherited concerns, and the imperfection of their intelligence. A people formed from all the peoples of the world, free as their conscience, as the air, without masters, without army, and without fortress-prisons is the result of all human, European, and Christian precedents. Their faults, then, must be those of the human race in a given period of development. But as a nation, the United States is the latest result of human logic. They have no kings, no nobles, no privileged classes, no men born to command, no human machines born to obey. Is not this result in keeping with the ideas of justice and equality that Christianity theoretically accepts? Well-being is distributed more widely than in any other country; the population increases according to laws heretofore unknown among other nations; production continues its astounding progress. Could freedom of action and a lack of government not account at all, as Europeans claim, for any of this? It is said that the effortless occupation of new territories is the cause for such prosperity. But then, why in South America, where it is equally easy, or even easier, to settle new lands, neither population nor wealth increases, and there are such stationary cities and even capitals that have not built one hundred new houses in ten years? A census has not been made in any nation of the intelligent capability of its inhabitants. Population is counted by the number of inhabitants, and from these figures its strength and value are deduced. Perhaps this statistic can be significant for war, considering man as a machine of destruction; but one peculiar trait of the United States makes this calculation faulty even in this case. If it comes to killing men, one Yankee is equivalent to many men of other nations, hence the destructive power of the nation can be counted as two hundred million men. The rifle is the national weapon, target practice the pastime of children in the states that have forests, and hunting squirrels in the trees, shooting them in the feet so as not to damage their skins, is an astonishing skill acquired by all.

United States statistics show the number of adult men as twenty million inhabitants, all educated, reading, writing, and enjoying political rights with some exceptions, albeit insufficient to distort the rigor of the inference: these are men with a home, or with the certainty of obtaining one; men beyond the reach of the claw of hunger and despair; men with hope in a future precisely as their imagination can invent it; men with political sentiments and needs; men, ultimately, who are their own masters, their spirit elevated by education and their sense of dignity. It is said that man is a rational being, inasmuch as he is capable of attaining and exercising reason; and in this respect no country on the face of the Earth has a greater number of rational beings, even though it may have ten times as many inhabitants.

It is not easy to show how liberty works to produce the wonders of prosperity that the United States displays. Can religious freedom produce wealth? How can the capacity of choosing one chapel or another, of believing in one dogma or another, work to develop productive forces? From the point of view of each religious sect, it is as if other sects did not exist, and therefore the liberty is in effect nonexistent for each of them separately. Europeans attribute this to the ease offered by a new country, with virgin lands that are easily acquired, which would be a satisfactory explanation if South America, as large as it is, did not have a greater area of virgin lands, the same ease for obtaining them, and yet its people are also more backward, poor, and ignorant than the European masses. Hence it is not enough to be merely a new country with vast spaces where the sphere of action can expand.

Many times I have turned to this moral and intellectual survey to try to explain the surprising social phenomena in America. At present I shall establish only one fact, namely, that the aptitude of the Anglo-Saxon race does not in itself account for the cause of the great development of North America. The inhabitants of both banks of the Niagara River are English. However, there where the English colonies make contact with the American population, they are visibly two different peoples. One English traveler, after describing various examples of industry and progress on the American side of the falls, added:

> Now I am once again under the jurisdiction of the English laws and government, and therefore I no longer think myself a foreigner. Although the Americans in general are civil and amiable, an Englishman, a foreigner among them, is harassed and upset by their boasts of feats in the last war, and of their superiority over all other nations

in terms of virtue, knowledge, bravery, liberty, government, and all other excellence. However, while they may merit ridicule for this foible, I cannot fail to admire the energy and spirit of enterprise that they display in all ventures, and I deplore the apathy of the English government as regards the improvement of these provinces. A single glance across the banks of the Niagara is sufficient to show on which side the more efficient government lies. On the United States side, great cities rise up, along with numerous ports with break-waters for protection of the harbor, stagecoaches run the length of the roads; and trade activity can be seen in wagons, carts, horses and men, moving in all directions. On the Canadian side, although divided by a river, in a *long-standing establishment,* and seemingly with *better land,* there are only two or three stores, a tavern or two, a port precisely as God made it and without constructions to defend it; one or two little boats at anchor, and a small quay.

Another traveler, after describing various signs of growing industry on the American side, adds: "In the country that we traveled across (on the Canadian side) the crops were at an advanced stage, without there being any signs of an attempt to harvest them. Wherever we stopped to change horses, we were assailed by gangs of children selling apples, and for the first time we saw on this side some *beggars.*" It was only a short time ago that a great number of immigrants who had gone to Canada emigrated again to the United States. As a means of wealth and civilization, the railroads are common to Europe and the United States, and as in both countries they date only from yesterday, it is possible to study in them the prevailing spirit in both societies. In France the leveling-out work, as with all work on the railroad, is carefully examined by engineers before the railroads are opened to transport; wooden fences protect both sides; dual tracks of cast-iron rails facilitate movement in opposite directions; if a local road crosses the course, strong gates guard the entrance, carefully closing a quarter of an hour before the train arrives in order to prevent accidents. There are guards posted at set distances all along the railroad to clear the space, announcing with different-colored flags if there is any danger or obstacle that might detain the train, which departs from the platform only four minutes after a phalanx of guards has ensured that all passengers have taken their places, the doors are closed, and the way is clear, and that there is no one within a yard's distance of the train. Everything has been planned, calculated, examined, so that one may sleep peacefully in that hermetically sealed prison. Let us now see what happens in the United States. The railroad cuts across leagues of primeval forests where no human dwelling has yet been established. As the company still lacks funds, the rails are wooden, topped with a thin sheet of iron, which frequently comes loose, and the eye of the engineer scrutinizes everything incessantly for fear of a disaster. A single line suffices for the going and coming of the trains, as there are sidings at fixed distances where the outbound train waits for the passing on the opposite side of the inbound train. There is not a soul who can speak of accidents having occurred there. The railroad runs through the villages, and the children are at the doors of their houses or in the middle of the road itself, watching the train pass for fun; as well as a street, the railroad is a local thoroughfare, and the traveler may see people moving out of the way to let the train pass, to then continue immediately on their way. Instead of gates on the local road-crossings, there is simply a written sign that says *Listen out for the bell when approaching,* a message that warns the cart driver that he will be split in two should he cross imprudently when the train is passing. The train departs slowly from the platform, and as it is moving passengers jump aboard, fruit and newspaper sellers jump off, while passengers move from one carriage to another, to entertain themselves, to feel free, even in the rapid flight of steam. Cows like to lie along the railroad, and the North American locomotive is fitted with a triangular snout that has the charitable mission of casting aside these indiscreet creatures which might be crushed under the wheels, and it is not unheard of for a sleeping boy to be thrown four yards by such a bump, which in saving his life might break or dislocate a limb. The physical and moral results of both systems are all too clear. Europe, with its old science and its riches accumulated over centuries, has not been able to open half the railroads that expedite movement in North America. The European is a minor under the protective watch of the state; his instinct for preservation is considered insufficient: fences, gates, guards, preventive signals, inspections, insurance, all has been put into use to preserve life; all except his reason, his discernment, his daring, his liberty; all except his right to look after himself, his intention, and his will. The Yankee looks after himself, and if he wants to kill himself nobody shall stop him; if he comes running after the train to catch it, and dares to take a leap and grab a handrail, avoiding the wheels, he is perfectly entitled to do so; if the rascally newspaper seller, in his desire to sell one more copy, has allowed the train to gather speed, he will take a running jump to the ground, everyone will applaud the skill with which he lands on his feet, and he shall continue on his way on foot. This is how the character of nations is formed and how liberty is used. Perhaps there are a few more victims and accidents, but at the same time there are free men, not disciplined prisoners with supervised lives. The word *passport* is unknown in the United States, and the Yankee who manages to see one of these European documents, in which is recorded each movement that the traveler has made, shows it to the others with horror and disgust. The boy who wishes to get on the train, the steamer, or the canal barge, the single girl who is to make a visit at some two hundred leagues' distance, will never come across anyone who will ask them with what purpose or with whose permission they stray from the paternal home. They use their liberty and their right to movement. Hence the Yankee boy shocks the European with his self-possession, his cautious prudence, his knowledge of life at the age of ten. "How goes business?" asked Arcos, my fellow traveler, of a smart lad who gave us an annotated inventory of the books, periodicals, and pamphlets he endeavored to sell to us. "It goes well; for the last three years I have made a living from it and I already have three hundred dollars[11] saved. This year I shall save the five hundred I need to form a partnership with Williams and set up a bookshop, and operate in the whole state." This merchant was nine or ten years old. "Are you a landowner?" we asked of a strapping youth traveling to the Far West. "Yes, I am going to buy land; I have six hundred dollars."

Beside the railroad track runs the electric telegraph, which to shorten distances sometimes splits off from the normal route and plunges into the dense forest to carry the most interesting news over two hundred leagues. When in 1847 the first trials were being carried out between Rouen and Paris, the press was proclaiming the existence of 1,635 miles of telegraph lines in the United States; when I arrived there were 3,000 miles; and as I crossed the country between New York and New Orleans, a company was formed and a line put into operation between the former of those two cities and Montreal in lower Canada, where I had been fifteen days earlier. Today there must be 10,000 miles, and within very few

11. See note 5, above. [E.N.]

years, the telegraph lines will cover the same 80,000 miles covered by the post. In France the telegraph is for the use of the government, and is a state affair; in the United States it is a simple affair of movement and activity, and correspondence is accepted from the administration only because the fee is paid. Can there be a greater inconsistency of ideas, for liberals and republicans to accept in France this monopoly, therefore going without the most expeditious of means of communication? In Harrisburg, with its population of forty-five hundred souls, the electric telegraph had such daily use that the clerk had barely enough time to operate it; while in France, not so much as a paltry trial had been made. I make these comparisons to show the different atmosphere in which the people are educated and the moral and physical energy that is expended. In France there are three categories of passenger car, in England four; nobility is gauged by the money they can pay for each one; and to degrade the man who can afford little, railway managers have accumulated comforts and luxury in first class, and left backless, narrow, hard boards for those in third. I know not why they have not set barbs in the seats to mortify the poor. In the United States, the passenger car is a room twenty yards long and spaciously broad, with seats with movable backs in order to form a small group of four seats with two going backward, with a gangway in the middle to ease movement, and the cars open at both ends, so that the curious may move from the first to the last while the train is in motion, and so that the air may flow freely throughout. The comforts and cushions are excellent and equal, and as a result, the fare is the same for all. I have been shown at my side a state governor, and the calluses on the hands of my other neighbor marked him out as a coarse lumberjack. Thus there is implanted a sentiment of equality, of respect for man. The Venetian aristocracy established equality in the bare poverty of the gondolas so as not to stir the envy of poor noblemen; the democracy of North America has distributed comfort and luxury in equal measure in all the cars to encourage and honor poverty. These simple facts suffice to measure the liberty and spirit of both nations. *The Times* once said that if France had abolished the passport, it would have made more progress in liberty than it has failed to make in half a century of revolutions and advanced social theories, and in the United States the effects are there to be seen.

This is a pale portrait of liberty in North America. In the middle of cities man is raised in the wild, if it is possible to say so; the woman of any given social background wanders the streets and sidewalks alone from the age of twelve, flirts up to the age of fifteen, marries whomever she pleases, travels, and buries herself away in the new home to prepare the family; the boy from a young age goes to school, is familiar with books and the ideas of men; he is a grown man by fifteen, and thenceforth all guardians disappear from sight. He has not seen soldiers, has no knowledge of gendarmes; the hubbub of the streets amuses him, exalts him, and educates him; his passions develop healthily and vigorously; he has a profession and is married by the age of twenty, sure of himself and his future. The general progress of the Union will carry him forward in spite of himself and he will advance his own business. And then, what grandiose dreams stir his mind, what paths open up in all directions toward his fortune! Is he a craftsman? A great company, a factory to cover the United States with the product of his craft, or even a European invention not yet introduced into the country, an improvement to known machinery or a new invention, because the Yankee today shrinks from nothing. For a long time I have believed that the wealth of North America was and will be for many years the appropriation and seizure of the progress of human intelligence. European science invents, and American practice popularizes the iron range, the Durand plow, the locomotive, the telegraph. There is nothing more natural, and yet, nothing could be further from the truth. The statistical data collected in recent years show that a proportion of the inventions and improvements adopted in England are of North American origin. They have modified the steam engine; improved the ship's keel; perfected the passenger car, to the extent that these articles are exported to Europe itself; and in Russia and other places there is a preference for American entrepreneurs and craftsmen in everything concerned with road-making. The Yankee wooden bridge, which sometimes crosses twelve blocks in one river and bears the weight of trains carrying agricultural produce, on seemingly flimsy pedestals and frames, is yet the fruit of the most extensive study of the laws of gravitation, impact, yield, and balance of combined forces. For the Yankee engineer bridge-building has become a mechanical art, and he builds them where he pleases to withstand floods, hurricanes, and enormous burdens; half of the farming tools are the invention of his own genius, and the steam mill, like the casks that he fills with flour, are the product of his factories and his schemes to produce immense results with highly limited means.

But where the North American's capacity for development shines through the most is in the possession of the land that is to be the nursery for a new family. In the midst of the most advanced civilization, the sons of Noah share out the depopulated land, the Nimrods lay the foundations of a new Babylon. I shall leave aside those who follow the ordinary pace of societies that grow by adding a new house to an emerging village, and newly cleared fields to the tilled farm.

The state is the faithful trustee of the great amount of lands belonging to the federation, and to provide each man with his part of the property there are neither speculating middlemen nor fluctuations in prices that close the door of acquisition to small fortunes. Land is worth ten reales[12] per acre; and this fact is the starting point for the future landowner. There is a procedure in the distribution of lands of such symmetrical beauty that only God could have devised it.

The state sends its engineers to outline saleable land, taking as the basis of their measurement a meridian of the sky. If at one hundred leagues' distance to the south or the north another portion of land is to be measured, the engineers will seek the same meridian, so that one day, two centuries later, there might appear, complete and without interruption, those lines that have divided the continent into areas, as if it were a small farm. This rectilinear surveying is exclusive to the American genius. Property in the province of Buenos Aires, on that Pampas as flat as a geometry table, was forced by the genius of Rivadavia[13] to fit into parallelograms, triangles, and easily measurable figures so that they might effortlessly be reproduced in the map provided by the topographical department every ten years, so that in comparing different editions, one could study with the naked eye the movement of property, seeking an average size, large estates subdivided by partitions among heirs, small properties accumulating, out of a need to devote them to cattle raising.

The fatal error of the Spanish colonization of South America, the deep affliction that has condemned current generations to immobility and backwardness, derives from the way in which land was distributed. In Chile, large expanses of land were shared out among the conquis-

12. See note 5. The price of public lands at the time was probably about a dollar an acre. [E.N.]

13. Bernardino Rivadavia (1780–1845), president of Argentina from 1826 to 1827. [E.N.]

tadors, measured from hill to hill, and from the bank of a river to the edge of a gully. Counties were founded among the captains, and in the shadow of their makeshift shelters refuge was sought by the soldiers, fathers of the tenant farmer, this landless laborer who grows and multiplies without increasing the number of buildings. The urge to acquire land in the name of the king meant that men took possession of entire districts, with such a distance between different landowners that in three centuries they have failed to clear the land in between.

In the meantime, cities were ignored in this vast plan, and what few villages that have been created since the conquest were done so by presidential decree, with at least one hundred villages in Chile founded artificially by this means. See how the North American proceeds, now in the nineteenth century called to conquer his piece of land to live in, because the government has been careful to leave to all successive generations their share of the land. Every year the conscription of young aspirers to property crowd around the auctioneer's hammer at the sale of public land, and with their numbered allotment head off to take possession of their property, waiting for the formal titles to arrive later from the offices in Washington. The bolder Yankees, the misanthropes, the wild ones, the squatters, in short, operate more romantically, more poetically, or more primitively. Armed with their rifle, they wander into the maze of the virgin wilderness; for fun they kill the squirrels that gambol tirelessly among the branches of the trees; a well-aimed bullet flies into the sky to bring down an eagle hovering with its majestic wings above the dark green surface formed by the tops of the trees; the ax, his faithful companion, with no more aim than exercising strength, brings cedars or oaks to the ground. In his rambling forays, the undisciplined planter seeks a fertile plot, a picturesque viewpoint, the bank of a navigable river, and when he has made his choice, as in the most primitive times of the planet, he says, "This is mine," and with no other formalities takes possession of the land in the name of the king of the world, which is labor and will. If one day the surveying of public lands reaches the limit that he has drawn out for his property, the auction sale will only serve to tell him what he owes for what he has grown, according to the price at which the adjacent uncultivated fields are sold; and it is not unusual for this indomitable, unsocial character, once the population has caught up with him in its advance across the desert, to sell his farm and move away with his family, his oxen, and his horses, seeking out the desired solitude of the forests. The Yankee has been born irrevocably a landowner; if he possesses nothing, nor has ever possessed it, he does not say that he is poor, merely that he is poor right now; business is bad; the country is going to the dogs; and then the primeval forests appear in his imagination as dark, solitary, distant; and at the heart of them, on the banks of an unknown river, he sees his future manor, the smoke rising from the chimney, the oxen that return to the fold at sundown with heavy tread, joy at last, his own property. From then on he speaks of nothing else but to go forth and people, settle new lands. He spends his nights hunched over the map, working out the journeys, drawing a route for his cart; and in the periodical he looks at nothing but the announcement of a sale of public lands, or of the new city that is being built on the shores of Lake Superior.

After sacking Tyre, Alexander the Great had to find a new center for world trade where the spices of the Orient could be brought together, to spill out immediately onto the coasts of the Mediterranean. The foundation of Alexandria brought him fame as proof of his perceptiveness, even though the trade routes were known and the Isthmus of Suez the indispensable market between the seas of India and Europe and Africa at that time. This feat is achieved every day by North American Alexanders who wander in the desert searching for places that an extensive study of the times to come will indicate as the future centers of trade. The Yankee, inventor of cities, professes a speculative science, which by induction leads him to estimate the place where a future city will blossom. With the map unfolded in the shadow of the trees, his deep eye measures the distances of time and place, maps out in his mind the route that public roads will later take, and finds on the map the necessary crossroads that must be formed. He has a head start over the invasive march of the population advancing across the desert, and calculates the time those from the north will take and those from the south will need for both to reach the point he is studying, which he has chosen at the confluence of two navigable rivers. Then with a steady hand he draws the route of the railroads that will join the trade system of the lakes with his expected metropolis, the canals that might feed the rivers and gullies that he finds at hand, and the thousands of leagues of river navigation which in all directions appear as spokes into the hub he imagines. If, after fixing these points, he finds a layer of coal or some iron mines, he sketches the plan of the city, gives it a name, and returns to the towns to announce through the thousand echoes of journalism the discovery that he has made of the location of a famous future city, the center of one hundred trade paths. The public reads the announcement, opens the map to verify the accuracy of the inducement, and if they find the calculations to be right, stampede to buy plots of land, here where piers and docks will stand, here around Washington or Franklin Square; and a Babel is raised within a year, in the middle of the forest, all toiling to be in possession on the day when the great destinies come true as predicted by the topographical science of the city. Roads are then opened up; the local newspaper tells of the progress of society, agriculture commences, temples are raised, along with hotels, docks, and banks; the port is filled with ships, and the city begins to branch out, and the urgency is felt to link up via railroads and canals with other great centers of activity. One hundred cities on the lakes, on the Mississippi and other remote points, had such wise and calculated origins, and almost all justify with their astounding progress the accuracy and depth of the economic and social studies that brought about their creation.

I know of two kinds of human beings in whom there survives, even amid our current moderation of moral character, the ancient heroic spirit of the earliest ages of man: the convicts of Toulon and Bicêtre,[14] and the North American emigrants. All the rest of the human species has fallen into the lethargy of civilization. The feats of Francisco Pizarro[15] and those of the Argonauts are repeated constantly by the unheard-of audacity of the freed convicts; valor, constancy, suffering, dissimulation, and violation of all moral laws, of all principles of honor and justice; everything is equal, without this excluding a certain greatness of the soul, a certain profound intelligence in the means, revealing human genius misused, an Alexander perverted and busy killing a handful of passers-by instead of ravaging nations and gunning down thousands, which now changes the scene and the names, war, conquest, et cetera.

In the United States those steely characters, who are spread out 1 percent everywhere, surrender themselves to their heroic instincts, though

14. Prisons in France famed for their abusive treatment of inmates. [E.N.]

15. Francisco Pizarro (1478–1541), Spanish conqueror of Peru, defeated the Inca Empire. [E.N.]

still nameless, to settle and multiply. The Yankee spirit feels hemmed-in in cities; he needs to see from the door of his home the extensive and shaded colonnade formed by the primeval oaks in the forests.

Why has this colonizing spirit died out among us, the descendants of official colonization? Since Columbus and up to an undoubtedly not so remote period, the foundation of a Spanish city was merely a stepping-stone to support the invasion of other more distant places. The conquest of Peru entailed the expedition of Almagro: when Mendoza was defending himself from the Araucanians in the south, sixty lancers under the command of Jofré [sic] were detailed in the east to cross the Andes and found two cities, San Juan and Mendoza, solitary in the middle of deserts, on the banks of the two rivers found there.[16]

Let me explain the whole system of these enterprises, which would require Hercules to undertake them, and you shall see whether those feats of our conquistadors of South America merit contempt for their motives and for their means. You know well how much irritation there was and what nonsense was spoken by both sides in the matter of the Oregon frontiers. All was left in peace after the Americans and the English had reached a reasonable understanding, except the Yankee spirit, which just as the condor smells blood had smelled arable land, rivers, forests, and ports in the talks. A debate is beginning again in the newspapers on the possibility of attracting trade from China via Oregon; on the ease of opening a railroad, eight days' journey, from the Pacific to the Atlantic, and the advantage of taking hot bread from Cincinnati, via Oregon, and a thousand other topics, unlikely and absurd to anyone but a Yankee, who is accustomed to believing anything is possible as long as he can conceive of it, since his mind is trained to conceive projects.

When the opinion is formed and the roads to be followed to that remote Dorado marked, the most apt season for traveling is indicated, and the starting point and the day designated by some emigrants who invite all the adventurers of the Union to accompany them on the glorious journey. On the day of the rendezvous, from all points of the hori-

16. Diego de Almagro (1475–1538), Spanish conquistador, discovered Chile; García Hurtado de Mendoza (1535–1609), Spanish governor of Chile and later viceroy of Peru, successfully fought the warlike Araucano Indians; Juan Jufré y Montera (1516–1578), Spanish conquistador, crossed the Andes to found the city of San Juan in Argentina. [E.N.]

zon lines of wagons can be seen arriving, loaded with women, children, chickens, pans, plows, axes, chairs, and all kinds of household objects; these are accompanied by a few herds of plague-ridden oxen and lame and crippled mules and nags, forming an overworked part of the expedition, and above all this group there prevails the sunburned, stressed, and serious faces of the Yankees, dressed in threadbare topcoats or frock coats or tailcoats, with a rifle as a walking stick and the tranquil gaze of the puritan and the farmer.

If I am to give an exact idea of these emigrations and of the Yankee spirit, I need now to keep to the facts and follow the daily incidents of one, among hundreds, of these stupendous marches through the desert, without soldiers, guards, public clerks, or human authority connecting them to the Union which these sons of Noah leave without regret.

In May of 1845 there had passed through Independence, the last populated boundary of the state of . . . several lines of wagons, which, in groups of thirty-eight, twenty-eight, or a hundred, headed at short intervals for Oregon. On the 13th day many of these parties, grouped in a convoy of one hundred and seventy wagons of the abovementioned description, found themselves surrounded from a distance by Indians who were prowling to raid the livestock amounting to around two thousand head. This led them to consider that it was time to organize the colony, and constitute this itinerant state, as the officers and public clerks until then active had to finish their functions in Big Soldier. The two officers who must first be named are the pilot (scout) and the captain. Throughout the journey this supreme question has been discussed in the conversations in the wagons and round the fire at the camps, and the rival candidates have formed their parties. On May 13th, each wagon throws into the fray at least two men, to meet in an elective assembly. Two candidates for pilot step forward. One is a Mr. Adams, who has ventured inland as far as Fort Laramie, possesses Gilpin's Notes,[17] and has with him a Spaniard who knows the country; Mr. Adams is also one of those who have most contributed to Oregon fever, that is, the desire to emigrate. Mr. Adams requests five hundred dollars to act as pilot if the honorable assembly chooses to elect him.

Mr. Meek is an old mountaineer in the style of Cooper's trapper; he

17. William Gilpin (1813–1894), explorer and politician, wrote memoirs of his travels in the Pacific Northwest. [E.N.]

has spent many years in the Rocky Mountains as a dealer and trapper and has proposed like the other man to pilot them as far as Fort Vancouver, for 250 dollars, of which he requested only 30 dollars in advance. A motion is passed to postpone the submission until the next day, when old Meek is seen coming at a gallop on his horse, his eyes and hand pointing toward the fields. The Indians are taking the livestock, he says hurriedly; the assembly is dissolved and within five minutes has turned into a cavalry squadron, armed with rifle and dagger, and marching in orderly fashion on the enemy. At a distance of two miles the village of the Indians can be made out; the army rabble attacks the wigwams, and the Indians take fright, the women crying, the children hiding, they know not what to make of that attack by the palefaces. The Indian chiefs come forward to offer the peace pipe, and protest vigorously against the accusation weighing upon them. A poor fellow, arriving at the village, is caught and taken prisoner. Judges are named and the prisoner stands at the bar. Asked straightforwardly if he is a criminal or not, he responds with a terrified grunt. His case is then heard accordingly; witnesses make their statements, and as there is insufficient evidence for the charges against him, he is acquitted completely, and it is proven on the contrary that it was a false alarm to postpone the election. With spirits calmed and rifles laid down, the electoral assembly is formed again and proceeds with the vote, resulting in the election of trapper Meek as pilot and Mr. Welch as captain, with all the other officers necessary for good government, such as lieutenants, sergeants, judges, etc., etc. The march begins on May 14th. Five miles on the 16th. On the 17th sixteen wagons split off and join the main corps. On the 17th they reach a wigwam of the Caw Indians, distinguished thieves who conduct themselves honorably with the group and provide it with provisions in exchange for products of the Union. On the 19th the minority defeated at the elections protests against the will of the majority. To satisfy their thwarted ambitions, it is agreed that the mass will divide into three groups, each of which will select its own chiefs and officers, recognizing no other general authority than that of the pilot and of Mr. Welch. Before separating it is agreed that the pilot be paid, and to do so a treasurer is appointed, who after giving the corresponding guarantees proceeds to collect the funds; some flatly refuse to pay, and other ex-citizens have no money. Having satisfactorily resolved these and other points, they proceed to the appointment of officers for each of the three groups, with regulations drawn up in each regarding the good government of the company, and the march continues on the 20th. On the 23rd the pilot notifies them that the place where they are is the last where spare parts can be procured for axle trees and wagon tongues.—The road is measured daily with a chain, and a diary is kept of all that occurs, the appearance of the country, features, pasture, firewood, water, timber, rivers, landscapes, buffaloes, etc., doves, rabbits, etc., etc. June 2nd: one company proposes that it be released from the commitment to wait for the others on the marches. The motion is rejected.—15th. Halt. A herd of buffalo falls under rifle fire, they kill some and make *jerky*. The scene that the countryside presents now is thus described in the travel diary: "The hunters, returning with the spoil, some erecting scaffolds, and others drying the meat. Of the women, some were washing, some ironing, many baking. At two tents, a fiddle was employed in uttering its unaccustomed voice among the solitudes of the Platte; at one tent I heard singing; one man reads his Bible; another, a novel. A Campbellist preacher was reading a hymn preparatory to religious worship."—June 24th: they reach Fort Laramie, 630 miles from Independence.

By day they busy themselves with reshoeing horses and gathering together provisions, sugar, coffee, tobacco. They give a banquet to the Sioux Indians, preceded by a speech:

> A long time ago, said the Indian chief, some white chiefs passed up the Missouri, saying that they were the red man's friends. This country belongs to the red man, but his white brethren travels through, shooting the game and scaring it away. Thus the Indian loses all that he depends upon to support his wives and children. The children of the red man cry for food, but there is no food. It was the custom when the palefaces passed through his country, to make presents to the Indians of powder, lead, etc. His tribe was very numerous, but most of the people had gone to the mountains to hunt. Before the white man came, the game was tame, and easily caught. Now the white man has frightened it; and the red man must go to the mountains. The red man needed longer guns.

A Yankee, who for the time being acts as white chief, expresses himself in these terms:

We are journeying to the great waters of the west. Our great father owned a large country there, and we are going to settle upon it. For this purpose we bring with us our wives and little ones. We are compelled to pass through the red man's country, but we travel as friends and not as enemies. As friends we feast them, we shake them by the hand and smoke with them the pipe of peace. They must know that we come among them as friends, for we bring with us our wives and children. The red man does not take his squaws into battle, neither does the paleface. But friendly as we feel, we are ready for enemies; and if molested we should punish the offenders. Some of us expected to return. Our fathers, our brothers, and our children are coming behind us, and we hope the red men will treat them kindly. We met peacefully; so let us part. We are not traders and have no powder or ball to give. We are going to plow and to plant the ground . . . !

September 3rd. "We traveled fifteen miles to Malheur." In this place the road splits in two, and the immigrants are fearful of taking the wrong road. "Mr. Meek, who had been engaged as our pilot as far as Oregon, led nearly two hundred families with the wagons and livestock to follow the trail to the left, ten days before our arrival at the crossroads. . . . Over a long distance they found en excellent trail, with plenty grass, fuel, and water; they then continued along some barren mountains where for many days they wanted for water, and when they found it, it was so bad not even the cattle could drink it. But even so it was necessary to make use of it. Camp fever, as it is called, soon broke out.

"They at length arrived at a marshy lake, which they attempted to cross, but found it impracticable; and as the marsh appeared to bear south, despite the opinion of the scout Meek, they turned north, and after a few days' travel they [arrived] at Falls river. The[y] traveled up and down this river endeavoring to find a passage, but it was impossible to cross.

"Their sufferings were daily increasing, their stock of provisions was rapidly wasting away, their cattle were becoming exhausted, and many attached to the company were laboring under severe attacks of sickness. At length Meek informed them that they were not more than two days' journey from the Dalles. Ten men started on horseback for the Methodist station with provisions for two days.

"After riding faithfully for ten days, they at last arrived at the Dalles. On their way, they encountered an Indian who furnished them with a rabbit and a fish; and this with the provision they had started with, was their only food for the ten days' travel. Upon their arrival at the Dalles, they were so exhausted in strength, and the rigidity of their limbs was so great, as to render them unable to dismount without assistance. At this place they met an old mountaineer usually called Black Harris, who volunteered his services as a pilot. He in company with several others, started in search of the lost company, whom they found reduced to great extremities, exhausted by fatigue, and despairing of ever reaching the settlements. They succeeded in finding a place where their cattle could be driven down to the river and made to swim across; after crossing, the bluff had to be ascended. Greater difficulty arose in the attempt to effect a passage with the wagons. A large rope was swung across the stream, and attached to the rocks on either side; a light wagon was suspended with pulleys from this rope, to which ropes were attached; this bed served to convey the families and loading in safety across. The passage of this river occupied some two weeks. The distance to the Dalles was 35 miles, where they arrived about the 13th or 14th of October. Some twenty of their number had perished by disease, and a like number were lost, after their arrival, from the same cause. . . ."

September 7th. "This day we traveled around twelve miles. The road exceeded in roughness that of yesterday. Sometimes it pursues its course along the bottom of the creek, at other times it wound its way along the sides of the mountains, so sidelong as to require the weight of two or more men on the upper side of the wagons to preserve their equilibrium. The creek and road are so enclosed by the high mountains as to afford but little room to pass along, rendering it in some places almost impassable. Many of the mountains viewed from this point seem almost perpendicular, and of course present a barren surface. The view is occasionally relieved by a few scrubby cedars; but along the creek the brush and briars are so impenetrable as to preclude ingress . . . but knowing that those who have preceded us have surmounted the difficulties, encouraged us to persevere."

November 1st. "We were now at the place destined at a not-so-distant period to be an important point in the commercial history of the Union, as a center of trade with China and India. Passing through the timber that lies to the east of the city, we beheld Oregon City and the Falls of the Willammette, at the same moment. We were so filled with gratitude that we had reached the settlements of the white man, and with admiration at the appearance of the large sheet of water rolling over the Falls, that we stopped, and in this moment of happiness recounted our toils, in thought, with more rapidity than tongue can express or pen write. From Independence to Fort Laramie, 692 miles; from there to Fort Hall, 585; to Fort Bois, 281; to the Dalles, 305; from the Dalles to Oregon City, 160 miles, making the total distance cleared 1,960 miles. . . .

"We had been so long among the savages that we resembled them much in appearance; but when attired in new apparel and shaved as became white men, we hardly knew each other. We had been long in each other's company; had undergone hardships and privations together, had passed through many dangers, relying upon each other for aid and protection. Attachments had grown up, which when we were about to separate were sensibly felt; but as we were yet separated from our families, where still stronger ties were felt, each one took his course, and in a few hours our party had scattered, and each traveling in a different direction."[18]

When one reads the narrative of such adventures as these, one no doubt feels proud to belong to the human race. None of the great passions caused by the wonders of history is at hand here to arouse the spirit, neither the despair of the remains of the great army, nor the love for the fatherland of ten thousand Spartans cast among the barbarians, nor the thirst for gold, for glory, and blood of the Spanish conquistadors. Men of that mettle in the United States had lands of public property on which to settle, families to help them, livestock to assist them in the hard toil of the land. They cross six hundred leagues of desert to fulfill a great idea; they, the cast-offs of the North American people, want the Union to shine its stars on the Pacific sky, to accomplish the golden dream of bringing India and China closer, and snatch away these markets from England. They offer their sacrifice, then, to an idea about the nation's future, because the Yankee knows that the first generation on the new plantations fertilizes the land with his sweat only so that future generations might enjoy it; when in Oregon many hundreds of fami-

18. *Journal of Travels over the Rocky Mountains to the Mouth of the Columbia River, Made the Years 1845 and 1846.* [A.N.] By Joel Palmer, published in Cincinnati (1847). The Spanish original is confusing. Large amounts of text have been omitted without notice. [E.N.]

lies have come together, the chiefs, leaving aside the ax with which they slowly destroy the forests to plow a field and create their property, will gather at a deliberative assembly "for the purpose of fixing the principles of civil and religious liberty, as the basis of all laws and constitutions of government, that may hereafter be adopted," and decree that:

Sec. 1. No person demeaning himself in a peaceable and orderly manner, shall ever be molested upon account of his mode of worship, or religious sentiments.

2. The inhabitants of said territory shall always be entitled to the benefits of the writ of habeas corpus and trial by jury, of a proportionate representation of the people in the legislature, and of judicial proceedings, according to the course of common law. All persons shall be bailable, unless for capital offenses, where the proof shall be evident, or the presumption great. No man shall be deprived of his liberty but by the judgment of his peers, or the law of the land. . . .

3. Religion, morality, and knowledge, being necessary to good government and the happiness of mankind, schools and the means of education shall be forever encouraged. . . .

5. No person shall be deprived of the right of bearing arms in his own defense; no unreasonable searches or seizures shall be granted; the freedom of the press shall not be restrained; nor the people deprived of the right of peaceably assembling and discussing any matter they may think proper.

6. The powers of the government shall be divided into three distinct departments:—the legislative, executive, and judicial, etc., etc.

Land law:

Any person now holding, or hereafter wishing to establish a claim to land in this territory, shall designate the extent of his claim by natural boundaries, or by marks at the corners and upon the lines of such claim, and have the extent and boundaries of said claim recorded in the office of the territorial recorder, in a book to be kept by him for that purpose, within twenty days from the time of making said claim; PROVIDED, That those who shall be already in possession of land, shall be allowed twelve months from the passage of this act, to file a description of his claim in the recorder's office;

and PROVIDED FURTHER, That the said claimant shall state in his record, the size, shape and locality of such claim.

Sec. 2. All claimants shall, within six months from the time of recording their claims, make permanent improvements upon the same by building or enclosing, and also become an occupant upon said claim within one year from the date of such record or, in case not occupied, the person holding said claim shall pay into the treasury the sum of five dollars annually, and in case of failure to occupy, or on failure of payment of the sum above stated, the claim shall be considered as abandoned; PROVIDED, that no nonresident of this territory shall have the benefit of this law; and PROVIDED FURTHER, That any resident of this territory, absent on his private business for two years, may hold his claim by paying five dollars annually to the treasury.

Sec. 3. No individual shall be allowed to hold a claim of more than one square mile, or six hundred and forty acres, in a square or oblong form, according to the natural situation of the premises. Nor shall any individual be allowed to hold more than one claim at the same time. . . .

Sec. 5. The boundary lines of all claims shall hereafter conform, as near as may be, to the cardinal points.[19]

As you can see, this people has organically in its mind, as if it were a political conscience, certain constitutive principles of association: political science turned into a complementary moral sentiment of man, of the people, of the mob; the municipality becomes the rule of spontaneous association; freedom of conscience and thought; trial by jury. If you wish to measure the road that this people has traveled, then gather together a group, not of the lower orders of the English, the French, Chileans, or Argentines, but of the educated classes, and ask them to form an impromptu association, and they will not understand what you want of them, even less set with precision, like those adventurers of Oregon, the bases on which the government of an emerging society must rest, and that due to the distance and the deserts that divide it from the rest of the Union is in fact and in law separate from the common

19. Oregon Organic Law, enacted July 5, 1845. [A.N.]

homeland.[20] Some years later a territory will arise from these scattered rudiments; and from the territory a state to add a new star to the constellation of the North American states, with its same laws, its practices, its civil and political institutions, and above all with that particular national character, marked with the determined stamp of that colossus.

There is a phenomenon occurring in the United States, which despite pertaining to fundamental principles inherent to the human species, has not until today been precisely established. Not even the right word can be found to indicate it in any language. To attempt to indicate it in two pages would be the index or the plan of a great book. What are morals? The code of precepts that, in six thousand years, has been brought about by the contact of one man with another, so they might live in peace without mutual harm, loving each other, seeking good. The morals that attach us to God through our fathers, are, after Confucius, Socrates, and Franklin, foreseen, found. If morals are lacking perfection through human study and the sentiments of the heart, they are completed by the revelation in terms of the part of man most separate from ourselves; namely, the neighbor, the foreigner, the enemy, a classification that distinguishes three degrees of separation; in the laws, one's neighbor is indifferent; the foreigner, the cloth from which the slave was always cut; for the enemy, all ties with the human family cease, death shall soon be upon him, without remorse, with glory. When man is called the enemy, he ceases to be part of our species; neither laws nor any religion whatsoever have been able to do anything to this day against the moral effects of this classification.

But morals refer to the actions of individuals only. What is the name of that other part of the life of man, as a member of a flock, of a hive, or of a shoal, given that he belongs to a species of gregarious animals? Ask the tsar of Russia, a lord of Parliament, ask Rousseau, Rosas, or Franklin, and each one will give you a handsome political system, with precepts, obligations, rights, and duties that act as rules for individuals in relation to the mass, to society. Some will claim that the *one* who governs will do everything he pleases for the common good; others will hold that the lords are those who have the right to do their sovereign will, and there

20. In the 1848 Message, the president of the United States demanded that the inhabitants of Oregon be invited to enter into a relationship with the Union and recognize the common authority as a territory. [A.N.]

will be no shortage of those who maintain that each individual has the right to interfere in the business of all, although this will depend on the number of goods that one has accumulated or the condition of one's reason. Human politics, then, has not made as much progress as human morals, and that primordial science can still be placed among the speculative sciences despite referring to the most ancient, long-lasting, most current fact, which is the society in which we live. The human species is lacking a sense, if it is possible to say so. To the *conscience* that rules the moral actions of man, it is necessary to add something else to indicate with the same certainty the duties and rights that constitute association, morals on a larger scale, affecting millions of men, among families, cities, states, and nations, to be completed later by the laws of all mankind. The city of Athens appears to have acquired this sentiment; later it was held by the Roman patricians; but it was destroyed by them, wounding it through the gap left by morals to this day, that is, in the classification of the *enemy;* and the Roman patricians were destroyed and scattered by the *plebs,* who acquired the same sentiment in the shadow of the patrician, and by the *foreigners,* who being first conquered enemies later wanted to become part of the Roman Senate.

Forgive me this pedantic tirade, without which I cannot explain my idea. The vast population of the United States has acquired this sentiment, this political conscience, as I know not what name to give it. As to how it has acquired it, you may conjecture from Bancroft's history of the United States.[21] It is a fact that has been four centuries in preparation; it is the practice of doctrines and parties defeated and rejected in Europe, and which has been developed, perfected, established with the Pilgrims, Puritans, Quakers, habeas corpus, Parliament, *juris,* unpopulated land, distance, isolation, the wilderness, independence, etc. In England there are political and religious freedoms for lords and tradesmen; in France for those who write or govern; the people, the brute mass, poor, disinherited, do not yet *feel* anything about their position as members of a society; they shall be governed by a monarchy, by an aristocracy, by a theocracy, depending on how landowners, lawyers, the military, and men of letters wish or fail to withstand.

21. George Bancroft, *History of the United States of America, from the Discovery of the American Continent.* The first three volumes, published 1834–1840, were probably the ones known to Sarmiento. [E.N.]

In North America the Yankee shall inevitably be republican, out of the perfection that his political sentiment acquires, which is now as clear and fixed as the moral conscience; because it is a dogma that morals are acquired, without which the revelation was futile, and no revelation whatsoever has been made to men to guide them in their relations with the masses. If one part of the Union defends and maintains slavery, it is because in that part the moral conscience concerning the foreigner as a race, imprisoned, hunted, weak, ignorant, places him in the category of *enemy,* and as such morals do not favor him; but in all the other states, in all classes, or rather, in the one class that society forms, the *political* sentiment that must be as inherent to man as reason and conscience is completely developed. So it follows that wherever ten Yankees meet, poor, ragged, stupid, before striking an ax at the foot of the trees to build a dwelling, they gather to set the bases of the association; the day will come when this pact is not written, because it will always be tacit; and this pact is, as you have seen in the Organic Law of Oregon, a series of dogmas, a Decalogue. Each man will believe what he wishes; each man will name whom he wants to govern him; each man will say out loud and in writing his thoughts; he will be judged by a jury, and will be granted safe bail for any misdeed that does not merit capital punishment.

But this part is only that which can be formulated, as there is another part that lies in the ideas and acquisitions made; and it is the most worthy of study. For example: a man attains the fullness of his moral and intellectual development only through education; hence society must complete the work of the father in raising his son. Free schools appear simultaneously and sometimes prior to the foundation of a town. Society needs to have its own voice, just as each individual has his own to express his sentiments, opinions, and desires; then there will be meetings and a House of Representatives to enact all the wishes, and a daily press that shall concern itself with the interests, passions, and ideas of the great masses. As society, even born in the heart of the forests, is the daughter and heir of all acquisitions of world civilization, it shall aspire to have immediately or as early as possible a daily post, roads, ports, railroads, telegraphs, etc., and piece by piece one comes to have the plow, clothes, kitchen utensils, improved and patented, the latest result of human science for all, for each one.

These details, though seeming trivial, nevertheless constitute a unique fact in the history of the world. I have just come from traveling in Europe, admiring her monuments, prostrating myself before her science, astounded still by the wonders of her arts; but I have seen her millions of peasants, proletarians, and artisans, base, degraded, unworthy of being counted among men; the crust of filth that covers their bodies, the rags and tatters they wear, do not reveal enough the darkness of their spirit; and in terms of politics, of social organization, such murkiness manages to darken the minds of the wise, of the bankers and the noblemen. Imagine twenty million men who know enough, who read enough every day to exercise their reason, their public or political passions; who have food to eat and clothes to wear, who in their poverty hold justified, feasible hopes for a happy future, who lodge on their travels in comfortable and spacious hotels, who travel seated on soft cushions, who carry a billfold and geographical map in their pocket, who fly through the air on wings of steam, who are kept abreast daily of all that is going on in the world, who debate unceasingly on matters of public interest that stir them vividly, who feel they are the legislators and makers of national prosperity; imagine this accumulation of activity, enjoyment, strength, progress, having an effect at the same time on twenty million, with very few exceptions, and you will feel what I have felt, on seeing this society on whose buildings and squares the sun seems to shine more brightly, and whose members show in their projects, enterprises, and labors a virility that leaves the human race in general far behind. The North Americans can be compared today only with the ancient Romans, with no other difference than that the former conquer rough nature itself with their own toil, while the latter seized through war the fruit created by the work of others. The same virile superiority, the same obstinacy, the same strategy, the same concern with future power and greatness.

Their ships are the best in the world, the cheapest, the largest. If on the high seas you should one day find close to the wind a ship hastened along by the squall, whose gusts swell to bursting the main, topgallant, wing, and anchor sails, the French, Spanish, or English captain of your ship who has reefed down the mainsail will tell you which nation it belongs to; he will tell you, grinding his teeth in anger, that it is a Yankee ship; he knows it from the size, from its audacity, and above all because it passes close by his ship without raising the flag to greet him. In European ports and docks, your eyes will come across a special section where the colossal frigates gather together, seeming something belonging to another world, to other men; they are the Yankee ships that began by

THE UNITED STATES (1847) : 109

growing in size in order to contain a greater number of cotton bales and have ended up forming a whole class in naval construction. Fifteen steamers of those that service the Hudson, joined by their keels and bows, make up a wooden street, one mile long. If on a stormy day you see in Le Havre or in Liverpool a ship endeavoring to take to sea, it is a Yankee ship whose departure was scheduled for that day, and which the honor of its flag, the glory of the stars on it, keeps it from waiting, as other nations' ships do, for the wind to die down. Which ships are those that hunt whales in polar seas? They are almost exclusively North American ones; and within that solitary hull, that squatter of the seas, you will find a small crew who do not drink liquor because they belong to the temperance society, men hardened by troubles who make a modest living from danger and death in order to settle in the United States when they return, to buy a plot and till their land and build a house, and tell their children, gathered around a cast-iron stove, of their adventures at sea. Last year, Queen Victoria, accompanied by Prince Albert, was sailing on her sumptuous yacht around Falmouth Bay. All the ships were decked out to honor the royal visitors. At the top of the highest mast of a North American frigate there could be seen a Yankee sailor standing on one foot, moving to and fro with the ship as it swayed on its anchors, and waving his hat in one hand in the air as a sign of greeting. This is the hieroglyphic expression of the Yankee sailor. The queen fell ill at the sight of that spectacle. An English sailor was stung by national pride into repeating the test. The queen forbad him with a show of horror. Would he have done it? He did not do it, and that is enough. It was an imitation of another man's daring; the man is capable of that and much more; but only the genius of one people inspires the idea and the courage to pull it off.

I linger on this point of the North American navy because the ship for the Yankee is his international means, the extension of his nation to make contact with all other nations on earth; and in this time of universal movement, the people that has the swiftest ships, the cheapest to build and therefore with lowest freight costs, is the king of the universe. In the Mediterranean, in the seas of India and the Pacific, they outshine, cut out, and drive away daily all other ships or trade except their own. Oh, kings of the Earth, you who have insulted for so many centuries the human race, you who have set the foot of your minions on the progress of reason and the political sentiment of uprising peoples; within twenty years the name of the North American Republic shall be for you like that of Rome for the barbarian kings. The theories, the utopias of your philosophers, discredited, ridiculed by tradition, by legitimacy, the fait accompli, naturally supported by half a million bayonets, so that the ridicule will be effective, will also find the fact enlightening and triumphant. When the states of the Union are in their hundreds, and their inhabitants in hundreds of millions, educated, dressed, and sated, how will you oppose the sovereign will of the great Republic in world affairs? Your guardians of beggars? But you forget that the American ships will blockade you in all the seas, in all the ports! God has wished in the end that there be united in a single fact, in a single nation, the virgin land that allows society to spread out into infinity, without fear of poverty; the iron that completes human endeavors; the coal that stirs the machines; the forests that provide the materials for naval architecture; popular education, which develops through general instruction the strength of production in all the individuals of a nation; religious liberty, which attracts the peoples en masse to join the population; political liberty that looks in horror on despotism and families of privilege; the Republic, ultimately, strong, rising like a new star in the sky; and all these facts link together: liberty and abundant land; iron and industrial spirit; democracy and the superiority of the fleet. Endeavor to break them apart with theories and speculation; say that liberty, popular education, do not enter at all into this unheard-of prosperity which leads inevitably to an indisputable supremacy; the *fact* will always be the same, that the European monarchies have gathered together decrepitude, revolutions, poverty, ignorance, barbarianism, and the debasement of the highest number. Spit at the heavens and let us ponder the advantages of the monarchy. The land turns barren beneath your feet, and the Republic brings corn to feed you; the ignorance of the masses is the basis of your thrones, and the crown that adorns your temples shines like a flower atop ruins; half a million soldiers keep the balance between the jealousy and envy of a few sovereigns while the Republic, placed by Providence on propitious land, like a beehive, saves those immense sums to turn them into means of prosperity which brings its return in the increase of power and strength. Your science and your vigil serve only to increase the splendor of the Republic. *Sic vos non vobis* you invented electric telegraphs so that the union would expedite its communications. *Sic vos non vobis*[22] you created the rails so that North American production and trade would be transported. Franklin had the boldness to present himself in the most splendid court in the world with his shoes marked by farm work and his clothes of coarse cloth; a day will come when you will hide your scepters, your crowns, and your golden trifles to present yourself to the Republic, for fear that it will leave you at the door like clowns or jesters from a fair.

Oh, I am exalted, my dear friend, by the idea of sensing the moment when the sufferings of so many centuries, of so many millions of men, the violation of so many holy principles by the material force of facts, elevated to theory, to science, will also find the *fact* that crushes them, that dominates them and demoralizes them! The day of the great uproar of the strong Republic, rich with hundreds of millions, is nigh! The progress of the North American population shows it; it grows by the hundreds, and the other nations only by ones; the figures will balance out and change the proportions immediately; and will not those numerical figures express what is embraced, in productive forces and physical and moral energy, by a people proficient in practices of liberty, labor, and association?

22. "Thus do ye, but not for yourselves" (attributed to Virgil). [E.N.]

2 | The Framework of the National Constitution (1852–1860)

JUAN BAUTISTA ALBERDI
Bases and Starting Points for the Political Organization of the Argentine Republic (1852) (Excerpts)

1

I. THE CONSTITUTIONAL STATUS OF THE RIVER PLATE

Victory at Monte Caseros alone[1] does not put the Argentine Republic in possession of all that it needs. The battle has set her on the path to organization and progress, in light of which this victory is as important an event as the May Revolution, which overthrew the Spanish colonial government.

Although it cannot be said that we are back where we started (for states do not tread the path of their suffering without some benefit), we find ourselves, as in 1810, in need of creating a general Argentine government, and a constitution to regulate the conduct of that government. — All the seriousness of the situation lies in this pressing requirement. A change of government presents fewer problems when there is a constitution that can regulate the conduct of the government created by the Revolution. But the Argentine Republic today lacks a government, a constitution, and the general laws that might take its place. This is the main difference between the recent revolutions in Montevideo and Buenos Aires: because a constitution exists in Uruguay, all evil has vanished since the new government has taken office.

The Argentine Republic, a simple, tacit, and implicit organization until now, must begin by creating a national government and a general constitution to regulate it.

But with which trends, purposes, or perspectives should this future constitution be conceived? What are the bases and starting points of the

---

Original title: "Bases y puntos de partida para la organización política de la República Argentina." Source: *Obras completas de Juan Bautista Alberdi* [Complete works of Juan Bautista Alberdi], vol. 3 (Buenos Aires: La Tribuna nacional, 1886–1887).

1. Name of the battlefield where on February 3, 1852, Rosas was defeated by General Urquiza, current president of the Argentine Confederation. [A.N.]

new constitutional order and the new government soon to come into power? — This book concerns itself with these questions, the result of many years' thought, albeit written with the urgency of the Argentine situation.

In it, I seek to assist the constituent deputies and press to lay the foundations necessary for progress on the constitutional question.

While applying myself to the Argentine question, I find it necessary to touch on the question of South America, to explain more clearly where the Argentine Republic has come from, where it is now, and where it is headed, in terms of its political and social destinies.

II. THE HISTORICAL NATURE OF SOUTH AMERICAN CONSTITUTIONAL LAW: ITS ESSENTIAL DIVISION INTO TWO PERIODS

All constitutional law of once Spanish America is incomplete and defective in terms of the means that should allow America to fulfill its great destiny.

I shall indicate those defects and the cause that may excuse them, so that my country might refrain from falling victim to this generally poor example. There must be some advantage to be had from being the last country to organize itself.

None of the constitutions of South America deserve to be taken as a model for imitation, for the reasons I shall list below.

Two essentially different periods make up the constitutional history of our South America: one beginning in 1810 and concluding with the war of independence from Spain, and the other, which dates from that period to the present day.

All the constitutions of the latter period are a reminiscence, a tradition, often word-for-word revisions of the constitutions of the earlier period.

These revisions were made with domestic aims; sometimes to strengthen power for the sake of order; other times to weaken it for the sake of liberty; sometimes to centralize the way in which it is exercised, other times to make power more local: but never with the aim of rooting out from the constitutional law of the earlier period all that which went against the growth and progress of the new states, nor with the intention of establishing means conducive to achieving this great goal of the South American revolution.

What obstacles are there in the first constitutional law, and what do they entail? I shall indicate them.

All the constitutions written in South America during the War of Independence were the full expression of the prevalent need at that time. That need was to put an end to the political power that Europe had wielded in this continent, beginning with the conquest and continuing with the colonial period; and as a means of ensuring that this power would be entirely extinguished, any kind of European influence in these countries was eliminated. Independence and freedom from abroad were the vital interests that concerned legislators in that period. In this, the legislators were right; they understood their times and served them well.

All the ills of America lay in and were defined as its dependence on a conquering government belonging to Europe; consequently, to remedy this ill South America sought to distance itself from the influence of Europe. While we fought with Spain, disputing inch by inch our American soil, and against the monarchical example of Europe, fighting for the democratic sovereignty of this continent, our legislators saw nothing further than the need to proclaim and ensure our independence, and impose the principles of equality and liberty as the bases for domestic government, instead of the monarchic system that had previously prevailed in the Americas and endured still in Europe. — Europe was hateful to us because of its domination and its monarchism.

During that period, in which democracy and independence were the whole constitutional purpose, wealth, material progress, trade, population, industry, indeed, all economic interests, were incidental things, secondary benefits, second-place interests, misunderstood, poorly studied and, of course, heeded even less. They were still written into our constitutions, but only as minor details intended to embellish the whole.

Under this spirit of reserve, prejudice, and fear toward Europe, the means of improvement through the action of economic interests forgotten and abandoned, the constitutions contemporaneous with San Martín, Bolívar, and O'Higgins were enacted. Inspired by those illustrious men, these constitutions were later repeated almost word for word and with insufficient judgment by subsequent constitutions, which endure to this day.

Two great revolutions, which served as a model for us, contributed to setting us on that road: the French Revolution of 1789, and the revolution of the United States against England. I shall indicate the form of their influence to prevent the erroneous imitation of those great models, to which we South Americans are still inclined.

In their wording, our constitutions imitated those of the French and the North American republics.

Let us see the result that this had on our economic interests, that is, in matters of trade, industry, navigation, immigration, on which all the future of South America depends.

The example of the French Revolution passed on to us its acknowledged incompetence in economic matters.

It is well known that the French Revolution, which proclaimed all liberties, refused to recognize free trade and abolished it. The Convention turned its customs into a war weapon, pointed especially at England, thus sterilizing the excellent measure of abolishing provincial customhouses, as decreed by the National Assembly. Napoleon continued pushing France onto that path with the continental blockade, which became the basis of France's and Europe's industrial and commercial regime during the life of the empire. As a result of this system, European industry grew accustomed to living off protection, tariffs, and prohibitions.

The United States was no better example to us in its foreign policy and in economic matters, strange though this may seem.

One of the major constitutional aims of the northern Union was the defense of the country against foreigners, who surrounded the nascent republic to the north and to the south, possessing more territory in the Americas than the USA, and professing the monarchical principle as their system of government. Spain, England, France, Russia, and almost all European nations had vast territories around the nascent confederation. It was thus right that it should seek to safeguard itself against the feasible return of those foreigners who had been defeated though not expelled from the Americas. Such fear today in the South American states would be groundless, as they have no European government in the vicinity.

Having separated from a maritime and manufacturing state, the United States had the aptitude and the means to be both these things, and it was in their interests to adopt a policy that sought to protect its industry and fleet against foreign competition by means of exclusions and tariffs. But we have neither factories nor fleet to defend by restricting foreign industry and fleets with prohibitions and regulations, when they seek us out for trade.

Furthermore, when Washington and Jefferson advised the United States to follow a foreign policy of abstention and reserve toward the political powers of Europe, it was during the commencement of the French Revolution and the terrible commotion of all Europe at the end of the last century. In this regard, those famous men gave their country excellent advice, distancing it from political alliances with countries burning in the flames of a struggle unrelated to American interests. They would speak of political links, not of trade treaties and agreements. And even in this regard, the United States possessed a fleet and manufacturing industry, and could be exempted from close alliances with maritime European nations and their manufacturing. But South America is entirely ignorant of the special nature of its situation and circumstances, when it invokes for itself the example of the foreign policy that Washington advised for his country in an entirely different time and circumstances. North America's liberal colonial system always attracted settlers to its soil in vast numbers, even before independence; but as heirs of an essentially exclusive system, we need a highly stimulating policy for foreign affairs.

Everything has changed in this age: a replica of a system that suited times and countries quite unlike ours would only serve to lead us into stupidity and poverty.

This is, however, what is offered by the constitutions of South America; and to better illustrate the truth of this observation of such importance in our destinies, I shall examine in particular the better-known constitutions tried or in force in South America, in those provisions regarding the question of *population,* for example, through *naturalization* and *residence;* our state education and our municipal improvements, through the admission of foreigners into secondary posts; *immigration,* in relation to religious matters; *trade,* through the regulations of our foreign trade policy; and *progress,* through reform guarantees.

I shall start with those of my country as evidence that I am guided in this critique by complete impartiality. . . .

X. WHAT THE SPIRIT OF THE NEW CONSTITUTIONAL LAW IN SOUTH AMERICA SHOULD BE

From the preceding outline, we can see that the constitutional law of South America is opposed to the interests of her material and industrial progress, on which all her future now depends. An expression of the needs of a South America from a bygone age, it is no longer in harmony with the new demands of the present. The time has come to revise it in relation to the current needs of South America. Let us hope that the Argentine Republic, the pioneer of fundamental changes on this continent, will have the good fortune to open a new era by setting an example with its next constitution!

Hereafter, constitutions must take the new situation of South America as their starting point.

The situation today is not that of thirty years ago. Needs that at other times were incidental are now pressing.

The South America of thirty years ago sought only liberty and independence; for these things she wrote her constitutions. She did well, for it was her mission at that time. The moment to cast off the European yoke from this continent was not the time to attract settlers from that feared Europe. The words *immigration* and *colonization* roused painful memories and fearful sentiments. Military glory was the most sought-after prize. Trade and material well-being were presented as lackluster things.—The poverty and sobriety of the republicans of Sparta were held up as virtues worthy of imitation by our first republicans. The grotesque apparel of our peasants was proudly contrasted to the rich cloth of Europe. Luxury was looked down upon and considered the ruin of morality and liberty.

All those things have changed and are looked on differently in the era in which we now live.

This does not mean that today's South America should forget liberty and independence as the great goals of its constitutional law, but rather that it should be more practical than theoretical, more thoughtful than zealous, as a result of maturity and experience. It should concern itself with facts rather than men, and not focus so much on the ends but on the practical means to truly achieve them. Today we seek the practical reality of what in other times we were content to merely proclaim and write.

Herein lie the goals of constitutions today: they must seek to organize and to constitute the great practical means of pulling the emancipated South America out of the dark and subordinate state in which it lies.

Those means must feature today at the head of our constitutions. Just as before we gave priority to independence, liberty, religion, so today we must favor free immigration, free trade, railroads, unhindered industry, not replacing those great principles, but as essential means of turning them from words to reality.

Today we must set ourselves up, if such language is permitted to us, to have population, to have railroads, to see our rivers made navigable, to see our states opulent and rich. States, like men, must start by developing and strengthening their bodies.

These are the means and needs that make up the particular features of our times.

Our constitutional contracts or pacts in South America must be a kind of mercantile contract of collective societies formed especially to settle these deserts, which we baptize with the pompous names of republics; to build railroads, which cut the distances that render impossible indivisible unity in political action, something our constitutions of South America have so innocently copied from the constitutions of France, where political unity is the product of eight hundred years of preparatory work.

These are the needs today, and constitutions must not express the needs of yesterday, or those of tomorrow, but those of the present day.

We should not aspire to a constitution expressing the needs of all times. Like the scaffolding the architect uses to construct buildings, they must serve us in the endless construction of our political edifice, placing them one way today and tomorrow another, according to the needs of the construction. There are constitutions of transition and creation, and definitive constitutions of preservation. What South America cries out for today is the first kind, for these are exceptional times.

XI. CONSTITUTION OF CALIFORNIA

I have the good fortune of being able to cite, in support of the system I propose, the example of the last famous constitution written in the Americas: the constitution of California, which confirms our constitutional foundations.

The constitution of the new state of California, enacted in Monterrey on October 12, 1849, by a convention of delegates of the people of California, is the simple and easy application of the dominant constitutional law of the United States to the government of the new state. This law forms a common direction, the reason of all men, for the inhabitants of those fortunate states.

Without universities, without academies or lawyer's associations, the improvised people of California have brought forth a constitution replete with foresight, good sense, and opportunity in every one of its provisions. It could be said that it has nothing in excess and wants nothing. — At least, there is no rhetoric, no phrases, no pompous tone in its form and style: it is all simple, practical, and positive, yet still dignified.

Five years ago, dissident religions, foreigners, and trade were excluded from that territory. All was desolation and distress under the republican system of Spanish America, until the neighboring civilization, provoked by those uncivilized and unjust exclusions, took possession of its rich soil and enacted therein its laws of genuine liberty and immunity. In four years, a country which for three centuries had remained a gloomy, impoverished village has been transformed into a state of the first republic in the world.

The gold of their *pleasures* may have helped to achieve this result; but, under the Mexican government, doubtless that gold would have produced nothing more than turmoil and scandal among the mobs arriving from everywhere, frenetically thronging together on a soil sown with gold, but with neither government nor law. Its free constitution, its tolerant and progressive government will do far more than gold for the greatness of this new Pacific state. The gold rush might bring thousands of adventurers together, but only the law of liberty may turn those masses and that gold into a civilized and blossoming state.

The fundamental law of California, a tradition of North American liberty, is designed to create a great people in a matter of years.

That law defines *the people of California* as all the people who dwell there, who are entitled to rights, privileges, and prerogatives of citizenship, in matters regarding civil liberty, personal safety, the inviolability of property, of mail and papers, of the home, of movement, of work, etc. (Article 1, sections 1 and 17).

It guarantees that no law will be enacted preventing *any person whatsoever* from inheriting property or diminishing the obligation and value of contracts (section 16).

It confers a passive vote to the naturalized foreigner, to obtain a seat in the legislature and in the state government, after only one or two years' citizenship (Articles 4 and 5). It is well known that the general laws of the confederation since the beginning of the Union open the doors of the Senate and of the House of Representatives to foreigners naturalized in the United States. The Americans knew that in England naturalized foreigners are excluded from Parliament. But "a different course," writes Story, "naturally arising from the circumstances of the country, was adopted in the American colonies . . . with a view to invite emigrations, and settlements, and thus to facilitate the cultivation of their wild and waste lands."—"It has been justly observed," Story adds, "that under the reasonable qualifications established by the constitution, the door of this part of the federal government is open to merit of every description, whether native or adoptive, whether young or old, and without regard to poverty or wealth, or any particular profession of religious faith."[2]

The California Constitution declares that no marriage contract may be made void because of a failure to meet the requisites of any religion, if it were otherwise honestly executed. Thus the constitution makes mixed marriages inviolable, which is the natural means to form a family in our America, which has a calling to populate itself with foreign men and women with good customs. To consider education without protecting the formation of families is to expect generous harvests from soil without fertilizer or preparation.

To complete the sanctity of the family (the breeding ground for the state and the republic, the only fertile means of population and of social regeneration) the *legislature shall protect by law* (these are its handsome words) from forced sale a certain portion of the homestead and other property of all heads of families (Article 9, section 15).[3]

The constitution obliges the legislature to encourage by all possible means intellectual, scientific, moral, and agricultural progress.

It directly and inviolably allocates a part of the property of the state for the support of public education, and thus guarantees the progress of its new generations against all abuse or neglect from the government. It

2. Joseph Story, *Constitution of the United States* . . . (abridged by the author) (Boston-Philadelphia, 1833), chap. IX, sections 321, 323. [E.N.]

3. Author's error. The provision cited is in Art. 11, section 15. [E.N.]

makes education one of the fundamental bases of the political pact. This is established by all of Article 10.[4]

It establishes the equality of taxation on all state property and lays the bases of the direct taxation system, which is the most suitable for countries that receive all their development from abroad, instead of customs tax, which is a tax burden imposed on the very civilization of these countries.

In support of true credit, it forbids the granting of privileges to set up banks by the legislature; it categorically prohibits the issue of all paper as money by banks, and only permits deposit banks (sections 31 and 35, Article 4).

I have not sought to analyze the California Constitution in all its provisions to protect liberty and order, but only those related to the progress of its population, of industry and culture. I have cited them to demonstrate that these are not indisputable new laws that I propose, but simple and rational bases for completely organizing a nascent country, which is capable above all of providing the means to develop its population, its industry, and its civilization, through the rapid acquisition of large numbers of men from abroad, and institutions of our own to attract them and help them settle advantageously in an empty and gloomy territory.

XII. FALSE POSITION OF THE SPANISH AMERICAN REPUBLICS.—THE MONARCHY IS NOT THE MEANS TO MOVE OUT OF THIS FALSE POSITION, BUT A POSSIBLE REPUBLIC BEFORE THE TRUE REPUBLIC.

Only those great economic means, that is, those that nourish and strengthen material interests, could be capable of getting South America out of the highly false position in which it is placed.

That position was caused by imposing in South America the republican form by law; the republic not being a practical truth on this soil.

The republic ceases to be a factual truth in South America because the people are not prepared to be ruled under this system, superior to their capacity.

Would a return to the monarchy of a bygone age be the way to give this America a suitable government for its capabilities? If the republic in

4. The article concerning education is Art. 9. [E.N.]

the present condition of our people is impracticable, does it follow that the monarchy would be practicable?

Decidedly not.

The truth is that we are insufficiently mature for the exercise of representative government, whether it be monarchical or republican.

The supporters of the monarchy in the Americas are not deluding themselves when they say we lack the aptitude to be republicans; but they are deluding themselves more than we republicans if they think we have more resources to be monarchists. The idea of a representative monarchy in Spanish America is deficient and ridiculous; it lacks, in my view, even common sense, if we examine above all the present moment and the state of affairs we have reached. Our monarchists from the earlier period may have had some excuse for their dynastic plans; the monarchical tradition was but a step away, and they still fancied it would be possible to reorganize it. But today it is something that nobody with common sense would consider. After an endless war to turn into monarchies what we have changed into republics with a twenty-year war, we would return happily to a monarchy more restless and turbulent than the republic.

The handsome example of Brazil should not deceive us; let us congratulate this country on its good fortune, let us respect its form, which is capable of protecting her civilization, let us coexist with her, and walk toward the common goal of all forms of government—civilization. But let us abstain from imitating her monarchical ways. That country has not known the republican form for a single day; her monarchical life has not been interrupted for so much as an hour. From a colonial monarchy she passed without interregnum to an independent monarchy.—But those of us who have practiced the republican form for forty years, albeit very badly, would be worse monarchists than republicans, because today we understand the monarchy even less than the republic.

Would this new monarchy of choice take root? It would be something never before seen: the monarchy is essentially of traditional origin, proceeding from facts. Would we choose counts and marquises from our friends who are our equals? Would we consent willingly to being inferior to our equals?—I would like to see the face of the man who considers himself competent to be chosen king in these republican Americas.—Would we accept kings and nobles of European extraction?—Only after a new conquest by war: and who could conceive of, never mind consent to, such madness?

The issue of a possible government in formerly Spanish America has only one sensible solution: it consists of raising our peoples to the heights of the form of government imposed on us by necessity; it consists of giving them the aptitudes they lack to be republicans; in making them worthy of the republic we have proclaimed, which we can neither practice nor abandon; the improvement of the government lies in the improvement of the governed; in the improvement of *society* to obtain the improvement of *power*, which is its direct expression and result.

But the road is long and we must wait a great deal to reach the end.— In this case, might there be a suitable government to cover this period of preparation and transition?—There is, fortunately, and without having to abandon the republican system.

Happily, the republic, so fertile in forms, recognizes many degrees and lends itself to all the demands of time and space. In knowing how to accommodate it to our own day and age lies the art of constituting it among us.

That solution has a happy precedent in the South American republic, and we owe it to the sound sense of the Chilean people, who have found in the energy of the president's power the public guarantees that the monarchy offers for order and peace, without going against the republican government. This profound and spiritual saying is attributed to Bolívar:[5] "The new States of formerly Spanish America need kings with the name of president."—Chile has resolved the problem without dynasties or military dictatorships, by means of a constitution monarchical in its foundations but republican in form: a law that links the chain of modern life to the traditions of past life. The republic cannot have any other form when it immediately follows a monarchy; it is necessary for the new regime to contain something of the old one; a people cannot leap from one extreme end to the other; the French Republic, offspring of a monarchy, would have saved itself by this means; but the exaggeration of radicalism would return it via the empire to the monarchy.

How, then, to turn our nominal democracies into real democracies? How to change into facts our written and nominal liberties? By what

5. Simón Bolívar (1783–1830), leader of the independence movement in northern South America. [E.N.]

means will we raise the real capacity of our peoples to the level of their written constitutions and proclaimed principles?

By the means that I indicate and that everyone knows; by the education of the people, carried out through the civilizing action of Europe; that is, through immigration, through civil, commercial, and maritime legislation, on suitable foundations; through constitutions in harmony with our times and our needs; through a system of government that supports the action of those means.

Such means are not original, it is true; the revolution has known them since the beginning, but has only practiced them incompletely, on a small scale.

I shall allow myself to say how these means should be understood and organized, so that they may lead to the yearned-for growth of these countries and the true republic with all that this entails.

XIII. EDUCATION IS NOT INSTRUCTION

Belgrano, Bolívar, Egaña, and Rivadavia understood in their era that only through education could these peoples one day deserve the form of government that need had imposed on them beforehand. But they confused *education* with *instruction,* the genre with the species. Trees are capable of being raised, but only rational beings can be taught. Today, public knowledge realizes this capital difference, and it is not so long since that celebrated moment when a deep thinker, M. Troplong,[6] highlighted this difference in the debate in France on freedom for teaching.

That error led to another: that of disregarding the education that comes with the spontaneous action of things, the education received through the example of a life more civilized than ours; fertile education, which Rousseau[7] understood in all its importance and named *education of things.*

It must take the place that we give to instruction in the present age of our republics, because it is the most effective and most suitable means for bringing them out rapidly from the backwardness in which they exist.

Our earliest publicists said: "How is the culture of the great European

6. Raymond-Théodore Troplong (1795–1869), French politician and jurist, president of the Cour de Cassation (French Supreme Court) from 1852 until his death. [E.N.]

7. Jean-Jacques Rousseau (1712–1778), French philosopher, author of *Social Contract.* [E.N.]

states promoted and fostered? — Principally through instruction: then we must start from this."

They did not see that our nascent peoples were in the act of being raised, or formed before being taught, and that if instruction is the means of culture of already developed peoples, education by means of things is the means of instruction that is best suited to peoples who are beginning to come into being.

As for the instruction given to our peoples, it was never adapted to their needs. Copied from one provided for peoples who are not in our position, it was always sterile and with no advantageous result.

The elementary instruction given to the people was rather more pernicious. What good was it to the common man to be able to read? As a reason to see himself swallowed up as an instrument in the management of a political life of which he had no knowledge; to be taught by the venom of the electoral press, which contaminates and destroys when it should be enlightening; to read insults, slanders, sophisms, and incendiary claims, the only thing that pricks and stimulates his uncultured, uncouth curiosity.

This is not to suggest that the people be denied elementary instruction, but rather that it is a powerless means of improvement compared with others, which have been neglected.

Higher education in our republics was no less sterile and unsuited to our needs. What have our institutions and universities of South America been, if not factories of charlatanism, sloth, demagogy, and titled presumption?

Rivadavia's attempts for secondary education were flawed in their preference for the moral and philosophical sciences over the practical and applied sciences, which are those that must make us fit to defeat this wild nature that dominates us everywhere, it being the main endeavor of our current culture to transform and defeat it. The main establishment was named *school of moral sciences.* — It would have been better if it had been *school of exact sciences and of arts applied to industry.*

I do not claim that morals should be forgotten. I know that without them industry is impossible; but the facts show that morality is achieved more swiftly through hardworking and productive habits provided by those honest notions than through abstract instruction. These countries need more engineers, geologists, and naturalists than lawyers and theologians. Their improvement will come with roads, with artesian wells, with immigration, and not with inflammatory or servile newspapers, or with sermons or slogans.

In our plans for schooling we must flee from the sophists, who make demagogues, and from a monastic tradition, which makes slaves and underhand characters. Let the clergy educate themselves, but they should not take upon themselves the training of our lawyers and statesmen, our salesmen, sailors, and soldiers. Could the clergy give our youths the mercantile and industrial instincts that must distinguish the South American man? Could they take from their hands that fever of activity and enterprise that might turn them into Spanish American Yankees?

Instruction, to be fruitful, must be reduced to applied arts and sciences, favoring practical things, such as modern languages and knowledge of practical and immediate use.

The English language, as the language of liberty, industry, and order, must be even more obligatory than Latin; no university diploma or degree should be awarded to the young man who does not speak and write it. — That one innovation would lead to a fundamental change in the education of youth. How can they receive the civilizing example and action of the Anglo-Saxon race without the general possession of its tongue?

Our plan for instruction must multiply commercial and industrial schools, opening them in market towns.

Our youth must be educated in industrial life, and for this it must be schooled in the auxiliary arts and sciences of industry. Our type of South American man must be the man trained to overcome the great and overwhelming enemy of our progress: the desert, material backwardness, the savage and primitive nature of our continent.

To this end we should seek to take our youths away from the inland cities, where the ancient regime endures with its habits of sloth, conceit, and dissipation, and attract them to the coastal towns, so they can be inspired by Europe, which comes to our soil, and the instincts of modern life.

The coastal towns, due precisely to their coastal nature, are more instructive schools than our pretentious universities.

Industry is the only means to bring youth to order. While England watched Europe burn in its civil wars, it did not deliver its youth to mysticism to save itself; it raised a temple to industry and paid homage to it, and made demagogues ashamed of their madness.

Industry is the sedative par excellence. It leads through well-being and wealth to order, through order to liberty: England and the United States are examples of this. Instruction in South America must fix its goals in industry.

Industry is the great means of moralization. By providing men with a living, it prevents crime, often the offspring of poverty and sloth. In vain shall you fill the intelligence of young men with abstract notions of religion; if you leave them lazy and poor, unless you deliver them into monastic mendicity, they will be dragged into corruption out of a taste for comforts they cannot obtain for want of means. They will be corrupted without ceasing to be fanatical. England and the United States have attained religious morality through industry; and Spain has been unable to attain industry and liberty out of simple devotion. Spain has never been guilty of the sin of impiety, but this has not been enough for her to escape from poverty, from corruption, and from despotism.

Religion, the bedrock of all society, must be a branch of education among us, not instruction. What we need are religious practices, not religious ideas. Italy has filled the world with theologians; there may not be a single one in the United States. But who would argue that Italian customs are not more religious than those of North America? South America does not need the Christianity of pamphlets, exhibitions, and parades. It does not need the academic Christianity of Montalembert,[8] or the literary Christianity of Chateaubriand.[9] It needs religious practice, not poetry; and that practice will come from practical education, not from sterile and verbose preaching.

As for woman, modest and powerful artificer who, from her corner, sets up private and public customs, organizes the family, prepares the citizen, and lays the foundations of the state, her instruction need not be brilliant. It should not consist of decorative talents and outer luxury, such as music, dance, and painting, as has happened heretofore. We need ladies, not artists. Woman must glow with the sheen of honor, of dig-

8. Charles de Montalembert (1810–1870), French journalist, historian, and politician, was one of a group of Catholic liberals who wanted a separation of church and state. [E.N.]

9. François-René de Chateaubriand (1768–1848), French romantic writer and politician. [E.N.]

nity, of the modesty of her life. Her destiny is serious; she has not come into the world to decorate the parlor, but to embellish the fertile solitude of the home. Attach her to her house and you save her; and for the house to attract her, one must make of it an Eden. It is well understood that the preservation of that Eden demands incessant attention and hard work, and that a hardworking woman does not have time to lose herself, nor the taste for squandering her time in vain gatherings. As long as woman lives in the street and among provocations, receiving applause as an actress, in the *parlor,* as a deputy brushing shoulders with that kind of public called society, she will raise her children in her image, she will serve the Republic like *Lola Montes,*[10] and she will be of as much use to herself and to her husband as a more or less decent *Messalina.*[11]

I have spoken about *instruction.*

I will now speak about how our *education* must be practiced.

XIV. CIVILIZING ACTION OF EUROPE IN THE REPUBLICS OF SOUTH AMERICA

The republics of South America are the product and the living testimony of the action of Europe in the Americas. What we call independent America is no more than Europe established in the Americas; and our revolution is nothing more than the dismembering of a European power into two halves, which today handle their own affairs.

All civilization on our soil is European; America itself is a European discovery. It was brought about by a Genoese mariner, and its discovery was promoted by a Spanish sovereign. Cortés, Pizarro, Mendoza, Valdivia,[12] who were not born in the Americas, populated it with the people who are today in possession, who are certainly not indigenous.

10. Stage name of Maria Dolores Eliza Rosanna Gilbert (1821–1861), an Irish-born dancer and actress of great beauty. [E.N.]

11. Wife of Roman emperor Claudius known for her influence on her husband and her promiscuity, Messalina was executed in A.D. 48 for conspiring to assassinate Claudius. [E.N.]

12. Spanish conquistadors and colonizers: Hernán Cortés (1485–1547) conquered Mexico in 1519; Francisco Pizarro (1478–1541) conquered Peru in 1531; Pedro de Mendoza (1487–1537) led the expedition that founded Buenos Aires in 1536; Pedro de Valdivia (1497–1553) conquered Chile in 1940 and founded Santiago in 1941. [E.N.]

We do not have a single important city that was not founded by Euro-peans. Santiago was founded by a European named Pedro Valdivia, and Buenos Aires by another foreigner named Pedro de Mendoza.

All our major cities took European names from their foreign founders. The name *America* itself was taken from one of its foreign discoverers, Amerigo Vespucci,[13] of Florence.

Even now, after independence, indigenous people are neither impor-tant nor numerous in our political and civil society.

We who call ourselves Americans are no more than Europeans born in the Americas. Skull, blood, color, everything is from abroad.

The indigenous man does us justice; to this day he calls us Spaniards. — I know not of any person of distinction in our societies carrying a Pe-huenche or Araucano[14] surname. The language we speak is European. To the humiliation of those who reject its influence, they must curse it in a foreign language. The Spanish language carries its name with it.

Our Christian religion has been brought to America by the foreigners. If it had not been for Europe, America today would be worshiping the sun, the trees, the beasts, burning men in sacrifice, and would not know marriage. The hand of Europe planted the cross of Jesus Christ in this once heathen America. Blessed be for this alone the hand of Europe!

Our ancient and current laws were enacted by foreign kings, and to their good graces we owe to this day civil, commercial, and criminal laws. Our national laws are copies of foreign laws.

Our administrative regime in terms of treasury, taxation, revenues, etc., is to this day almost entirely the work of Europe. And what are our political constitutions if not the adoption of European government systems? What is our great revolution, in terms of ideas, if not another aspect of the French Revolution?

Enter our universities and show me knowledge that is not European; enter our libraries and show me a useful book that is not foreign.

Look at the suit you are wearing, from head to toe, and it is unlikely that the soles of your shoes be American. What do we call good taste if not European taste? Who has dominion over our fashions, our ele-

13. Amerigo Vespucci (1451–1512), navigator in the service of Portugal and Spain, was the first to realize that the land discovered by Columbus was a new continent. [E.N.]

14. Indian tribes from the south of Argentina and Chile. [E.N.]

gant and comfortable customs? When we say *comfortable*, suitable, *bien, comme il faut*, are we alluding to Araucanian things?

Who knows of a gentleman among us who boasts of being a pure Indian? Who would marry his sister or his daughter with an Araucanian nobleman, and not a thousand times with an English shoemaker?

In America, all that which is not European is barbarian: and there is no other division than this. First, the native, that is, the savage; second, the European, that is, we who were born in America and speak Spanish, we who believe in Jesus Christ and not in Pillan (an Indian god).

There is no other division of the American man. The division of city men and country men is false, it does not exist; it is reminiscent of Niebuhr's studies of the early history of Rome.—Rosas ruled not with gauchos[15] but with the city. The main Unitarios were country men such as Martín Rodríguez, the Ramos, the Miguens, the Díaz Vélez; in contrast, Rosas' men were the Anchorenas, the Medranos, the Dorregos, the Aranas, who were educated in the city. The Mazorca[16] was not made up of gauchos.

The only subdivision that the Spanish American man admits is the *man from the coastal region* and the *inland* or *Mediterranean man*. This division is real and runs deep. The first is the fruit of the civilizing action of Europe in this century, exerted by trade and by immigration in the towns of the coast. The other is the product of sixteenth-century Europe, of Europe at the time of the conquest, which is preserved intact as in a jar in the inland towns of our continent, where Spain placed him with the object of preserving him thus.

Between Chuquisaca and Valparaíso there is a difference of three centuries, and it is not the Institute of Santiago that has created this difference in favor of the city. It is not our inadequate schools that have placed the coast of South America three hundred years ahead of inland cities. In fact, the coast lacks universities. It is to the living action of modern Europe, exercised through free trade, through immigration, and through industry, in towns on the coast, that it owes its immense progress compared with others.

15. Horsemen from the Argentine Pampas. [E.N.]

16. Militia renowned for cruelty that acted as police during the Rosas dictatorship. [E.N.]

In Chile, the likes of Portales, Rengifo, and Urmeneta,[17] highly influential statesmen, did not graduate from the national institute. The two Egañas,[18] illustrious organizers of Chile, were inspired by Europe's fertile work. More than once the heads and professors of the institute have taken from Valparaíso its most brilliant and useful inspirations for government.

From the sixteenth century to this day Europe has not ceased for a single day to be the source and origin of civilization on this continent. Under the old regime, Europe performed that role through European rule. This nation brought us the last expression of the Middle Ages and the beginning of the renaissance of civilization in Europe.

The South American Revolution brought an end to the Spanish European influence on this continent, but it was replaced by the Europe of England and France. We South Americans today are Europeans who have swapped masters: the Spanish initiative has been followed by that of the English and French. But Europe is always the creator of our civilization. The means of action has changed, but the product is the same. Official or governmental action has been supplanted by social action, the action of the people, of the race. Modern Europe does nothing more in South America than complete the work of the Europe of the Middle Ages, which is kept in an embryonic state, half-formed. Its current means of influence will not be the sword or the conquest. America has already been conquered; it is European and thus unconquerable. A war of conquest implies rival civilizations, opposed states—the savage and the European, for example.—This antagonism does not exist; the savage is defeated, in America he has neither dominance nor ascendancy. We, Europeans in blood and civilization, are the owners of America.

It is time to recognize this law of our American progress and call again for help from Europe for our incomplete culture. We have fought

17. Diego Portales (1793–1837), conservative politician, minister of state and later of war, influential in the consolidation of the Chilean republic; Manuel Rengifo (1793–1845), minister of finance in 1830, successfully organized the Chilean economy; Jerónimo Urmeneta (1816–1881), liberal politician, minister of finance and later of foreign affairs. [E.N.]

18. Juan Egaña (1769–1836), politician and jurist, participated in the War of Independence and wrote the 1823 Chilean constitution; his son, Mariano Egaña (1793–1846), politician and legislator, was the main author of the 1833 Chilean Constitution. [E.N.]

and defeated Europe with arms on the battlefield, but we are far from victory in the fields of thought and industry.

Feeding occasional grudges, there are some who are alarmed by merely the name of Europe; there are those who still fear ruin and slavery.

Such sentiments constitute a state of disease in our South American spirits, most unfortunate for our prosperity, and therefore worthy of analysis.

The Spanish monarchs taught us to hate as *foreign* all that was not *Spanish.* The liberators of 1810, in turn, taught us to loathe under the name of *European* all those not born in America. Spain herself was included in this hatred. The question of war was set out in these terms:— *Europe* and *America*,—the old world and the world of Columbus. That hatred was called loyalty, and ours *patriotism.* At the time, such hatred was a useful and opportune means; today they are concerns that darken the prosperity of these countries.

The press, instruction, history, prepared for the people, must work to destroy concern with foreign things, as this is an obstacle that fights head-on the progress of this continent. The aversion to the foreigner is barbarianism in other nations; in those of South America it is something else, it is the cause of ruin and dissolution of the Spanish type of society. That ruinous tendency must be fought with the arms of credulity itself and of the coarse truth, which are within the reach of our masses. The press that initiates and sponsors the true spirit of progress must ask the men of our people whether they consider themselves of the indigenous race, of Pampa or Pehuenche Indian origin, if they believe themselves to be descendants of savages and pagans, and not of the foreign races that brought the religion of Jesus Christ and the civilization of Europe to this continent, the erstwhile land of heathens.

Our apostolate of civilization must draw attention, in all its material nakedness in the eyes of our good people poisoned beforehand against what constitutes their life and progress, to the following facts of historic evidence:—Our Holy Father Pope Pius IX, the current head of the Catholic Church, is a foreigner, an Italian, the same as all the popes that have preceded him and those that will succeed him in the Holy See. The saints on our altars are foreigners, and every day our faithful people kneel before those worthy foreign saints who never set foot in the Americas, nor spoke Spanish in most cases.

Saint Edward, Saint Thomas, Saint Gall, Saint Ursula, Saint Mar-

garet, and many other Catholic saints were English; they were foreign
to our nation and our tongue. Our people would not understand them
if they heard them speak English, which was their language, and they
would perhaps call them gringos.

Saint Raymond Nonnatus was a Catalan; Saint Lawrence, Saint Philip
Benitius, Saint Anselm, Saint Sylvester were Italians, of the same origin
as those foreigners that our people scornfully dub *carcamanes*,[19] forgetting that we have numberless *carcamanes* on our altars. — Saint Nicholas
was Swiss, and Saint Casimir Hungarian.

Lastly, the Man–God, Our Lord Jesus Christ, was not born in the
Americas but in Asia, in Bethlehem, a small town in Judah, a country
twice as distant and foreign to us as Europe. Our people, on hearing his
divine word, would not have understood him, because he did not speak
Spanish; they would have called him a foreigner, and indeed he was: but
that divine foreigner, who has brought down borders and made all the
peoples on the Earth a family of brothers, does he not consecrate and
ennoble, so to speak, the condition of foreigner, through the fact of
being one himself?

Let us remind our people that the homeland is not the soil. We have
had soil for three centuries, and we have had a homeland only since 1810.
The homeland is liberty, it is order, it is wealth, civilization, organized
on the native soil, under its banner and in its name. — However, this has
been brought to us from Europe; that is, Europe has brought us the
notion of order, the knowledge of liberty, the art of wealth, the principles of Christian civilization. Europe, then, has brought us the homeland, if we add that it even brought us the population that makes up the
people and the body of the homeland.

Our patriots from the early period do not have the best ideas about
how to bring prosperity to this America, which they so successfully removed from Spanish rule. The notions of patriotism, the artifice of a
purely American cause, which they employed as a means for war that
suited the times, still prevail over them and possess them. Thus we have
seen Bolívar up to 1826 raising alliances to check Europe, when Europe
had no such pretensions, and General San Martín applauding Rosas' resistance in 1844 to the accidental claims of some European states. Although they filled a real and pressing need in the South America of that

19. A derisory term usually applied to a conceited person. [E.N.]

era, our patriots are to some extent oblivious today to the new demands of this continent. Military glory, which absorbed their whole lives, continues to be of greater concern for them than progress.

However, the need for glory has been now replaced by the need for prosperity and comfort, and the heroism of the warrior is no longer the proper instrument for the prosaic needs of trade and industry that are now the life of these countries.

Enamored of their deeds, the patriots of that earlier era fear anything that might endanger them.

But we, more focused on the work of civilization than on the patriotism of a bygone era, see without fear the advent of all that America can produce in terms of great events. Understanding that the current situation is one of transition, that our future destinies are as great as they are unknown, nothing scares us and we hold the highest hopes of improvement for all. America is not well; she is deserted, solitary, poor. She needs population, prosperity.

Where will this come from in the future? From the same place as before: from Europe.

XV. ON IMMIGRATION AS A MEANS OF PROGRESS AND CULTURE FOR SOUTH AMERICA—MEANS OF FOSTERING IMMIGRATION—FOREIGN TREATIES—SPONTANEOUS, NOT ARTIFICIAL, IMMIGRATION—RELIGIOUS TOLERANCE— RAILROADS—TAX EXEMPTION—FREE RIVER NAVIGATION

How and in what form will the life-giving spirit of European civilization come to our soil in the future? As it has always done: Europe will bring us her new spirit, her habits of industry, her practices of civilization in the immigrants she sends to us.

Every European who comes to our shores brings us more civilization in his habits, which he then passes on to our inhabitants, than in so many philosophy books. The perfection that cannot be seen, touched, or felt is not well understood. A hardworking man is the most effective catechism.

Do we wish to implant and acclimatize in South America the liberty of the Englishman, the culture of the Frenchman, the industry of men from Europe and the United States? Let us bring living pieces of it in the customs of their inhabitants, and let us settle them here.

Do we wish for the habits of order, discipline, and industry to prevail in our America? Let us fill it with people who possess these habits in full. They are communicative; at the side of the European industrialist, the South American industrialist is swiftly formed. The tree of civilization does not grow from a seed. It is like a vine, it grows from a grafting. This is the only means for this American desert to swiftly become a world of opulence. Reproduction alone is a very slow means.

If we wish to see our states grow in a short time, let us bring from abroad the best-formed and -prepared elements.

Without large populations there is no culture or development, major progress cannot be made; everything is small and miserly; nations of half a million inhabitants may be great by their territory, but by their population they will be provinces, villages, and all their things will always carry the miserly, provincial stamp.

Important notice to South American statesmen: — elementary schools, high schools, universities are, alone, very poor means of progress without great enterprises of production, the daughters of large portions of men.

Population—a South American necessity that represents all its other needs—is the precise measure of the competence of our governments. The minister of state who does not double the census of these peoples every ten years has wasted his time on trifles and trivialities.

Let the *roto,* the gaucho, the *cholo,*[20] primary unit of our popular masses, run through all the transformations of the best education system, in one hundred years you will not make him an English laborer who works, consumes, lives decently and comfortably.—Give a million inhabitants, the average population of these republics, the best possible education, make them as educated as the canton of Geneva in Switzerland, as the most cultured province of France, will that make a great and blossoming state? Certainly not: for is a million men in a territory comfortable for fifty million anything more than a miserly population?

Others argue that in educating our masses, we will have order; and in having order, the population will come from abroad.

I say to them that they invert the true method of progress. You shall have order and popular education only through the influence of masses introduced with habits rooted in that order and good education.

20. *Roto,* in Chile, a poor peasant; *cholo,* Indian or part-Indian peasants in Bolivia and Argentina. [E.N.]

Multiply the serious population and you will see the vain agitators, disregarded and alone with their frivolous revolutionary plans, in the middle of a world absorbed by serious occupations.

How can all this be obtained? — more easily than spending millions on miserly attempts at interminable improvements.

FOREIGN TREATIES

Sign treaties with foreign countries in which you give them guarantees that their natural rights to property, civil liberty, security, buying, and movement will be respected. Those treaties will be the most beautiful part of the constitution; the external part, which is the key to progress in these countries, which are to receive their growth from abroad. For this branch of public law to be inviolable and long-lasting, sign treaties for an indefinite or very long time. Do not fear to be attached to order and culture.

To fear that treaties will be perpetual is to fear that individual guarantees will perpetuate on our soil. Argentina's treaty with Great Britain prevented Rosas from turning Buenos Aires into another Paraguay.

Do not be afraid of placing the remote future of our industry in the hands of civilization when there is a risk that it may be snatched away by barbarians or domestic tyranny. The fear of treaties is a remnant of the first warring period of our revolution: it is an antiquated principle that has run its course, or an ill-advised imitation wrongly taken from the foreign policy that Washington advised to the United States under circumstances and for reasons entirely different from those that concern us.

Treaties of friendship and trade are the honorable means for placing South American civilization under the protection of world civilization. Indeed, would you not wish for our constitutions and all the guarantees of industry, property, and civil liberty established by them to live inviolably under the protection of the weapons of all peoples, without affecting our nationality? — Set down the rights and civil guarantees, which they grant to their inhabitants, in treaties of friendship, trade, and navigation with foreign countries. Fulfilling treaties, and having the foreigner fulfill them, will mean fulfilling our constitution. The more guarantees you give to the foreigner, the more rights you will have ensured in your country.

Have dealings with all nations, not with a few; grant to all the same guarantees so that none may dominate you, and so that one serves as an obstacle against the aspirations of the other. If France had had in the River Plate a treaty equal to that of England, there would have been none of the emulation concealed under the shroud of an alliance that for ten years wrought discomfort on the affairs of the Plate, operating by half measures and always with one eye on preserving exclusive and partial advantages.

IMMIGRATION PLAN

Spontaneous immigration is genuine, great immigration. Our governments must foster it, not by acting like entrepreneurs, not with miserly concessions of land habitable only by bears, in misleading, extortionate contracts that hurt the population more than the settler, not with handfuls of men, with shady deals to do business with some influential speculator; that is a lie, a farce rather than fruitful immigration. Immigration should be done on a large scale, impartially, such as that which brought California to life in the space of four years, through generous liberties, through exemptions that make the immigrant forget he is a foreigner, persuading him to settle in this homeland; facilitating, without limits or rules, all legitimate aims, all useful trends.

The United States is such an advanced people because it has been made up incessantly of European elements. At all times the United States has received a most abundant immigration from Europe. Those who believe this only dates from the time of independence are wrong. Legislators from every state very wisely sought this, and one of the reasons for their permanent break with the mother country was the barrier or hindrance that England sought to place on this immigration which imperceptibly was converting her colonies into a colossus. This reason is invoked in the very act of the declaration of the independence of the United States. One can see for oneself, therefore, whether the accumulation of foreigners prevented the United States from gaining independence and creating a great and powerful nation.

RELIGIOUS TOLERANCE

If you want moral and religious settlers, foster not atheism. If you seek families that shape private customs, respect the worship of every belief. Spanish America, limited to Catholicism, to the exclusion of any other religion, represents a solitary and silent convent of monks. The dilemma is unavoidable: either exclusively Catholic and unpopulated, or populated and prosperous, and tolerant in terms of religion. To summon the Anglo-Saxon race and the populations of Germany, Sweden, and Switzerland, and deny them the right to follow their religion, is tantamount to summoning them only out of ceremony, out of liberal hypocrisy.

This is true to the letter:—to exclude the Protestant religions from South America is to exclude the English, the Germans, the Swiss, the North Americans, who are not Catholic; that is, the settlers that this continent needs the most. To bring them without their religion is to bring them without the agent that makes them what they are; it is to make them live without religion, make them become atheists.

There are aspirations that lack common sense, and one such aspiration is to seek population, families, customs, and at the same time hinder the marriage of the Protestant settler: it means joining morals with prostitution. If you cannot destroy the invincible affinity of the sexes, why take away the legitimacy of natural unions?—It is to increase the number of concubines instead of wives; to condemn our South American women to the ridicule of foreigners; to make South Americans be born in sin; to fill all South America with bastards, prostitutes, disease, impiety, in a word. That cannot be aspired to in the name of Catholicism without insulting the splendor of this noble church, which is so capable of joining in all human progress.

Is it right to want to foster morals in everyday habits, and persecute churches that teach the doctrine of Jesus Christ?

In supporting this doctrine I do no more than praise a law of my country that has been validated by experience. Religious freedom has existed in Buenos Aires since October 1825, but it is necessary that the concession in that province be extended throughout the Argentine Republic under the constitution as a means of spreading the settlement of European immigration further inland. It already exists under the treaty with England, and no local or interior constitution should make an exception to or repeal the national agreement contained in the treaty of February 2, 1825.

Spain was wise to employ the tactic of Catholic exclusivity as a means of monopolizing its power over these countries, and as a means of civilizing the indigenous races. Hence the Code of the Indies began by ensuring the Catholic faith in the colonies. But our modern constitutions must not copy the Laws of the Indies, because it would reestablish the ancient regime of monopoly to benefit our first Catholic settlers, and jeopardize the broader and more generous aims of the new American regime.

INLAND IMMIGRATION

Heretofore, European immigration has remained in coastal towns, which has given rise to these towns' cultural superiority in South America over inland towns.

Under the independent government the system of the Laws of the Indies has continued, which excluded foreigners from the inland regions, under strict penalties. Title 27 of the *Recopilación Indiana*[21] contains thirty-eight laws intended to hermetically seal inland South America from non-Iberian foreigners. The mildest of these was law 7, which imposed the death penalty for having any dealings with foreigners. Law 9 ordered the *cleansing* of foreigners from the land, in order to maintain the Catholic faith.

Who can fail to see that the centuries-old influence of that legislation remains latent to this day at the core of the new government? What else could be the origin of such resistance, which even to this day the foreigner encounters in the inland areas of South American countries?

It is up to the new regime to reverse the colonial system, to remove the inland regions from their seclusion, thwarting the spirit of reserve and exclusion that had formed in our customs with laws opposing and reacting against those of the Indies.

But the most effective means of raising the capacity and culture of our inland peoples to the level and capacity of maritime cities is to bring them to the coast, so to speak, through a large and liberal transport system, putting them within reach of the civilizing action of Europe.

The great means for introducing Europe into the inland countries of our continent on a scale and proportion powerful enough to bring about a portentous change in a few years are the railroad, free inland navigation, and free trade. Europe comes to these faraway regions through trade and industry, and seeks the riches of our continent. Wealth, like

21. *Recopilación de Leyes de los Reynos de las Indias.* A compilation of the laws enacted by the Spanish monarchs for their American possessions, approved in 1680 by Charles II. [E.N.]

population and culture, is impossible wherever means of communication are scarce, small, and costly.

Europe comes to America thanks to the ease that the ocean affords her. Let us prolong the ocean to the interior of this continent with land and river steam power, and the inland regions will be as full of European immigrants as the coast.

RAILROADS

The railroad is the means to set right what Spanish colonizers set backward in this continent. Spain placed the heads of our states where the feet should be. For its purposes of isolation and monopoly, this system was wise; for our intentions of expansion and commercial liberty, it is disastrous. It is necessary to bring the capital cities to our shores or take the coast inland into our continent. The railroad and the electric telegraph eliminate distance, bringing about this prodigy better than all the magnates of the Earth. The railroad innovates, reforms, and changes the most difficult things, without decrees or riots.

The railroad will bring unity to the Argentine Republic better than all the congresses. The congresses may declare the republic *one and indivisible;* but without the railway to bring its most remote parts closer, it will forever be divisible and divided, contrary to all legislative decrees.

Without the railroad there will be no political unity in countries where distance makes the action of central government impossible. Do you want the government, the legislators, and the courts of the coastal capital to legislate and judge the affairs of the provinces of San Juan and Mendoza, for example? Bring the coast to those places by railroad, and vice versa. Place those extremities at three days' distance, at least. But to have the metropolis or capital twenty days away is in practice tantamount to having it in Spain, as when the old regime ruled, which we destroyed especially because of this absurdity. Therefore, political unity must begin with territorial unity, and only the railroad can turn two areas separated by five hundred leagues into a single area.

Nor would it be possible to take into the inland regions of our countries the action of Europe via immigration, which today is regenerating our coasts, without such powerful vehicles as the railroads. They are or will be to the local life of our inland territories what great arteries are to the lower limbs of the human body: sources of life. The Spanish knew this, and in the latter days of their reign in America they occupied themselves seriously with the construction of a transcontinental road across the Andes and the Argentine desert. This was even more audacious than the Andes canal imagined by Rivadavia, who was troubled by the same need. Why would we deem utopian building a route that in other times was even considered by the Spanish government, so slow and sparing in its great works of improvement?

In 1804, Viceroy Sobremonte returned to the old Spanish project of canalizing the River Tercero, to bring the Andes nearer to the Plate; and in 1813, under the patriot government, the same idea arose. With the modest title of *The Navigation of the River Tercero,*[22] Don Pedro Andrés García wrote a book to rival the work of M. Michel Chevalier,[23] on ways of transport as a means of government, trade, and industry.

There are abundant means to build railroads in these countries. Negotiate loans from abroad, pledge your revenues and national assets to enterprises that will make them prosper and multiply. It would be puerile to wait for ordinary revenues to cover such costs; invert that order, start with expenditure, and you shall have revenues.—If we had waited until we had revenues capable of covering the costs of the war of independence against Spain, we would still be colonies to this day. With loans we had cannons, rifles, ships, and soldiers, and we were able to gain our independence. What we did to leave slavery behind is the same as that which we must do to leave backwardness behind, which is tantamount to servitude. Glory must not have more importance than civilization.

But you shall not obtain loans if you have no national credit, that is, credit based on the securities and liabilities of all the people of the state together. With credits from town councils and provinces, you shall not build railroads, or anything of size. Unite as the body of a nation, consolidate the liability of your present and future revenues and fortune, and you will find someone who will lend you millions to provide for your local and general needs; because though you do not have money

---

22. Pedro Andrés García (1758–1833), "Memoria sobre la navegación del Tercero y otros ríos que confluyen al Paraná," in Pedro de Angelis, *Colección de obras y documentos relativos a la historia antigua y moderna de las provincias del Río de la Plata,* vol. 3 (Buenos Aires: Imprenta del Estado, 1836). [E.N.]

23. Michel Chevalier (1806–1879), French politician and statesman, advocated a liberal free-market economy. [E.N.]

today, you have the means to be opulent tomorrow.—Scattered and splintered, expect nothing but poverty and contempt.

EXEMPTIONS, PRIVILEGES

At the same time, protect private enterprises for the construction of railroads. Lavish them with advantages, privileges, all imaginable favors, stopping at nothing. Prefer this means over all others. In Lima, a whole convent and ninety-nine years of privilege have been granted to the first railroad between the capital and the coast: half of all the existing convents would have been given had it been necessary. The railroads are to this century what the convents were to the Middle Ages: every era has its agents of culture. The village of the *Caldera* has sprung up around the railroad, as in other times they did around a church. The interest remains the same: to bring man closer to his Creator through the perfection of his nature.

Is our capital insufficient for these enterprises?—Deliver them then to foreign capitals:—Let the wealth from abroad, like its men, take up residence on our soil. Surround foreign capital with immunity and privilege, so that it may become naturalized among us.

South America needs capital as much as population. An immigrant without money is a soldier without weapons. Make the pesos migrate into these countries of future riches and current poverty. But the peso is an immigrant that demands many concessions and privileges. Give them, because capital is the left arm of progress in these countries. It is the secret with which the United States and the Netherlands gave a magical drive to their industry and trade. The Laws of the Indies to civilize this continent through religious propaganda, just like in the Middle Ages, filled the convents with privileges as a means of fostering the settlement of these advanced guardians of civilization in that period. Our laws must do likewise to fuel industrial and commercial development, lavishing favor on industrial enterprises that raise their daring flag in the deserts of our continent. Privileges for heroic industry are the magical incentive to attract riches from abroad. That is why the United States assigned to the general Congress, among its major functions, that of fostering the prosperity of the confederation through the concession of privileges to authors and inventors; and that land of freedom has been fertilized by, among other means, the privileges given by freedom to the heroism of enterprise, to the talent of improvement.

INLAND NAVIGATION

The great rivers, those *roads that move,* as Pascal said, are another means of pushing inward the civilizing action of Europe through the immigration of its inhabitants into the inland regions of our continent. But those rivers that are not navigable are as good as if they did not exist. To make them the exclusive domain of our poor and impecunious flags is equivalent to no navigation. For them to fulfill the will of God and populate the interior of the continent, it is necessary to give them up to the law of the seas, that is, absolute liberty. God has not made them as big as inland seas so that only one family might sail on them.

Proclaim the freedom of their waters. And to make it permanent, so that the unstable hand of our governments does not repeal today what was agreed yesterday, sign perpetual treaties of free navigation.

To write those treaties, do not read Wattel or Martens,[24] do not remember the Elbe and the Mississippi. Read in the book of South America's needs and, whatever they dictate, write it with the arm of Henry VIII, without fear of derision or disapproval over inability. South America is in a situation at once critical and exceptional, and only by means never previously seen will it successfully escape from it; the fate of Mexico is a warning of what a system of hesitation and reserve will bring.

May the light of the world penetrate every corner of our republics. With what right do we hold in perpetual brutality the most beautiful parts of our regions? Let us give to the civilization of present-day Europe what our former masters denied it. To exercise the monopoly that was the essence of their system, they gave only one entrance to the Argentine Republic; and we have conserved in the name of patriotism the exclusivity of the colonial system. An end to exclusion or bans, whatever the flag. An end to exclusivity in the name of the homeland.

THE NEW DESTINY OF INLAND AMERICA

May every inlet be a port; may every navigable tributary receive the civilizing light of the flag of Albion; on the banks of the Bermejo and the

24. Emerich de Vattel (1714–1767), Swiss philosopher and author of *The Law of Nations,* whose work laid the foundations of international law. Friderich Martens (1635–1699), a German naturalist, published his observations in *Spitzbergische oder groenlandische Reise Beschreibung.* [E.N.]

Pilcomayo may there shine intermingled with the other flags the same flags from everywhere that brighten the waters of the Thames, the river of England and of the world.

What about customs!—hollers routine. Aberration! You wish to stupefy the country in the name of the treasury? But is there nothing less fiscal than backwardness and poverty? States were not made for customs, customs were made for states. Do you fear that by dint of population and wealth there will lack resources to pay for the authorities, which are indispensable for protecting such wealth? Idiotic economy, which fears thirst amid the sweet torrents of the Paraná River! And do you not remember that free trade with England since the time of the colonial government had a financial or fiscal origin in the River Plate; that is, liberty was created in order to bring revenue?

If you wish for trade to populate our deserts, do not kill the traffic with inland customs. If a single customhouse is one too many, what shall we say of fourteen customhouses?—Customs is prohibition; it is a tax that should be deleted from South American revenues. It is a tax that burdens the civilization and the progress of these countries, whose elements come from abroad. It should be banned for a twenty-year trial, and use loans to fill the deficit. That would be to spend on liberty, which fertilizes, a little of what we have spent on war, which sterilizes.

Nor should you fear that nationality might be compromised by the accumulation of foreigners, or that the national type might disappear. That fear is narrow-minded and apprehensive. Much foreign blood has been spilt in defense of American independence. Montevideo, defended by foreigners, has earned the name of New Troy. Valparaíso, populated by foreigners, is the jewel of the Chilean nationality. The English have been the most conquered people of all; all nations have set foot on their soil and mixed in it their blood and their race. It is the product of an infinite mixture of castes; and precisely because of that the Englishman is the most perfect of men, and his nationality so pronounced that it makes ordinary people think that his race is pure.

Do not fear, then, the mixture of races and tongues. Out of a babel, out of chaos, South American nationality will come forth bright and clear. The soil adopts men, it attracts them, assimilates them, and makes them its own. The immigrant is like the colonist; he leaves his mother country for the homeland of his adoption. It is two thousand years since these words were spoken that form the motto of this century: — *Ubi bene, ibi patria.*[25]

And in the face of European complaints over the nonobservance of treaties that you sign, do not run for your sword or cry "Conquest!" So much sensitivity does not sit well in new peoples, who need the whole world in order to prosper. Every age has its particular honor. Let us understand that which belongs to us. Let us take a good look at ourselves before drawing the sword: not because we are weak, but because our habitual inexperience and disorder make us presumed guilty before the world in our external conflicts; and above all because peace is worth twice as much to us as glory.

Victory will give us laurels; but the laurel is a sterile plant for America. The example of American greatness is not Napoleon, it is Washington. And Washington does not represent military triumphs, but prosperity, growth, organization, and peace. He is the hero par excellence of order in liberty.

For his war victories alone Washington would today be buried and forgotten by his country and the world. Spanish America has numberless generals with feats of arms more brilliant and numerous than Washington's. — His claim to immortality lies in the admirable constitution that has made his country a model for the universe, and which Washington sealed with his name. — Rosas held in his hands the means to do this in the Argentine Republic, and his greatest crime is to have wasted this opportunity.

To reduce in two hours a great mass of men into an eighth of what they were through the action of the cannon: this is a bygone, dated heroism.

On the contrary, to multiply a small population in a few days is the heroism of the modern statesman; the greatness of creation, instead of the savage greatness of extermination.

The size of the population is the measure of the aptitude of South American ministers.

Since the mid-sixteenth century, inland America has been an impenetrable tabernacle for non-Iberian Europe. The time has come for its absolute and general enfranchisement. In three hundred years there has been no more solemn period for the world of Columbus.

---

25. Where one is well off, there is his country. [E.N.]

The Europe of today does not come to fire cannon shots at slaves. It aspires only to burn coal far upriver, rivers that today flow only for the fishes. Open their doors wide to the majestic entrance of the world, without arguing whether it is by concession or by right; and to prevent problems, open them before arguing. When the bell of the steamboat has rung out before virginal and solitary Asunción, the shadow of Suárez will be astonished in the presence of the new missionaries, who endorse enterprises unknown to the Jesuits of the eighteenth century. The birds, owners today of the enchanted forests, will take flight in fear; and the savage of the Chaco, leaning on the bow of his arrow, will contemplate with sadness the course of the formidable machine that heralds his abandonment of those riverbanks. Wretched remnant of primitive creatures: bid farewell to your past dominion. Reason now unfurls its sacred flags in the country that will no longer protect the bestiality of the most noble of races with undeserved asylum.

On the picturesque banks of the Bermejo a grateful nation will one day raise a monument on which shall be engraved:—To the Congress of 1852, liberator of these waters, from grateful later generations.

XVI. ON LEGISLATION AS A MEANS TO STIMULATE THE POPULATION AND DEVELOPMENT OF OUR REPUBLICS

Civil and commercial legislation, the regulations of industrial and mercantile policy, must not repel the foreigner whom the constitution attracts. It would matter little that he should find easy roads and open rivers to penetrate inland, if it were only to collide with civil laws that block him. Whatever progress was made on one side would be lost on the other.

Nobler would it be to openly exclude him, as the Laws of the Indies did, than to let him in with fallacious promises, to make him the victim of an entirely colonial and hostile state of affairs. The new government on the coast and the old system inland, liberty in the constitution and chains in the regulations and civil laws, that is a sure way of discrediting the new system of government and conserving the backwardness of these countries.

It will be necessary, then, for the civil laws of procedure and trade to be modified and conceived in accordance to the trend followed by the constitution; in the final analysis, the various branches of private law are nothing but organic laws.

The economic and industrial demands of our times and of South America must serve as the basis for the reform of our internal legislation, as they will be used for the enactment of its constitutional law.

The constitution must guarantee that its organic laws will not be exceptions that revoke the great principles consecrated by the constitution, as has been seen more than once.—It is necessary that administrative law be not a fallacious means to eliminate and revoke constitutional liberties and guarantees. For example:—The press is free, according to the constitution; but there may come an organic press law that creates so many obstacles and limitations on the exercise of that liberty as to make it an illusory fallacy.—*Suffrage is free,* says the constitution; but there may come an organic electoral law that with exceptional requisites and limitations will turn the freedom to vote into a lie.—*Trade is free,* says the constitution; but the treasury comes with its regulations, and like the Madrid printer's law mentioned by Figaro,[26] organizes such freedom by saying: "Provided that no vessel from abroad docks without paying port duties, anchorage dues, lighthouse dues; that no goods enter or leave without paying customs duties; that no man may open a brothel without paying for an annual license; that no man trades inland without paying toll duties; that all credit documents be signed on stamped paper; that no trader enter or leave without a passport, no goods without a dispatch form, paid in full to the treasury; aside from these and other *limitations, trade is completely free,* as established by the Constitution."

In the promulgation of our national laws, we have heretofore followed French legislation as the favored model. The French Civil and Commerce Codes have a great deal of good, and deserve to be applied as they have been in half of Europe. But it has been rightly noted that they are not in harmony with the economic needs of this age, which differ so from the age when Roman legislation was written, of which the modern Civil Code of France is an imitation, and so are our ancient Spanish laws.

The provisions of Roman law, patrician in inspiration, were more concerned with real estate than with goods and chattels, which are prevalent in our century of trade. With a wise perspective for those times, it burdened the buying and selling of real estate with numberless formalities, and those formalities, copied by our modern codes and applied to the

26. Pen name of Spanish poet, liberal politician, and journalist Mariano José de Larra (1809–1837). [E.N.]

circulation of goods and chattels, divest it of the swiftness required by trade operations. South American civil law must facilitate industry and trade, simplifying procedures and reducing the requisites for the buying and selling of goods, reducing the system of proof for cases in which the origin of property is dubious, regulating procedures at law on broad foundations of publicity, brevity, and economy.

Where justice is expensive, nobody seeks it, and all is delivered unto the dominion of iniquity. — Between cheap injustice and expensive justice there is no choice.

Property, life, and honor are nominal goods when justice is bad. There is no incentive to work in the buying of goods that are to be at the mercy of the scoundrel.

Law, constitution, and *government* are empty words if they are not reduced to deeds by the hand of the judge, and it is ultimately the judge who makes the law a reality or a lie.

The South American procedure law must allow foreigners to form part of the lower courts.

In administration as in industry, the foreigner's cooperation is useful for our practical education.

To the benefit of the population of our republics, for foreign immigration, our civil laws must undertake especially:

1. To remove the obstacles and impediments of a bygone age that make mixed marriages impossible or difficult;
2. To simplify the civil conditions for buying property;
3. To give the foreigner the entitlement to civil rights, without the condition of an absurd reciprocity;
4. To bring an end to *jus albinatus,*[27] giving the foreigner the same civil rights as the citizen to dispose of his posthumous assets by testament or other means.

To the benefit of industry, our civil law must reform the mortgage system, on the foundations of publicity, specialty, and equality, reducing the number of privileges and mortgages in favor of those incompetent as a cause of precedence in bankruptcy proceedings brought against insolvent debtors.

---

27. Medieval law by which the property of a deceased foreigner was appropriated by the state. [E.N.]

The law must seek securities for the incompetent, not at the expense of private credit, which causes national wealth to flourish, but through independent means.

Private credit must be the pampered child of American legislation; it must have more privileges than the incompetent, because it is the heroic agent summoned to civilize this bare continent. Credit is the availability of capital; and capital is the magic wand that must give us population, roads, canals, industry, education, and liberty. Any law against private credit is a law against America.

The trade of South America, so original and peculiar because of the nature of the goods it produces, and because of the operations it usually involves, requires more suitable laws than local regulations passed two hundred years ago in the town of Bilbao, which consisted at that time of fourteen thousand souls in Spain.

Legislation must also be readjusted, for the good of the security, morality, and brevity of mercantile business. Where culpable insolvency is tolerated, or there are delays in the realization of the assets of the bankrupt debtor, there can be no development of trade, no attachment to property, trust is missing in business, and with it the principle on which the life of trade rests. The Commercial Code is the code of life itself in these countries, and above all in the Argentine Republic, whose existence in the past and the present is represented by the mercantile industry.

For the benefit of domestic and foreign maritime trade, our mercantile laws must make it easier for the foreigner to buy, in his name, the property of national vessels, the sale of naval properties, and permit vessels sailing under the national flag to be crewed by foreign seamen, waiving any advantage as such which under treaties would have been obtained in European countries on condition of restricting our fleet.

To bring about these changes so necessary to our progress, it is not advisable to think of complete codes.

Partial and swift reforms are the most convenient. — It is the way in which free peoples legislate. The mania for codes derives from the vanity of the emperors. England does not have a single code, and practically there is no interest that is not legislated for.

Argentine civil and commercial legislation must be as uniform as it has been heretofore. — It would be irrational for us to have as many trade codes, as many civil laws, and as many mortgage systems as we have provinces. The uniformity of legislation, in those branches, does not damage in the slightest the attributions of local sovereignty, and highly favors the development of our Argentine nationality.

Thus far, I have indicated the aims or general trends in view of which the constitutions and laws of South America should be conceived. Limiting myself now to the Argentine Republic, I shall indicate the foundations on which, in my opinion, the planned constitution should stand.

XVII. FOUNDATIONS AND STARTING POINTS FOR THE CONSTITUTION OF THE GOVERNMENT OF THE ARGENTINE REPUBLIC

Fraternity and unity of all political parties.— Justo J. de Urquiza[28]

There is a formula, as common as it is profound, that can be used as the preface of almost all known constitutions. Almost all constitutions start by declaring that they are enacted in *the name of God, supreme legislator of the nations.*—This great and beautiful phrase should be taken not in the mystical sense, but in its deep political sense.

God, indeed, gives each people its constitution or normal way of being, as he gives it to each man.

Man does not discretionally choose his constitution to be stout or slim, nervous or sanguine; nor do the people choose *at will* a monarchical or republican, federal or centralist constitution. Man receives these dispositions at birth: he receives them from the soil of wherever he dwells, from the number and condition of the original inhabitants of that soil, from the previous institutions and from the facts that make up its history, in all of which his will acts only in the direction given to the development of those things in the most advantageous way for his providential destiny.

Our revolution took from the French Revolution this definition of Rousseau's:— *The law is the general will.*—In contrast to the former principle that the law was the will of kings, this maxim was excellent and useful to the republican cause. But it is a narrow and materialistic definition because it allows the human legislator to ignore the starting point for his task of simple interpretation, so to speak.—It is a kind of sacri-

28. Justo José de Urquiza (1801–1870), Argentine general and statesman, governor of the province of Entre Ríos 1841–1852, defeated Rosas at the Battle of Caseros and became first president of the Argentine Confederation (1854–1860). [E.N.]

lege to define the law, the general will of the people. The will is power-less before the facts, which are the work of Providence. Would the will of a congress, the expression of the people, be law if, taking into account the scarcity and advisability of manpower, it ruled that Argentines be born with six arms? Would a law be the will of the people, expressed by a constituent congress, if it obliged all Argentines to think with their knees and not with their heads? The same impotence, more or less, would then assist it for changing and disturbing the action of the natural elements that come together to form the normal constitution of that nation. "Fatal is the illusion into which the legislator falls," said Rivadavia, "when he expects his talent and will to change the nature of things, or replace it by enacting and decreeing creations."[29]

The law, whether constitutional or civil, regulates the existence of collective beings called states; and its author is ultimately none other than that very existence governed by the law.

The constituent Argentine Congress will not be summoned to make the Argentine Republic, nor to create the rules or laws of its normal organism; it will not be able to reduce its territory, nor change its geological constitution, nor change the course of its great rivers, nor turn agricultural lands into mineral. It will study and put into writing the natural laws in which all of that may be combined and developed in the most advantageous way for the providential destinies of the Argentine Republic.

This is the meaning of the well-known rule that all constitutions must suit the country for which they are intended; and all of Montesquieu's theory about the influence of climate in the legislation of peoples has no other meaning than this.

Thus, the facts, the reality, which are the work of God and exist because of the action of time and previous history of our country, will be the ones that give shape to the constitution that the Argentine Republic receives from the hands of its constituent legislators. Those facts, those natural elements of the normal constitution, which the Republic already has as the product of time and of God, should be studied by the legislators, and the bases and foundations of their work of simple study and writing, let us say it thus, and not of creation. Anything else would be to legislate for one day, wasting time on inept and puerile speculation.

And naturally, by applying this method to solving the most difficult

29. Speech of February 8, 1826, on his inauguration as president. [A.N.]

problem that the political organization of the Argentine Republic has raised up to this day—which entails determining what would be the most apt foundation for the organization of its general government, whether *centralist* or *federative;*—the Congress shall find that these two bases have traditional precedents in the prior life of the Argentine Republic, that both have coexisted and coexist to form the two elements of the political existence of that Republic.

The Congress must surely obtain this result if, driven by good methods of observation and experimentation, it begins in awareness of the facts and classifies them suitably, to deduce from them the knowledge of their respective power.

History shows us that the political precedents of the Argentine Republic, concerning the form of the general government, are divided into two classes, which refer to the two *federative* and *centralist* principles.

Let us begin by enumerating the *centralist precedents.*

The centralist precedents of the Argentine government can be divided into two types: some correspond to the era of colonial government, and others belong to the period of the revolution.

The *centralist precedents* belonging to our earlier colonial existence are:

1. Unity of Spanish origin in the Argentine population.
2. Unity of religious beliefs and worship.
3. Unity of customs and language.
4. Political unity and unity of government, as all the provinces were part of a single state.
5. Unity of civil, commercial, and criminal legislation.
6. Judicial unity, in procedures, jurisdiction, and scope, as all the provinces of the viceroyalty recognized a single appeals court, based in the capital, with the name of *Royal Audience.*
7. Territorial unity, under the denomination of *viceroyalty of the River Plate.*
8. Financial unity, or unity of revenues and public expenditure.
9. Administrative unity of all other aspects, as the central action came from the viceroy, supreme head of state, established in the capital of the viceroyalty.
10. The city of *Buenos Aires,* established as the capital of the viceroyalty, is another centralist precedent of our former colonial existence.

Let us enumerate now the *centralist precedents from the time of the revolution.*

1. Unity of political beliefs and republican principles. The nation has thought as one man in terms of democracy and republic.
2. Unity of sacrifices in the War of Independence. All the provinces were united in blood, pain, and perils in that enterprise.
3. Unity of conduct, of efforts, and of action in said war.
4. The different pacts of general union, celebrated and interrupted during the revolution, constitute another centralist precedent of the modern era of the country, which is set down in its laws and its treaties with foreign states. The first of these is the solemn act of the declaration of independence of the Argentine Republic from the dominion and vassalage of Spain. In this act the Argentine people stands melded into a single people, and that act prevails and will prevail perpetually for their glory.
5. The general congresses, presidencies, supreme directories that, for more or less long intervals, were seen during the revolution.
6. External or international diplomatic unity, established in treaties signed with England, Brazil, France, etc., which acts shall form part of the external constitution of the country, whatever it may be.
7. The unity of glories and reputation.
8. The unity of symbolic colors of the Argentine Republic.
9. Unity of coat of arms.
10. The implicit, intuitive unity that is revealed every time one says, unthinkingly: Argentine Republic, Argentine territory, Argentine people, and not the republic of San Juan, nation of Buenos Aires, state of Santa Fe.
11. The very word *Argentina* is a centralist precedent.

By virtue of these precedents, the Argentine Republic has formed a single people, a great and single consolidated state, a unified colony, for more than two hundred years, under the name of the viceroyalty of the River Plate; and during the revolution in which the people of the provinces were called upon, for the creation of an independent and American sovereignty, the precedents of bygone monarchical centralism held an invincible influence over modern politics, as they do to this day, preventing us from thinking that the Argentine Republic could be anything else but *one single state,* albeit federative and made up of many provinces, endowed with relative and subordinate sovereignty and liberties.

Let us be wary, then, of believing that unity of government has been but one episode in the life of the Argentine Republic; on the contrary, this unity has been the distinguishing feature of her existence for more than two centuries.

But let us turn now to the equally normal and powerful precedents that make the *indivisible unity of the Argentine domestic government* impossible, and that will oblige any central government system to divide and harmonize its actions with provincial sovereignties, which in turn are limited the same as the central government in terms of domestic administration.

The following facts are *federative precedents of the Argentine Republic,* both colonial and as an independent nation, set down in its history and proven by their fame:

1. Diversities, provincial rivalries, sown systematically by colonial domination and renewed by republican demagogy.
2. The long interregnums of isolations and provincial independence, as occurred during the revolution.
3. Provincial special features, derived from the soil and the climate, that lead to other differences in terms of character, habits, accent, in the products of industry and trade, and in their situation in relation to abroad.
4. The enormous and costly distances that separate provinces from each other, in a territory of 200,000 square leagues, inhabited by our population of one million.
5. The lack of roads, canals, of means of organizing a communication and transport system, and of prompt and easy political and administrative action.
6. The habits already acquired concerning laws, law courts, and provincial governments. For many years the laws of Argentina have not been made in Buenos Aires, nor are the lawsuits of the inhabitants of the provinces dealt with there, as was the case in another era.
7. The partial sovereignty that the May Revolution recognized in each of the provinces, and which no central power has disputed in the modern era.

8. The extensive municipal immunities and the great breadth given to the provincial government by the former Spanish regime, in the towns of the Argentine Republic.

9. The de facto impossibility, without blood or violence, of subduing the provinces or their governors to voluntarily abandon a prerogative that, having been kept for a single day, is unlikely to be abandoned thereafter: the power of self-determination, sovereignty, or local liberty.

10. Treaties, partial alliances, signed by several provinces during the period of isolation.

11. Monetary provincialism, of which Buenos Aires set the most notable precedent with the paper money of that province.

12. Lastly, the agreement of the provincial governments of the confederation, in San Nicolás on May 31, 1852, ratifying the Pacto del Litoral of 1831, which establishes the federative principle of government.

All the aspects shown are part and parcel of the normal and real life of the Argentine Republic, in terms of the basis of its general government; and no constituent congress would have the power to make them disappear instantaneously with its decrees or constitutions. They must be taken as bases and consulted judiciously in the written constitution, which must express the real, natural, and feasible constitution.

The respective power of these prior aspects, both centralist and federative, leads the public opinion of that Republic to the abandonment of any exclusive system and away from the two trends or principles, which having aspired in vain to govern the country exclusively, during a sterile battle fed over many years, seek today a parliamentary merger in the heart of a mixed system, embracing and reconciling the *liberties of each province* and the *prerogatives of the whole nation:*—an inevitable solution and the only solution, which comes about from the application of the two great parts of the Argentine problem—*Nation* and *Province*—and from the formula summoned today to preside over modern politics, which consists of the harmonious combination of *individuality* with generality, of *localism* and *nation,* or *liberty* with *association:* the natural law of any organic body, whether collective or individual, be it state or be it man; according to which the organism has two lives, so to speak, one local and another general or common, akin to what is taught

about the physiology of animate beings, whose life recognizes two exis-
tences, a partial one for each organ, and in turn a general one for the
whole organism.

XVIII. CONTINUATION OF THE SAME MATTER.
AIMS OF THE ARGENTINE CONSTITUTION

Just as the congress should be guided by observation and the study of
normal facts to determine the basis that best suits the general Argentine
government, so too must it use observation and the study of facts to analyze the most suitable aims of the constitution.

All of the present book comes down to expounding the aims that the
new South American constitutional law should put forward; however,
we shall enumerate them more precisely in this chapter, in relation to
the Argentine constitution.

In the presence of the desert, in the high seas, at the beginning of unknown roads and uncertain and great undertakings in life, man needs
the support of God, and delivers unto his protection half of the success
of his aims.

Religion must today be, as in the sixteenth century, the first object of
our fundamental laws. Religion is to the constitution of the people what
pure blood is to the health of the individual. In this political work, it will
only be considered as a means of social order, a means of political organization; since, as Montesquieu said, it is admirable that the Christian
religion, which provides the happiness of the other world, should also
provide happiness in this one.

But on this point as in many others, our modern constitutional law
must separate itself from the Laws of the Indies or colonial law, and
from the constitutional law of the first period of the revolution.

The colonial law was exclusive in terms of religion, as it was in terms
of trade, population, industry, etc. Exclusivity was its essence in all that
it ruled, and suffice it to recall that it was a colonial law of exclusion and
monopoly. The exclusive religion was used in that law as a means of the
state. — Furthermore, Spain excluded the Protestant religions from its
domains, in exchange for concessions that the pope gave to its kings on
interests of their time. — But our modern American politics, which instead of excluding should seek to attract and to concede, cannot ratify
and reestablish the colonial system of religious exclusion without damaging the ends and purposes of the new American system. It should

maintain and protect the religion of our fathers, as the first necessity of our social and political order, but it should protect it through liberty, through tolerance, and through all the means peculiar to the democratic and liberal system, and not like the former Laws of the Indies that excluded and prohibited other Christian religions. The United States and England are the most religious nations on Earth in their customs, and they have reached that result via the same means that we precisely wish to see adopted in South America.

In the first days of the South American Revolution, our constitutional policy did right in respecting Catholicism's earlier privileges and exclusions on this continent, as it proceeded with the same discretion protesting to the Spanish throne that the revolution be carried out in its favor. They were tactical concessions required for the success of the enterprise. But South America could not persist today in the same constitutional policy without rendering illusory and ineffective the aims of its revolution of progress and liberty. It will be necessary, therefore, to establish Catholicism as the religion of the state, but without excluding the public exercise of other Christian religions. Religious liberty is as necessary to the country as the Catholic religion itself. Far from irreconcilable, they need each other and complement each other. Religious freedom is the means to populate these countries. The Catholic religion is the means to educate their populations. Fortunately, on this point the Argentine Republic will have no choice but to ratify and extend throughout its territory what has already existed in Buenos Aires for twenty-five years. All the bishops received in the Republic in the last twenty years have sworn obedience to these religious freedom laws. It would be too late for Rome to object to this point in the modern constitution of the nation.

The other great aims of the Argentine constitution today will be, as this book has shown, different from those of the first period of the revolution.

At that time it was a matter of strengthening independence through arms; today we must try to secure it through the material and moral growth of our people.

Political aims were the pressing needs of that period; we should now be principally concerned with economic aims.

To distance ourselves from Europe, which had kept us in slavery, was the great constitutional aim of the first era; to attract her so that she may civilize us as free men with her populations, as she civilized us as slaves with her governments, must be the constitutional aim of our times. On this matter our South American constitutional policy must be as original as the situation of South America, and must be ruled by that situation. To imitate foreign regimes of ancient nations, now civilized, abundant in population but lacking in territory, is to fall into a coarse and disastrous absurdity; it is to apply to an exhausted body the diet fitting for a man suffocated by excess and obesity. As long as South America has no foreign constitutional policy suited to its highly specialized needs, it shall not leave behind the dark and subordinate condition in which it finds itself. The application to our foreign economic policy of international doctrines that govern the relations of European nations has damaged our progress as much as the havoc of the civil war.

With scarcely a million inhabitants populating a territory of 200,000 square leagues, the Argentine Republic is a nation only in name and in territory. Its distance from Europe is enough for it to be considered an independent nation. The lack of population preventing it from becoming a nation also prevents it from acquiring a full general government.

With this in mind, the population of the Argentine Republic, today bare and desolate, must be the great and primary aim of its constitution for many years. It must guarantee the execution of all the means of obtaining that vital result. I shall call these means *public guarantees of progress and of growth*. On this point the constitution must not be limited to promises; it must give guarantees of implementation and reality.

Thus, to populate the country, it must guarantee religious liberty and facilitate mixed marriages, without which there will be population, but scarce, impure, and sterile.

It must lavish citizenship and a home on the foreigner without imposing it. I say *lavish* because this word expresses the means necessary. Some South American constitutions have adopted the conditions with which England and France grant naturalization to the foreigner that those nations do not need in order to increase their excessive population. It is a case of imitation taken to an idiotic and absurd level.

The constitution must assimilate the civil rights of the foreigner, whom we greatly need, to the civil rights of the national, without impossible, illusory, and absurd conditions of reciprocity.

It must give them access to secondary-level public jobs, more as a benefit for the country than for them, as in this way the country will take advantage of their aptitude for the management of our public affairs, and will promote the public education of our citizens by a practical example, the same as in private industrial business. In the municipal government this system will be highly advantageous. A former English or North American municipal worker, established in our country and incorporated into our town halls or local councils, shall be the most edifying or instructive monitor in that branch in which we Spanish Americans generally perform so badly and ineffectively, as in the policy of our own private houses.

As the main element of Argentina's growth and most motivating incentive for much-needed immigration is the development and exploitation of the rich resources of the Republic, its constitution must recognize, among its main aims, the inviolability of the right to property and full liberty of work and industry. To promise and set down these guarantees is not to establish them. One aspires to reality, not to hope.— Serious constitutions should not consist of promises, but guarantees of implementation. Thus the Argentine constitution should not be limited to declaring the private right to property inviolable, but should guarantee the reform of all civil laws and all colonial regulations still in place, despite the Republic, that render this right illusory and nominal. With a republican constitutional law and a colonial, monarchical administrative law, South America takes away with one hand what it gives with the other: liberty on the surface and slavery underneath.

It must then give guarantees that no organic or civil law shall be enacted that alters, through regulatory exceptions, the force of the right to property established among its main principles, as does the Constitution of California.

The main aim of our colonial law was to guarantee not the individual's property but the property of the treasury. The Spanish colonies were formed for the treasury, not the treasury for the colonies. Their legislation was adapted to their purpose: they were machines for creating fiscal revenue. In the eyes of fiscal interest, the interest of the individual was nil. When the revolution began, we wrote into our constitutions the inviolability of private rights; but we have left the previous worship of fiscal interest as a lasting presence. Hence, despite the revolution and independence, we have continued to be republics made for the treasury. It is necessary to guarantee that this will be reformed, and that the words of the constitution on property rights will become a practical reality under organic and regulatory laws, in harmony with modern constitutional law.

The freedom of work and industry established in the constitution will be no more than a promise unless it guarantees at the same time the abolition of all the former colonial laws that enslave industry, and the enactment of new laws to implement and bring about that industrial freedom set out in the constitution, without destroying them with exceptions.

Of all the known industries, maritime and land trade is the special vocation of the Argentine Republic. The Republic derives this vocation from the shape, production, and extent of her soil; her colossal rivers, which make the country the organ of change throughout South America; and her situation in regard to Europe. — It therefore follows that liberty and the development of domestic and foreign trade, whether maritime or terrestrial, must feature in the primary aims of the Argentine constitution. — But this great aim will remain illusory if the constitution does not at the same time guarantee the execution of the means to effect this. Domestic trade freedom will exist in name only as long as there are fourteen inland customhouses, which are fourteen denials of freedom. — There must be one single national customs, in terms of the product of its revenue; and in terms of its regulatory system, the colonial or fiscal customs, the inquisitorial customs, illiberal and miserly from another age, the intolerant customs, of monopoly and exclusion, must not be the customs of a system of freedom and national growth. It is necessary to establish guarantees to reform both aspects, and solemn promises that freedom of trade and of industry will not be sidestepped by fiscal regulations.

Freedom of trade without freedom of river navigation is a contradiction, since all Argentine ports are river ports, so to close the rivers to foreign flags is to block the provinces and hand over all trade to Buenos Aires.

These reforms must become duties imposed by the constitution on the general government, designating a peremptory deadline, if possible, for their execution, and with grave and specific liabilities for their nonexecution. — True and high ministerial responsibilities lie in the performance of those duties of power, more than in any other part of the constitution of nascent countries.

Those ends that in other times were accessory, or rather disregarded, must today be placed at the head of our constitutions as their primary aims.

Second in importance in the aims of the constitution, after great economic interests, is independence and the means to defend it against improbable or impossible attack from the European powers. It is not that these aims are second in importance, but that economic means are those that must bring us to their attainment. With Europe's military defeated and distant from our southern continent, we must not set ourselves up to defend ourselves from its remote and feeble attacks. On this point we must not follow the example of the United States of America, who have in their vicinity European states with larger territory than theirs, who were enemies in another era and today are rivals in trade, industry, and navigation.

As the past, present, and future origins of our civilization and progress lie abroad, our constitution must be designed, on the whole and in its details, to stimulate, attract, and facilitate the action of that external influence, instead of checking and excluding it. In this respect the Argentine Republic will only have to spread and extend to all foreign nations the precedents that it has already established with England. There should not be more than one foreign public law; any distinction or exception is detestable. The Argentine constitution must contain an article aimed specifically at fixing the principles and rules of public law concerning foreigners in the River Plate, and those rules must be none other than those contained in the treaty with England, signed on February 2, 1825. To all foreigners the following guarantees must be applicable, which are only established in favor of English people in the treaty. All must be entitled *constitutionally,* not under treaties:

To freedom of trade;
To the franchise of traveling safely and freely with their ships and
    cargos to ports and rivers, accessible by law to all foreigners;
To the right to rent and occupy houses for the purposes of their
    trade;
To no obligation to pay differential rights;
To manage and practice in their name all acts of trade, without
    obligation to employ persons from the country to this effect;
To exercise all *civil rights* inherent to the citizen of the Republic;

To no obligation to military service;

To be free of forced loans, exactions, or military requisitions;

To keep all these guarantees in force, regardless of any break with the nation of the foreigner residing in the Plate;

To enjoy full freedom of conscience and worship, and the entitlement to build churches and chapels in any place in the Argentine Republic.

All this and more is granted to British subjects in the Argentine Republic by the treaty signed on February 2, 1825, for an indefinite period of time; and there are many reasons why it is advisable for the country to extend and apply these concessions to foreigners of all nations of the world, whether or not they have treaties with the Argentine Republic. The Republic needs to grant these guarantees due to an imperious need of its population and culture, and must grant them immediately, through the constitution, without aspiring to the illusory, vain, and puerile advantages of a reciprocity that for many years will be useless.

Today, more than ever, the adoption of this system would be advantageous, as it is intended to receive populations who, driven out of Europe by civil war and industrial crisis, bypass the rich regions of the Plate, to seek in California the fortune that they may find more easily there, with fewer risks and without venturing so far from Europe.

Peace and inner order are other great aims that the enactment of the Argentine constitution must keep in mind; because peace is necessary to the development of the institutions, since without peace all the efforts made for the prosperity of the country would be vain and sterile. Peace, by itself, is so essential to the progress of these countries in the making, that any constitution that gave no other benefit than peace would be admirable and fertile in its results. Later I shall return to this point of decisive interest for the fate of these republics, which march toward their extinction on the path of civil war, through which Mexico has now lost the most beautiful half of its territory.

Lastly, due to its nature and spirit, the new Argentine constitution must be absorbing, attractive, endowed with such strength of assimilation that it makes any foreign element that comes to the country its own, a constitution designed especially and directly to bring four to six million inhabitants to the Argentine Republic in a matter of a few years; a constitution that seeks to move the city of Buenos Aires a step closer to

San Juan, La Rioja, and Salta, and carry these cities to the fertile banks of the Plate, via railroad and electric telegraph, which reduce distances; a constitution that in a few years will turn Santa Fe, Rosario, Gualeguaychú, Paraná, and Corrientes into as many Buenos Aires in terms of population and culture, via the same means that has made this city great, namely its immediate contact with civilized and civilizing Europe; a constitution that, taking inhabitants from Europe and assimilating them into our population, in a short time makes our country so populous that it cannot fear the governments of Europe.

A constitution having the power of the fairies, who could build palaces in a single night.

California, contrived in four years, has made the fable come true, and has shown the true way to shape the new states of the Americas, bringing from abroad great chunks of population, fully formed, accommodating them in the body of the nation and giving them the American flag. Montevideo is another valuable example of this law of rapid population. And it is not gold that has brought about this miracle in North America: it is liberty, which before contriving California contrived the United States, which has existed just a single day in the political life of the world and yet represents one-half of it in greatness and prosperity. And while it is true that gold has contributed to the creation of this wonder, for the truth of the system that we offer, the fairy that brings together populations is better than riches.

Convinced of the need that these and no other, more limited, aims be the goals of the constitution that the Argentine Republic requires, I cannot deny that the program proposed in the preamble of the San Nicolás agreement seems to me to be rather limited, declaring its objective as the meeting of Congress to *enact the political constitution to regularize the relationships that must exist between the Argentine peoples, as belonging to the same family; to establish and define the high national powers, and secure the domestic order and prosperity and outward respectability of the nation.*

These aims are no doubt excellent; any constitution that did not have them in mind would be useless; but they are not the essential aims that the Argentine constitution should propose.

I do not expect the constitution to embrace everything; I would rather that it be too reserved and concise. But it is necessary that in what little it includes, it should not lack that which constitutes today the salvation of the Argentine Republic.

XIX. CONTINUATION OF THE SAME MATTER—ON THE
GOVERNMENT AND ITS FORM—PURE UNITY IS IMPOSSIBLE

We have just seen what aims the constitution should propose. But ends cannot be sought without using the means to obtain them; and to obtain them seriously and effectively it is necessary for the means to match the ends.

The first of these would be the creation of a government as general as the objectives and ends taken into account, and as permanent as the life of the constitution.

The constitution of a country implies a government responsible for enforcing it: no constitution, no law, is upheld by its own virtue.

Thus, the constitution itself is no more than the organization of the government considered in the subjects and things covered by its action, in the way it is to be elected, in the means or faculties it will have at its disposal, and in the limitations it must respect.

Therefore, the idea of constituting the Argentine Republic means nothing more than the idea of creating a general, permanent government, divided into three primary powers intended to make, interpret, and apply both constitutional and organic laws.

The articles of the constitution, as Rossi[30] said, are *like titles of chapters of administrative law.* All constitutions are made effective by means of organic laws. It will be necessary, then, to have a permanent legislative power responsible for passing these laws.

Both those laws and the constitution will be susceptible to doubts in their application. A permanent, general judiciary will be indispensable to the Argentine Republic.

Of the three essential recognized forms of government, *monarchical, aristocratic,* and *republican,* the latter has been proclaimed by the American Revolution as the government of these countries. There is, then, no question as to the form of government.

As for the *foundation* of government, this lies originally in the nation,

---

30. Pellegrino Rossi (1787–1848), a politician and jurist born in Carrara, Italy. After teaching in Geneva, Switzerland, he was invited to teach in Paris at the Collège de France. Appointed ambassador to the Papal States in 1845, after the 1848 revolution in France he became minister of the interior in Rome under Pius IX. His moderate liberal policies did not satisfy the conservatives or the radicals. He was assassinated November 15, 1848. [E.N.]

and *democracy*, among us, more than a form, is the very essence of government.

Federation or *unity*, that is, a greater or lesser centralization of the general government, is incidental, a secondary complement of the government form. However, this accessory matter has heretofore dominated the whole constitutional question in the Argentine Republic.

Events have led to federalism prevailing, as the rule of general government.

But the word *federation* means *alliance, union, bond.*

As an alliance, as a union, the federation may be more or less close. There are different degrees of federation according to this. What is the correct degree for the Argentine Republic? — This will be seen in its historical precedents and the normal conditions of its physical and social way of being.

Thus, on this issue of the constitution, as in previous issues and in all others, the observation of the facts and the power of the precedents in the country should be the rule and starting point of the constituent congress.

But, since we are speaking of *constitution* and of general *governments,* we already know that the federation will not be a simple alliance of independent provinces.

A constitution is not an alliance. Alliances do not imply a general government, as a constitution essentially does.

This means that the dominant ideas and desires are on the right path.

According to the law of precedents and the rule of the present situation, the Argentine Republic will be and could be nothing but a federative state, a national republic made up of various provinces, at once independent and subordinate to the general government created by them. — The terms *federal, central,* or *general* government mean the same in the eyes of scholars of constitutional law.

A federation conceived in this way will have the advantage of bringing together the two rival principles into a *merger,* whose roots lie in the natural and historic conditions of the country, and which has just been proclaimed and promised to the nation by the victorious voice of General Urquiza. — The San Nicolás agreement has lately served to remove any doubts on this issue.

The idea of pure unity should be abandoned in good faith, not via concession but via conviction. It is a beautiful ideal of government, but in the present situation of our country it is impossible in practice. That which is impossible belongs not to the domain of politics; it belongs to the university, or if it is beautiful, to poetry.

The foremost enemy of pure unity in the Argentine Republic is not Don Juan Manuel Rosas, but the space of 200,000 square leagues in which the handful of our scarce population of one million is diluted, like a drop of red paint in the Paraná River.

Distance is the origin of local sovereignty, because this replaces strength. Why is the gaucho independent? — Because he inhabits the Pampas. Why does Europe recognize us as a nation when we have less population than the ancient province of Bordeaux? — Because we are three thousand leagues away. For the same reason, our inland provinces are sovereign, separated from Buenos Aires, their ancient capital, by three hundred leagues of desert.

The Unitarios of 1826 had no knowledge of the practical conditions of political unity; nor did their predecessors in previous congresses.

Generally speaking, the legislators of South America imitated the constitutions of the French Revolution, enacting *indivisible unity* in vast desert countries that, while capable of *one government,* are not capable of an *indivisible government.* — Rivadavia, leader of the Unitario Party in that period, brought from France and from England the zeal and the admiration of the system of government that he had seen used so successfully in those ancient states. But neither he nor his supporters took into account the conditions that had led to the existence of centralism in Europe, or the obstacles for applying it in the Plate.

The reasons they gave in favor of its admission are precisely those that made it impossible: such were the great size of the territory, the lack of population, of enlightenment, of resources. Those reasons might justify their suitability or need, but not their *feasibility.*

"The internal security of our Republic," said the commission writing the centralist constitution bill, "could never be sufficiently established in a country of such an immense size and as unpopulated as ours, unless by giving the government's power easy, rapid, and strong action, which it cannot have in the complicated and feeble organization of the federal system." — Yes; but how would one give to government power easy, rapid, and strong action over scarce populations scattered over the surface of a country of immeasurable size? How to conceive the speed and ease of action over vast, unexplored territories, without population, roads, and resources?

We do not have enough enlightenment or riches in the people to be federal, they said.—But do you believe that unity is the government of the ignorant and the poor? Is it poverty that has led to the consolidation of the three kingdoms of Great Britain into a single national government? Is the ignorance of Marseille, Lyon, Dijon, Bordeaux, Rouen, etc., the origin of French unity?

No, certainly not. What is true is that France is centralist, for the same reason that the Union of North America exists: because of wealth, because of population, the practicability of the territory, and the culture of its inhabitants, which are the basis of all general government.—We are incapable of perfect federation or unity because we are poor, uncultured, and few.

We have obstacles for all systems, and for the representative republican system as much as for any other. However, we have been cast into it, and know none other more applicable, despite our disadvantages. Democracy itself is hard to come by with our means, and yet we are in it and are incapable of living without it. The same will happen with our federalism or general system of government; it will be incomplete, but at the same time inevitable.

Furthermore, is pure unity the daughter of agreement?

What is unity or consolidation of government? It is the disappearance, the absorption of all local governments into a single national government. But what government agrees to disappear?—The sword and conquest are what suppress it. Thus was the consolidation of the United Kingdom of Great Britain; and the sword has added one by one the provinces that today, after eight centuries of effort, make up the unity of the French Republic, more worthy of reform than of imitation in that respect, according to Thierry and Armand Carrel.[31] How was our own unity formed under the ancient regime, the unity of the viceroyalty of the Plate? By the free vote of the people?—Certainly not; through the

31. Augustin Thierry (1795–1856), French historian, promoted the use of original documents and chronicles for the study of history; Armand Carrel (1800–1836), French journalist, was Thierry's secretary and an ardent republican. [E.N.]

labor of the conquistadors and the royalist, central power on which they depended.

Might this be the way to form our unity? No, because it would be unfair, ineffective, and excessive, since there are other possible means of organization.—If local power is not given up to the point of disappearing, it can be delegated, at least in part, as a strong and better means of existing. This would be the means possible to form a general government, without local governments disappearing.

Unity is not the starting point, it is the finishing point of governments; history says so, and reason proves it. "On the contrary, any confederation," said Rossi, "is an intermediate state between the absolute independence of many political individualities and their complete merger into one and the same sovereignty."

It will be necessary to pass through this intermediate stage in order to achieve national unity.

The Unitarios have not represented a bad principle, but a principle that is impracticable in the country, in the times, and to the extent that they desired. Besides, they were following a trend, an element that may be essential in the organization of the Republic. *The pure theorists, as statesmen, have no other defect than that of being precocious,* as one great writer said: *it is an honorable defect, the privilege of high intelligence. . . .*

XXV. CONTINUATION OF THE SAME ISSUE—RELATIVE SCOPE OF EACH OF THE NATIONAL POWERS—ROLE AND MISSION OF THE EXECUTIVE POWER IN SOUTH AMERICA— EXAMPLE OF CHILE

This would be the place to speak of the respective functions that the three powers (executive, legislative, and judicial) of the confederation's government should have. But as it is the object of this book to designate the bases and general aims, in view of which the new constitution is to be conceived, without dealing with the details, I shall not occupy myself with studying the scope of the respective power of each of the branches of general government, as this is a matter of logical application, and separate from my work on general bases.

I shall only draw attention, without going beyond my objective, to two essential points that must be kept in mind in the constitution of the *executive power,* whether national or provincial. This is one of the features in which our Hispano-Argentine constitution must differ from the example of the federal constitution of the United States.

"The Viceroy of Buenos Aires must continue in full with the superior authority and absolute powers granted to him by my royal title and instruction, and the Laws of the Indies," stated the second article of the Ordinance of Mayors for the viceroyalty of Buenos Aires.

Such was the vigor of the executive power in our country before the establishment of the independent government.

It is well known that we did not make the democratic revolution in South America to reestablish the system of government that existed before, nor is there any question of doing so; but if we want the executive power of democracy to have the stability of the royalist executive power, we must pay some attention to the way in which this was organized in order to carry out its mandate.

The goals of the revolution will be saved by establishing the democratic and representative origin of power, and its constitutional and responsible nature.

As for its energy and vigor, the executive power must have all the faculties made necessary by the precedents and the conditions of the country, and the greatness of purpose for which it is instituted. Otherwise, there will be government in name but not in reality; and if there is no government there can be no constitution; that is, there cannot be order, or liberty, or Argentine confederation.

The times and the men who received as their mission to proclaim and establish in South America the dogma of the radical sovereignty of the people would not have been suitable for setting up a derived and delegated sovereignty for the government. The revolution that took sovereignty away from the kings to give it to the people could not then get the people to delegate it to national governments as respected as royal governments; and South America was left between anarchy and the omnipotence of the sword for many years.

Two systems have been tried in the southern extreme of the former Spanish Americas to get out of this position. Buenos Aires placed the omnipotence of power in the hands of a single man, raising him to the position of being law and code of law. Chile used a constitution instead of the discretionary will of one man; and that constitution gave the executive power the means to have it respected with all the effectiveness of which a dictatorship would be capable.

Time has shown that the Chilean solution is the only rational one in republics that only a short time earlier were monarchies.

Chile has shown that between an absolute lack of government and a dictatorial government there is a possible regular government; and it is that of a constitutional president who can take on the powers of a king at the time that anarchy disobeys him as a republican president.

If order—that is, the life of the constitution—demands in America that flexibility of power necessary to enforce the constitution, it is all the more demanded by the enterprises interested in the material progress and growth of the country. I do not see why in certain cases extensive powers cannot be given to overcome backwardness and poverty when they are given to overcome disorder, which is no more than the offspring of the former.

There are many issues in which the special powers given to the executive power can be the only means of carrying out certain reforms of long, difficult, and uncertain execution, if they are given to legislatures made up of citizens more practical than educated, and more divided by petty rivalries than disposed to working toward a common way of thinking.

Such are the reforms of civil and commercial laws, and in general all those works which because of their considerable size, the technical nature of their subject, and the need for unity in their plan and execution, are performed better and faster in the hands of a competent few than in many ill-prepared hands.

I will not hesitate in stating that the fate of the states of South America depends especially on the constitution of the executive power.

As this power is designed to defend and preserve order and peace— that is, the observance of the constitution and of the laws—it could be said that government is reduced almost to the executive only in these countries of former Spanish America. What does it matter that the laws are brilliant, if they are not to be obeyed? What matters is that they be put into practice, whether good or bad; but how will this be achieved if there is not a serious and efficient power to do it?

Do you fear that the executive will be their main offender? In such a case there is no other remedy than to suppress it completely. But could you live without a government? Is there an example of any people on Earth who subsist in regular order without any government whatsoever? No: therefore you have vital need of a government or executive power. Would you make it absolute and all-encompassing, to make it more responsible, as was seen sometimes during the anxiety of the revolution? No: instead of giving despotism to a man, it is better to give it to the law. It is already an improvement that severity be exercised by the constitution and not by the will of a man. The worst part of despotism is not its harshness but its inconsequence, and only the constitution is immutable.

Give to the executive power all power possible, but give it through a constitution.

This development of the executive power constitutes the dominant need of the constitutional law of our time in South America. The attempts at monarchy, the impulses that sought to trust public fate to a dictatorship, are the best proof of the need that we indicate. Those movements prove the need, despite being wrong and false in terms of the means to fulfill it.

The division that we have made before of Spanish-American constitutional law in two periods is also applicable to the organization of the executive power. In the first constitutional era one sought to weaken power as much as possible, believing that this would somehow help liberty. Individual liberty was the great aim of the revolution, which saw in government an enemy element, and saw it rightly because it had been thus under the defeated regime. Individual and private guarantees were proclaimed, and nobody remembered the public guarantees, which give life to the private guarantees.

That system, the offspring of circumstance, made the establishment of government and order impossible in the American states rebelling against Spain. All was anarchy and disorder, when the sword was not itself government. That state of affairs is relevant to this day (1852).

But we have come to times and circumstances that clamor for change in the constitutional law of South America, as regards the way to constitute the executive power.

The individual guarantees proclaimed with such glory, won with such blood, will turn into vain words, into glaring lies, if they are not made effective through public guarantees.—The first of these is the government, the executive power invested with the strength to make constitutional order and peace a reality, without which liberty, the institutions, wealth, and progress are impossible.

Peace is the need that dominates all the public needs of South America. — The continent needs only peace to make great progress.

But do not forget: peace comes only along the path of the law. The constitution is the most powerful means of pacification and order. Dictatorship is a perpetual provocation to fight; it is a sarcasm, a bloody insult to those who obey without reserve. Dictatorship is anarchy constituted and converted into a permanent institution. Chile owes peace to its constitution, and there is no lasting peace in the world that does not lie in an explicit pact reconciling public and private interests.

Peace in Chile, those eighteen years of continuous peace amid storms abroad, is an honor for South America. It does not come from the type of soil, or from the nature of the Chileans, as has been said; it comes from their constitution. Before it, neither the soil nor the national character prevented Chile from living in anarchy for fifteen years. The constitution has brought order and peace, not by chance, but because this was its purpose, as stated in its preamble. It has brought peace through a vigorous executive power, that is, a powerful guardian of order — mission essential to power, when it really is a power and not a name. This feature constitutes the originality of the Chilean Constitution, which, in my view, is as original in its way as the United States Constitution. This feature was connected to the historic power base in Chile, and received from this tradition the vigor that it enjoys. Chile was able to innovate in this tactfully, which other republics have never experienced. The inspiration came from the Egañas, and the philosophy dates from 1813. At that time Don Juan[32] wrote: "A balance of power is an illusion. Balance between the moral and the physical sphere reduces all power to nil." — "Nor can balance be formed from the division of the executive and the legislature, nor can this sustain the constitution." — "What is true is that in antiquity, and today in England, the executive power shares formally the legislative faculties." — "The present constitution is as adaptable to a mixed monarchy as to a republic." — "In great dangers to the Republic, domestic or external, censorship or the government can propose to the governing body, and it will decree, *that all the powers of the government or of the civic council be concentrated and united in a single president, with all other magistrates surviving with their respective*

---

32. Juan Egaña, see note 18, above. [E.N.]

faculties, being this kind of dictatorship for a limited time and declared by the governing body.[33]

Here is the seed, planted in 1813, that formed, better digested and developed, the originality and excellence of the constitution in force in Chile, illustrated by twenty years of peace, due to its Articles 82 (especially subsections 19 and 20) and 161.

Free of any connection with the political parties of Chile, as both contain persons I am fond of and friendly with, I speak thus of the constitution out of the need I have to propose to my country, which is now being constituted, what experience has taught me as worthy of imitation in the field of the constitutional law of South America. I limit myself to the constitution of the executive power, not to the use that rulers have made of it; and thus in honor of the institution whose imitation I recommend, I must say that the rulers have not done for the country all the good that the constitution gave them the opportunity to do.—Otherwise, no different affection has ever changed my way of seeing this constitution; loyal from afar to the opposition or the government, I have always looked on it in the same way.

With the same impartiality I indicated at the start of this book the major defects that this constitution suffers from, and with the useful purpose of preventing my country from imitating it, on points in which its reform is imperative for the prosperity of Chile.

33. Notes that illustrate some articles of the Chilean Constitution of 1818, or laws that can be deduced from it, by Don Juan Egaña. [A.N.]

JUAN BAUTISTA ALBERDI

The Economic and Revenue System of the Argentine Confederation According to Its Constitution of 1853 (Excerpts)

INTRODUCTION

The federal Argentine Constitution contains a complete system of economic policy, in that it guarantees with strict provisions the free action of *labor, capital,* and *land* as the main agents of *production;* ratifies the natural law of balance governing the phenomenon of the *distribution* of wealth; and circumscribes within reasonable and fair limits actions related to the phenomenon of public *consumption.* All economic matters are contained within these three great divisions.

Scattered about the Constitution, its provisions do not appear therein as parts of a system. Yet they form it more completely than any other known constitution in both the New and Old Worlds.

My aim is to gather together these provisions into a methodical body of science, arranging them into a system suggested by the relationships of mutual provenance and dependency that connect them in order to spread knowledge and expedite the implementation of the Constitution for the sake of greater interest for the current and future destinies of the Argentine Republic. Wealth is important for the prosperity of the nation and the existence of power. Without revenue there is no government; without government, without population, without capital, there is no state.

The economy, like legislation, is universal when it is concerned with economic facts from a general philosophical perspective; and national or practical when it occupies itself with the modifications those things receive from the age, soil, and special conditions of a given country. The former is *pure economics:* the latter is *applied or positive economics.* The

Original title: "Sistema económico y rentístico de la Confederación Argentina, según su constitución de 1853." Source: *Obras completas de Juan Bautista Alberdi* [Complete works of Juan Bautista Alberdi], vol. 4 (Buenos Aires: La Tribuna nacional, 1886–1887).

present text, limited to the study of the rules and principles laid out by the Argentine constitutional law for the development of the issues that concern the wealth of that country, belongs to applied economics, and it is more a book on *economic policy* than on *political economics*. In it I disregard the examination of any theory, of any abstract formulas that are usually the subject of economic writings, because this work on applied, positive economics assumes that the doctrines of pure economics are known to the reader; and above all because the Constitution already provides the principles with which all economic questions in the field of Argentine legislation and politics are to be resolved.

The legislator, the statesman, the publicist, the writer need only study the economic principles adopted by the Constitution to take them as a mandatory guide in all works of organic and regulatory legislation. They cannot follow other principles, or economic doctrines other than those already adopted in the Constitution, if they are to put into practice that Constitution and not another that does not exist.

To test new systems, to embark into the domain of new ideas, is to turn away from the Constitution at the point where it should be most observed. It is to distort the beautiful sense of its provisions and throw the country into disorder and delay, hindering the material interests that are necessary to help the country out of the uncertain and subordinate position in which it finds itself.

But as political economics is chaos, an interminable and complicated dispute in which no two schools agree with each other on how to understand and define wealth, production, value, price, revenue, capital, currency, credit, it is very easy for the legislator and the publicist, depending on the school where they were educated, to deviate from the Constitution and alter its economic viewpoints and principles, without intending or desiring it, by merely adopting principles opposed to the laws and organic regulations enacted to bring the Constitution into effect.

To avoid this danger, it is useful to bear in mind to which school of economic science the doctrine of the Argentine Constitution belongs; and which schools profess rival doctrines opposed to those that the Constitution has followed in its economic and revenue project.

Let us first see, for our objectives, the main point that divides them.

There are three elements involved in the formation of wealth:

1. *Productive forces or agents,* namely *labor, land,* and *capital.*
2. The *mode of application* of these forces, which has three forms: *agriculture, commerce,* and *manufacturing industry.*
3. Lastly, the *products* of the application of these forces.

For each of these elements the following question has arisen, dividing economic systems: in the interest of society, is liberty worth more than regulation, or is regulation more fertile than liberty? For the development of production, is it better for each person to dispose of their *land, capital,* or *labor* with full liberty, or is it better for the law to limit some of those forces and increase others? Is it preferable for each person to apply them to the industry they choose, or is it better for the law to expand agriculture and restrict commerce, or vice versa? Should all products be free, or should some be excluded and prohibited for protective reasons?

This is the gravest question of political economics in relation to public law. An error of the system on this point means prosperity or ruin for a country. Spain has paid for the error of her economic policy with the loss of her population and her industry, having sought to resolve those questions in a manner opposed to liberty.

Let us now see how this question has been resolved by the four main schools into which political economics is divided.

The *mercantile school,* represented by Colbert,[1] minister of Louis XIV, which saw wealth only in *money* and admitted no other means of earning it than manufacturing and trade, naturally followed the restrictive protectionist system. Colbert formulated and codified the economic system introduced in Europe by Charles V and Philip II.[2] That school, belonging to the infancy of economics, contemporary with the greatest political despotism in countries of its Franco-Spanish origin, represents the limited and despotic intervention of the law in the exercise of industry.

This school is similar to the *socialist economics* school of our day, which

1. Jean-Baptiste Colbert (1619–1683), secretary of state and general controller of finance under Louis XIV of France, followed an interventionist economic policy by creating and protecting state industries. [E.N.]

2. Charles V of the Holy Roman Empire (Charles I of Spain), born 1500, became king of Spain in 1516, was elected Holy Roman Emperor in 1519, abdicated in 1556, and died 1558. Philip II, his son, born 1527, king of Spain 1556, died 1598. [E.N.]

has preached and requested state intervention in the organization of industry, based on a new social order more favorable to the greater number. For diverse reasons and with different ends, the two go hand-in-hand in their tendency to limit individual freedom in the production, possession, and distribution of wealth.

These two schools are opposed to the economic doctrine on which the Argentine Constitution rests.

In contrast to these two schools, on the side of liberty, we find the *physiocratic* school, represented by Quesnay,[3] and the great *industrial* school of Adam Smith.[4]

Eighteenth-century European philosophy, closely tied to the origins of our revolution in the Americas, was the origin of the physiocratic school, or school of the economists, which was weakened by not recognizing any other source of wealth than land, but which had the merit to profess liberty as a principle of its economic policy, reacting against monopolies of any kind. To this school belongs the formula that recommends to governments: *laissez faire, laissez passer,* regarding all intervention in industry.

Amid the noise of the independence of America, and on the eve of the French Revolution of 1789, Adam Smith proclaimed the omnipotence and dignity of labor; of free labor, of labor in all its applications—*agriculture, trade, manufacturing*—as the essential principle of all wealth. "Inspired by the new social era, which was opening up for both worlds (though he may not have suspected it)," writes Rossi,[5] "giving labor its citizenship and noble titles, the fundamental principle of science was established." This school, very closely tied to the American Revolution, because of its banner and the period when it was born, and which sixty

3. François Quesnay (1694–1774), French economist and physician; for his physiocratic school, the laws of economics operated in the same way as the laws of physics. [E.N.]

4. Adam Smith (1723–1790), Scottish philosopher and economist, author of *The Wealth of Nations.* [E.N.]

5. Pellegrino Rossi (1787–1848), a politician and jurist born in Carrara, Italy, taught in Geneva, Switzerland, and was invited to teach in Paris at the Collège de France. Appointed ambassador to the Papal States in 1845, after the 1848 revolution in France he became minister of the interior in Rome under Pius IX. His moderate liberal policies did not satisfy the conservatives or the radicals. He was assassinated on November 15, 1848. [E.N.]

years later has had Robert Peel as its neophyte in the last days of his glorious life, preserves to our present day the dominion of science and the respect of the greatest economists. His most lucid apostle, his most brilliant expounder, is the famous Jean-Baptiste Say,[6] whose writings preserve that eternal freshness that comes with works of genius.

The economic doctrine of the Argentine Constitution belongs to this school of liberty, and outside of that one must not seek comments or auxiliary means for the enactment of the organic law of that Constitution.

The Constitution is, in economic terms, what it is in all branches of public law: the expression of a revolution of liberty, the consolidation of the social revolution in America.

And, indeed, the Constitution has consolidated the principle of economic liberty, being a political tradition of the May Revolution of 1810 against Spanish rule, which made that liberty the main reason for the war against the colonial or prohibitive system. Dr. Moreno,[7] the main agent of the 1810 Revolution, wrote the program for our economic regeneration in a famous petition, which he presented to the last Spanish viceroy in the name of the landowners of Buenos Aires, requesting freedom to trade with England, which the unwary viceroy accepted, with a result that promptly gave us the revenue to send him back to the other continent.

Our revolution embraced economic liberty, because that liberty is the source that science recognizes as the wealth of nations; because liberty was especially suited to the needs of the uninhabited Argentine Republic, which had to attract with liberty population, capital, and industries, which to date she still lacks, at the risk of her independence and liberty, forever vulnerable to losing them, in the same pitfall in which Spain lost her dominance:—in destitution and poverty.

Therefore the economy of the written Constitution is the faithful expression of the real and normal economy that must bring prosperity to Argentina; which does not depend on a system or on an internal political party, as the Republic, whether centralist or federal (the form is irrelevant), does not have and will not have any other way of escaping

6. Jean-Baptiste Say (1767–1832), French liberal economist, author of *Traité d'économie politique.* [E.N.]

7. Mariano Moreno (1778–1811), a lawyer and journalist, was secretary of the Primera Junta (first governing body, installed May 25, 1810). [E.N.]

from the desert, poverty, and backwardness, than liberty granted in the broadest way to industrial labor in all its forces (*land, capital,* and *labor*) and in all its applications (*agriculture, trade,* and *factories*).

This is precisely the reason why the distinguishing feature of the Argentine Constitution is its economic system, placing it above all the republican constitutions of South America. Understanding that the most vital needs of the country and South America are economic, as these are the needs of its population, land, and river viability, and the import of capital and industries, the Constitution has taken great pains to bring together all the means to satisfy these needs, inasmuch as they depend on state action.

What Argentine public need does not depend on an economic need? The country lacks roads, bridges, canals, docks, a fleet, palaces for its authorities. Why does it lack all these? Why does it not purchase them, why does it not possess them? Because it lacks the means to obtain them, namely, capital, funds, wealth. — Why are private industries not exploited on a large scale? For the same reason. Why does this land sleep deeply and lie in darkness so close to indigence, this land where silk, cotton, and cochineal grow freely, which has more navigable routes than could be made with millions of pesos; hundreds of leagues of the Andes Mountains, which have given a fabulous renown to Mexico, Peru, and Copiapó? Because of a lack of capital, labor, population, accumulated wealth.

It is therefore necessary that Argentina begin by leaving poverty behind, in order to have homes, education, government, liberty, dignity, and civilization, as all these are acquired and preserved by means of wealth. Therefore its present destiny is economic; and wealth, capital, population, material welfare are the priorities it should occupy itself with now and for a long time.

What has the Argentine Constitution done in order to enjoy these assets? It has studied and become aware of its rich resources; and guided by the advice of science, which has demonstrated the nature and place of those origins, it has surrounded their spontaneous and natural course with guarantees and securities.

Indeed, who makes wealth? Is wealth the work of the government? Is wealth decreed? The government has the power to hinder or help the production of wealth, but the creation of wealth is not the work of the government.

Wealth is the child of labor, of capital, and of land; and as these forces, considered as instruments of production, are no more than faculties that man puts into use to create means of satisfying his natural needs, wealth is the work of man, imposed by his instincts of preservation and improvement, and obtained by the faculties he is endowed with to fulfill his destiny in the world.

In this respect, what does wealth demand of the law in order for it to be produced and created? What Diogenes demanded of Alexander: not to cast his shadow on him. To ensure full *liberty* in the use of man's productive faculties; to exclude no one from that liberty, which means the *civil equality* of all *inhabitants;* to protect and *ensure* each man of the results and fruits of his industry: therein lies all the work of the law in the creation of wealth. All the glory of Adam Smith, the Homer of true economic science, lies in having *demonstrated* what others had felt, that in free work lie the basic rudiments of wealth.

The freedom of *labor,* in this respect, includes its means of action, *land* and *capital,* and the whole circle of its threefold use — agriculture, trade, manufacturing — which are nothing more than variations of labor.

According to this, organizing labor is no more than organizing liberty; to organize labor in all its branches is to organize agricultural liberty, the liberty of trade, the liberty of manufacturing. This organization is mostly negative; it consists in systematic abstention, in decrees that parallel those of the old prohibitive system, which carry the precept of *laissez faire* to all the points in which others *did for themselves* or *prevented doing.*

Fortunately, economic liberty is not political liberty; and I say fortunately, for in the exercise of economic liberty there is no circumstantial reason that might legitimize restrictions that, in matters of political liberty, divide scientific opinion into rival camps of good faith and good reasons. To exercise economic freedom is to work, acquire, transfer private assets: therefore everybody is fit for it, regardless of the system of government. To use political liberty is to take part in government; to govern, albeit only through suffrage, requires education, if not science, in handling public affairs. To govern is to manage the destiny of all; which is more complicated than handling one's individual and private fate. Therein lies the domain of economic liberty, which the Argentine Constitution assimilates to the *civil liberty* granted equally to all inhabitants of the country, whether nationals or foreigners, under Sections 14 and 20.

With this fertile liberty thus placed in the hands of all, it becomes the great source of wealth for the country; the most powerful incentive for populating it through the introduction of foreign men and capital; the liberty summoned to clothe, feed, and educate the other liberties, its brethren and pupils.

But wealth is not born for its own sake: its purpose is to satisfy the needs of man, who forms the wealth. So it is that as soon as it exists, one must find out how to *share* or *distribute* it among those who have come together to produce it. For this it is produced; and if the producer does not receive the share that matches his contribution, he ceases to contribute in future, or works feebly, wealth declines, and with it the prosperity of the nation. Therefore it is necessary that natural law be followed, which makes each producer the owner of the benefit or profit corresponding to the service of his labor, his capital, or his land, in the production of common and divisible wealth.

What assistance does the producer request from the law in the *distribution* of profits? — The same as for production: the fullest liberty of man; the abstention of the law in regulating the profit, obeying in its distribution the justice accorded freely by the will of each man.

Consumption is the purpose and conclusion of wealth, which has the objective of disappearing in the service of the needs and enjoyment of man, or to be used for its own reproduction: hence consumption is divided into *unproductive* and *productive.* Consumption can also be distinguished as *private* and *public.* The law has no place in *private consumption,* but may make rules and guarantees so that *public consumption* or state expenditure does not devour the country's wealth; so that the national treasury, whose role it is to defray these costs, is formed, administered, and applies itself for the good and usefulness of the nation, and never to the detriment of the taxpayer. The sum of these guarantees forms what is called the revenue or financial system of the confederation.

Therein lies all the purpose of the law, the whole circle of its intervention in *production, distribution,* and *consumption* of public and private wealth; it comes down purely and simply to guaranteeing its greatest independence and liberty in the exercise of those three great functions of the Argentine economic organism.

The 1853 Argentine Constitution is the codification of the doctrine that I have expounded above in a few words, and which I shall examine in its practical applications to organic law in the course of this book, which shall be divided, like the economic subject, into three parts:

> The first is devoted to examining the provisions of the Constitution that refer to the phenomenon of the *production* of wealth;
> The second is devoted to expounding and studying the constitutional principles referring to the *distribution* of wealth;
> And lastly, the third is devoted to examining the provisions related to the phenomenon of *public consumption,* or the formation, administration, and use of the national treasury.

PART 1. PROVISIONS AND PRINCIPLES OF THE ARGENTINE CONSTITUTION REGARDING THE PRODUCTION OF WEALTH

CHAPTER 1. GENERAL CONSIDERATIONS

The preamble in which the Constitution briefly expresses the major viewpoints that cover its provisions enumerates, among various others, that of *promoting general welfare, and securing the blessings of liberty to our-selves, to our posterity, and to all men of the world who wish to dwell on Argentine soil.*

The liberty whose benefits the Constitution seeks to ensure is not exclusively political, but liberty of all kinds, both civil and religious, both economic and intellectual, as otherwise it would not promise it to *all the men of the world who wish to dwell on Argentine soil.*

All interests contribute to *general welfare,* but none more immediately than material interests. This principle, which is true in London and Paris, the heart of European opulence, is doubly so in uninhabited countries where material welfare is the starting point and the summary of present prosperity.

For this reason the Argentine Constitution (Section 64, subsection 16), giving the legislative government the power to do all that is *conducive to the prosperity of the country, to the advancement and welfare of all the provinces, and the progress of enlightenment,* categorically fixes and indicates as means conducive for the purposes of all welfare and improvement "*the promotion of industry, immigration, the construction of railroads and navigable canals, the colonization of lands of national property, the introduction and establishment of new industries, the import of foreign capital and the exploration of inland rivers, under protective laws for these ends.*"

As industry, meaning *labor,* immigration and colonization, meaning *manpower,* and *capital* are no more than agents or instruments for the *production* of wealth, it can be inferred that the laws that protect these means are equally *protective of production.*

The laws that protect production already have their principles in the Constitution; they cannot be arbitrary, nor must they be anything other than organic laws of the constitutional economy. In the course of this first part, we will expound the principles that the Constitution recognizes and guarantees as origins of Argentine *production.*

But before moving on, let us pause to observe one matter that constitutes the most profound and fundamental change that the Constitution has introduced into Argentine economic law. This matter consists of the superior scale or range that the Constitution gives to the *production* of national wealth, over the formation of the treasury or fiscal wealth. Who would have thought that forty years after the start of the fundamental revolution, this would be a novelty in formerly Spanish America?

The Argentine Constitution is the first to distinguish the wealth of the nation from the wealth of the government; and which, considering the latter as an accessory branch of the former, finds that the true way to get abundant contributions from taxpayers is to make the nation rich and opulent.

Indeed, can there be a rich treasury in a poor uninhabited country? Enriching the country, populating it, filling it with capital, is this nothing more than enlarging the fiscal treasury? Is there any other means of feeding the arm than fattening the body of which it is a limb? Or is the nation made for the treasury and not the treasury for the nation?

It was important to set down this matter in the fundamental code of the Republic, because this alone constitutes almost all the Argentine revolution against Spain and its colonial government.

Until now the worst enemy of the wealth of the country has been the wealth of the treasury. We owe to the old colonial regime the legacy of this fundamental error of the Spanish economy. We are countries of a fiscal complexion, peoples organized to produce royal revenues. Simple tributaries or colonists for a period of three centuries, to date we are the product of this precedent, which has more power than our written constitutions. Having been machines of the Spanish treasury, we have become machines of the national treasury: herein lies all the difference. Having been colonists of Spain, we have been the same to our own governments: always fiscal states, always servile revenue machines, revenues that never come because poverty and backwardness yield nothing.

The economic system of the Argentine Constitution puts to death this principle of our old and modern annihilation, placing the nation before the government, public wealth before fiscal wealth. But in economy, more than in any other branch, establishing a principle is nothing; what matters most, what is hardest, is to put it into practice. No regime is annihilated by a decree, constitutional though it may be, but rather by the slow action of a new regime, the creation of which takes the same time as the formation of the bad regime, or even longer, because the destroying and forgetting are prior tasks. The modern regime is in our hearts, but the colonial regime is in our habits, and our habits are usually more powerful than the abstract desire for the best.

There is, therefore, a danger to which the beautiful system of the Argentine Constitution might succumb, if it is not taken into account by the legislator who must regulate the implementation of the new system in relation to the production of national wealth.

To serve this purpose, I will first expound the table of constitutional guarantees to protect *production,* and beside them the pitfalls and dangers, in the two following chapters.

CHAPTER 2. RIGHTS AND GUARANTEES TO PROTECT PRODUCTION
The production of wealth is brought about by the combined action of three agents or instruments, which are:

Labor,
Capital,
And land.

By land, economists mean the soil, rivers, lakes, plants, mines, and wildlife. In this sense there may be, indeed there are, riches that are not *produced.* Taking this word in its technical sense, it means the modification by which the value of something is produced or *increased.* In these riches, which are called *natural* riches, the Argentine Republic is admirably abundant, as it has rivers that represent vast sums as vehicles of communication; productions not created by man, such as natural dyes, cotton, silk, gold, and silver; an infinite variety of wood, salt, coal, and fields fertilized by a climate superior to all industry. All of these riches enter into the domain of constitutional provisions.

The action of these three productive agents or forces, nearly always in combination, occurs in three modes or forms of industrial work, namely:

Agriculture,
Manufacturing,
And trade.

Outside of these three modes of production, outside of these three great divisions of man's industry, there is nothing more. It is important to remember that agriculture, in its highest economic sense, includes besides tilling the land, mining, hunting, as well as fishing, timber, and the rural production or raising of livestock.

Each of these three modes of production is the object of special provisions of the Argentine Constitution; and all three are the object of provisions that they share in common.

To expound them clearly and methodically, I shall divide this chapter into four articles: the first addresses the guarantees of production in general; the second addresses agricultural production; the third, manufacturing production; and the fourth, commercial production.

Article I. Guarantees and liberties common to the three
instruments and the three modes of production.
These are guarantees common to all types of industry and the exercise of all industrial force:

Liberty,
Equality,
Property,
Security,
Education.

These guarantees have two aspects, one moral and political, the other material and economic. Here they will be considered as guarantees granted to the production of Argentine wealth. In four separate paragraphs I shall show that in establishing them, the Constitution has sought to ensure several other sources or principles of wealth and material welfare for the country.

I. *On liberty in relation to economic production.* This is widely established by Section 14 of the Argentine Constitution, which provides that: All the inhabitants of the confederation are entitled to the following rights, in accordance with the laws that regulate their exercise, namely: to work and perform any lawful industry; to navigate and trade; to petition the authorities; to enter, remain in, travel through, and leave Argentine territory; to publish their ideas through the press without previous censorship; to make use and dispose of their property; to associate for useful purposes; to profess freely their religion; to teach and to learn.

Let us consider these rights in their economic application and in their practical results on Argentine wealth.

Economic freedom is for *all inhabitants,* for nationals and foreigners, and so it should be. To limit it only to the offspring of the country would be to sterilize that source of wealth, given that the use of economic freedom, more than that of political freedom, demands, to be productive and fertile, the aptitude and intelligence that usually accompany the foreign worker and are lacking in the Argentine worker at present.

Right is the name and rank that the Constitution gives to economic liberty, which is of immense importance, since liberty, as Guizot says, is an illusory gift when it is not a right that can be claimed with the Constitution in hand. Neither the law nor any power can take away from Argentine industry its right to constitutional liberty.

Economic liberties are granted *in accordance with the laws that regulate their exercise.* This provision leaves in the hands of the legislator, formerly a Spanish colonist, the great danger of repealing the Constitution with regulations, by merely ceding to the instinct and routine of our colonial economy, which governs our habits but not our spirits. To regulate freedom is not to confine it. When the Constitution makes its exercise dependent on rules, it does not intend these rules to be a means for enslaving its scope and movements, as in such a case liberty would be a false promise, and the Constitution, free in words, would be oppressive in fact.

All regulation that is a pretext for organizing economic freedom in its exercise, restricts it and hampers it, committing a double attack on the Constitution and on national wealth, which has its most fertile principle in that freedom.

The right to work and to exercise all lawful industry is a liberty that embraces all means of human production, with no other exception than *illicit* or criminal industry, that is, industry that attacks the freedom of others and the right of a third party. All the great school of Adam Smith can be reduced to demonstrating that *free work* is the essential principle of all created wealth.

The freedom or right to petition is a safeguard of economic production, as it offers the way to obtain the implementation of the law that protects capital, land, and labor, without the security of which wealth would lack stimulus and production a purpose.

The freedom or right to locomotion assists in such an indispensable way the practice of all industry and the production of all wealth, that without it, and with restrictions placed on its practice, it would be impossible to conceive the practice of trade, for example, which is the production or increase of value of something through its transport from the point of production to that of consumption; and it is no less difficult to conceive of agricultural or manufacturing production, where the right to transport such production, which gives production encouragement and stimulus, is missing.

The freedom to publish in the press is of primary importance for economic production, whether considered as a means to exercise literary or intellectual industry, or as a guarantee protecting all guarantees and liberties, both economic and political. Experience shows that the production of wealth is never abundant where there is no freedom to denounce and combat in the press the errors and abuses that encumber industry; and, above all, of bringing to light all the truths with which the physical and exact sciences contribute to extending and perfecting the means of production.

The freedom to make use and dispose of one's property is a complement to the freedom to work and the right to property; an additional guarantee of great use against the tendency of the socialist economy of this era, which, under the pretext of organizing those rights, seeks to restrict the use and availability of property (if not negate the right for it to exist) and make the work of the imbecile equal to the work of the genius.

The freedom of association applied to industry is one of the most powerful resources that modern economic production can recognize; and in the Argentine Republic it is a guarantee of the only means for fulfilling the need of the country to undertake the construction of railroads, to promote European immigration, to set up establishments of private credit, through the action of associated or united capitals, to work in the interests of those ends and objectives.

The freedom of association implies the practice of the other economic liberties; because if credit, labor, the use of property, and movement are not all free, what use is the freedom of association in industrial matters?

The right to freely profess one's religion is a guarantee of importance for the production of Argentine wealth, as much as for its moral and religious progress. The Argentine Republic will not have immigration, population, or manpower if it demands of dissident immigrants, who are the most apt for industry, the immoral sacrifice of the religion in which they have been raised, as if a religion learned at a mature age had any power and were capable of replacing what was received with the mother's milk.

The freedom to teach and learn is strongly related to the production of wealth, whether the former be considered a productive industry, or both be seen as the means to improve and broaden industrial education, or as a repeal of the ancient laws on masters and contracts of apprenticeship. In this regard, laws restricting the freedom to teach and learn, besides offensive to the Constitution that establishes it, go against the interests of Argentine wealth.

Besides those principles mentioned above to favor the production of wealth, the Argentine Constitution establishes another principle, which in seeking to fulfill only a moral and religious need serves the interest of industrial labor, curing it of a shameful affliction. Slave labor lessens the advantage and honor of free labor. The man-machine, the man-thing, the man-alien, is a thing of sacrilege, with which the slothful and immoral owner of his brother obliges to sell cheap the product of a free man, who cannot compete with the slave, as he works for nothing because he works for another.

The Argentine Constitution prevents this disorder in Section 15, conceived thus: "In the Argentine confederation there are no slaves; and a special law shall regulate whatever compensation this declaration may give rise to. Any contract for the purchase and sale of persons is a crime for which the parties shall be liable, as well as the notary or officer authorizing it." The freedom of labor receives its last sanction under Section 19 of the Constitution, which provides that: "The private actions of men, which in no way offend public order or morality, or injure a third party, are reserved to God and are *exempted from the authority of judges*. No inhabitant of the confederation shall be obliged to perform what the law does not demand, or deprived of what it does not prohibit."

We see, from all the above, that liberty, considered by the Constitution in its effects and relations with economic production, is both the beginning and the source of public and private wealth, and a condition of moral welfare. Any law—according to this, any decree, any act that in any way restricts or compromises the principle of liberty—is a more or less serious attack on the wealth of the citizen, on the treasury of the state, and on the material progress of the country. Despotism and tyranny, whether of power, of laws, or of regulations, annihilate at its source the origin of wealth—which is free labor; they are the causes of poverty and of scarcity for the country, and the origin of all degradation that poverty entails.

II. *On equality in its relation to production.* The terms in which the Argentine Constitution establishes the principle of equality give this guarantee an immense influence in the production and distribution of wealth.

Under Section 14, cited above, all the inhabitants of the confederation enjoy the same liberties in accordance with the law.

Under Section 15, also cited above, "in the Argentine Confederation there are no slaves."

Section 16, most explicitly of all, provides in favor of the principle of equality that:

"The confederation does not permit prerogatives of blood or birth; in it there are no personal privileges or titles of nobility. All inhabitants are equal before the law. Equality is the basis of taxation and of public burdens."

The Constitution extends the guarantee of equality to include foreigners. "Foreigners (reads Section 20) enjoy in the territory of the confederation all the civil rights of citizens."

The Constitution does not specify which law all inhabitants are equal before, which demonstrates that it refers to civil, economic, and fiscal law, the same as to the political law regarding nationals of the country.

Having thus established equality, we find that our fundamental economic law disregards absolutely the distinctions of the old royalist law, which divided people, for economic purposes, into:

Freemen and slaves,
Nobles and commoners,
Common and privileged,
Workers and idlers by class and birth,

Foreigners and nationals,
Taxpayers and those free of burdens and taxes,
First-born and younger sons, etc.

All are equal today under the law of labor, which presides over the production of wealth.

In raising slaves to the level of free men, the Constitution does a powerful service to production, because it prevents the disastrous competition between the free worker who produces for himself and the slave worker who produces for his owner; and it rehabilitates and dignifies work, degraded in the hands of the slave, making it shameful in the eyes of the free man. Ennobling, glorifying labor in this way, the Constitution sets the citizen on the path to his true independence and personal freedom, as labor is the source of fortune, by which means man shakes off any servile yoke and becomes truly lord of himself. The destitute man is free in name; he does not have opinion, vote, or color. He gives everything in exchange for his bread, which he is unable to earn through intelligent and manly work. Voltaire said that he loved wealth as a means of independence and liberty, and thus it is rightly loved wherever there are free men.

In making foreigners and nationals equal in their enjoyment of civil rights to exercise all kinds of industry, labor, and profession, the Argentine Constitution (Section 20) gives national production a powerful boost, because the labor of the foreigner, more advanced than we, as well as more fertile in production by being more intelligent, active, and capable, contributes through his example to the education of the Argentine producer.

The civil consequences of the principle of equality established by the Constitution in the inheritance law are of great importance to economic production, because they exclude the existence of entailed estates, the institution of which takes away from industry the general use of land, its most powerful agent, and it also facilitates its use by subdivision of property.

We must also consider as postulates of the principle of equality in the economic sphere, because they effectively are, the extinction of the licenses and guilds of various branches of industry, and of indefinite monopoly patents which to some extent contradict the guarantee of equality.

Also contrary to the principle of economic equality as established by the Constitution are the protectionist laws and regulations for certain types of production, through direct prohibitions or high taxation, which are tantamount to indirect prohibitions.

Equality, as a principle of taxation established by Section 16 of the Constitution, frees production of enormous burdens, which weighed on the least able of the population in the era of divisions of classes and ranks. Today exemptions must be granted to immigrants, the importers of industries, or machinery and mechanical procedures, exemptions that in another era were granted to idle nobles or unproductive soldiers.

The differential laws in Argentine maritime law, for reasons of the foreign nationality of the trader, would go against the spirit and economic trend of Section 20, which makes the civil condition of the foreign industrialist equal to that of the national industrialist, as a means of multiplying the forces and faculties of national production.

In conclusion from the above, given that economic equality, under our Constitution, is more a means of enrichment and prosperity than an end in itself, any law or regulation against the principle of equality is harmful not only to the Constitution, but also to the wealth and welfare of the Argentine Republic.

III. *On property in relation to industrial production.* Property, as a guarantee of public law, has two aspects: one legal and moral, the other purely economic and material. Considered as a general principle of wealth and as a merely economic fact, the Argentine Constitution establishes it under Section 17 in the most advantageous terms for national wealth. It reads: "Property may not be violated, and no inhabitant of the confederation can be deprived of it except by virtue of a sentence based on law. Expropriation for reasons of public interest must be authorized by law and previously compensated. Only Congress levies the taxes mentioned in Section 4. No personal service can be requested except by virtue of a law or sentence based on law. Every author or inventor is the exclusive owner of his work, invention, or discovery for the term granted by law. The confiscation of property is hereby abolished forever from the Argentine Criminal Code. No armed body may make requisitions or demand assistance of any kind."

The most advanced and perfected political economy could not request fuller guarantees in favor of property as an elemental principle of wealth.

It has been seen that wealth, or rather production, has three instruments or agents that bring it into being: *labor, capital,* and *land.* To compromise or confiscate *property*—that is, the exclusive right of each man to make use and dispose fully of his labor, of his capital, and of his lands to produce what is apt for his needs or enjoyment—is to do no more than to leave production without its instruments, that is, to paralyze its fecund functions, rendering wealth impossible. Such is the economic importance of any attack on property, on labor, on capital, and on land, for whoever knows the play or mechanism of the right to property in the generation of general wealth. Property is the motive and stimulus of production, the incentive of labor, and a remunerative end of the motives of industry. Property has no value or attraction, it is not truly wealth unless it is inviolable by law and in practice.

But it was not enough to recognize property as an inviolable right. It can be respected in principle and disregarded and attacked in its most precious aspect: in the use and availability of its advantages. More than once have tyrants used this sophistic distinction to confiscate property that they dared not challenge. Socialism, a hypocritical and timid doctrine, also not daring to negate the right of property, has employed the same sophism attacking the use and availability of property in the name of the organization of labor. Taking into account this and the concept that property without unlimited use is a nominal right, the Argentine Constitution has established under Section 14 the broadest right to *use and dispose of one's property,* with which it has cast an iron bolt on the advances of socialism.

The Constitution has gone further than establishing the principle of property, providing remedies to cure and prevent other ills that often beset property.

The individual thief is the weakest of the enemies that property can recognize.

Property can be attacked by the state, in the name of *public usefulness.* To put a stop to this defect, the Constitution has demanded that Congress, that is, the highest representation of the country, qualify under law the need for *commandeering,* or rather, for *expropriation,* as in some ways there is no expropriation because property must be *previously compensated.*

Property may be attacked by arbitrary or exorbitant taxation by the government. To prevent this ill common to nascent countries, the Constitution attributes exclusively to Congress the power to levy taxes.

Intellectual property can be attacked by plagiarism, because an idea divulged by the press or other means of publicity is easily spread. To remedy this, the Constitution declares that *every author or inventor is the exclusive owner of his work, invention, or discovery, for the period that the law grants.* This is what is commonly called an *invention patent or privilege,* which, as can be seen, is not a monopoly or limitation on the right to property, unless property itself can be taken in the same sense.

Labor and the personal faculties for his work constitute man's most genuine property. The *property of labor* can be attacked in the name of a necessary service to the Republic. To prevent it, the Constitution declares that *no personal service is demandable except by virtue of the law or a sentence based in law.* It is understood that the law or sentence is not the cause, but the means to demand the service whose cause is a freely stipulated personal commitment.

Property can be attacked by criminal law under the name of *confiscation. To prevent it,* the Constitution *has removed confiscation from the Argentine Criminal Code forever.*

Property tends to undergo peculiar attacks in times of war, which are common in the Argentine Republic, under the name of *requisitions and assistance.* To prevent it, the Constitution states that *no armed body may make requisitions, or demand assistance of any kind.*

The Constitution stresses the power conceded to protective guarantees of property, declaring under Section 29 "Congress may not vest in the national executive power—nor may the provincial legislatures vest in the provincial governors—extraordinary powers or the total public authority; it may not grant acts of submission or supremacy whereby the wealth of the Argentine people will be at the mercy of governments or any person whatsoever."

In all these principles and guarantees with which the Constitution defends the right to property against attacks that persecute it in various ways, the Constitution does a great service to public wealth, which has in property one of its most fertile sources.

IV. *On personal safety in relation to the production of wealth. Labor* cannot exist without man, because it is no more than the action of the human faculties applied to the production of wealth: that application is indirect in the action of machines, whose labor ultimately comes down to the labor of man. No machine makes itself or sustains its own activity without the assistance of man. *Capital,* which is the second force that produces wealth, is no more than a result of previous labor; and *land* is impotent and barren without labor and capital, that is, without man's assistance, which makes it produce by means of those forces.

Hence it follows that *labor, capital,* and *land* cannot perform their productive functions, nor can wealth be developed when man is not assured of his rule over his person by the support of the Constitution against the aggressions of law, authority, and individual interest.

Taking this into account, the Argentine Constitution has passed in favor of individual safety the precious guarantees contained in Section 18, as follows: "No inhabitant of the confederation may be punished without previous trial based on a law enacted before the act that gives rise to the process, or tried by special committees, or removed from the judges appointed by law before the act for which he is tried. Nobody may be compelled to testify against himself, or be arrested except by virtue of a written warrant issued by a competent authority. The defense by trial of persons and rights may not be violated. The domicile may not be violated, as well as the written correspondence and private papers; and a law shall determine in which cases and for what reasons their search and occupation shall be allowed."

"No personal service can be requested except by virtue of a law or sentence based on law," states Section 17.

Section 19 completes the inviolability of the home, stating that "the private actions of men that in no way offend public order or morality, or injure a third party, are reserved only to God and are exempted from the authority of judges. No person shall be obliged to perform what the law does not demand or deprived of what it does not prohibit."

Section 29 denies Congress itself the power to concede to the national or provincial executive extraordinary powers that place the life of a man at the mercy of any government or person whatsoever.

These guarantees, which appear to be only of political and civil interest, are of immense importance in the exercise of economic production, as can be easily demonstrated.

There is no security or trust in the promises of a trader whose person may be set upon at any instant and imprisoned or deported.

There can be no trade or commerce where the roads abound with dangers for the traders.

It is impossible to conceive of rural, agricultural, or mining production where men can be carried away from their labors to serve in the army.

The inviolability of the home includes that of the workshop and that of the factory. Respect for correspondence and private papers concerns the good success of trade businesses and of industry, as without it business over distance would be impossible.

Furthermore, the worst insecurity for persons is that which is born from bad laws and from the arbitrariness of magistrates, because the insuperable strength of public power brings with it moral prestige of authority. Hence Section 18 of the Constitution is careful to establish the bases of a trial, in order that the law or the authority shall not have the means to exercise against any person the slightest tyranny under the appearance of legality.

V. *On education in relation to economic production.* Thus far we have seen that the Constitution intervenes in favor of production, with the sole purpose of guaranteeing and ensuring the free and broad exercise of its natural forces, which are labor, capital, and land. It stipulates a single duty for organic and regulatory legislation regarding industry, which is summed up in this famous maxim: *laissez faire, laissez passer.*

However, the law goes further in its support, without compromising the liberty that acts as the basis of its economic system. By studying its provisions in relation to each one of the branches of industry, we will see what positive effect it has in favor of wealth, without diminishing liberty.

Let us see here the service that it provides to production in general, intervening in favor of free public education.

Section 5 of the federal Constitution requires that each province *ensure* through its local constitution *free elementary education.*

Section 64 gives powers to Congress, among others, "to provide what is conducive to the prosperity of the country and the welfare of the provinces, and the progress of enlightenment, providing plans for general and university education, and promoting industry and immigration, the construction of railroads and navigable canals, and the colonization of lands belonging to the nation, the introduction and establishment of new industries, the import of foreign capitals, and the exploration of inland rivers, by means of laws protecting these ends and temporary concessions of privileges and stimulus payments."

The same power is attributed by Section 104 of the federal Constitution to the provincial legislatures, without detriment to that vested in the national Congress for the ends indicated.

So that general and free education have the effect attributed to it, among others, by the Constitution, that is, to assist the prosperity and material welfare of the country, it will be necessary to focus on the instruction of the new generations in the practical exercise of the means of production. Commercial instruction, the teaching of arts and crafts, practical methods for tilling the soil and for improving breeds of useful animals, a taste and inclination for mechanical subjects, should be the great objective of popular teaching of these societies eager for superficial glory and savage enough to kill men who have a different opinion, instead of the honor of defeating wild nature and populating the desert with towns.

The best school for the Argentine producer is the practical example of the European producer. Grasping this, the Constitution itself has drawn up the method of education that best suits our industrial classes, charging the Congress with promoting immigration (Section 64) and declaring that "the general government shall foster European immigration; and may not restrict, limit, or burden with any tax whatsoever, the entry into the Argentine territory of foreigners who arrive for the purpose of tilling the soil, improving industries, and introducing and teaching arts and sciences" (Section 25).

The laws protecting these purposes, through which the state must intervene, in accordance with the Constitution, to serve industrial education, must protect those ends in no other way than through the fullest liberty and security, as this is the only system of protection that the Constitution admits, the basis of its economic system having been studied extensively. As for the *privileges and stimulus payments* that it also admits as a means of protection, these are applicable to the invention and import of innovations of great use, in which case they are rather the recognition of a property or some kind of intellectual property (Section 17) than the award of a monopoly restricting economic freedom.

We have examined up to here the protective guarantees of the different modes of production; let us now see the guarantees related to each kind of production in particular.

Article II. Constitutional principles and guarantees
related to agricultural production.

Agriculture, in its broadest economic sense, covers not only the growing of vegetal products, such as cereals, sugarcane, cotton, hemp, etc., but also rural production or rearing of livestock and animals of use to man, timber, exploitation of mines, hunting and fishing, and all that the Earth contributes as a main instrument of production.

In this sense, agriculture is the industry par excellence for the Argentine Republic of the present times, due to the prodigious suitability of its lands for agricultural production in all the branches mentioned.

However, it can be seen that agriculture has not been the object of special constitutional guarantees of the type with which the Constitution has been so generous toward commercial industry. Why? Because since agriculture was the only industry permitted under the old regime, the modern regime has not had to emancipate it from the essentially colonial and monopolistic shackles that kept our former trade chained up.

If there are no more regulations or special arrangements for agriculture than the above-mentioned principles and guarantees of property, liberty, equality, security, and education, which the Constitution provides for all forms of production anyway, it is to be deduced that all the agricultural constitutional law of the Argentine Republic can be reduced to regulatory and legislative nonintervention or, in other words, a *laissez faire, nonobstructive* system, which is the most positive formula for industrial liberty.

It also follows that mining legislation, hunting and fishing regulations, agrarian laws, and rural statutes that existed until now in the Argentine Republic should be considered repealed inasmuch as they are irreconcilable with the principles of economic freedom granted by the modern Constitution. And the regulations and laws subsequently enacted about agricultural interests of any kind should be adapted to such principles.

To organize agriculture in accordance with the outlook of the modern Constitution is to organize its liberty. The only intervention that, according to the Constitution, can be exercised by the law in this branch of national industry must have the objective of removing any hindrance or obstacle to agricultural work, facilitating all means to make available to it the opulent resources and sources of wealth found in our land worthy of the name of *Argentina,* which it holds as an expressive symbol of its incomparable wealth.

Many types of production and crops for which our soil is highly suitable fell into decline under the old regime as a result of the economic errors of Iberian politics, which believed it would serve the interests of its monopoly by prohibiting us from growing such crops as sugarcane, cotton, linseed, etc., etc.

Article III. Principles and provisions of the Constitution regarding commercial production.

Is there a *production* that can be called commercial? Does commerce *produce,* in the sense that this word has in political economics? There is not today a single economist who would not give an affirmative answer to this question.

Production is understood by economists not as the material creation of something that previously did not exist (man does not have such a power), but as the transformation of objects by industry, making them suitable for satisfying some need in man and acquiring therefore a value. In this regard, trade contributes to production to the same degree as agriculture and machines, increasing the value of products through their transfer from one place where they are worth less to another place where they are worth more. A hundredweight of copper from Coquimbo has a greater value in a warehouse in Liverpool, due to the work of the trader who transported it from the country in which it was not needed to the country where it is of greater use.

Trade is a means of civilization, above all for our continent, as well as a means of enrichment; but it is under this latter aspect that we will consider it here.

None of our national sources of wealth were more blocked than this one; and as a result, if trade is the industry that has received the most liberties from the Constitution, it is because no other industry needed them so much, since it was trade that bore the brunt of our old colonial regime, which can be defined as the code of our mercantile and maritime oppression.

To destroy the work of the old colonial law, which made our trade a monopoly of Spain, the Argentine Constitution has made trade and navigation the public and fundamental right of all inhabitants of the

202 : JUAN BAUTISTA ALBERDI

confederation. All have the right to navigate and trade, Section 14 categorically states.

And so that freedom of navigation and trade, declared a constitutional principle, does not run the risk of being repealed by regulations enacted involuntarily by the routine that governs the economic notions of all ex-colonist legislators, the Constitution has rightly enacted the other liberties that assist and sustain freedom of trade and navigation.

The right to trade and to navigate, admitted as a principle, has been and could be attacked by exceptions that excluded foreigners from practicing them. Our Laws of the Indies were modeled on this system, which continued to coexist with the Republic. So as not to take from trade its most expert and capable manpower, Section 20 of the Constitution grants foreigners the right to trade and navigate in the same degree as nationals. "Foreigners," as mentioned above, "enjoy within the territory of the confederation all the civil rights of citizens; they may exercise their industry, trade, and profession; own real estate, buy and sell it; navigate the rivers and coasts; practice freely their religion, etc."

The right to navigate and trade had been and was liable to being annulled by exceptional restrictions imposed on the freedom to leave and enter, to remain and to travel within the territory, which is nothing less than a highly important accessory of commercial freedom. The Constitution makes this abuse impossible, declaring in Section 14 "the right in favor of all inhabitants of the confederation to enter, remain, travel, and leave Argentine territory."

The right to trade and navigate, established as a fundamental principle, was liable to being annulled by exclusions of flags in the navigation of our inland rivers and maritime coasts. For internal navigation to genuinely exist in the fullest sense, Section 26 of the Constitution declares that "navigation of inland rivers of the confederation is free for all flags, subject only to the regulations issued by the municipal authority."

Trade, navigation, and inland traffic, declared free under the principle of constitutional law, were liable to and indeed were attacked during the republican revolution by provincial regulations that fixed duties for inland customs. The May Constitution had sought to make this attack on free trade impossible, declaring four times instead of once that inland trade and navigation cannot be burdened with any type of taxation whatsoever. Sections 9, 10, 11, and 12 of the Constitution are four versions of the same precept of commercial freedom.

"Throughout the territory of the Confederation," reads Section 9, "there shall be no other customs than national customs, in which the tariffs enacted by Congress shall be in force."

"Within the Republic," reads Section 10, "the circulation of goods of national production or manufacture is free from duties, as well as the circulation of articles and merchandise of all kinds cleared in foreign customs."

"Goods of national or foreign production or manufacture," reads Section 11, "as well as livestock of all kinds, that may pass through the territory of one province to another, shall be free from transit duties, the same as the carriages, vessels, or beasts in or on which they are transported; and no other duty, whatever its name may be, shall be imposed on them by reason of their passing through the territory."

"Vessels sailing from one province to another," Section 12 states, "shall not be bound to enter, anchor, or pay transit duties."

By these provisions it is evident that all these measures were taken in the Constitution so that they would not be repealed by regulatory law. For greater security, it has added a new guarantee of irrevocability through Section 28, which provides that: "The principles, guarantees, and rights recognized in the preceding sections shall not be modified by the laws that regulate their enforcement."

But a constitution irrevocable by organic law could be repealed by another constitution regarding freedom of navigation and trade or any other point. To safeguard free trade from any reactionary change, Section 27 of the Constitution declares: "The federal government is under the obligation to strengthen its relationships of peace and trade with foreign powers, by means of treaties in accordance with the principles of public law laid down by this Constitution."[8]

The treaties thus considered are an international remedy, advised by experience, against the ill of versatility of our South American democracy, which alters and destroys everything, without preserving or carrying out anything of use or import, due to the fickleness of its institutions, without root or guarantee.

---

8. In compliance with this section of the Constitution, the government has guaranteed freedom of navigation and trade forever in the confederation, signing treaties to this end with England, France, the United States, Portugal, Sardinia, Chile, and Brazil. These treaties are anchors of the federal Constitution as regards its basic principle: the freedom of trade and river navigation. There all ports are river ports. [A.N.]

In all those liberties assured to trade and navigation, the Constitution has admirably served the production of Argentine wealth, which recognizes in commercial industry its richest and most powerful influence. In other words, those liberties are not only rights granted to economic production: liberty is the *means,* not the *end* of the politics of our Constitution.

When we say that the Constitution has made *liberty* a means and a condition for economic production, we mean that the Constitution has imposed the obligation on the state to not interfere with restrictive decrees or laws in the practice of commercial and maritime production or industry; as in political economics, individual freedom and governmental nonintervention are two ways of saying the same thing.

Article IV. Constitutional principles and provisions regarding the manufacturing industry.
I. *Manufacturing situation in Argentina.* The economic organization of the Spanish colonies, which today are the republics of South America, has its origins in the well-known system of Charles V and Philip II, to whom are attributed the ruin of economic liberty in Europe, and the establishment of a policy of prohibition and exclusion, which has caused so many stupid wars in Europe. "This was the epoch of all bad ideas," says Blanqui, "of all bad systems in arts and manufactures, in politics, and in religion. We do not today commit a single error, or follow a single industrial prejudice, that was not bequeathed to us by that mischievous power which was strong enough to convert into law its most fatal aberrations. No, never will science find terms strong enough, nor humanity tears enough to stigmatize and to deplore the ill-omened acts of such a reign! Philip II, of unfortunate memory, only carried them to their results; it was Charles V who laid their foundations."[9]

This single precedent is enough to appreciate the economic complexion that we owe to the politics of our origin, and how much work and time will be necessary to change to our advantage our native, ancient way of life.

9. Jérôme-Adolphe Blanqui (1798–1854), French liberal economist. Alberdi quotes from his *Histoire de l'économie politique en Europe depuis les Anciens jusqu'à nos jours* (1837); see *History of Political Economy in Europe,* trans. Emily J. Leonard (New York, 1880), pp. 215–16. [E.N.]

Satisfied with the gold of the Americas, Spain neglected and lost its factories.

To impose on us the consumption of its manufactured products, it prevented us from obtaining them from abroad, and forbad us from establishing manufactories, building vessels, and educating our sons in any other European country but Spain.

Herein lies the double origin of our absolute lack of manufacturing industry.

We find ourselves in the act of creating it, as does all of Spanish America.

To do so, what system shall we adopt? There are two options: that of prohibitions and exemptions, and that of promotions reconcilable with freedom. Manufacturing history may be divided on this point, even though the economic science of our days may not, whose truths are of all the ages like the phenomena of chemistry.

This question has ceased to be so for the Argentine Republic, whose Constitution has determined the only means for state intervention in the creation and promotion of manufacturing industry.

These means are:

Education and instruction.
Stimuli and ownership of inventions.
Freedom of industry and trade.
Abstention from prohibitive laws and the duty of repealing existing
    ones.

Let us examine these means in as many paragraphs.

II. *The Argentine Constitution admits two types of industrial education for our working classes; that which is obtained through professional instruction, received in public or private schools; and that which is brought about by the action of the example of trained workers from industrialized countries.* In support of the former, Section 14 declares the freedom of teaching and learning; Section 5 makes it the duty of the provincial governments to provide free elementary education to the people; and Section 64, subsection 16, of the Constitution obliges Congress to provide for the progress of enlightenment through the organization of general and university education.

The state could take great advantage of the practice of these means of instruction in favor of the manufacturing industry by founding schools of arts and trades for the free teaching of the working classes. More than intelligence of the arts, it is important that the youth learn in these schools to honor and love work, to know that it is more glorious to know how to manufacture a rifle than to know how to use it against the life of an Argentine.

Herein lies the main means that the state has to promote the manufacturing industry in the Republic: it consists of spending part of the public treasury on teaching the working people about the different products and manufactures that the country needs.

The other, more urgent and effective way at present consists of the immigration of industrious classes with good knowledge of their work. The power of state intervention on this point is outlined by the following sections of the Constitution: "The federal government," reads Section 25, "shall foster European immigration; and may not restrict, limit, or burden with any tax whatsoever, the entry into the Argentine territory of foreigners who arrive for the purpose of tilling the soil, improving industries, and introducing and teaching arts and sciences.

"It is the responsibility of the Congress," reads Section 64, subsection 16, "to provide encouragement for the prosperity of the country, the advance and welfare of all the provinces and the progress of enlightenment . . . promoting industry, immigration . . . the introduction and establishment of new industries . . . through laws protecting these aims, and through temporary grants of privileges and stimulating rewards."

Section 104 of the Constitution similarly establishes this in regard to the power of the provinces in fostering industry.

III. *Protective laws, temporary concessions of privileges, and stimulating rewards are, according to the section cited, another means that the Constitution places in the hands of the state to foster the manufacturing industry about to be born.* This means is highly delicate in practice, due to the errors into which the inexpert legislator or statesman can be led by a superficial or nominal analogy with the fateful protectionist system of privilege-based exclusions and monopolies.

To know what kind of *protection,* what kind of *privileges* and *rewards* the Constitution offers as *means,* it is necessary to study the *ends* that it intends to attain with these means. Let us read again its text, with a view to investigating this important point for the life of manufacturing freedom. *It is the responsibility of Congress* (reads Section 64) *to provide encouragement to the prosperity of the country, etc., by fostering industry,*

immigration, the construction of railroads and navigable canals, the coloniza-
tion of lands of national property, the introduction and establishment of new
industries, the import of foreign capitals, and the exploration of inland rivers
(by what means?)—The Constitution continues, *through laws that pro-*
tect these AIMS, *and through temporary grants of privileges and stimulating*
rewards (equally protective of those AIMS, one assumes).

According to this, the AIMS that laws, privileges, and rewards are
called to protect are:

Industry,
Immigration,
The construction of railroads and navigable canals,
The colonization of lands of national property,
The introduction and establishment of new industries,
The import of foreign capital,
And the exploration of inland rivers.

It is sufficient to mention these AIMS to recognize that the *means of*
protection that the Constitution provides for them are *liberty* and the
privileges and *rewards* reconcilable with liberty.

IV. *In fact, might a law that protects industry through restrictions and pro-*
hibitions be suitable, when Section 14 of the Constitution grants all inhabitants
of the Confederation the freedom to work and exercise all industry? Such restrictions and prohibitions would be a means of attacking that principle
of the Constitution through the protectionist laws that contain them;
and this is precisely what the Constitution has sought to prevent when
it states in Section 28: "The principles, guarantees, and rights recognized
in the preceding sections shall not be modified by the laws that regulate
their enforcement." This provision closes the door on the enactment of
any protectionist law, in the sense that is usually given to this word, that
is, *prohibitive* or *restrictive.*

Can you conceive a law that protects immigration through restrictions and prohibitions? Such a law would attack the means that the Constitution itself indicates to protect this end. Indeed, the Constitution
states in Section 25: "The federal government shall foster European immigration; and may not restrict, limit, or burden with any tax whatsoever, the entry into the Argentine territory of foreigners who arrive for
the purpose of tilling the soil, improving industries, and introducing
and teaching arts and sciences." This section allows the state to employ

any means it wishes to foster immigration, except those of restrictions and limitations.

Nor is it conceivable how the law could attain the introduction of new industries and the import of foreign capital, barring them from the country with prohibitions, or limitations and restrictions equivalent to an indirect prohibition. The law that protects those ends has no other means to obtain them, according to the intentions of the Constitution, than the fullest liberty. Money is powerful enough itself without the law protecting it with prohibitions; the only protection that the law can give it is liberty.

Nor has the Constitution sought that the construction of railroads and navigable canals, the colonization of national lands, the establishment of new industries, and the exploration of inland rivers be protected by laws that prohibit and restrict liberty, which the Constitution itself provides in Section 14, of working and performing any industry, of navigating and trading, of movement in the territory, of making use and disposing of property, of association for useful purposes; because that would be to admit that it sought to repeal with legislative exceptions what it has rejected expressly and vigorously in Section 25, which is quoted word for word above.

The *exclusive privileges* that the Constitution admits as a means of industrial protection are, more than privileges, simply derived forms of intellectual property rights. Section 17 of the Constitution, establishing the inviolability of property, declares that *any author or inventor is the exclusive owner of his work, invention, or discovery, for the term granted by the law.* This *exclusive property* for a *determined time* receives the name of *temporary privilege* in Section 64, subsection 16.

Extending, under a universally received jurisprudence, the meaning of the *invention* or *discovery* to the introduction of a whole new industry and the application of a whole mechanism unknown in the country, although it may be known elsewhere, the Constitution considers as exclusive owners of their introduction and application the entrepreneurs or authors of such enterprises; and the temporary privilege that is granted to them amounts to no more than this transitory property. The same would apply, under our Constitution, to the *exclusive privileges* with which the law *might protect* the efforts of companies and capitals that may undertake the construction of railroads and canals, the colonization of our desert lands, and the import of foreign capital to establish private banks.

The *stimulating rewards* admitted by the Constitution are another means of protection that the law could use with the purpose of fostering the manufacturing industry without the slightest attack on liberty; as none of its ends are compromised in the slightest by the concession of medals, bonuses, honors, lands, pecuniary rewards, and remunerative exemptions, with which the state may contribute to the establishment and progress of national manufactories, without the need to resort to prohibitions and exclusions, more disastrous for the manufactories that it seeks to protect than for the industrial liberty attacked by them.

V. *In fact, the usual means of stimulus employed by the protective or protectionist system, which consist of prohibiting imports of certain products, in the indefinite monopolies granted to certain manufactures and in the imposition of heavy import duties, are prohibited in all respects by the Argentine Constitution, as attacks on the liberty that it guarantees to all industries in the broadest and most loyal manner, as unconstitutional hindrances on the liberty of private consumption, and, above all, as ruinous to national manufactures, which the Constitution seeks to help bring into existence and advance. Such means are the protection of stupidity and laziness, the clumsiest of privileges.*

Abstaining from its use, hindering it in all legislative attempts to introduce it, and promoting the repeal of the endless number of protectionist laws bequeathed to us by the old colonial regime are other means that the Constitution gives to the state to intervene negatively, but highly effectively, in favor of the manufacturing industry of the Argentine Republic.

It can be said that in this branch all the work of the legislator and statesman comes down to protecting national manufactories, less through the enactment of new laws than through the repeal of existing ones. Repealing our colonial manufacturing laws moderately and systematically is the way to introduce logic and harmony between the enacted Constitution and our industrial legislation, which, while it is in place, will keep the Constitution in limbo, ruling the land of ideas while the colonial laws preserve their dominion over the facts.

Such is the political obligation arising from Section 28 of the Constitution, which states: *The principles, guarantees and rights* (of liberty) *recognized in the preceding sections, shall not be modified by the laws that regu-*

late their enforcement. This section refers to past laws as much as it refers to future ones: it prohibits the latter from coming forth and orders the former to disappear. What it desires is that there be no laws, old or new, that alter the principles, guarantees, and constitutional rights with the excuse of regulating or organizing their practice.

And while Section 64, subsection 11, has given Congress the obligation to enact civil, commercial, and mining codes, it has done nothing more than impose on it the duty of reforming our legislation, royalist and colonial in origin and purpose, in order to harmonize it with the new principles of the republican Constitution, which holds the code of our new national existence. Finally, Section 24 of the Constitution completes the enactment of this legislative duty, stating that *the Congress will promote the reform of current legislation in all its branches.*

To facilitate the practical exercise of this highly important branch of our economic policy, we shall dedicate the following chapter to the examination of diverse means of exception with which all liberties that protect production can be annulled in their results by organic laws and regulations.

CHAPTER 3. PITFALLS AND DANGERS TO WHICH LIBERTIES
THAT PROTECT PRODUCTION ARE EXPOSED
*Article 1. On how the economic guarantees of the Constitution
might be repealed by the laws made to organize its exercise.*
These dangers and pitfalls of constitutional liberty in economic matters reside in the organic laws regulating their exercise. Both laws enacted after the Constitution to put it into practice and those prior to its enactment are organic laws of the Constitution. They shall be the object, respectively, of two articles into which chapter 3 shall be divided.

1. *Liberty proclaimed is not liberty put into practice.* To establish economic liberty in the Constitution is merely to *write it,* to proclaim it as a principle and nothing more; to transfer it from there to organic laws, to decrees, regulations, and ordinances is to *enforce* it, and there is no other way to turn liberty in writing into liberty in fact.

No Constitution is enough by itself; none is put into effect by itself. Generally it is a simple *code* of the *principles* that must be the bases of other laws intended to enforce these principles. Rossi, with typically profound reason, has said in relation to this that *the provisions of a consti-*

tution are as many chapter headings of administrative law. Section 64, sub-section 28, gives the Congress the power to make all appropriate laws and rules to put into effect the aforementioned powers, and all other powers granted by this Constitution to the government of the *Argentine Confederation.*

According to this, to have economic liberty written in the Consti-tution is a precious acquisition without the slightest doubt: but it is to have the *idea,* not the *fact;* the *seed,* not the *tree* of liberty. Liberty takes on body and life when it enters the field of organic laws, that is, of laws of action and accomplishment; of laws that *do* what the Constitution merely *says* or *declares.*

Tyrants are usually accused of being the cause when the liberty writ-ten in the Constitution does not go as far as facts. They may have a great part to play in this: but one must not forget that the worst tyranny is that which lies in our habits of economic oppression, strengthened by three centuries of existence; in economic errors, which we have inherited through eight consecutive generations; and above all in our political, administrative, and civil laws prior to the American Revolution, which are simple organic means of putting into practice the principles of our old system of colonial government, rated by current science as the full-est expression of the prohibitive and restrictive system in political eco-nomics. We are the product of those royal precedents, not of the written declarations of the revolution. Those customs, those notions, those laws are weapons of oppression that still exist and that will lead to the rebirth of economic tyranny because they were made precisely to consolidate and sustain that tyranny.

It is necessary to destroy them and replace them with habits, notions, and laws, which should be as many means to put into practice the liberty proclaimed in economic matters. To change the law of the viceroys is to disarm the tyrants, and there is no other means to put a stop to them. The tyrant is the product, not the cause, of the tyranny; our economic tyranny is the product of our legislation, handed down from Charles V and Philip II, present in our instincts and practices in spite of our bril-liant declarations of principles.

As long as you let our republican governors and presidents administer the economic interests of the Republic according to the laws and orders that we owe to those frenzied enemies of freedom of trade and industry, what will it lead to in the truth of facts? That we will have the colonial system in economic matters, living de facto beside the *written* liberty in the republican Constitution.

As a matter of fact, all economic liberties of the Constitution can be annulled and reduced to golden deceptions, simply by leaving in place a large part of our old economic laws and enacting other new ones that, instead of following the new principles, follow our old revenue and fiscal habits, usually stronger than our principles.

II. *The danger of inconsistency comes from colonial education and from the Constitution itself.* This danger has two sources: First, our primitive economic context, our colonial constitution, essentially exclusive in matters of trade and industry; second, the reserved manner in which our Constitution has declared the liberties that are of interest for wealth.

Embodied in our traditional notions and habits, the prohibitive system drags us involuntarily to repeal by law, by decree, by regulations, the liberties that we accept under the Constitution. We fall into this inconsistency, to which the foreigner is witness, without realizing it. We believe ourselves the supporters and owners of economic liberty because we see it written in the Constitution; but in putting it into practice, we reestablish the old regime in ordinances taken from it, because they are the only ones we know, and we thus repeal the modern regime with the best intentions of organizing it.

And if any reproach should be raised in the depths of our republican conscience over this inconsistency toward the new regime, there will be no lack of economic schools that in the name of socialism will absolve us and justify this restoration of the prohibitive system with the mask of liberty and civilization; which represents a third pitfall for our desired freedom.

Let us see how the Constitution contributes to facilitating its reproduction, subjecting the exercise of the economic liberties that it proclaims to the conditions of existing or possible, old or new organic law (the Constitution makes no distinction).

The *liberty* of industry, the right to work, the freedom or right to navigate and trade, the right to petition, locomotion, and travel, to print and publish, to use and dispose of one's property, the right of association, worship, teaching, and learning: how are these precious and stupendous liberties granted by the Argentine Constitution? *In accordance with the laws that regulate their exercise,* says Section 14.

Property is also subject to the conditions of the law. According to Section 17 no person may be deprived of it *except by virtue of a sentence based in law.* Expropriation for reasons of public interest *must be authorized by law.* No personal service can be requested *except by virtue of law.* Literary ownership lasts *for the term granted by law* (Section 17).

Section 18 of the Constitution declares that *the domicile may not be violated, nor written correspondence and private papers,* but trusts that a law shall determine *in which cases and for what reasons their search and occupation shall be allowed.*

No action is obligatory if *the law does not demand it,* says Section 19.

The *navigation of inland rivers* is declared free under Section 26, and *subject only to the regulations* issued by the national authority.

This reserved and conditional way of proclaiming economic liberty leaves the two models standing: the new and the old; freedom and slavery: liberty in the *Constitution,* oppression in the *law*; liberty in the *written word,* slavery in *practice,* if the law is not adapted to the Constitution.

Under the absolute monarchs of Spain, all those *liberties and guarantees,* subject to laws that they enacted according to their interests, did not cease to exist. The *person,* the *liberty,* the *property* shine like sacred rights in the words of more than one old Spanish code that is still in force among us. What problem could this cause to political absolutism since liberty was granted only as limited by the law or the will of the sovereign? Thus was the name of *freedom of trade* given to the authorization granted in the mid-eighteenth century, to many ports of Spain to trade with many ports of the Americas, always excluding foreigners from enjoying this privileged freedom. This franchise was a *liberty,* compared with the regime that had preceded it. Spain, not content with excluding all nations from trade with Spanish America, excluded even its own ports, permitting only Seville to dispatch goods to the West Indies. This *single port* system lasted two centuries—from 1573 to 1765—until the establishment of the system that was called *liberty,* because the chains had been loosened within the prison.

To grant liberty in accordance with the law is to leave liberty to the discretion of the legislator, who has the power to restrict it or extend it. Blessed with good intentions, this regime may suit the exercise of political liberty; but with neither good nor bad intentions can it ever suit the exercise of *economic liberty,* always harmless to order, and summoned, as I have said elsewhere, to nourish and educate the other liberties.

I do not share the inexperienced and at times hypocritical fanaticism that requests lavish political liberties for people who know how to use them only to create their own tyrants. But I desire for our people un-limited and abundant *civil liberties,* which include the *economic liberties to buy, sell, work, navigate, trade, transit,* and practice all *industry.* These liberties, shared by citizens and foreigners (under Sections 14 and 20 of the Constitution), are summoned to populate, enrich, and civilize these countries, not political liberties, an instrument of concern and ambition in our hands, and never desired or useful to the foreigner, who comes to us in search of welfare, family, dignity, and peace. It is heartening that the most fecund liberties should be the most practicable, above all as they are accessible to the foreigner who comes to Argentina already educated in their exercise.

Through this method of being free with permission from the law, the constitutional law of formerly Spanish America has led, in economics above all, to thousands of laws and ordinances akin to the well-known Figaro's law, according to which the right to write, like the right to trade, was established in Madrid. Beaumarchais humorously said, "There has been established in Madrid a system of liberty that is extended even to the press, by virtue of which, provided nothing is written about the au-thorities, or religion, or politics, or morals, or government officials, or corporations, or the opera, or other public performances, or persons in reference to anything whatsoever, anything can be printed freely, under the inspection of three censors."[10]

Not in jest but very seriously did their colonial laws of *freedom of trade* write: "Provided that the *goods* are *Spanish* and not from elsewhere; that they leave a legally authorized *Spanish port* and go to a legally au-thorized American port; that they go in a specially *authorized vessel,* and under the charge of an *authorized person* for this passage, subject to infor-mation about blood, conduct, beliefs, etc., trade in the Americas is free, in accordance with the laws."

With the Americas now free, her constitutions have declared freedom of trade in accordance with the laws; but as her commercial and fiscal legislation has remained the same as before, the freedom of trade pro-

---

10. Alberdi takes the quotation from Beaumarchais' *The Marriage of Figaro,* act V, scene III, from the heading of the journal published by Mariano José de Larra (1809–1837), Spanish poet and journalist, who used the pen name Figaro. [E.N.]

claimed by the Republic has remained organized thus: "Provided that no vessel from abroad ceases to pay lighthouse dues, port duties, anchorage dues, quay dues (even if there is no quay); that they do not bring prohibited or monopolized goods; that these goods are unloaded according to legal procedures, and pay customs duties, storage, warehouse, or transit dues; that no man may open a brothel without paying for a license, under pain of closure or the confiscation of his constitutional liberty; that any inland dealer pay the right to use roads that are not roads; that all credit documents, to be authorized, be signed on stamped paper; that no trader enter or leave without a passport, no goods without a dispatch form, trade is free under the Constitution, in accordance with the laws."

While economic liberty is granted in this way in South America, it shall be only a false liberty or simply for show. As long as the constitutions rule *in accordance with the law,* and the law is the same as before the liberating revolution, it means that we shall be *free* as when we were slaves: free *in general* and slaves *in particular,* free according to *general principles,* slaves according to *exceptional laws;* free as a people, colonized as individuals.

It is important to bring *liberty,* that is, the *revolution,* or rather the *reform* to organic law, in which the government of the Spanish monarchs still remains. I repeat that I speak of *economic liberty;* and both for my country and for South America as a whole on this point. What is most important is always to keep in mind the danger of annulling each and every economic liberty of the Constitution for laws that regulate its exercise.

And as these liberties have the object and social role of populating, pacifying, enriching, and improving the material and moral condition of our scarce and backward people, it follows that any law that repeals those liberties, in full or in part, is an attack on the real and genuine prosperity of the Republic, on its wealth, its welfare; that is, on the high-minded and generous intentions of the Constitution stated in its preamble.

3

Part 1 of the Constitution of the Argentine Nation (1853–1860–1866)

Sanctioned by the Constituent General Congress in May 1853, reformed by the National Convention "ad hoc" September 25, 1860, and with the Reforms of the Conventions of 1866 and 1898.

PREAMBLE

We, the representatives of the people of the Argentine nation, gathered in General Constituent Assembly by the will and election of the provinces that compose it, in fulfillment of preexisting pacts, in order to form a national union, guarantee justice, secure domestic peace, provide for the common defense, promote the general welfare, and secure the blessings of liberty to ourselves, to our posterity, and to all men of the world who wish to dwell on Argentine soil: invoking the protection of God, source of all reason and justice: do ordain, decree, and establish this Constitution for the Argentine nation.

PART 1

CHAPTER 1. DECLARATIONS, RIGHTS, AND GUARANTEES

Section 1: The Argentine nation adopts the federal republican representative form of government, as this Constitution establishes.

Section 2: The federal government supports the Roman Catholic Apostolic religion.

Section 3: The authorities in charge of the federal government shall reside in the city to be declared capital of the Republic by a special law of

Original title: Constitución de la nación Argentina: Primera parte. Source: International Constitutional Law Web site.

Congress, once settled the cession of the territory to be federalized by one or more provincial legislatures.

Section 4: The federal government provides for the expenditures of the nation with the funds of the national treasury, composed of the proceeds of export and import duties, the sale or lease of lands owned by the nation, the revenues of the posts, other taxes equitably and proportionally levied on the population by the national Congress, and of whatever loans and credit transactions Congress may order in case of national emergencies or for enterprises of national interest.

Section 5: Each province shall enact its own constitution under the republican, representative system, in accordance with the principles, declarations, and guarantees of the national Constitution, ensuring its administration of justice, municipal regime, and elementary education. Under these conditions, the federal government shall guarantee each province the full exercise of its institutions.

Section 6: The federal government may intervene in the territory of the provinces in order to guarantee the republican form of government or to repel foreign invasions; and at the request of their constituted authorities, it may intervene to support or reestablish them, should they have been deposed by sedition or invasion from another province.

Section 7: The public acts and judicial proceedings of one province are worthy of full faith in the others; and Congress may, by general laws, prescribe the manner in which such acts and proceedings shall be proved and the legal effects thereof.

Section 8: The citizens of each province shall be entitled to all rights, privileges, and immunities inherent in the condition of citizen in the other provinces. The extradition of criminals is a reciprocal obligation among all the provinces.

Section 9: Throughout the territory of the nation there shall be no other customs than the national ones, in which the tariffs enacted by Congress shall be in force.

Section 10: The circulation of goods of national production or manufacture is free from duties throughout the Republic, as well as the circulation of articles and merchandise of all kinds cleared in the national customs.

Section 11: Goods of national or foreign production or manufacture, as well as livestock of all kinds, that may pass through the territory of one province to another, shall be free from so-called transit duties, the same as the carriages, vessels, or beasts in or on which they are transported; and no other duty, whatever its name may be, shall be imposed on them by reason of their passing through the territory.

Section 12: Vessels sailing from one province to another shall not be bound to enter, anchor, or pay transit duties; and no preference shall be granted in any case to any port over another, by means of trading laws or regulations.

Section 13: New provinces may be admitted into the nation; but a new province shall neither be established within the territory of another province or provinces, nor be formed from several, without the consent of the legislatures of the provinces concerned as well as that of Congress.

Section 14: All the inhabitants of the nation are entitled to the following rights, in accordance with the laws that regulate their exercise, namely: to work and perform any lawful industry; to navigate and trade; to petition the authorities; to enter, remain in, travel through, and leave the Argentine territory; to publish their ideas through the press without previous censorship; to make use and dispose of their property; to associate for useful purposes; to profess freely their religion; to teach and to learn.

Section 15: In the Argentine nation there are no slaves: the few who still exist shall become free as from the swearing of this Constitution; and a special law shall regulate whatever compensation this declaration may give rise to. Any contract for the purchase and sale of persons is a crime for which the parties shall be liable, as well as the notary or officer authorizing it. And slaves who by any means enter the nation shall be free by the mere fact of entering the territory of the Republic.

Section 16: The Argentine nation admits neither blood nor birth prerogatives: there are neither personal privileges nor titles of nobility. All its inhabitants are equal before the law, and admissible to employment without any other requirement than their ability. Equality is the basis of taxation and public burdens.

Section 17: Property may not be violated, and no inhabitant of the nation can be deprived of it except by virtue of a sentence based on law. Expropriation for reasons of public interest must be authorized by law and previously compensated. Only Congress levies the taxes mentioned in Section 4. No personal service can be requested except by virtue of a law or sentence based on law. Every author or inventor is the exclusive owner of his work, invention, or discovery for the term granted by law. The confiscation of property is hereby abolished forever from the Argentine Criminal Code. No armed body may make requisitions or demand assistance of any kind.

Section 18: No inhabitant of the nation may be punished without previous trial based on a law enacted before the act that gives rise to the process, or tried by special committees, or removed from the judges appointed by law before the act for which he is tried. Nobody may be compelled to testify against himself, or be arrested except by virtue of a written warrant issued by a competent authority. The defense by trial of persons and rights may not be violated. The domicile may not be violated, as well as the written correspondence and private papers; and a law shall determine in which cases and for what reasons their search and occupation shall be allowed. Death penalty for political causes, any kind of tortures and whipping, are forever abolished. The prisons of the nation shall be healthy and clean, for the security and not for the punishment of the prisoners confined therein; and any measure taken with the pretext of precaution that may lead to mortify them beyond the demands of security, shall render liable the judge who authorizes it.

Section 19: The private actions of men that in no way offend public order or morality, or injure a third party, are reserved only to God and are exempted from the authority of judges. No inhabitant of the nation shall be obliged to perform what the law does not demand or deprived of what it does not prohibit.

Section 20: Foreigners enjoy within the territory of the nation all the civil rights of citizens; they may exercise their industry, trade, and profession; own real property, buy and sell it; navigate the rivers and coasts;

practice freely their religion; make wills and marry under the laws. They are not obliged to accept citizenship or to pay extraordinary compulsory taxes. They may obtain naturalization papers residing two uninterrupted years in the nation; but the authorities may shorten this term in favor of those so requesting it, alleging and proving services rendered to the Republic.

Section 21: Every Argentine citizen is obliged to bear arms in defense of the fatherland and of this Constitution, in accordance with the laws issued by Congress and the decrees of the national executive power to this effect. Citizens by naturalization are free to render or not this service for a period of ten years as from the date they obtain naturalization papers.

Section 22: The people neither deliberate nor govern except through their representatives and authorities established by this Constitution. Any armed force or meeting of persons assuming the rights of the people and petitioning in their name commits the crime of sedition.

Section 23: In the event of domestic disorder or foreign attack endangering the full enforcement of this Constitution and of the authorities hereby established, the province or territory that is in a turmoil shall be declared in state of siege and the constitutional guarantees shall be suspended therein. But during such a suspension the president of the Republic shall not pronounce judgment or apply penalties on his own. In such case, his power shall be limited, with respect to persons, to their arrest or transfer from one place of the nation to another, should they not prefer to leave Argentine territory.

Section 24: Congress shall promote the reform of the present legislation in all its branches, and the establishment of trial by jury.

Section 25: The federal government shall foster European immigration; and may not restrict, limit, or burden with any tax whatsoever the entry into Argentine territory of foreigners who arrive for the purpose of tilling the soil, improving industries, and introducing and teaching arts and sciences.

Section 26: Navigation of the inland rivers of the Nation is free for all flags, subject only to the regulations issued by the national authority.

Section 27: The federal government is under the obligation to strengthen its relationships of peace and trade with foreign powers, by means of treaties in accordance with the principles of public law laid down by this Constitution.

Section 28: The principles, guarantees, and rights recognized in the preceding sections shall not be modified by the laws that regulate their enforcement.

Section 29: Congress may not vest on the national executive power — nor may the provincial legislatures vest on the provincial governors — extraordinary powers or the total public authority; it may not grant acts of submission or supremacy whereby the life, honor, or wealth of the Argentine people will be at the mercy of governments or any person whatsoever. Acts of this nature shall be utterly void, and shall render those who formulate them, consent to them, or sign them liable to be condemned as infamous traitors to their fatherland.

Section 30: The Constitution may be totally or partially amended. The necessity of reform must be declared by Congress with the vote of at least two-thirds of the members; but it shall not be carried out except by an assembly summoned to that effect.

Section 31: This Constitution, the laws of the nation enacted by Congress in pursuance thereof, and treaties with foreign powers are the supreme law of the nation; and the authorities of each province are bound thereby, notwithstanding any provision to the contrary included in the provincial laws or constitutions, except for the province of Buenos Aires, the treaties ratified after the Pact of November 11, 1859.

Section 32: The federal Congress shall not enact laws restricting the freedom of printing or establishing federal jurisdiction over it.

Section 33: The declarations, rights, and guarantees that the Constitution enumerates shall not be construed as a denial of other rights and guarantees not enumerated, but rising from the principle of sovereignty of the people and from the republican form of government.

Section 34: The judges of the federal courts cannot at the same time hold an office in the provincial courts. The federal service, whether civil or military, shall not grant a right of residence in the province in which it is performed unless it is where the employee habitually resides, this provision being understood as pertaining to the right to choose employments in the province in which he accidentally happens to be.

Section 35: The denominations successively adopted from 1810 up to the present, namely: "United Provinces of the River Plate," "Argentine Republic," "Argentine Confederation," shall henceforth be official names to be indistinctly used for the designation of the government and territory of the provinces, the words "Argentine Nation" being used in the making and enactment of laws.

3 Liberalism in a New Nation (1857–1879)

1

BARTOLOMÉ MITRE
Protection of Agriculture (1857)

We need not state that we are not protectionists. Everyone knows that there are no more ardent defenders of the freedom of trade than ourselves, whether in government, in the press, or in public speech, and that many of the economic laws under which we live, based on the most liberal principles, bear the mark of our ideas, starting with the customs law and finishing with the maritime pilots law.

If, when the customs law was first discussed after the victory at Caseros, protective agricultural duties had not existed, we would certainly have opposed their passing into law. But those duties existed, and, under their shelter, agriculture had developed and interests had been created, whose future depended on the continuation of that system, and entire regions such as Chivilcoy and other country districts had become agricultural areas thanks to the protection of the law. It was therefore neither fair nor fitting to destroy interests created under the guarantee of the law, dashing the hopes of cereal producers, worthy of consideration though the consumers' rights may have been, and however true the economic doctrine was to which those interests were sacrificed.

Thus, as radical reformists in economic matters, we yielded the logic of principles when faced with a matter worthy of consideration, and in this respect we were conservatives.

Today the daily *El Orden*, whose economic doctrines have almost always been in agreement with ours, requests that the matter of agricultural protection should bow to the logic of principles, and that the protective duties that add a surcharge on foreign flour to benefit wheat from Chivilcoy and other agricultural districts in our countryside be deleted from the customs law.

We said because of this that the idea of *El Orden* could be formulated in this way: *May Chivilcoy and the agriculture of Buenos Aires perish, rather*

Original title: "Protección a la agricultura." Source: *Los Debates*, July 6 and 7, 1857.

than the principle, a paraphrase of the renowned expression *let the colonies perish, rather than the principle.*

El Orden does not accept this formula and replaces it with another: "Save the principle so that Chivilcoy and the agriculture of Buenos Aires should prosper more than today, without the people who are consumers ever being exposed to suffering the effects of scarcity and monopoly."

Having accepted this new formula, let us reflect on it.

The first question to arise is, of course, this: If the protective duties of the customs law are abolished, will the agriculture of Buenos Aires succumb or not?

We believe that it will.

El Orden also believes this.

It says that "the government owes agriculture the protection it is in need of, meaning roads, bridges, navigable rivers, that is, facilitating transport and lowering freight costs, and also providing labor, lowering the average salary by means of foreign immigrants, and not disturbing the laborer in his peaceful work."

This amounts to recognizing that our agriculture needs protection in order to exist.

Working on the basis of this principle, we argue that while bridges and roads are not built, while the rivers are not navigable, nor freight cheaper, while willing hands are lacking and wages are not lowered, agriculture in Buenos Aires will perish if the protective duties of the customs law are repealed.

Today, despite protective duties, harvests are being burned in Chivilcoy as a consequence of the high price of freight, a high price whose origins lie mainly in the lack of good roads.

Everyone knows how difficult it is to resolve the roads problem in Buenos Aires, and that on only three roads adjacent to the city, altogether measuring less than six leagues, half a million pesos are spent every year, and in winter they cannot even be traveled by horse.

In what way, then, would protection of any other kind be effective, when it is materially impossible for it to yield results for many years?

Were the protective duties that today shore up the agricultural industry to be abolished, it would not survive before a road could be built from Buenos Aires to the town of Mercedes, and we would have sacrificed valuable interests, created under the guarantee of a law, and representing immense capital in the form of land, population, seed, farming implements, grinding mills, and bakeries, that greatly exceed the amount bread consumers pay for at the end of the year.

Let those bridges and roads be built, lower the cost of freight by means of another type of protection, and we will agree to the protective duties of the customs law being repealed, but until this be done, let us preserve the market for our cereals, unless we seek to immolate the interests of a hugely important industry on the logic of a principle.

It would be an illusion to believe that another type of protection for agriculture, consisting in lowering freight costs by opening decent roads, would not also be paid for by the consumer, nor can it be believed that it would cost less than at present.

The monies with which the roads must be built come from the taxpayer, and it is the taxpayer who ultimately pays for everything, either when buying bread or paying taxes.

Furthermore, it is a proven fact that all taxes balance out in the end, and that it is not right to say that one social class or another is more highly taxed than another, whether the tax is directed at the consumer or whether it targets the producer. If in consequence of the protective duties on cereals the consumer has to buy bread at a higher price, he will clearly charge for his labor according to his needs, and ultimately everyone will end up paying that surcharge, whether the tax be levied at customs when the foreign flour is introduced, or in the marketplace when our wheat is sold, or, alternatively, when a tax be levied to open a road from Buenos Aires to Chivilcoy.

As long as no direct protection be forthcoming from easier transport, what we want is for the current protective duties to remain in place so that Chivilcoy and the agriculture of Buenos Aires should not perish, the mills are not ruined, and the progress made in this direction does not become infertile.

The protection that we are calling for, furthermore, boils down to very little. Here is our formula: *That the duty levied on the entry of foreign flour be equal to the surcharges our cereals receive in transportation from the center of production to the market where they are sold.*

The day it costs as much to bring a bushel of wheat from Chivilcoy by land or water as it does today to bring a bushel of wheat from anywhere else in the world, when that day comes our cereals will be able to compete freely in the marketplace, quality shall determine preference, and protective duties can and must be abolished. But to obtain that result it is indispensable that this other protection of *bridges and roads* should come into effect. However, as long as this is not the case, one cannot reasonably call for the repeal of protective duties, which would be the ruin of the agricultural industry, as those who are calling for it acknowledge, declaring themselves against a protectionist system by substituting it for another one that they deem *necessary*. If protection is necessary in any form so that agriculture may survive, let us stick to the present form while the promises offered are not fulfilled.

But, it will be asked, is there a need for agriculture to survive? Why does agriculture deserve more protection than any other industry?

Yes, it is a necessity that agriculture should survive, and it deserves preferential protection because its existence and its prosperity are important for the state of Buenos Aires not only as an economic, but as also a great social matter.

Agriculture is a necessity in a country devoured by the desert, where to establish habits of order and discipline it is essential to settle the nomadic population that corrupts, barbarizes, and impoverishes societies.

Because agriculture civilizes populations.

Because it fixes populations and builds families.

Because it transforms the soil, multiplying the value of the land.

Because it reacts peacefully against disorder and tyranny.

Because it raises new population centers and mellows customs.

Because it helps to spread well-being throughout the industrious classes of the people and puts within their reach means of work that are proportionate to their means.

Because it divides up property and complements rural industry, which, left to its own devices, would lead us into barbarism.

This is why we do not want our agriculture to succumb, why we want Chivilcoy to prosper and be wealthy, and why we ask that, as long as freight costs are not adjusted, the current duties on foreign flour be kept.

It is not much to ask.

Aside from the protection accorded it by the customs law, agriculture is a deprived industry among us. Not only must it struggle with poor roads, lack of labor, high wages, and high transport costs, but it is also harried by large landowners and even by the law itself, which prevents them from acquiring land.

Land law is calculated to protect the landowner, and this protection costs the state more than is at present afforded to agriculture.

This is yet another reason not to abolish current duties on foreign flour.

May a land law be passed so that all farmers may acquire land to grow their grain.

May new roads be opened to bring down transport costs.

May wages be lowered.

Agriculture needs no further protection to prosper.

But as long as none of this is done, it is a duty, it is a need, it is in our interests to support the agricultural industry so that something other than the system currently followed be possible. We therefore disagree with *El Orden,* which requests the abolition of duties on foreign flour, which, in the current state of affairs, would be tantamount to a death sentence for agriculture.

2

BARTOLOMÉ MITRE
On Trade (1869)

The Argentine Republic, gentlemen, is the only South American nation that has not been populated because of the incentive of precious metals, the only one that does not owe its formation, development, and gradual prosperity to the magic of gold and silver locked up in its bosom, which has attracted European immigration to American shores ever since the discovery of the New World. Mexico with its rich mines, Peru with its mountains of gold, Chile with its silver, Brazil with its gold and precious stones, the pearls of the Antilles and Tierra Firme, the emeralds and opals of Central America, and more or less all the other regions whose names can be read on the map of this continent owed their growth and their origins to this type of riches, which we lacked. For a long time their wealth was measured by their heaps of gold, silver, and precious stones, which brought out our poverty all the more, while today those heaps of gems are the slag heaps of long-dead furnaces in comparison with the wealth that trade and industry have created and which gold can no longer measure alone.

We, the dispossessed of this golden rain, did not have even the rich output of the tropics which provided new settlers with such bountiful profits. Weed-covered plains, landlocked between sterile mountains, stoneless rivers, and chaotic terrains that hemmed them in, the colonization of the River Plate area is a phenomenon worthy of our attention, as it is the only colonization in South America since the times of its discovery that was born and grew asking the land only for its daily bread by means of productive work—the only one that was born and grew amid hunger and poverty, despite being christened with a name that only the

Original title: "Discurso al comercio de Buenos Aires [Speech to the Buenos Aires Chamber of Commerce] (February 21, 1869). Source: *Obras completas de Bartolomé Mitre* [Complete works of Bartolomé Mitre], vol. 16 (Buenos Aires: H. Congreso de la Nación Argentina, 1959).

future would justify. The name of the River Plate was a shining promise that trade has made a reality.

This poor colony, saved by labor after supplying the most primary needs in life, was condemned to vegetate in obscurity and poverty, and most likely perish, had trade not come to inject it with that spirit of immortal life that increases the hardiness of societies over the passing of time. But the development of trade was impossible due to the restrictive laws that were the basis of the colonial system of the mother country. Its ports closed, its fruits rotting, condemned to be supplied with European artifacts that had traveled by land across the length of southern America, our trade system was a violation of natural laws, a sorry waste of labor in which life was spent without increasing social capital. It was an order of things in which ultimately the colony should have succumbed in sterility.

Trade saved it from death, and injected it with new life, and—oddly enough—the hostilities aimed at the colony so as to wound the mother country were those that most directly contributed to reestablishing the balance of economic law, sending out output along roads traced by the hand of the Creator. The walls of Colonia del Sacramento, built as protection against smuggling, served as a shelter for trade. There it was fortified, there it unfurled its flag and endured the siege against monopoly, until at last the trade launched via its natural roads came to be a moral function for these countries, something that could not be suspended without compromising their very lives.

The smugglers of all the world, and the trade and military expeditions from England at the start of this century contributed to bring down the last barriers of monopoly, until the revolution came and gave universal trade its legal status.

Under the auspices of these noble origins, the sons of this land and all the traders here present, regardless of which country in the world they were born in, must recognize each other as the sons of the same fertile and generous mother. Whether they belong to the virile Anglo-Saxon race that has broadened the sphere of human activity, whether they come from the regions where the Phoenicians sailed, inspired by the spirit of trade, whether they be possessed of the mercantile spirit of those Italian republics of the Middle Ages, whether they descend from the industrious Flemish or build statues to a herring salter, whether they call themselves British, Belgian, French, Italian, Dutch, German, Spanish, or Portuguese, or are included under the common name of Americans, we must all recognize each other as brothers.

And we must recognize each other as brothers not only for our shared origin and for having all suckled at the same maternal bosom, but because we also all profess the same religion of duty under the auspices of the austere and holy law of mutual, shared labor.

Trade is a job and a fertile job that civilizes, enriches, and improves the human condition, participating with the dual nature of material power and moral greatness that makes it more worthy of admiration and respect. And this is why I said before that I would speak with my heart and with my convictions.

For this reason I bow to trade, not because of its innumerable merchant vessels that sail the seas of this globe, not for the value of its merchandise, nor for the power of its capital, nor for the multiplicity of its transactions, nor the real influence it bears on the physical and political order, but rather for its effective influence on human progress, its direct action on man viewed as a moral being, and above all the balance that it keeps and the harmonies that it brings between the physical and the moral worlds.

Trade is advocated by some and maligned by others.

It is advocated for its most visible and vulgar trait, namely its direct influence over production and wealth, and its immediate effects on the well-being of societies and individuals. But not all are equal to the higher law presiding over its development, and its latent, constant, and powerful action on our consciences.

It is stigmatized as a condemnation of selfishness by moral sectarians who believe themselves spiritualists because they speak in the name of a misunderstood generosity, while falling victim to the aberrations of the coarsest materialism. To them, the art of buying and selling goes against the law of charity, forgetting the severe words of the Apostle of the Gospel who made him who did no work unworthy of bread. And the beauteous ideal for them is a gratuitous life in the common enjoyment of riches acquired by others.

What causes the greatest astonishment and warrants the attention of us all is what we would call the mechanical potency of trade, which removes weights, counterbalances masses, directs forces, and operates complex machinery of production or credit. What most captivates the thinker's attention, meditating on the transcendental mechanisms of trade, is its elemental function, what might be called the generating principle of its whole mechanism, that is, the buying and selling of things. Trade is great and noble precisely because it is the art or science of buying and selling, because buying and selling is the logical and natural evolution for producing wealth, creating capital, increasing man's productive capacity, increasing simultaneously the intellectual and moral joys, rendering him answerable to the laws of creation and the ends for which the Creator intended him. If things were not bought and sold, man would lie in isolation and poverty, and in the most deplorable moral wretchedness. If objects did not have a value that could be bought or sold, the changes of the products of nature would be sterile to produce the phenomenon of capitalization, which is the purpose of trade.

Indeed, gentlemen, wealth can be created only by snatching it away from nature and putting it at the service of man, and at the same time enriching him. Capital can be created only by laboring over the elements of conquered wealth. And as wealth and capital can be acquired only through work and savings, one can preserve one and fertilize the other only through successive transformations wrought by changes. Without buying and selling, one would have nothing durable; everything created would be consumed and we would go back to being slaves to nudity and poverty, from which we were emancipated by labor. Above all it would paralyze the active and fertilizing action of circulating capital, which is the great lever governing trade, and which buying and selling drive, perpetuating and enlarging the rich inheritance passed down from generation to generation, incorporating the labor and sweat of those who have preceded us in our task, passed on not as a gratuitous gift, but on the condition of persevering in such fatigue.

Only those who falter at the manly task of life, only those who have neither the energy nor the capacity to produce, only those who expect from the efforts of others what they cannot attain by themselves, are those who preach the cowardly and shameful theory of gratuitous enjoyment not achieved from the sweat of their brows.

It would truly be a calamity and the ruin of humankind if things were not bought and sold, and everything were given away for nothing. We would all have a daily banquet as splendid as this one; the rich wines would flow from the cups and mankind decked out in a flowery crown would deliver itself unto the delights of a feast as brilliant as it were fleeting. What would happen next? As wealth and capital are the result of work accumulated by many generations, the day they became gratis we would start to consume created capital without replacing it with new work and new creation, without accumulating savings, until all the created and accumulated capital were consumed, the fountain of life drunk dry, movement paralyzed and man transformed back into that sort of beast in a primitive state that was civilized by the division of labor, that slave of brute nature redeemed by accumulated capital, that vegetative being with no moral or material value who, thanks to the gifts he owes to uninterrupted labor, now dominates creation and governs himself only because he buys and sells, that is, because he has an intrinsic value and because he gives value to things, and with them he creates and feeds social capital, which is the principle of life in the economy of the human species, just as circulating capital is its blood.

We, the legitimate sons of labor, can, with a calm hand and serene conscience, break the daily bread in the banquet of life, imbued with the knowledge that we are doing good and that we profess a healthy and moral doctrine worthy of strong souls, when we raise cooperative work above idleness, and when we advocate the greatest value that sweat and human intelligence incorporate into the objects that it creates and the work that it presides over, whatever its nature may be.

It can be said that morally we who are represented at this table are two great guests: trade and politics. On the one hand, the workers from a given period in politics according to the law of democratic renewal, that is, the rulers, administrators, and legislators, those chosen by the people to preside over the work of a period, and, on the same level as them, the soldiers who have fought in the front line with the sword in favor of our principles. On the other hand, the day workers, those who in working for themselves work for everyone, increasing public wealth, the traders who come to greet us at the end of our tiring day of work and toast us with the feasting cup, merging in a single sentiment, thus setting workers from the bureau and workers from the office on an equal footing with workers on the battlefield.

We have all been workers at the service of the good cause, and in the contemporary struggles in which we have all acted, not only has the efficient action of the government made itself felt on the same level as the powerful action of capital, but also the irresistible and beneficent action of the principles professed by some and proclaimed by others, and practiced by all in the name and in the interest of freedom and justice.

In the war with Paraguay[1] which is now over, or can be considered over, not only has the Argentine Republic triumphed in its political capacity as a nation, not only has the triple alliance triumphed in the vindication of its rights, but so too have the great principles of free exchange, which are the principles that give life to trade. For trade too, the threatening fortresses have been pulled down. For trade, the chains obstructing the River Paraguay have also been broken. For and because of trade, the free navigation of the upper rivers has been won, freedom of trade and the defeat of monopoly and the exploitation of peoples by their tyrants. For trade too, the present and future peace has been won in these regions, bringing greater guarantees to the development of labor, which today can enjoy the time and space to exercise its influence.

In all places, work represented by trade must defeat resistance and must fight valiantly among combatants in the front line. But among us this occurs more frequently, for we are still in a period of experiment and development. Therefore, as well as the olive crown symbolizing its peaceful triumphs, it also has its laurel wreath for its triumphs, which in its name, in its interests, and through its more or less direct action has been achieved by others with the arms of civilization at the expense of fatigue, danger, and blood generously spilled.

When our warriors return from their long and glorious campaign to the deserved ovation from the people, trade will see inscribed on their victorious banners the great principles that the apostles of free exchange have proclaimed for the greater glory and greater happiness of men, for those principles have triumphed too.

And so I raise my glass to the moral and material greatness of trade, to its fertile and peaceful triumphs, to the conquests made by the arms of civilization in its interest and in its name, and, as the representative of its principles, to the outstanding trade of Buenos Aires in particular and of Argentina in general, worthy of the dual crown that, each day, becomes green again, watered by the fertilizing sweat of the workers.

---

1. In the War of the Triple Alliance or War of Paraguay (1864–1870), Brazil, Argentina, and Uruguay were allies against Paraguay. [E.N.]

3

BARTOLOMÉ MITRE
Chivilcoy Speech (1868) (Excerpt)

Delivered at the banquet offered to him by the people of Chivilcoy on the occasion of finishing his term as constitutional president.

October 25, 1868

... Let us turn to another example, not so far from home.

The occupation of territory and the ownership of land are two great conquests that civilization has achieved among us. What methodical plan preceded this occupation? What preconceived idea led to property? By what means did one bring about the other? The need for expansion and the survival instinct of social needs are what led to this conquest, with the assistance of the cattle and horses that occupied the desert and populated it as God helped them. They had no railroads to travel by steam, they had no population to settle the desert with their dwellings, and so they pushed on with the useful animals that accompany man, increasing his well-being and his wealth. This was how they saved the frontiers drawn out by the military sword of the conquest, this was how they pushed the Indian back, this was how they valiantly marched in search of the promised land and preceding the military expeditions that came to steal their glory as conquerors of the desert, they drew the new borders that the law had to confirm as the limits of Christian property. This was pastoral civilization, marching on four legs, if you will, but it was civilization as only we could extend it, marking the boundary of the property with men, putting cattle amid them, and having the cattle represent wealth and well-being, thus multiplying production and consumption. If we had not so proceeded, we would today be reduced to a

Original title: "Discurso de Chivilcoy." Source: *Obras completas de Bartolomé Mitre* [Complete works of Bartolomé Mitre], vol. 16 (Buenos Aires: H. Congreso de la Nación Argentina, 1959).

tenth of the populated territory, and the savage Indian who not so long ago came to set fire to the huts of Chivilcoy would dominate the territory of Buenos Aires from Pergamino to Chascomús, leaving behind him the Salado River.

Such is the result to which some of our learned men unthinkingly aspire, calling this rudimentary civilization barbarian. But incomplete though it may be and for all the problems it may have, it is ultimately what has produced the greatest and best results to date, given the conditions in which we have been living.

To implement the beautiful ideal of those who speak ill of stock breeding and preach crop farming above all else, it would be necessary to limit ourselves to a narrow strip of land, confine ourselves to the banks of the rivers, resettle the populations, and live as slaves to the land, waiting for whatever it produced. And as there would only be room for men, we would have to kill our fifty million sheep, our ten million cattle, and dismount our horses, releasing them into the desert to be seized by the Indians, thus giving them new weapons against civilization, that is to say that this beautiful ideal consists of diminishing the populated territory, expanding the desert, disarming ourselves, and reducing the wealth and, consequently, the productive, military, and consumer strengths of the Argentine man.

It is a disastrous mistake that, disseminated by some and heard by people such as ours who have the humility to believe in the words of their oracles, may lead us into ruin and misery if we do not react with perseverance against it, popularizing this truth now demonstrated by experience: that stock breeding is the basis of our wealth and that the growing of crops can progress only if done hand-in-hand with this. Twenty years ago the United States had fewer than six million head of cattle, while England had ninety million and France eighty million, yet today it is one of the major world powers in cattle, and when this is twinned with crop production, it leads to the creation of a new North American world in the Far West. Without the production of wool and leather we would be the most wretched country in the world, even if we had an area sown with cereals four times the size of the land taken up by farming today.

This vast expanse of thinly populated land, having at its service such a considerable and cheap means of production, is what today constitutes our superiority over the others of the globe. It is what makes us one of the most productive and high-consuming peoples in the world. European science cannot account for this phenomenon, and our plagiarists, who accept the theories that rest on differing and contrary facts with closed eyes, know only how to sing hymns to crop farming, calling for cattle to be slaughtered as enemies of civilization. However, it is to them, it is to the occupation that, with them, we have made of our soil to which we owe the fact that the province of Buenos Aires with 400,000 thousand inhabitants should produce almost as much and consume more than the Republic of Chile, with 1,600,000 inhabitants, for all that Chile is essentially a crop-farming country and has such rich silver mines.

When a handful of men occupy, maintain, and defend such a vast expanse of land in the name of property, fighting against time and space, when they make the soil produce more riches than millions of men with land favorable to agriculture, when they consume more than them, spending their wealth accumulated through their work and capitalization, I say that this people may have a long way to go to resolve its economic and social troubles; but it deserves to call itself civilized and cannot be called barbarian because it struggles with more problems and possesses less wheat and has more cattle, more sheep, and more horses, and is therefore richer and happier following its instincts than obeying the conventional rules that time has left behind. [*Applause.*]

Property has asserted itself among us through the virility of poor peasants and capitalists who went out to populate the land beyond the frontier with their livestock, and where they remained until the Congress passed the first law on the matter in the year 19 and established it. And this deed was more powerful than later laws on emphyteusis, in which Rivadavia,[1] one of our great and genuine sages, also paid his tribute to human fallibility: for, where emphyteusis has retreated, defeated by the spear of the savage, property has been maintained by withstanding the blows of the barbarian.

Though livestock farming was fought against by those who believed themselves more knowledgeable than shepherds, it has triumphed and, fertilized by the introduction of sheep, that Rivadavia had the glory of

1. Bernardino Rivadavia (1780–1845), President of Argentina 1826–1827, passed a law of emphyteusis (see note 6 in the introduction). [E.N.]

promoting, and by the crop farming that is developing in its shadow, it today constitutes the heart of our wealth, and these facts prove that there are ignorant men who know more than economists, or those who claim to be such. [*Applause and laughter.*]

But let us turn to things closer at hand, let us speak of crop farming in Chivilcoy, and let us see the part that to each is due in the progress that has been made in this piece of land. Here we will see the folly of those so-called sages, we will see them get things right by getting things wrong, demonstrating that they knew less than the farmhands of the old farms of this district. [*Marked attention.*]

Who was the first man to sow the first grain of wheat in the fertile soil of this district? I could tell you who it was that now, after 350 years, planted the first cereal seed in the River Plate. But it is a secret I am keeping to bring to light at a better opportunity. [*Laughter.*] In the meantime I believe there is no one who could satisfy my curiosity.

I suppose that that obscure benefactor of Chivilcoy was some poor man from a remote province. [*Applause and laughter.*] From that humble germ grew forth this town, the railroad that brings it to life, and all the rest of the progress that does it such honor.

Blessed be that seed that enclosed so many good things in its bosom!

Blessed be the errors that it has led to, for without them Chivilcoy would vegetate over its wheat and burn the corn from its harvests to feed the flames!

When that event occurred, no sage had thought to provide the means for the people to enjoy their daily bread. So the countryside of Buenos Aires ate no bread. It was necessary for that poor, obscure provincial — I repeat he must have been so [*laughter*] — to drop that blessing from his rough hand, saying to the fellow men of my province, the Porteños who are so proud of their progress: "Brothers, for you too bread is kneaded in this world." [*Laughter.*] And only since then has bread been eaten in our countryside!

This in itself was undoubtedly a great leap forward, but this is not the most curious part of the tale. This chance or deliberate deed, this partial progress which at most would have given rise to a badly located agricultural district too far from its natural market, and which therefore could not afford its transport costs, this error in some ways led to another error of the sages, and thanks to it we have the joy of great feats being performed, obtaining results that are the opposite of what was intended. In this case we can say that God writes straight on crooked lines, and often uses humble means to humiliate the self-satisfaction of arrogance!

When wheat was seen to grow in greater abundance here than elsewhere, due to the simple fact that more was sown here, our agricultural scientists instead of attributing it to its only true cause, without taking the trouble to study the nature of the soil, believed in good faith that this land in Chivilcoy was different from all the others, that only here could cereals grow, and, on this arbitrary supposition, they based a whole system of land division and soil use, in which, as usual, good was derived from results that were the opposite of what was anticipated.

The emphyteuts, the usufructuaries of the land, started to sublease, charging for every one hundred meters what they were paying for every league, prohibiting the small farmers from building houses so they would not put down roots there. The poor man tilled, sweated, harvested, and paid up. But after a certain amount of time he stood firm on that land, asserted his title as holder, and disputed his rights with the obsolete emphyteut. Five hundred farmers from the district, holders of various portions of Chivilcoy land, came forward one day to petition the government for protection and preference in their possession, and the government broke the ties between them and the emphyteut and offered them the property that today is a fact. And so it was that those impoverished in spirit and money, serfs to the slaves of the land, were redeemed of their slavery to outdated laws, giving a powerful core and a foothold to those who desired the subdivision and sale of the land. Since then, Chivilcoy has belonged to the movement of new ideas and progress, and since then it has grown and prospered on the revitalizing wind of progress. But behold, in the presence of this agricultural progress the sages, obeying erroneous or incomplete ideas, combine new plans and by getting it wrong, get it right again, like he who unknowingly wrote prose, without suspecting that he who exercised his intelligence was none other than that neglected worker, who may then have been sleeping the sleep of eternity in his wheat fields, and governed them from the grave.

Given that Chivilcoy produces wheat on this land, they said to themselves, let us build a railroad from Buenos Aires to Chivilcoy, to give them an outlet and encourage crop farming. This was the innocent idea that led to the construction of the Western Railroad, and there must be very few who did not take part in it in their time. Today we can applaud the completion of the railroad, but we laugh at the idea that it was not even based on a study of agricultural statistics. If anyone had told you then that that railroad could, in one week, transport all the wheat and corn produced by Chivilcoy, your jaws would have dropped, and it is likely that it would not then have been built, for they believed in good faith that the railroads had been invented only for wheat. [*Laughter.*]

It must be twelve years since I was last in Chivilcoy. The town was already founded, and a new opinion was beginning to form in it. I was interested in learning about its production, and I learned to my surprise that Chivilcoy produced only half the wheat harvested in the province. At that time Buenos Aires consumed 360,000 bushels[2] a year, that is, about 1,000 a day. The 240,000 bushels that the country produced were not enough. The rest came from abroad, so Chivilcoy only contributed to domestic consumption with a little over 100,000 bushels, and this was the extent of its cereal production. I was very careful not to divulge this secret, lest it occur to them not to continue the railroad they had started. [*Applause.*]

Thanks to this error, the railroad today reaches Chivilcoy, and we must be grateful to that obscure provincial mentioned earlier, who with a grain of wheat produced this miracle, fooling the sages and benefiting his hardworking descendants. [*Applause.*]

The railroad arrived here, and the economists who had based their calculations on the transport of grains were left a little dumbfounded when the people of Chivilcoy gave them the news that they had changed their minds a little, and presented them with sheep and wool as well as corn and wheat, their astonishment growing when they came across a new product that they had not taken into account: they came across a town instead of a wheat field, and above all they came across men, who are worth more than wheat, and these men with exact ideas about their convenience, moved by a progressive spirit, who, without contradicting the laws of wealth, found a practical solution to a thorny economic problem, making good by the consortium of livestock with agriculture, a route that, theoretically, was foolishly created for the sole object of transporting a few bags of wheat. [*Loud applause.*]

2. We have translated the Spanish word *fanegas* as bushels, though it is not an exact equivalent (a bushel is about two-thirds of a *fanega*). [E.N.]

Far be it from me to advocate the vulgar, coarse idea of giving preference to instinct over reason, to material fact over scientific theory.

My aim has been solely to give each his due, reestablishing the balance I believed somewhat altered in terms of the appreciation of the intelligent forces of society. Every people possesses a given sum of intelligence, just as it possesses a given sum of circulating capital, and just as money is in everyone's hands, in greater or lesser quantities, intelligence is in all heads in the proportion and the conditions that God and upbringing have distributed it.

Intelligence is like water, it has a level. It is good that rulers should in some respects appreciate the governed and look down a little, be inspired by opinion, and understand what is happening in the modest regions where events occur that teach practical lessons to the wise and the powerful.

It is good that the rulers, remaining within the bounds laid out by the law and without ignoring the superiority of talent, virtue, and knowledge, and considering some as atoms and others as units of public reason, learn to weigh the knowledge of men and of ideas, just as they can tell a false coin from a good one.

It is good that we should all be aware for this reason that the hammer that multiplies the power of the hand, the needle, that elemental machine that in the beginning was a fish bone, the saw, the file, the screw, the tongs, the shovels, the plow, and even the art of smelting metal to build these outstanding arms that have provided man with new organs, are, like the first grain of wheat sown in Chivilcoy, anonymous inventions that the collective intelligence can take as its own.

It is one more reason for the people to be educated, so that all should aspire, if not to be great sages, at least to be educated men who cultivate their intelligence by expanding the sphere of their moral pleasures and preparing themselves to manage with greater benefit their material interests, because education is like capital never spent and always producing, that by making us richer makes us happier.

I can say this in Chivilcoy without it seeming preaching in the desert, here where there are six municipal schools with the seventh being built to complete the number of spiritual works of mercy. They started by feeding the hungry, and they finished by bringing blessings to the poor, who will be sure of the kingdom of heaven and also that of the Earth if they are nourished with the daily bread of education.

Thus we shall have free peoples and good governments, and here we see how we tread unthinkingly on the field of politics where so many more or less noble interests are stirred, and in whose tempestuous area must always be heard the tranquil voice of love for one's fellow man, of charity toward one's neighbor, so that it may fall like a balm on hearts sore with hatred and the wounds of contemporaneous struggles.

We already know how to fight and kill, we know how Cain and Abel fall bloodied in the field of slaughter, we know how peoples and men are destroyed, with fire and swords, we know how governments are undone, in struggles that had their reasons, in battles between good and evil, painful but necessary victories. It remains for us to learn the hardest part of practical politics, which is how the peoples are regenerated by civic virtue, by perseverance in their purpose, by the growth of education and wealth, how freedom is consolidated in order, how free governments are founded by giving to the people what belongs to the people, and to power what belongs to power, treating each other with reciprocal benevolence and righteous spirit. We already know all this, and we say, to put an end once and for all to the sages and the impoverished of spirit, what one thinker said: "Do not count on me to conspire for the demolition of the established powers, let us try to improve the existing government, legitimizing it for its advantages and glorifying it for the greatness of its works." [*Applause.*]

Let us build instead of destroying.

Let Chivilcoy be the popular platform from which these great practical truths that preserve and perfect societies are proclaimed.

Let this be the soil where the seed of truth falls and sprouts, and may the harvest be abundant.

Let this be a field of peaceful struggle and fertile labor, where combat is done with the arms of work and the sap of life circulates vigorously, improving conditions for all.

Let them come here, the politicians, the economists, the traders, the industrialists, the writers, and the immigrants who seek their well-being among us, to breathe a healthy atmosphere in the order of ideas and deeds, as healthy as the air we breathe, purified by these beautiful groves. [*Applause.*]

Honor and happiness for Chivilcoy!

I would be lying and making a coarse compliment if I said of Chivilcoy that it is great in the present. It is an alluring promise, it is well-prepared land, it is an outline for a great town, it is what is called a society—cultured, rich, and happy—and this must encourage it in its work. It carries in it the seeds of future greatness: it has a love for work, improved machinery, the outline of a magnificent city, a progressive spirit, a municipal spirit, the holy love of the shared fatherland, a thirst for public education, stock breeding, and crop farming in harmony, the union of its residents, and it has energetic and hardworking men inspired with the virile spirit of the robust laborers of human progress. May God be with them and with their people! Meanwhile, let us toast the future greatness of Chivilcoy! Its moral greatness in the present! [*Tripled and prolonged applause. Cheering.*]

4

BARTOLOMÉ MITRE
Governments as Business Managers (1869)

Governments are said to be poor business managers. If governments become merchants to wrestle with the public, and use the people's revenue to compete with private industry; if they divert government forces and resources into works that jeopardize the interests of the community, not only are governments being poor business managers, but they are usurping powers that are not theirs and openly violating their mandate. But there are a number of enterprises that must, out of necessity and public convenience, be located in the government, mainly those connected to taxes, road links, and major trade and shipping facilities, works that governments must perform and can carry out only by consulting the interests of all rather than the profit of a few. That is why I said before that works of the nature that concerns us should have been performed preferably by the public powers rather than private enterprise, and I shall demonstrate this.

Necessity has forced mandatory taxes to be levied on goods and persons, for states need revenues to live. There is no other way of explaining the reason for taxing production, capital, consumption, personal labor, and even the growth of private wealth. It is the supreme law, the daughter of supreme necessity.

What reason is there for erecting a building called a customhouse and, from everything that passes through it with four casks, taking one away for the government?

What reason is there for the state to filch from the consumer's plate and devour a fourth or fifth of his food?

Original title: "Gobiernos empresarios." Source: "Discurso tercero, cuestión puerto de Buenos Aires, pronunciado en el Senado Nacional el 14 de septiembre 1869" [Debate on the port of Buenos Aires at the national Senate, extract from third speech, session of September 14, 1869], in *Obras completas de Bartolomé Mitre* [Complete works of Bartolomé Mitre], vol. 16 (Buenos Aires: H. Congreso de la Nación Argentina, 1959).

What reason is there for taking one or two pesos from every tax-payer's pocket for every ten pesos he has in it?

It is necessity and nothing but necessity. True, it is as compensation, with the condition of returning that sum in the form of security and benefits for the taxpayers. True, the tax is nothing more than the association of small capital, which would be insignificant in isolation, but when brought together produces great results, multiplying their action and their effectiveness. But it would be better if the tax were more logical, if the state, like individuals, were to live on what it earned, seeing profits as the compensation for the real services it provided to society. This should be the economic ideal of free peoples and governments.

An economic poem, one might say! Yes, an economic poem written in numbers and commented on by one of the most sensible economists of our century: an economic poem that has nonetheless been partly accomplished by a people who have the intelligence of practical life, and which every day adds new songs in honor of the truth of such a system.

When Chevalier[1] the economist was in the United States, he had the opportunity to witness the prodigious spectacle of New York's development in terms of public works, and to see for himself its portentous results. What most seized his attention was the observation of the new spirit presiding over the new state's economic movement, giving its constitution an elasticity that, for both peoples and individuals, is the condition of a long and prosperous existence. He tells us in his celebrated *Letters on North America* that, while publicists in Europe argued over whether it was correct for a government to undertake works, their kings, who had not hesitated over their right to raise thousands of millions in taxes from the peoples to cover them in blood and devastate them, lent an attentive ear to the debate to persuade themselves whether it was lawful to enrich the people by means of creative works, as in New York. Meanwhile, the modest authorities of this "miniature empire," as he calls it, "undertook the *execution* of *public works* [these are his own words],[2]

1. Michel Chevalier (1806–1879), professor of political economy and a Saint-Simonian economist and supporter of free trade, was commissioned by the French government to visit the United States in 1833 to report on its transportation system. He published, like Tocqueville, an analysis of North America in a series of letters. He also negotiated with Richard Cobden in 1860 a free trade treaty between France and Great Britain. [E.N.]

2. Inserted by the author. [E.N.]

and has found its advantage in them; after having executed them, it has managed them itself on its own account, and found even greater advantages in this."[3] (See *Lettres sur l'Amérique,* et cetera, vol. 3, p. 212.)

When Governor Wit [*sic*] Clinton conceived the plan for the stupendous Erie Canal, which would join Lake Erie with the Hudson River, a distance of 146 leagues, the first men of the Union hatched the most sinister predictions about the results of such an enterprise. Jefferson wrote to Clinton that it would take a century to undertake such an enterprise. Madison wrote to him at the same time that it was madness to undertake a work in New York State that all the treasures of the Union could not pay for, only with its own resources. Unmoved, Governor Clinton threw himself into the enterprise and, sharing with his compatriots his noble confidence in the country's future, dug the first shovelful on the Erie Canal on July 4, 1817. Eight years later, in 1825, the canal was completed, and 146 leagues and a half of new navigable waters connected the Far West with the Atlantic, pouring new sap of life into the innards of society. At the end of that day, Governor Clinton dropped dead amid his triumph, and this unfortunate circumstance meant that he was not elected president of the Union, for his perseverance and works had placed him highly in the public esteem. . . .

Today the revenue from the canals accounts for a third of the product of general revenue. In 1861, the main revenue of the state reached 10.5 million, including 3,331,655 pesos (I even remember the small change) corresponding to the sum of schools that are used only in education, meaning that we already have two-thirds of revenues as the product of real services provided by the government. Would it be impossible for the other third of revenues to be defrayed by the greater product of the canals after the debt is paid, and the revenue applied to such an object? Apparently not.

When this happens the economic poem we had been concerned with will be fully concluded, and there will be a people in the world that has achieved the ideal of levying tax only for effective services, living hon-

3. The English translation is from Michel Chevalier, *Society, Manners and Politics in the United States: Being a Series of Letters on North America,* translated from the third Paris edition (Boston: Weeks, Jordan & Co., 1839), from the Online Library of Liberty, http://oll.libertyfund.org/index.php?option=com_staticxt&staticfile=show.php%3F title=2135&layout=html. [E.N.]

estly from its paid work, to repay social gains. Such a result will be due to the great works of public use made by governments, governments as business enterprises, that is!

But without paying attention to any of this, it is said that all nations and all governments have followed the opposite system, handing over works of this type to private interest, without any other reason than the fact. Another common error, in which even the very fact cited is false!

To dispel this error it is best to adopt certain points of view to reach the end that we propose.

Take the London docks, for example, built by the West Indies Company. This is the hobbyhorse of those who contend that governments should not build so much as a humble jetty, and that they should give all sorts of privileges to a handful of individuals, even when this is to tyrannize with them the vast majority of private individuals. I shall cite the minister in order to refute an authority that he cannot deny, as it is a book that he respects and from which he has learned much of what he knows: I am referring to Coquelin's *Dictionary of Political Economy*.[4]

In that work, it can be seen that when authorization was given to build those docks, the privilege conceded to them did not in any way clash with established uses, for at the time, under the name of legal docks, a large amount of the banks of the Thames enjoyed similar prerogatives, and those docks were exploited by the same customhouse. (See *Diccionario de Economía Política, v*ol. 1, p. 570.) . . .

The Liverpool docks, a further argument of the enemies of public powers as builders of public works, were made by the municipality, and this means that the public enjoys them in common after obtaining the benefit of building an artificial port on the Mersey.

England, for all that a federal system is not proclaimed there, is ruled by principles of administrative decentralization that expand the action of public powers, rendering more effective the action of the towns; and the general tendency is always to subdivide government without abdicating its prerogatives and duties to society. . . .

The great port of Genoa, which the minister reminded us of, is made at the expense of the province of Genoa, and is the responsibility of the

4. Charles Coquelin (1802–1852), French economist, editor together with Guillaumin of the *Dictionnaire de l'économie politique contenant l'exposition des principes de la science* (1852). [E.N.]

provincial municipality and the general government. The same is true of the port of Livorno.

The docks of Antwerp are made jointly by the municipality and the government, which receive the proportional duties from them.

And on the subject of Antwerp, I shall say that the same thing has happened in Belgium as in New York: its government has made itself an undertaker of public works and has exploited them by itself, and both it and the public have fared more than well. Thanks to the government's railroads, an economic miracle is taking place there: it costs less to tour Belgium by rail than it would to replace the soles of one's shoes if one were to travel the same route on foot.

5

JOSÉ HERNÁNDEZ
Governments as Business Managers (1869)

In the last sessions of the Senate, on the occasion of the debate on the matter of the port, which has not yet been resolved, General Mitre gave several speeches in support of the province's right to set itself up as the manager of said works.

"They are mistaken," said General Mitre, "those who contend that governments should not be business managers."

And as if this simple denial were sufficient, General Mitre believes himself to be exempt from entering into further explanations to demonstrate the foundation of his extraordinary claim.

I can understand why he does not stoop to provide evidence, because we know not on what basis he might have upheld such a patent denial of the most obvious principles of science and economic liberty.

Though we were and still are in diametrically opposed ranks, though we fought him like a fatal antagonist, it wounds us to see General Mitre descend from the heights where fortune has elevated him in order to make use of untenable sophisms and articulate words bereft of any meaning in politics, at the service of the most retrograde doctrines in the economic and social order.

Our people, who can be said to have grown up in the midst of revolutions and anarchy, are generally strangers to the principles of economic science, and have not managed to elucidate clearly and succinctly those problems that hinder their progress.

But, with their instinctive insight, they have understood for some time that the purely administrative mission of governments tends to be increasingly narrower and more simplified, while the people improve themselves in the practical schooling of democracy, regaining strength and exercising their rights.

Original title: "Gobiernos empresarios." Source: *El Río de la Plata,* September 17, 1869.

In the most advanced civilizations, which have borne the flag of liberty and progress furthest, which are conscious of their political mission, power is relegated to strictly limited functions.

Not many years ago, the Buenos Aires press, concerning itself with Paraguay and faced with the prospect of a possible impolitically provoked rupture, marked out the people of Paraguay as a strange and singular aberration amid the political progress of the continent, and marked out for satire and ridicule that dismal government that monopolized for itself the only important branch of trade in that country: *yerba mate.*

And, upon my soul, the press had more than enough reason, all the more so, because of the greater injustice and absurdity of the new arguments that today resolutely support the provincial government, derailed from the progressive and moral track along which it was progressing with such determination.

To try to turn governments into business managers is to set up a monstrous theory that amounts to the falsification of all the healthy principles on which economic and administrative science rests.

It amounts to the enthronement of privilege, monopoly, plundering, but no longer to benefit individuals, as we have seen thus far, but to benefit the government, responsible for guaranteeing all liberties and all franchises of our liberal institutions.

It amounts to turning against the country the laws that should guarantee it and, in a word, legalizing injustice and pillage.

On what basis, on what precept of law can a government stand and claim for itself the exercise of an individual right, when it thus exploits the most important branches of social activity?

Where might it find set down those powers alien to its mandate, to want to destroy the benefits of free competition in one fell swoop, extinguishing the spirit of enterprise and making the works of progress and future depend on the unstable movements of politics that absorb our governments' time?

The Constitution empowers them to promote the enterprises on which the province's moral and material progress depends, but that does not mean handing on a power that is alien to the nature and character of governmental functions.

To govern is not to trade, nor is it to speculate, and if we were to permit our governments to embrace the branches of commercial activity and launch themselves down the difficult paths of speculation, we would wholly pervert the origin and foundation of the government of the states, distracting their efforts from truly legitimate and constitutional objectives.

We cannot allow this demoralizing result, and it is necessary for us to raise our vigorous voices to prevent the results toward which our politicians are headed in their determination to hinder the political progress of those governments who oppose their aspirations.

El Río de la Plata was the first to argue in the press the theory that governments cannot and must not assume the role of business managers, and, since General Mitre's words in the Senate contradict this doctrine, we must see in them an allusion to our periodical, and we carry out the duty of replying to that allusion, feeling that Mr. Mitre has been concise in the expression of his ideas to the extent of not presenting us with a single argument in support of them.

We have devoted several articles to this important question and shall keep returning to it until it is finally resolved.

We trust in the erudition and sense of the majority of citizens in the Senate and hope that the ideas issuing forth are appreciated in their true importance, ultimately understanding that, rather than broadening the sphere of government, they should seek by legal means to reduce and simplify it.

In these general conditions we also address the patriotic and enlightened spirit of the representatives of the province of Buenos Aires, who must not seek the strength of the government in the absorption of individual faculties, but on the contrary, in the strengthening of individual and social action, which leads to the benefit of the state.

6

BARTOLOMÉ MITRE
Immigration (1870)

The government of which I was the head was of the belief that the best system of immigration was a spontaneous one, and it promoted that indirectly while laying the ground for the fertile seed of the population so imported to prosper in our country all the more. True to this fundamental idea, it rejected any proposal for development or bounties that did not tally with it, thus heralding the beginning of the sole true system accredited by science and experience, acting within its powers without the need to reduce to written law what used to be a law of society observed for its own sake, and without imposing serious hardships on the country, while spending a very small amount and distributing said amount fairly and indirectly among the mass of immigrants. This is how the great results that I predicted in the early days of my administration have been achieved and how they have become a reality that has exceeded expectations.

There are four great currents of immigration converging on the Río de la Plata from divers points of the globe: from Ireland, Italy, Spain, and France, nor is the English contingent missing, nor Germany or Switzerland unrepresented in the promotion of our population and industry. By studying the action of these human currents that obey natural forces, it will become clear that without their assistance we would be lagging far behind on the road to prosperity and that we owe more to this spontaneous force than to the cogitations of our sages or the intelligence and foresight of our legislators.

To this is due a further, even more singular phenomenon that proves there is no bounty to compare with the advantages offered by Argentina

Original title: "Discurso en el Senado de la Nación (septiembre de 1870)" [Speech at the national Senate (September 1870)]. Source: *Obras completas de Bartolomé Mitre* [Complete works of Bartolomé Mitre], vol. 16 (Buenos Aires: H. Congreso de la Nación Argentina, 1959).

to the man who trusts in us and in himself without the need for artificial stimuli. We have all seen immigrants arriving with no more capital to their names than their health and their bare arms, who on arrival became capitalists overnight, with their futures solidly secured. How was such a singular miracle worked in the world? Through the demand for these arms that is born of the increase in production and its values. Our newspapers have thus been full of advertisements for sharecroppers—partners, that is—to lure them with the gains of another man's capital; and the great landowners and sheep farmers have been seen going to the immigrants' shelters to track down a sturdy, willing man to make him an offer of land, a roof over his head, and food, and put him in charge of a flock of two thousand sheep, the produce from which was to be divided between the landowner and the immigrant, in most cases Irish.

The increased value of the land is also due to this immigration and the production fertilized by it: not too many years ago, in a fifty-league radius around Buenos Aires, the price of a square league was twenty thousand pesos. Today it is worth anything up to one million and a half, or two million, and it is generally Irish immigrants who are paying those prices, for, grown rich on sheep farming, bringing with them a passion for property and a desire to settle permanently in the country that welcomed them so warmly, they thus contribute to multiplying the social capital through the increase in the value of property. For, of the thirty thousand Englishmen and Irishmen in our midst, rare is the man who looks to the city; they all live in the countryside.

Let us turn now to the Italians.

Who are the people who have made the ten leagues of arable land encircling Buenos Aires fertile? To whom do we owe the green belts surrounding all our towns along the coast of our great rivers, and even those oases of wheat, maize, potatoes, and woodland that break up the monotony of the uncultivated Pampas? To the Italian planters from Lombardy and Piedmont, or even from Naples, who are the most able and hard-working farmers in Europe. Without them we would have no vegetables, and, finding ourselves among the globe's most backward peoples where horticulture is concerned, like Virgil's peasant, we would not even know what an onion looked like.

To whom do we owe the development of our coastal shipping fleet, and the ease and cheapness of river transport? Who are the sailors that man the thousand ships flying the Argentine flag on their masts, or even the crews of our warships? They are the Italian descendants of the ancient Ligurians, the fellow countrymen of the discoverer of the New World, expressly excluded by this scheme from the benefit offered to other races, who, whatever their qualities, have not contributed to our workforce the way the Genoese have done and still do.

Let us run over the benefits this immigration has brought: it has, to a considerable degree, multiplied the reproductive power of the species and considerably contributed to the growth of the population; it has raised the production that is the basis of our wealth from its dejection; it has improved agriculture; it has nourished shipping; it has lent greater value to landed property; it is the nerve of commerce as an agent of production and consumption; its deposits form the basis of our great credit establishments; it promotes immigration and spontaneous settlement of its own steam, without burdening the treasury. Yet this is not all it has done. It has also contributed to improving the cultivation of vineyards and the manufacture of wine in Mendoza, San Juan, and La Rioja, the cane crop and sugar production in Tucumán, the tanneries, the working of mines, and other industries in the divers provinces of the Republic, and, most especially, it has led us to occupy the first rank in South America and second in the world as a field of work open to the human race.

I am not suggesting we exclude the colonies formed by national groups or spontaneous affinities from our population program, provided that such associations are built on spontaneity and freedom. For, bearing within them those fertile seeds, they will be our brothers from the first day and their children will be our children in keeping with our law, which makes natural citizenship obligatory. The Welsh colony of which I spoke earlier, the English colony of Córdoba, the German colony of Baradero, the Swiss, North American, Italian, and French colonies of Santa Fe and Entre Ríos, built on that foundation, are models worthy of imitation, belonging as they do to the order of spontaneous settlements, in which the action of local government contributes only what is of common use for nationals and foreigners alike. This is what a good law of colonization that aims to conquer the desert for civilization must lean toward. But let us not make artificial immigration the basis of our future population, as is currently the plan, and, if we have the means, as they say, to spend two million on buying a hundred thousand settlers, let us use them unflinchingly to bring equal benefit to the mass of one hundred thousand immigrants that will soon be arriving on our shores every year following the natural law of emigration and spontaneous immigration.

We will then be able to inscribe on our flag of immigration the famous legend of the North American system, "Freedom and property," and the last effort will have been made and the last word spoken.

Meanwhile, the soil, the climate, the economic laws irresistibly contribute to their progress and development, together with the moral laws written by God in the human conscience making it free, endowing it with deliberate willpower, and tempering the soul with the virile forces that make for the greatness of nations and the happiness of individuals.

Artificial and morbid ideas that are out of tune with these laws, and sustained more by thoughtlessness than hatred of them, will be unable to contain their expansion; they are the stones amid the current that only serve to reveal the living force running through the inert masses, producing merely a spray swiftly dispersed.

7

NICOLÁS AVELLANEDA
On Laws Concerning Public Lands:
Conclusion (1865)

SUMMARY—NEW NATURE OF AGRARIAN
LEGISLATION—WORDS BY DR. PAZOS—
ECONOMIC POLICY MODEL

I

We have reached the end of our task; and there only remains, in conclusion, for us to briefly set out the consequences we have
established in the preceding pages by listing the provisions of our laws,
reviewing them critically, or expounding the most proven doctrines and
the examples worthy of imitation. Leasing weakens the powers of man
and sterilizes the productive power of the soil. And it is therefore necessary to proscribe it from our public land laws, in the interests of its
cultivation, of free institutions, and of the population, which can put
down no roots because only property produces "that love of the land
that passes on to the object owned some part of the thought and soul
of the owner."[1] Argentine agrarian law, whether provincial or national,
cannot sensibly employ another model for the placement of public land
than that of property by sale.

But having adopted this starting point, the organization of the system will render it sterile unless all its provisions are subordinated to
the prime intention of making the acquisition of property easier and
quicker, while at the same time giving it complete security after it has
been constituted. That lofty and beneficial purpose must preside over
the formation of future laws and the reform of existing laws, being the
criterion and the guide, the basis of judgment, and the outcome sought.

Original title: "Estudio sobre las leyes de tierras públicas: Conclusión." Source:
Nicolás Avellaneda, *Estudio sobre las leyes de tierras públicas* [Study about laws on public
lands], 2d ed. (Buenos Aires: La facultad, de J. Roldán, 1915).

1. Vacherot, *La démocratie,* p. 211. [A.N.] Étienne Vacherot (1809–1897) was a French
philosopher and politician. The quotation, from *La démocratie* (1860), is on p. 208. [E.N.]

No property is secure when it is exposed to involvement in litigation. It is essential, therefore, that a general and methodical measurement should always precede a sale so that the location of the deeds, their paths, and their bounds never raise any questions.

Property is not rapidly acquired when one has to go through slow or expensive procedures to obtain it. The procedural steps established by our laws must therefore be simple, not burdensome, modeled where possible on the norm of U.S. laws, which have in this point achieved truly admirable simplicity.

Any high price is a hindrance to selling. Therefore, if one sincerely wishes to establish private property on empty lands and make it more accessible for all hard-working men, native or foreign, the high prices imposed on public land will find no place in the new laws. It is also advisable that the price, when it has been fixed, should be maintained without change for long periods in order to encourage the worker, who would be disconcerted in his plans to settle and build a future by an unexpected hike. The stability of land prices shows the persistence of a superior thinking in the laws that govern us, equally showing that it is not sacrificed to conventions as ephemeral as they are fallacious.[2]

How can property be considered secure when the laws that have created it and which should only seek to consolidate it, instead harass, restrict, or annul it? Such laws constitute the opprobrium of a nation. Constitutional jurisprudence declares them null and void; good faith calls them laws of betrayal, for they violate sacred commitments; and their results mark them as an agent of ruination for they have never led anywhere but to commotion and disaster. Is it still necessary to say that it is impossible to imagine that their sinister shadow will come to darken the pages of our legislation?

II

These ideas carry with them the power of propagation derived from the experience that has proven them everywhere, and the heartfelt need that demands their realization. And, driven by the progress of public reason,

---

2. We will discuss the theory of *high* and *low* prices further in the *Appendix,* considering it in relation to fiscal interests. We will also include there some ideas on *payments,* as we have deliberately omitted for this reason to set out the conditions of the sales system. [A.N.]

they will soon come to inspire a new spirit in our laws, making them architects of prosperity, population, and wealth. Then, and under their beneficent inspiration, our agrarian legislation will break loose from the incoherence surrounding it today, and adopting their character it will also have found its final path. A fiscal interest possessed by the greed of the moment, which, like all transitory interests, is variable and without scope, will never bring consistency to its resolutions, or nobility to its purpose. It is a guide blinded by greed, and worse than blind, it is capricious.

Landed property, easily obtained and cheap, must be the emblem of future laws so as to defeat the desert in its name and with its labor, and transform the barbarian face of our countryside. We need to step into the stream of ideas and deeds that govern the world. Immigration will not rush here, however much we invite it with our sterile promises, if, in looking into the causes that determine it, we do not open up the course along which it might flow. For immigration is not an adventurous evolution born from fantasy or whim, but rather a reflexive movement that obeys the rules governing all other human acts. Among these rules, observation has designated the first as the easy securing of landed property, which offers its share in the world's dominion to all the dispossessed of Europe. With property comes the home that ennobles man, and which brings the family together. And the feeling of the home established in a town, no matter how new, is the invincible force that stamps a secular vigor on it, giving it, like the United States, the power to overcome one of the greatest catastrophes witnessed in centuries, and which would have eroded the foundations of the strongest nations of the Old World.

III

To write these pages we have had to spend long hours going over our old Congressional Records: an arduous task, as it is impossible to resist an impression of sadness that slowly invades the spirit when we note the deathly silence that, after so few years, has fallen now on those debates, so lively and ardent, and whose actors thought were destined to leave their fiery mark on the memory. How many forgotten things so worthy of eternal life: vigorous patriotism that thinks it defeats all danger with its valor; eloquence forever disposed to tackle all questions; treasures of intelligence and sentiment, buried in this necropolis of thought, on which every event and every new day throws a new handful of dust! But we have come out of this reading convinced of our opinions, on seeing that they have always been maintained by the more upright and enlightened men in the Republic, and that we could, were objections made to our inadequacy, answer with their prestigious authority:

"The state," Dr. Agüero[3] used to say, "sells its land once; but it levies taxes on the real estate every year and for all time. The permanent advantage of collecting the tax should not, then, be sacrificed in any form to the possible advantage of the sale." This formula contains the most complete demonstration of the ideas we have been developing, without taking any other point of view than that of fiscal interest itself.

In another of the sessions of the same Congress of 1826, Dr. Pazos, rising to the heights of eloquence and political wisdom, delivered these magnificent words, which would have been the envy of Webster or Benton, who maintained the same ideas in the U.S. Senate.

"The state is not so much interested," said Dr. Pazos, "in apportioning its land, whether in emphyteusis or any other manner, for the lease or price that it immediately receives, as it is in populating the country and in future increase of the treasury's income due to the opulence of the nation. This should be the first objective of the Republic: populating its land, and populating it with the system that makes its population richer and better. Let the soil be occupied, let it be sown, let beautiful cities be erected, the population gathering together wherever, with attractive land for farming, the opportunity for exporting their fruits can be found."

"I will not see it," he added later, moved by the prospect of the country's future; "I will not see it, but it shall be seen by those who come later. When in the calm of peace the Republic attracts copious waves of industrious people, then new establishments will be formed, creating industries, cultivating the useful arts. And in these, and in other means to prosperity, the state shall find abundant taxable material, to gain from it wealth and advantages infinitely greater than it could today obtain from leases. This is what we must above all concern ourselves with:

3. Julián Segundo de Agüero (1776–1851), a Catholic priest, active as a leader of the Unitario party after independence, elected deputy for the province of Buenos Aires to the General Congress of 1824, became Minister of State under President Rivadavia in 1826. [E.N.]

namely, that the fostering of well-being and the population should be taken into account when it comes to distributing land."[4]

IV

A new light has appeared on the South American people's horizon to provide a way forward for their efforts, a norm for their constitutions, and a direction for their politics. And the light that shines in both worlds is the great example of the Anglo-American people. The thinking men of Europe have turned their eyes to admire it and try to account for the mystery of this miracle, while the South American people greet it from the darkness that surrounds them as a savior and as a guide. It has appeared as a providential design to help them overcome the difficult panorama they now face, struggling under all kinds of uncertainties, eager to break with the past, but fluctuating now timidly, now boldly from one experiment to another, without finding either their political personality or the true path of their industrial progress.

The European schemes about political power, the theories of her writers, have produced the same disillusionment in the Americas as in Europe, in addition to the internal breakdowns that strike the nascent peoples in every contrast because of the weakness and dispersion of the elements that constitute them. It is said that Sieyès,[5] dubbed the law-maker of France, contemplating the vanity of his own work and that of all his contemporaries, let slip this phrase in a moment of bitterness, which admirably defines his time and his country: "Our words are wiser than our ideas. We have done nothing": a sad verdict, but one that must remain as the epitaph of so many falsely glistering theories and so many solutions aborted in the unfulfilled attempt to establish liberty.

But even supposing the efficacy of European doctrines, which the results have not proven, they could only give us the knowledge of political institutions. Democracy, meanwhile, more than a political institution, is

---

4. *Congressional Records, no.* 32. Speeches from pages 5 to 11. [A.N.] The author is quoting Juan José Paso (not Pazos) (1758–1833), lawyer and politician, member of the Primera Junta and of other governing bodies in the first decades after independence. The reference to the *Congressional Records* should be no. 132 (not 32). Cf. Emilio Ravignani, *Asambleas Constituyentes Argentinas*, vol. 2, 1825–1826 (Buenos Aires, 1937), pp. 1213, 1215. [E.N.]

5. Emmanuel-Joseph Sieyès (1748–1836). [E.N.]

a social organization; and to become incarnate in deeds, to develop and live, it requires essential conditions that embrace the life of the people in all its phases. What sense is there, for example, in declaring popular sovereignty, establishing universal suffrage, if it is delivered to barbarian multitudes wallowing in ignorance or enslaved by poverty?

In order to survive, democracy needs to inspire the whole existence of the people, making all social elements in its image and for its support. And in this respect the nations of Europe can show us no examples worth imitating either in their present or in their past. Europe does not suffer our ills, and we do not have hers. It is therefore necessary, abjuring the worship of old idols, to turn our gaze to other peoples, other examples, other horizons. It is necessary to seek out democracy and the study of the conditions that sustain it there where it is not only a written phrase, an institution in outline, but where its spirit brings life to a whole people, where political dogma and the living law that presides over the relations of men have become flesh and blood.

Thus called to study both the institutions and the life of the North American people, our economic policy, following the new direction, will be the first to find its definitive path. The starting point and the purpose sought over here, carried out over there, are the same. They were few. Today they are many. They were poor. They are rich. They suffered the ills of the desert, and have learnt to subdue it. Where else could our economic laws find safer and more appropriate models?

Agrarian legislation must, above all, docilely attend this fertile school, the only one that can show the way to salvation. It is impossible to say what forms the future expressions of our economic phenomena will take. But we know that the desert is a curse and that we need to combat it. We know too that the desert is vanquished only through population, and that in order to populate it is necessary to occupy the land. What is the best system for encouraging the occupation of the soil? This is a practical problem, for which Anglo-American laws have the solution. Let us make them ours, then, and adopt them at least in their spirit and their tendencies, which far from opposing the particularities of our own way of life are a rational and necessary consequence of it.

It is not enough to implement North American democracy by adopting her political constitution. The constitution is nothing more than an emblem. And, after proclaiming it, there remains for us still the laborious, never-ending task of forming the economic, moral, and social conditions that will turn it into a living and long-lasting fact. Otherwise, this light that we greet today, which has come to raise our fading convictions and lead the way for the peoples and the men disoriented in this formless chaos of South American politics, will only have been a dazzling, but misleading phenomenon, like the aurora borealis, which delights the inexperienced sailor cast adrift by the storm on northern seas, who thinks it heralds the birth of a day that is far distant and that he will not see dawn.

LEANDRO N. ALEM

Investigation into the National Secondary School of Buenos Aires (Excerpt from Speech to Legislature of Buenos Aires Province, 22nd Ordinary Session, June 28, 1876)

8

. . . I challenge those who contest the bill to quote a single article from the Constitution that establishes, I do not say categorically, but in a way that can be deduced by arguing fairly, that the obligations and powers of the central power in these matters are of such an absolute, exclusive character as is claimed by these gentlemen.

There is no such article, Mr. President. The duty of providing instruction *in establishments such as the national high school*—I insist on this phrase—is one of those general duties that it has with its correlating attributions, to promote the prosperity of the provinces in every way, their progress and their growth, exercising them, as I have said before, in certain conditions and in all situations of those provinces where their action and initiative is safeguarded because they have the same duties and the same rights. In fact, they have preferential duties and rights because the central power can and must take action only when they cannot do so.

Yes, Mr. President: it is they who must first provide and develop education for their people, and, depending on their efforts and resources, they will be assisted by the nation or left to their own efforts, which will then be invigorated and go far beyond where they would if they were to expect everything from the general government.

Mr. President, I am not of the authoritarian school either.

Precedents are always held up as supreme, decisive; always the subservience of ideas, so often a hindrance to healthy reforms and genuine progress.

I am not so fatuous as to spurn precedents and expect my poor intelligence to impose itself on everything; but as I do not relinquish my own discretion, my individual judgment, I set my faculties to work by inquir-

Original title: "Investigación sobre el Colegio Nacional." Source: Roberto Etchepareborda, *Leandro Alem: Mensaje y destino,* vol. 5 (Buenos Aires: Editorial Raigal, 1955).

ing whether therein lie reason, truth, and justice, and if I believe I have found them I abide by them and bow to them. But if I am convinced that therein lies an error, I stand aside and fight these precedents—I never accept them blindly, for that is a poor, poor method. Error belongs to mankind and, what is more, Mr. President, something that happens in one place and in one period, an idea, a theory that arises from it, they may be useful and have a reason to exist in that place and at that time, while applying them at other times and in other places may be unsuitable and harmful. And, among ourselves, it is more dangerous still in matters of this nature, for, it can be said, we are still learning about our political life, continually wrapped up in discussions, vacillations, trying to consolidate and render practical the institutions stated in our fundamental code.

Mr. President: having considered the issue that is the reason for this bill, from the point of view of the suitability and development of education among us, the ideas of those of us who support it are also advantageously positioned.

Anyone who reads the beautiful pages of the notable publicist Charles Hippeau,[1] whose books on elementary and higher education in Germany and the United States are peerless, must be persuaded, Mr. President, of the truth of our doctrines.

Leaving aside events in Germany, with whom we have nothing in common in our political ways, I shall for a moment cast an eye over the enlightened peoples of the American Union.

It is well known, Mr. President, and perhaps in no other country in the world has education been developed more strongly and splendidly than there. Hundreds and hundreds of elementary schools and educational establishments of all kinds are to be found in American territory, containing in their bosom an incalculable number of pupils.

And so, Mr. President; the central power may have encouraged somewhat, no doubt, that development, while neither financing nor running any of those establishments exclusively, but the main idea is almost entirely due to the efforts of the federal states, the efforts of the commune, the municipality, the neighborhood, and even individual initiative. The

1. Alem is referring to Célestin Hippeau (1803–1883), French philologist and literary historian; commissioned by the French government, he studied education in several countries and published his observations. [E.N.]

ideas practiced there have been the powerful agent of that salutary work. And where the happy results of this way of being and proceeding are most noted is in recent times and as a result of the emancipation of the colored population, as a result of the abolition of slavery. In an instant, Sir, and as if by magic, new and innumerable schools populated the states of the Union, attended by thousands of children and adults of those wretches to receive the food of the spirit—the first light that ought to elevate them to the category that the stubborn white men of the South denied them. And all this, Mr. President, due to this particular initiative, to those generous efforts of the local councils and neighborhoods. It could not, surely, have been the central power, whose action is slow and weighted down by so much other business, and whose treasury is under strain from the war, that could have done such work.

Phenomena that many cannot yet explain and that provoke everyone's admiration take place continuously there. Today insignificant villages are founded with a dozen humble cabins, and in a short length of time, in a meager period of years, we find populous cities, rich and enlightened, becoming part of the great family of the Union with important political characters, respectable and respected, and exercising the legitimate influence that befits them in the country's general political movement. They are self-made, they owe nothing to any man, expect nothing from any man, and maintain their autonomy without blemish, exercising their rights within the constitutional limits. And so, Mr. President, if these fast and surprising manifestations of a precocious and vigorous life can be seen there, it is because an order of ideas is being obeyed such as the one we the authors of this bill have maintained. And if here we still see life held back, if I may so express myself, the skeletal and sickly life of certain provinces, it is also because another order of ideas is being obeyed by the minister and other members who accompany him. And do not believe, Mr. President, that we love freedom, independence, and autonomy any less than the Yankee. No, Sir. We too love and invoke and demand this at every moment, not only as individuals but as federated states, for this is in the sense I have been talking about. But this is where the evil lies: we cannot get used to living alone, by our own efforts; alone, we immediately confuse, irritate, and annihilate ourselves, and raise our eyes and hands in search of higher protection. So much so that, when we seek to adopt a measure like this, we instantly raise our voices to heaven, exclaiming: what will become of higher education if the central government is not responsible for it! It is a matter of withdrawing a subsidy, or simply reducing it, for, strictly speaking, the province is no longer fit to receive it, and by God, it is said, how the administration will fill up, how public needs will be satisfied if the nation does not give us its monies! But, by God, I would and do say in turn, work a little, stir yourselves, follow your own personal impulses; develop your faculties, apply your activity to the sources of your riches, and you will soon have the necessary resources and will naturally fix the path of your greater glory, rise up as important figures to exercise the influence that is yours in the political movement of the country, without inspiration from outside! Yes, develop your wealth, acquire economic status and with it enlightenment, and you will have political status too and you will contribute to establishing the balance among all the states and between them and the general power, a balance that is the true and solid basis for our institutions!

The honorable member, Colonel Mansilla,[2] has sought to give us a lesson in constitutional law by establishing or claiming to establish I know not what substantial differences between our Constitution and our political nature, and American institutions. And I say he has sought to teach us a lesson, for, through the story of a duelist defending a poet, he amply demonstrated to us that we constantly speak of the Constitution without understanding it.

This claim to know everything and better than everyone has its advantages and its drawbacks; advantages, because those violent and overwhelming manifestations tend to impose themselves on certain spirits; and drawbacks, depending on the locale or assembly they are made in and the people who hear them.

I am well aware that Colonel Mansilla is familiar with and knows more than military tactics and ordnance; his aptitude is proven and he can compete on an equal footing with the most learned person in any subject, just as there are learned persons who can also show and teach some military men what must be done and how it must be done on the battlefield. But it is unwise to steer the discussion in this direction.

As I was saying, Colonel Mansilla wished to establish certain differ-

2. Lucio Victorio Mansilla (1831–1913), military officer (later a general), politician, and writer; his best known book is *Una excursión a los indios ranqueles,* where he narrates a peaceful expedition he undertook to the Indian tribes of Argentina. [E.N.]

ences, which, frankly, I did not understand; my own fault, perhaps, or perhaps because he did not explain himself properly. All I heard and understood from him was that the North Americans' system of government was mixed. I do not know what nature he attributes to ours.

But whatever the deputy's ideas may have been in this respect, they are indubitably mistaken. We know, Sir, that neither here nor there is there a pure federation, because the Confederate states do not retain their independence and absolute sovereignty delegating certain powers to a central power—arguably the same powers. But the underlying political nature, the kind of institutions, is the same, and our Constitution is cast in the mold of the American one. It is, with a few small variants and details, almost a copy of it.

There is a difference, but in another sense, Mr. President, and one that favors the claims of the bill's backers. There the Union of states was formed with the idea or principle of autonomy already perfectly understood, and its leaders had sometimes to curb certain exaggerated manifestations of that principle that might jeopardize the Confederacy; while no one can be ignorant of how we came to life, with that autonomous principle unrecognized or hidden, if I may express myself thus; with the thought of unity and the centralizing tendency dominating in superior spirits, in the conspicuous characters of our revolution; a tendency that has been holding its fatal, pernicious sway, and that can still be felt as I have already shown to this chamber. Our efforts, then, have had to be different in this respect, and it is the ideas the commission upholds that should be instilled and spread to prevent this sickness.

Weaken federal ties, so it was said, and we jeopardize nationality. Let us embrace each other, and strengthen the central power.

What a lamentable confusion and contradiction of ideas, Mr. President. The one is indeed incompatible with the other.

It is no way to come closer to each other strengthening those ties, if we stay so close to the trunk, which is called the central power, if we go on equating ourselves with it, or rather if we continue to be absorbed by it.

As we broaden its sphere of action by having it intervene in local matters; as we enlarge its functions and powers in this way, so too do we restrict the action and powers of local authorities, whose autonomy and life we weaken, whose strength we enervate, and whose activity we numb. In these conditions, with their political and even economic importance—for their progress will be very slow—abated, and adversely affected, we remove, as I have said and will not tire of repeating, the balance that has to be sought in order to consolidate the confederation, and which should not be nominal but effective.

Mr. President: deliberating and resolving the issues on this matter that are submitted to Congress, I am not guided or impressed by the species of some backstreet clique or the murmurings of certain brooders.

It is not there where one receives the echoes of true public opinion. Rest assured, then, Deputy Mansilla, that neither this province nor the others are to *raise their ponchos,* to use your words, because of measures of this kind.

Indeed, three of us deputies who signed this project, which is of interest only to Buenos Aires, have been elected by the people of this province, and no precedent makes us suspect of being bad patriots or disrupters, and none of the five deputies was elected by the Argentine people as a whole.

And indeed, Sir, one of those deputies has suffered many privations, many hardships, and some danger to contain and defend that Argentine nationality, his integrity, and his honor, without wavering at any moment from the post where duty had placed him. I have been forced to this unburdening.

I now turn, Mr. President, to matters of the economy.

A few days ago, a member of the national Cabinet, the minister of finance, was telling us that it was necessary to normalize not only political progress but also, and more pressingly, the nation's financial progress, for, while the treasury's situation was urgent, it was to a large extent due to expenditure and costs that were not essentially national and had been run up in abundance.

Having demonstrated that Buenos Aires Province does not need this protection to educate its youth, that besides the national secondary school there is a perfectly well-organized establishment where the same studies are followed, and which with very little more effort and spending will meet the new demands on the school's students, in such a way that no harm should be suffered, why, then, this insistence on maintaining it and continuing to run up this expenditure, which, due to all these circumstances, is no longer of an essentially national character, as was clearly spelled out to the minister? This is spending from excess or whim, and solely to increase employment and broaden the remit of the Ministry for Religious Affairs.

And I must point out to the minister that the saving is not limited to six months of this year: the national treasury will save many hundreds of silver pesos over subsequent years, and our sights should be set much higher in this respect. It is not in one, or two, or in four years that we will reestablish the treasury balance. We have to save a great deal over a long period of time, and not extract a gram without examining the need to which it is allocated. Many details form an important group; many small savings will make a strong economy, and thus it is that we are proceeding and to which all these bills brought by the executive correspond, some signed by the minister for religious affairs.

9

DOMINGO FAUSTINO SARMIENTO
The Social Contract in the Argentine
Republic (1879)

WEAKNESSES AND DEVIATIONS

A few years ago, in a letter from El Chacho,[1] I was surprised to find the phrase: *magnificent future.* In Los Llanos[2] in La Rioja, amid simple peasants, magnificent future!

A phrase of Rivadavia's and the subject of his enemies' mockery! The magnificent future that awaited the Republic! The phrase now forgotten would have passed into folklore!

Some days ago we found in an old newspaper, rejuvenated with its gray hairs dyed to look as if it belonged to this day and age, the phrase *social pact,* Rousseau's social contract, the pact signed by the first men to form a society, the pact of Thomas Payne[3] in the United States, and we rubbed our eyes, once, twice, to make sure that it did say pact: and indeed, in 1879 a writer says social pact, under the rule of a written constitution; and it says pact in such a way that it draws the consequences of any *quid pro quo* pact or *barter* contract, under which "we must only respect *legitimate governments — we refuse to obey,* and as is natural, we shall not let ourselves be exterminated."

We have thus the social contract of Rousseau, who to provide the reason of the social contract established what appeared to be truth, at the time, protesting against historical events and in vindication of human dignity, "that man is born free, and everywhere he is found in chains."

Original title: "El contrato social en la República Argentina." Source: *Obras completas de Domingo Faustino Sarmiento* [Complete works of Domingo Faustino Sarmiento], vol. 40 (2001 reprint of 1948–1950 edition). Originally published in *El Nacional,* January 14, 1879.

1. Angel Vicente Peñaloza (1798–1863), "caudillo" of the province of La Rioja. [E.N.]

2. A district in La Rioja Province. [E.N.]

3. Incorrect spelling for Thomas Paine (1737–1809), author, revolutionary, and pamphleteer, and one of the Founding Fathers of the United States. [E.N.]

A century later, the sciences of nature join together to prove that man was a monkey, that over thousands of centuries he has gradually been perfected; but even if fossil evidence has not yet been found of this gradual transformation, the imperishable traces left by primitive man, prehistoric man, show indisputably that he was a miserable savage in Europe, more naked, wretched, and ignorant than Catriel, Pincen,[4] and their tribes brought to Buenos Aires today and spread out among the population. Once the cacique is taken prisoner, the tribes have voluntarily come forward, for in the destitution and helplessness of primitive man this is the primitive notion of government: attachment to the cacique, who is like the embodiment of society, that is, personal authority, which still has vestiges among ourselves and in Europe, and can go some way to explaining the support of those who follow a party leader, whether defeated or beaten, whether a criminal or a righteous man, and legitimize or undermine governments that are not those of the cacique.

We have a great deal from our ancestors the Indians, from Catriel, Rosas, Quiroga . . . I shall not go on, as the list is a long one.

It was therefore proposed to the world that we reestablish the imaginary primitive social pact and destroy the iniquities that centuries, conquest, and usurpation had accumulated upon the heads of the *people;* and one day the (French) *people,* twenty-four million men, most of them ignorant, fanaticized by the idea of the social contract, undertook, suddenly breaking the historic chain, and bringing down the framework of traditional government, to return man to his original equality, and for this they sent one and a half million men to the guillotine, considered less equal for being clergy, noblemen, rich, enlightened, or just indifferent, and since knowing how to read also was a form of inequality, and a gaping one in a generally ignorant people, they declared those who knew how to read and write *aristocrats.*

The revolution to render equality, fraternity, and liberty a universal law led to the empire of one fortunate soldier, and the free people knew no other law than the military discipline of the armies, nor any other equality than that of one attaining the rank of marshal, for every one hundred thousand who died on the battlefields, nor more fraternity than that of killing another one and a half million men, to extend through-

4. Indian caciques. [E.N.]

out Europe not liberty, but conquest at the mercy of the ambition of a sublime madman and his backward ideas of government. We shall not follow these *people* in their forty-year pilgrimage through the desert, arriving only now, mutilated, defeated, hopeless, disenchanted with the social pact, to seek the bases of government in other ideas.

Meanwhile, there was a good example to follow. Another nation, one that defeated and humiliated the French, with its unshakeable power base: England, free for centuries, had not sought to make all men equal, reform her government along rational bases, but accepted the government of her conqueror, who proclaimed himself king, with his generals who called themselves lords. They divided up power, made it hereditary, and on that evil basis a government developed, between the king and the lords, the conquered people gradually acquired liberties and some representation in another Parliament where they could make their complaints heard, *on their knees to the speaker,* as is the name heretofore given to the president of the Commons (of the unprivileged), until they were given the power to enact laws and taxation on the people, which neither the king nor the lords could do.

And with these simple principles, with almost the majority of the people deprived of the right to elect deputies, a right held only by certain corporations, villages, and cities, they have come to the present day, without starting revolutions, as the people advanced little by little in electoral franchises, and in security and justice, until they have given their institutions to the world, to geography a *republic* such as the United States, and to their own country the dominion of India, Africa, and the possession of *ten thousand* islands in all the seas, ruled by their ships.

The English colonies were populated by those persecuted by the motherland because of religious opinions, Puritans, Catholics, Quakers, Anabaptists, etc. They were already nations when, in the name of the right to be represented in the chamber, which is the only power that can impose laws, and represented by a Congress of the colonies, of delegates of the people and not the people themselves or a military man such as Washington, they were forced to create a general government, after winning their independence. There then came the time, unique in the world, to sign a social pact.

SOCIAL PACT

The contracting parties, thirteen states, signed a contract of confederation, which was turned into a public deed and proclaimed not under the title of constitution, a word that did not yet exist, but as the Nine Articles of the Confederation, under which each contracting party would be governed by its own laws, each one of them undertaking the obligation of providing a proportional contingent of soldiers for defense and representation abroad, and payment of debts incurred, a pact that seemed to be the eighth wonder of the world, the federal pact, the social contract.

But as the fulfillment of pacts is entrusted to the voluntary execution of each contracting party, experience over time showed that any state that was very poor, or careless, did not send contingents for the army, so that the Indians continued with their pillaging, and the navy could not defend the coasts. Having vast debts, and a large number of bills of credit, and lacking resources because of the voluntary pact, the bill was given at *two thousand pesos* for one, and the army was ultimately reduced to *forty-five* soldiers.

All this in nine years of experience, with which it became clear that government is not founded by pacts between the governed and a limited authority, but that a *coercive* power is needed, by virtue of *law,* mandatory for all and with the *strength* to enforce it.

CONSTITUTION

Hence a government constitution was enacted that was not based on voluntary pacts, but on a mandatory law, creating an executive power with material strength to oblige states and individuals to obey, without asking them whether they found the law to be good or just, or the authority legitimate or illegitimate by virtue of the Constitution; and seventy years of remarkable prosperity have now passed, without disturbance. This is not to say that of the thousand governors nominated by the parties in that period of time, there have not been one hundred or more who were bad, ignorant, badly elected, as the common people are greater in number than educated people, and things are the same the world over.

But with the social and industrial antagonism between the peoples of the South and those of the North, the former with slave labor, the latter with wages, the old doctrine of the social contract began to be revived twenty years ago, with Calhoum[5] claiming in his famous work *Principle on Government* that the union of the states was a pact and not a law; that the peoples who signed it could revoke it, if it was not in their interests to continue. The ground thus prepared, ten states split or attempted to split, by other means than those prescribed by the all-obliging constitution, and swore not to obey the president.

After one million lives and seven million pesos had been spent, the victory of the Constitution, imposed by the force of arms and coercion, showed that constitutions are not pacts that the contracting parties may break at will, but laws, to which all are obliged, on pain of punishment for him who violates it before its amendment by the representatives in Congress.

While Greemke[6] says something contrary to this, it is because Greemke wrote in 1848, in Cincinnati, influenced by the ideas of the South.

In 1865, there could not be found in the law bookshops of New York or Boston, unknown by the booksellers, an author of circumstances and polemic more despised by the statesmen of the North.

As in France, as in the United States, as in Buenos Aires, the idea of the constitution as a pact and not a law has meant only the making of revolutions, to separate from the nation and give arms to the anarchists, such as those who today maintain that they will obey only the governments that they judge legitimate, with such effrontery that it would be enough for the first ambitious person to say: this government is de facto in my opinion, be it in Mexico or in Buenos Aires, to unhinge society.

---

5. Incorrect spelling for John C. Calhoun (1782–1850). Twice vice president of the United States (under John Quincy Adams and Andrew Jackson), he defended the right of the states to secede from the Union. Sarmiento is probably referring below to *A Disquisition on Government* (1851). [E.N.]

6. Incorrect spelling for Frederick Grimke (1791–1863), Ohio Supreme Court judge from 1836 to 1842, author of *Considerations upon the Nature and Tendency of Free Institutions* (1848). [E.N.]

4 | Liberalism in Government and in Opposition (1880–1910)

1

LEANDRO N. ALEM
Speech on the Federalization
of Buenos Aires (1880)

. . . Given the nature of our system of government, on what should we focus more? I firmly believe that we should focus on the respective position of the federal states with the central power, because this is an unquestionable truth: when the general power "by itself" should have more strength than all the federal states combined, the regime shall be written into the Constitution, but it could easily and will gradually be subverted in practice and, in the end, completely overwhelmed at any time of turmoil.

The supreme power in the federally constituted republic, which recognizes the political status of the various groups that form it, must be "relatively" strong and have at its disposal only the elements necessary for the general goals of the institution, for it is inadmissible that all the states should rise up without reason or justice against that authority in its legitimate function. But if it holds and centralizes the greater sum of vital elements and effective forces, the republic will depend on its good or bad intentions, on its good or bad will, on the passions and tendencies that drive it. A dictatorship would be inevitable whenever a bad ruler should wish to establish one, for there would not be sufficient strength to control him and keep him in line.

. . . I have said, Mr. President, that all those fears that are expressed are imaginary, and that the danger lies, precisely, in the tendency and purpose that such evolution entails. And I must examine, briefly, the conditions in which under our charter the central power stands, together with all the elements that the Constitution provides for it.

Original title: "Discurso sobre la federalización de Buenos Aires." Source: "Discurso en la legislatura de la provincia de Buenos Aires, en el mes de noviembre de 1880" [Speech in the Legislature of Buenos Aires Province, November 1880], in Leandro N. Alem, *Obra parlamentaria* [Parliamentary works], vol. 3 (La Plata: Camara de Diputados, 1949).

Our national Constitution is more centralist than those of the USA and Switzerland. Our legislation is centralist, unlike the former, and the faculties attributed to the army are not found in the latter. I may venture to say that our executive is stronger still than the executive of England itself, despite that nation being a monarchy.

The president of the Argentine Republic is the commander-in-chief of a significant army on sea and land, and can place it where he sees fit. This army has no limits indicated by the Constitution, and the Congress may increase it as it sees fit.

The national treasury is well stocked, as it has the main revenues produced by the states, most of which comes from Buenos Aires—perhaps sixty or seventy percent of the revenue that this province produces.

The national executive forms its cabinet at will and maintains it in the same way, without any legal force impeding this.

The provinces cannot raise or maintain troops, or arm ships, and ultimately the national government has the right to intervene in them.

And I ask and expect an answer with an unprejudiced spirit. Is it possible in view of all that has been surveyed, to contend, as it has been said, that the basis of national authority is fragile and hesitant? Is it possible, proceeding as one should and applying the law impartially, to ever endanger the existence of this authority and of Argentine nationality, through disturbances and events more serious than those that have just occurred?

No, Mr. President. The national authority has all the powers and all the elements necessary to survive in any emergency, to keep order and bring down any irregular movement.

... Having dominated previously in this capital city, through its agents and allies, who will be able to contain it afterward?

It is a natural tendency of power to extend its dominance, expand its sphere of action, and grow larger in every sense. And if we already observe shadows cast continuously over the autonomy of certain provinces, the national authority noticeably influencing acts of politics and the internal regime of those provinces, what won't happen when it believes itself and feels so powerful and without any control over its proceedings?

I firmly believe, sir, that the fate of the Federal Argentine Republic will be left to the will and passions of the head of the national executive.

... Willful and ill-inclined rulers on more than one occasion have made the pernicious effects of centralization felt on the people. Interfering everywhere, taking their action to all places, governing them according to their will through their agents, their authority was unbreakable and they dominated everything and could subjugate it without meeting any effective resistance.

Decentralization was demanded by the people, who felt they had the aptitude to direct communal matters by themselves, and did not wish to remain under the guardianship of an all-absorbing power.

The Constitution of '73[1] responded to these legitimate aspirations and authorized the autonomy of the communes, emancipating them from that noxious interference that strangled initiative and weakened their activities, leaving their lot and their fate to the will of a leader.

Thus, freedom was secured with order. Neither one nor the other was dependent on the bad ruler. The communal groups, masters of themselves and responsible for their acts, would be the first to forge a normal situation that secured their rights, encouraging the progress and development of their legitimate interests.

Let us decentralize, then, in the province, and we will have warded off all danger for the future, but let us not centralize at the same time in the nation, incurring in inexplicable contradictions and engendering the same evil with even graver consequences.

But the solution that we give to this political issue, its supporters reply, is the solution recommended by history and tradition: Buenos Aires is the traditional and historical capital of the Argentine Republic.

This is not exactly so; and it seems incredible, Mr. President, that some distinguished souls make such a lamentable confusion of ideas.

First, it is a bad method to take tradition as the supreme and decisive reason for the solution to these problems of high political philosophy. It comes from the conservative school and I would go so far as to call it static, which still rises up against the rational and liberal school.

Tradition, taken in this sense, wants to keep us with our sight fixed only on the past, without shifting it ever to the future. It wants to bind us with inflexible ties to situations and eras that have disappeared, raising a barrier on the road to progress and ignoring modern demands.

It is not the system that we should adopt if we wish to advance frankly on the path that our elders indicated to us, when they fought with en-

---

1. Alem is referring to the constitution of the province of Buenos Aires. [E.N.]

thusiasm and enlightened by great hopes, to break the monarchic domination and bequeath us a virile nation, which was to be an example in this continent for the peoples who wanted to live in liberty.

"To maintain the institutions free in their true spirit," writes one of the most distinguished American publicists, "it is essential to make a high distribution of political power, with no consideration for the circumstances that have led to the formation of the government. This is a great problem of political philosophy and not a simple, accidental question in the history of a particular class of institutions."[2]

... The supporters of centralization are wrong in the results they expect. They commit a grave philosophical error in their appraisals.

The concentration of power does not produce vigor and greater vitality in a country. It will have at its disposal a greater number of elements, but the strength of these will be gradually weakened, for it is thus that its own initiative and its own activity is weakened, which is the true driver of progress.

Centralization, attracting the most effective elements, all the vitality of the republic, to a given point, will necessarily weaken other places. And, as Laboulaye[3] rightly said, it is the apoplexy in the center and the paralysis in the limbs. And it is necessary that all public men, the far-sighted politicians, do not forget that apoplexy in politics tends to be called revolution.

Yes: concentration and revolution are two words from the same date; they are two names for the same disease.

The mission of the modern legislator is, precisely, in the direction opposite to where the authors of this evolution are going. It consists of developing the activity of the individual, the family, the association, the district, the department, and the province throughout the republic, while keeping in mind that the state is a living organism and that the strength of all its members is the strength of the body as a whole.

Centralization also has one very serious disadvantage: that as it brings

2. This quotation is in all probability from Francis Lieber, *On Civil Liberty and Self-Government* (1853), but we have been unable to find the original text. Alem apparently quotes from memory (or rather paraphrases) from a Spanish or French translation of *On Civil Liberty*. [E.N.]

3. Édouard René de Laboulaye (1811–1883), French jurist, writer, and liberal politician. An ardent republican, he was an admirer of the American institutions. [E.N.]

all the elements and the vitality of the country to a single point, when that point hesitates, when it is shaken, the entire nation is rocked profoundly. It does not have aptly distributed forces: everything is there, the heart is there; there the blow is struck to the entire nation.

... There is no such centralizing tendency, I repeat. In economics as in politics, the two closely tied together, for there is no economic progress if there is no good policy, a liberal policy that gives the necessary space to all forces and all activities. In economics as in politics, as I was saying, the theory that leading thinkers propound, the most distinguished men of the old and the new continent, a theory that is inculcated, so to speak, in the heart of all societies, can be condensed, and they synthesize it in this simple formula: "Do not govern too much." The idea might better be expressed as "Govern as little as possible."

Yes: Govern as little as possible, for the less external government a man has, the more freedom advances, the more he governs himself, and the more his initiative strengthens and his activity develops.

The ancient republics, the republics of Greece, did not understand the system, did not discover the secret for raising and perfecting their institutions. And thus we have seen sometimes fall victims of despotism, and decay prematurely. There the citizen was free, but within the state, to which he was inflexibly tied and to which he belonged exclusively.

Liberty is a strength, says Laboulaye, that can be harnessed for good or for evil. Oppressed, it breaks out by necessity. Let it move forward, for it will produce beneficial results, according to the hand that directs it. The Americans have understood this idea well, treating political liberty as natural liberty, because it is the same liberty. And it is "individualism," political and religious, that is the secret and the cause of their well-being and their prosperity; autonomy, that is, starting with the individual, guaranteed in its "regular expressions," but only guaranteed, without protection or harmful guardianship of the superior power.

2

JUAN BAUTISTA ALBERDI
The Omnipotence of the State Is the Negation of Individual Liberty (1880)

... Now, as the mass or the whole of those private individuals is what, in the common sense of the word, is called the people, it follows that it is not the government but the people who are devoted to the gradual work of their progress and civilization on account of the conditions of South American society. And the people's favorite engine for performing this work is civil or social liberty, equally distributed among the native and foreign individuals that make up the association or people of South America.

If this natural and inevitable law of one's own individual growth is termed egotism, it must be accepted that egotism is summoned to precede patriotism in the hierarchy of the workers and servants of national progress. The country's advance must necessarily march in direct proportion to the number of its intelligent, industrious, determined egotists, and to the talents and guarantees that their fecund and civilizing egotism finds to exercise and develop.

South American society would be saved and assured of freedom and progress in its future from the moment intelligent egotism rather than egotistical patriotism were to be entrusted with the construction and building of the republics of South America.

And as it is unnatural for healthy egotism to neglect the work of its own individual growth, thus damaging its primary interest, the future progress of South America can quite genuinely be said to be guaranteed and assured by being under the watchful protectorate of individual egotism, which never sleeps.

... The omnipotence of the Fatherland inevitably becomes the omnipotence of the government in which it is embodied. This is not only

Original title: "La omnipotencia del estado es la negación de la libertad individual."
Source: *Obras completas de Juan Bautista Alberdi* [Complete works of Juan Bautista Alberdi], vol. 8 (Buenos Aires: La Tribuna nacional, 1887).

a negation of liberty, but also of social progress, as it suppresses private initiative in the works of such progress. The state absorbs all activity of individuals when it absorbs all their means and efforts to better themselves. In order to absorb them the state recruits into the rank and file of its employees those individuals who would be more capable if devoted to themselves. The state intervenes in everything, and everything is done under its initiative in the administration of its public interests. The state becomes manufacturer, builder, entrepreneur, banker, trader, and publisher, and thus deviates from its essential and sole mandate, which is to protect the individuals that make up the state from any attack, be it from without or from within. In all roles that are not essentially governmental, it acts like an ignorant fool, a harmful rival of individuals, making service to the country worse instead of better.

The field or service of public administration becomes an industry and a way of life for half the individuals that make up the society. The exercise of this administrative and political industry, which is a mere way of life, goes under the name of patriotism, for the service each individual does for the Fatherland to earn a living takes on the appearance of service to the Fatherland. Naturally, then, it takes on an appearance of love for the Fatherland—a great sentiment that is in its essence disinterested—a love for the hand that gives it its daily bread. How could one not love the Fatherland as one loves one's life, when it is the Fatherland that allows one to live?

Hence patriotism is not religion as in the old Greek and Roman days, nor is it even superstition or fanaticism. It is often mere hypocrisy in its claims of virtue and, in reality, a simple industry to earn a living.

And as the best industrialists, the most intelligent and active, are immigrants from the civilized countries of Europe, who, being foreigners, cannot exercise this government/industry, the poor performance of state industrialism ends up damaging them, limiting immigration and having an adverse effect on nationals who have no work in the privileged workshops of political administration.

If more than one young man, instead of competing for the honor of receiving a wage as a salaried employee, agent, or servant of the state, preferred to remain master of himself in the running of his farm or rural property, the Fatherland would henceforth be able to follow the road to greatness, liberty, and true progress.

. . . Another of the great drawbacks of the Roman notion of Fatherland and patriotism in the development of liberty is that, as the Fatherland was originally a religious cult, it engendered zeal and fanaticism, that is, blinding heat and passion.

Hence our hymns to the Fatherland, viewed in a mystical light, have outdone the religious songs of ancient pagan patriotism.

According to free England, through the pen of Adam Smith, zeal is the worst foe of science, which is the source of all civilization and progress. Zeal is a poison that, like opium, closes the eyes and blinds the understanding; against it there is no antidote but science, says the king of economists.

In South America, poisoned with that venom, zeal is a commendable quality rather than a dangerous disease.

Liberty has a cool and patient disposition — rational and thoughtful, not zealous, as is shown by the example of the Saxon peoples, who are truly free. The Americans of the North, like the English and Dutch, carry out their political dealings not with the fervor of religious matters, but as the most prosaic thing in life, which are the interests that sustain life. Never does their modern fervor go so far as fanaticism.

Zeal engenders rhetoric, luxury of language, the poetic tone, which is so bad for business, and all the violence of the word that leads to violent and tyrannical behavior.

In that rich pomp of the written and spoken word that is peculiar to zeal, the idea, which can live only through thoughtful deliberation and cold science, vanishes.

So it is that the North Americans, English, and Dutch are strangers to that patriotic poetry, that political literature, exhaled in songs of war that intimidate and dispel freedom instead of attracting it. The North Americans do not sing of liberty but rather practice it in silence.

Liberty to them is not a deity; it is an ordinary tool, like the crowbar or the hammer.

What South America lacks in order to be as free as the United States is that cool, peaceful, gentle, patient disposition to deal with and resolve the most complicated political affairs — a quality shared by the English and Dutch — which does not, at times, exclude fervor, but never goes so far as fanaticism that blinds and misleads. France enters into liberty insofar as it adopts this truly virile, that is, cold, mettle.

. . . Patriotic zeal is a sentiment peculiar to war, while freedom is fueled by peace. War itself has become more productive since it has changed zeal for science, but it is more the offspring of zeal than of science.

Through what mysterious bond have the notions of Fatherland, freedom, zeal, glory, war, and poetry been brought together in South America, as a result of which today public questions are treated with such passion and left unresolved precisely because they are not treated with the serenity and temperance that would make them so expeditious and straightforward?

It is not hard to conceive. If the Fatherland is seen as it was considered by Greek and Roman societies, in whose eyes it was a religious and holy institution, the cult of the Fatherland filled hearts with the inexplicable zeal of holy things. Zeal was only a small step from fanaticism. The Fatherland was worshiped as a kind of divinity, and its worship produced a zeal as fervent as that for religion itself. The Fatherland's natural and essential independence from abroad, was regarded as all its liberty, and its omnipotence was seen as the negation of all individual liberty capable of limiting its divine authority. Thus the warrior was the champion of its liberty against the foreigner, seen as the natural enemy of the Fatherland's independence, and human glory lay in the triumphs of wars waged to defend the freedom of the Fatherland against all domination from abroad.

War thus took its sanctity from the sanctity of its favorite object, namely, the freedom of the Fatherland, the defense of its sacred soil and of the sanctity of its banners, which were the blessed symbols of the Fatherland, its soil and its altars understood in a religious sense as the Greeks and the Romans did. From this point of view, the Fatherland was inseparable from these things, and zeal was instilled by holy and sacred things. The omnipotent and absolute Fatherland absorbed the personality of the individual, and the freedom of the Fatherland eclipsed the freedom of man, leaving no other legitimate or sacred object for war than the defense of the Fatherland's independence or freedom from abroad, and its omnipotence over individuals who were members of the Fatherland.

So it was that at the birth of the new states of South America, San Martín, Bolívar, Sucre, O'Higgins, the Carreras, Belgrano, Alvear, Pueyrredón, who had been educated in Spain and gained their notions of Fatherland and liberty there, understood American liberty in the Spanish sense, and made this liberty consist entirely of the independence of the new states from Spain, just as Spain had understood liberty as liberty from France during the war with Napoleon I.

These great men were undoubtedly champions of South American freedom, but freedom in the sense of the Fatherland's independence from Spain. And if they did not also defend the omnipotence of the Fatherland over its individual members, neither did they defend individual liberty, understood as the limit of the Fatherland's or the state's power, because they did not understand or know liberty in that sense, which is its most precious sense. From where or from whom could they have learned it? From Spain, which never knew it, in the time in which they were educated there?

The opposite was true of Washington and his contemporaries. They were more familiar with individual freedom than with the independence of their country, because they had been born, bred, and raised from the cradle depending on free England, enjoying the freedom of man.

So it was that after gaining the independence of their Fatherland, the individual members of it were as free as they had been since the foundation of that people, and their constitution as an independent nation only confirmed their old inner freedoms, which they already knew and wielded as veterans of liberty.

The glory of our great men was more dazzling, being born from the zeal that led to the war and the victories of independence for the Fatherland, born omnipotent over its individuals, as the mother country had been under her kings' absolute regime of government, which the Fatherland personified. Because it was born out of zeal for the Fatherland, which had been their entire object, and because they understood it in the quasi-divine sense of Ancient Rome and Ancient Spain, the glory of our great historical figures of the war and independence of the Fatherland and the omnipotent glory of our great warriors of independence continued to eclipse true liberty, which is the liberty of man, the zeal for those symbolic men going so far as to place them in the very altars of liberty itself.

... This is the ground on which the direction of our organic politics, and our political and social literature has traveled until now, where the liberties of the Fatherland have eclipsed and cast into oblivion the freedoms of the individual, who is the factor and unit from which the Fatherland is made.

Where does individual freedom derive its importance from? From its action in the progress of nations.

It is a varied and multifarious freedom that breaks down and works in the following several ways:

Freedom to want, choose, and elect.

Freedom to think, speak, and write: to hold and publish an opinion.

Freedom to act and move on.

Freedom to work, acquire, and dispose of what is one's own.

Freedom to stay or go, to leave and enter one's country, freedom of locomotion and circulation.

Freedom of conscience and worship.

Freedom to emigrate or not move from one's country.

Freedom to bequeath, hire, transfer, produce, and acquire.

As it contains the whole circle of human activity, individual freedom—the primary freedom of man—is the principal and immediate creator of all his progress, all his improvements, all the triumphs of civilization in each and every nation.

But the most dread rival of that beneficent fairy of the civilized peoples is the omnipotent and absolute Fatherland, inevitably embodied in absolute and omnipotent governments that do not want it, as it is the sacred limit of their very omnipotence.

It is, nevertheless, advisable to remember that as individual freedom has nurtured the Fatherland, so too does the Fatherland's freedom safeguard the liberties of man, who is an essential member of that Fatherland. But what Fatherland could be more interested in preserving our persons and our personal rights if not that Fatherland of which we are a fundamental part and unit?

To say it all in one final word, the freedom of the Fatherland is a part of the freedom of civilized man, which is the foundation and purpose of the entire social edifice of the human race.

3

JULIO ARGENTINO ROCA
Presidential Messages (1881–1886)

The legislative term ahead of you will be extremely toilsome and will require every last bit of perseverance, Honorable Gentlemen.

We would seem to be a people newly born to national life, for you have to legislate about all that constitutes the nation's attributes, means, and power—so great was the lack of a permanent capital for the Republic.

You may now pass your laws in complete freedom and in the knowledge that they will ultimately be obeyed, without fearing that any provincial governor, breaking with all practice, might come to voice protest in these precincts or try to force your decisions.

There is an urgent need, first and foremost, to complete the federalization of this city, to provide laws governing the administration of justice, municipality, and common education, and to settle the manner and form of their representation in Congress.

Greater importance has been given in Europe than among ourselves to the triumph of national authority over the authority of a province, and to the designation of Buenos Aires, the trading center of the River Plate, as the Republic's permanent capital, for, in that continent, age-old peoples who have spent long centuries forging national unity, have a better notion than we do of what government ought to be like in established countries.

... It is not by trusting to the enthusiasms of the public square, or in

Original title: "Mensajes presidenciales (1881–1886)." Source: Heraclio Mabragaña, *Los Mensajes. Historia del desenvolvimiento de la nación argentina redactada cronológicamente por sus gobernantes, 1810–1910* [History of the development of the Argentine nation, written chronologically by its rulers, 1810–1910], vol. 4 (Buenos Aires: Talleres Gráficos de la Compañía General de Fósforos, 1910).

the raptures of the moment that nations retain their independence and integrity — but by means of peace within their frontiers, the civic virtues of the citizen and respect for the principle of authority, and the observance of the Constitution and the laws.

(1881)

. . . With true satisfaction I can repeat my message of last year to you: "The Republic keeps itself in peace and friendship with all foreign powers, cultivating its relations on the basis of reciprocal benevolence."

The course of our diplomacy is more conspicuous every day for the uprightness of our conduct, and the Republic's name is gaining status and consideration among other peoples.

The question of boundaries with the Chilean Republic that used to give such cause for concern and has gone through diverse and dangerous uncertainties, reached an amicable conclusion, as you will know, and our relations with that nation now rest in the most complete harmony.

(1882)

. . . May this be our public aspiration: peace and order. Let us fulfill this program, and the light that begins to shine bright on the Republic shall become a beacon announcing to the world, like another star from the East, that there is, here in the Far South of the American continent, spanning four times the area of France and no less fertile, a nation that is open to all currents of the spirit, a nation with no castes, and no religious or social fixations, no tyrannies or Commune — a new temple on the face of the earth, consecrating all the freedoms and all the rights of Man.

(1883)

. . . Safe and stable governments are powerful agents of progress in new peoples, but the healthy application of the law by judges, which is tied more closely to the individual interests of citizens, reflects a still more eloquent state of civilization guaranteeing the regular development of social life.

. . . This is the fourth time I have had the satisfaction of opening your term of sessions in the most complete peace and tranquility, without misgivings from without or dangers from within.

The exercise of freedom and the federal institutions, with no revolts or riots, is the normal state of the country, due mainly to the progress of public reason, which has understood, through painful experience, that disorder will always entail poverty, backwardness, and disrepute.

There will be many gaps left, there will be defects or moles, or short-comings, if you will; but can we abruptly aspire to perfection, young nation that we are?

If we proceed with sound judgment these gaps and deficiencies will, little by little, be satisfied and corrected with the support and goodwill of all, rulers and governed alike.

Bad governments come to an end, and if another bad one comes along it soon passes away too. But revolutions are like wildfires: they scorch estates, devour the seed, and sap the lifeblood for many generations, and make the ground barren for centuries to come. You congregate from all points of the Republic, and can communicate your impressions of what you have seen and observed in your own provinces and on your journey, with the implementation of the vote, in our Constitutional Assembly, that counseled the people sixty years ago to bring revolution to an end and open the way to order.

(1884)

... In order to judge if we have taken the same path, if we have pro-gressed in equal proportion in the moral and political order; in order to judge if we have more or less freedom now, more or fewer constitutional franchises, more or less regularity in the exercise of our constituent laws, more or less respect for national authority and of this authority for the rights of provinces and citizens; in order to judge ourselves in this order, we must not take our measure dispensing with our past, or according to the ideal forged by patriotism, or by the example of other peoples older than ourselves that have entered independent life better prepared than the Argentine Republic and all the other American nationalities of Latin origin; we must come to terms with our recent past and the model of what we have been in previous administrations.

... There is talk of fraud, violence, abuse of authority. The higher government is not responsible for the doings and conduct of every offi-cial of the Republic who participates in the electoral mechanism, and it would be a danger perhaps for our form of government for the federal government to interfere in order to correct electoral acts in the prov-inces. The ultimate judge, in that case, is you.

We must consider, furthermore, that, however swift our progress, it is not possible to demand that even the lingering aftertaste of the past be extinguished in a flash — a time so full of this kind of irregularity and so recent in our lives. This fraud, this violence, this abuse . . . will, little by little, be tempered and corrected by the pleasures of peace, the education of the political parties, and the influence of public reason that is every day more enlightened and profits more from experience and the spread of learning.

(1886)

4

PEDRO GOYENA
Speech on the Common Education Act (1883)

. . . And let it not be said that the tradition I have referred to has therefore been abandoned and the religious concept of Catholic dogmas and doctrines disregarded, for to *support* the Apostolic Roman Catholic religion according to the correct use of the words and clauses of the Constitution in keeping with the above statement does not merely mean, as has been claimed, to give the Church a more or less limited sum of money to pay for the external aspect, the material aspect of worship. No! By virtue of the constitutional provisions, Congress approves funds not only to cover this material part of religion, but also to teach Catholic doctrine to young people who will become the clergy, for bishops' visits to their dioceses, for missions among the Indians, that is, for a spiritual end that the Argentine Constitution and Congress, which legislates under the former, have considered necessary for the well-being and morality of the people. When the Constituent Congress of '53 anticipated the nation of the future, it wanted the indigenous peoples to be part of it, those groups of men still immersed in the limbos of barbarism. And so they would become an element homogeneous with the civilized part of society, persuaded of the goodness and efficacy of Catholicism, it ruled in favor of promoting the conversion of those tribes to this religion. The Constituent Congress understood that an arbitrary philosophy or any sect would not have been effective for this object.

That constitutional ruling amounted to saying: this society is Catholic; in the future this society, remaining faithful to its glorious tradi-

Original title: "Discurso sobre la ley de educación común." Source: *Debate parlamentario, ley 1420, 1883-1884* [Parliamentary debate, law 1420, 1883-1884] (preliminary study, selection, and notes by Gregorio Weinberg), vol. 1 (Buenos Aires: Centro Editor de América Latina, 1984).

tions, must maintain the unity that gives life, that gives energy, that gives the character of nationality to civilized peoples.

. . . The Argentine Constitution obeyed healthy principles when it set out the provisions I have referred to, for in penetrating the domain of philosophical considerations, treating the question no longer in the sphere of historical precedents, but rather in the sphere of law, doctrine, and intellectual speculation, it is inconceivable, Mr. President, that there exist a state without God, that there exist a state that, when legislating on the education that is to shape its future citizens intellectually and morally, citizens who are to prolong the fatherland in the future, could leave aside religious notions, that could dispense with religion.

What is the state, Mr. President?

The word has two main meanings: either the state is simply taken as an assemblage of public powers, or it is considered as a society brought together under the same laws, under the same authorities.

In neither concept can it be claimed that the state should be neutral or nonparticipating in matters of religion; and these words, *neutral* and *nonparticipating,* are euphemisms to avoid the direct, true word, the precise and dread word: atheist!

The state cannot rationally be atheist.

The public powers are meaningless, unintelligible, illegitimate, unless they start from the bottom of that very society, express it, and govern it according to its nature, so that it might be steered toward the achievement of the ends befitting great groupings of men, that is, of intelligent, free, responsible, moral beings. And even when the functions of the state are only performed externally, and even when they are especially functions acting as guarantees so that each individual's external activity should not hinder or disturb the activities of others, and society, instead of plunging into anarchy, is kept in order and develops harmoniously, it will not mean that these functions are exercised properly if it casts into oblivion or spurns the guarantee of the guarantees, the basis of individual and social security, the supreme explanation of law, namely, religion.

. . . If we consider the state as a group of individuals who have a collective life, a harmonious life, something that gives it unity and energy, I ask: when does the world present groups of this kind, unless moved principally by those beliefs of which our history holds such glorious expressions and to which I was referring a moment ago? All those who speak of the homeland, do they not understand that this homeland, as well as the land, as well as the light, as well as the air into which we have been born, also represents a shared feeling, a shared thinking, the belief, the hope of the generations that succeed each other in the theater of History? And of all the ideas, all the sentiments that stir the human heart, which could be higher and more worthy of consideration than the idea and the sentiment that tie us to an immortal fate, to eternity, and to God?

. . . When we legislate on schools, we legislate on society's renewal, on the forces that are to act in it, and decisively influence its existence. Obviously, then, this legislation must tend to ensure that these forces are not blind, but conscious forces led by the higher principle of morality, and, consequently, the teaching of religion must be established in public schools.

In opposition to this, it is observed that religious education should be provided in the home and at church; that the state has no reason to concern itself with what pertains to the family or the priest.

The basis of this argument is false, as has just been seen. If it were said that the state must dispense with religious education because religious matters are none of its concern, I have just shown that this is not true in terms of doctrine, nor is it historically the case.

But looking more closely at the argument that the state, while respecting religion, prohibits the schoolmaster in the public school from providing religious education for children and leaves this to the actions of the family and the priests, it is, of course, necessary to note the malice in which crafty publicists have enveloped this doctrine. Under the somewhat deceptive appearance of respect for religion and the family, this doctrine in very many cases nullifies religious education, which, according to the principles of good legislation and mere good sense, should be extensively provided to all children.

Indeed, it is the duty of parents to teach their children religion. The priesthood was established to preach the Christian truth to all. But let us, as practical men, consider the conditions of this teaching in our country. Let us consider the enormous number of children with ignorant and impoverished parents, children deprived of receiving religious education at church—owing to the scarcity of our clergy—because of the impossibility of indoctrinating them, if they had no prior knowledge of the catechism — because of the territorial distribution of the population, unsuited for it; and let us see what results would be produced from the omission in the law of an article such as the one proposed by the committee. That omission would leave a great number of children devoid of religious education, children for whom it is of special interest that they be instructed and raised to the level of Christian civilization, children who have no means in their families to pull themselves up from that situation in which they would be thoughtless voters and dangerous citizens, as claimed at the previous session.

What we want, then, is for the child whose father or priest cannot provide a religious education to find at school the light to replace what is lacking at home, to replace the lack of a priest, something that, as I have said, is unfortunately all too frequent in our special conditions.

The Church wants religious education at school, it wants the catechism to be taught everywhere, and it particularly desires it there where the clergy are scarce, its constant determination being to bring to all people the light of revealed truth.

. . . Doctrines designated with the name of liberal Catholicism have been condemned. There is no place in the Church for liberal Catholics, Catholics who place the teaching and rights of the Church behind the idolatry of the state; and it is a Catholic of this kind, a Catholic who considers the state to be above religion, that the honorable member wishes to make of the president in calling him a *constitutional Catholic.*

The honorable member's aim, irreconcilable with orthodoxy, goes against our very own fundamental code, that says that the president must belong to the Catholic communion, that is, the Catholic Church, which means being subject to its divine teaching, professing all that it professes and teaches. The Constitution does not demand of him any other theology, any other morals than Catholic theology and Catholic morals. It does not demand of him an Argentine or constitutional theology or morals, to speak in the style of my honorable colleague.

And if there is something to be observed in the president of the Republic — from the point of view of religion — it is that he must be truly inspired with the Catholic spirit, have love and sincere respect for it, because of the functions he performs as patron that the Constitution confers on him to discharge them in good faith, as a son of the Church, not with the aim of hostility and ill will toward it, which would be abhorrent to that position.

. . . The Church has not, then, condemned an acceptable doctrine, but has spoken well when it has argued that there are other authorities that must intervene in the education of our youth, and those authorities are the authority of the Church, of the Church, Mr. President, with which it cannot be denied that the Argentine public powers have official relations.

When it is said that there are bishops, when the existence of these prelates is acknowledged in the Argentine Republic, when they are provided with endowments, they are not acknowledged as such, or provided with these resources, so that they be enclosed in the walls of the church; they are acknowledged with the full force of the functions that their dignity encompasses. Those functions are clearly determined in the law and are well known in history. To acknowledge a bishop so that he is praying in church, without allowing him to practice in society the teaching mission entrusted to him by the Church and which the Church cannot resign, would surely be a gross mockery, a repugnant farce.

. . . What is the progress, what is the liberalism, what is the civilization that the *Syllabus* condemns when it says that the Roman pontiff cannot and must not tolerate them?

Sir, the liberalism that is condemned is what in our day is understood as such, having taken as a label a word that deceives by its analogy with *liberty* and that indeed covers up the opposite of it; the liberalism that is condemned is the *idolatry of the state.*

Liberalism contains a concept of the state whereby it can legislate while entirely dispensing with all idea of God and any religious notions.

Liberalism is a way of conceiving of social life, administration, government, completely disconnected from religion.

From there arises a system of legislation, a set of laws of which the bill presented in place of the one advised by the committee would be one of the forerunners.

When the state is conceived as an entity above individual rights, one that does not respect the duty and the right of the father of the family to educate his children—one that does not respect the Church's teaching mission, nor the principle of religion—what happens? The state fills it all, killing all initiative, and proud of its predominance with the desire to preserve it, it legislates in this manner.

. . . Behold modern civilization. What is it if not the absorbent predominance of material interests? Can it be true that amid the pomp of the arts, amid the wealth and abundance, man may have satisfactorily developed as an intellectual and moral being? The answer cannot be affirmative. While it is true that man has progressed materially, it is not true that he shines with the splendor of his virtues.

Science, to which the Church has never been hostile, has taken the wrong path, due to the influence of a foolish pride. The men who penetrate the mysteries of the world; who thrust themselves into and sail through the air endeavoring to mock the adverse currents, who sail the seas and cross the land with the speed of steam power, who send with yet greater speed, no longer the silent sign of thought, but the vibrant word along telephone lines, who paint with brushes of pure light unknown to the ancients, as one Argentine orator said, who analyze the faraway stars, who discover life in organisms unknown because of their minute size—the men who perform such marvels are no more loyal because of it, are no more self-sacrificing than at other moments of history; on the contrary, their selfishness is increasingly refined and powerful. And contemporary societies offer a shocking imbalance between their material greatness and the paltriness, poverty, and weakness of their moral makeup!

It is a surprising phenomenon, where this human duality appears! Never has man been greater, one might say, than in the nineteenth century: governing matter, dominating nature, which now appears to obey him in servile fashion. But this is not the case. Man is, because of his pride, at once abased to that very matter whose docility would be thought a terrible perfidy, and the soul sighs imprisoned in narrow bonds, the sky has no promises of hope, the brilliant star does not symbolize faith, the gaze uncovers only what is useful and profitable for an ephemeral and fleeting existence. The horizon shrinks, man grows smaller, and degrades himself!

. . . The bill of the honorable members to whom I am referring is unacceptable both from a doctrinal and from a practical point of view.

It is unacceptable from the doctrinal point of view because the fact of excluding religion from the number of subjects whose study is demanded as mandatory, permitting only its teaching outside official classroom hours, amounts to considering religion as something futile, as something unnecessary, and disconnecting it from public schools because of a legal ruling.

The bill is equally unacceptable because the fact of leveling out into a common permit the teaching of the different religions can be explained only by the concept that, as far as the state is concerned, they are all alike; and as it is absurd that they could all be true, this amounts to placing in the same category of false religions that which the public powers must uphold under the national Constitution.

The honorable members' bill is, therefore, unconstitutional: it implies a grievous insult against the Catholic religion and is the first step on the road to implanting irreligious legislation in the varied relations of civil life.

It starts with this disconnection of the school regarding the religious principle. It is then declared in law that it is enough for the state that the child, the future citizen, should know how to read and write, grammar, history, and geography, while being ignorant of his duties to God. And logically the day will come when, as I observed a few moments ago, the basis of the family will be for the state a simple contract performed before a civil servant. If one wishes to add a religious ceremony, if one wishes to add the sacrament of marriage, so be it, I care not a jot; the source of rights and obligations lies solely in the contract.

5

DELFÍN GALLO
Speech on the Common
Education Act (1883)

. . . Progress, institutions, and freedom itself will be compromised and distorted in their legitimate hopes of development the day that the political parties responsible for putting those aspirations into practice unite and fight under the banner of religious ideas as the main goal of their efforts, religious ideas that are so liable to fall into aberrations in the masses. The political banner might easily become the bloody standards of other eras, the scandal of the century and of modern civilization.

The social questions that are the mission of the people and their government have never been properly resolved when the solutions were inspired by the interests of a sect or considerations of a purely religious nature.

Happily, we have, until now, avoided that kind of danger, and have done so because our public figures, understanding the depth of the abyss we could have found ourselves dragged into, have skirted around those kinds of questions, always taking prudent solutions, in which the true situation of the minds in the Republic could be seen, reconciling, wherever possible, the demands of liberty and the interests of the dominant church in the country.

Unfortunately, this rule of conduct has been forgotten in this case: the question comes to the Chamber, and I said that I considered it with much apprehension, as with the passions it arouses and amid the ardent atmosphere which has built up, I fear it may be the spark that ignites a perilous blaze.

. . . Mr. President: I have said it before from this very stand, and be-

Original title: "Discurso sobre la ley de educación común." Source: *Debate parlamentario, ley 1420, 1883–1884* [Parliamentary debate, law 1420, 1883–1884] (preliminary study, selection, and notes by Gregorio Weinberg), vol. 1 (Buenos Aires: Centro Editor de América Latina, 1984).

lieve it necessary to repeat it on this occasion. I have the deepest respect
for the Catholic religion. It was the faith of my parents, that is, of those
who instilled in my soul all the sentiments of virtue and honor that I can
cherish, and it is the religion of the vast majority of the people whom we
represent in this Chamber. Nor am I one of those who believe Catholicism irreconcilable with freedom.

. . . But here we reach the fourth point, a key one in this discussion:
the secular nature of education.

The doctrine of the Church regarding secular or religious teaching
has been set down with great eloquence by the speaker who preceded
me on the floor.

Yes, Mr. President, what the Church prefers, above all, is that education be religious, Catholic, and that such Catholic religious education be
provided by the state, which in that case will only be—in the words of
one thinker—the general, the armed wing of the Church.

That is its doctrine.

. . . It appears to me that after all the progress made by humanity, nobody could maintain the advisability, the usefulness to the Argentine
Republic, of spiritual power, of the power of the popes, coming to rule
over, to prevail over, temporal power, that is, over the sovereignty of the
people, which is today the basis of all political government.

. . . But it is not only the extirpation of religious sentiment that can
bring decay to societies: it is also the deviation of that same sentiment,
being led along a wrong course.

And I also say to you: Attack atheism, but attack intolerance and fanaticism as well. Attack atheism, which can produce barbarism in the
midst of civilization, but also attack fanaticism, which is the death of
conscience and the gloomy silence of tombs.

Fanaticism means Spain, still struggling to shake off that leaden
shroud that has covered it for so many centuries; the Papal States, the
Two Sicilies, the whole of Italy, that is, the most beautiful regions in
Europe, where the sun shines with the greatest splendor, where the land
bears the best fruits, where, having been the seat of nations that have
held the scepter of the world, they have become poor, dejected, and humiliated, falling apart like the walls of an old convent, whose dwellers,
in rapturous contemplation of God, must have forgotten the laws and
the needs of existence.

I would not, for all these reasons, wish the suppression of religious feeling on our people. On the contrary, I want the atmosphere of Argentine schools to be a religious atmosphere, to use Guizot's beautiful phrase.

But could our bill possibly have such an outcome? Could our bill lead to a suppression of religious sentiment in our society? I have taken it and examined it from all sides and, frankly, I cannot find any of these drawbacks.

Our bill begins by saying: "the teaching of morals shall be compulsory."

What does the study of morals mean?

Is it perhaps the morals of self-interest, the morals of Condillac, the morals of selfishness? No, Mr. President, it is not the study of those morals that we decree. We decree the study of morals based in God, based in human responsibility, that is, in the great dogma of the immortality of the soul.

. . . Our bill does not seek to stamp out religious sentiment. We prescribe that morality be taught, and we also open the doors of schools so that religious ministers may complete the work of the state in matters religious. The only difference between the honorable members who defend the committee's bill and we who attack it lies here: must the atmosphere of schools be solely a religious one, or must it also be a Catholic atmosphere?

Herein, in precise terms, Mr. President, lies the true nature of the question; herein lies the only way in which, in my opinion, the question must be dealt with. And with the question posed as such, I contend that the committee's bill runs counter to the Constitution, counter to freedom of conscience, which is above all the constitutions of the world because it is the right of mankind. It goes against the mission of the state in matters of education, and it goes even against the correctly understood interests of the Church.

. . . Mr. President: the preamble to the Constitution states that its object is to ensure the benefits of freedom for ourselves, our children, and all men on Earth who wish to come and inhabit our soil.

This is the primary aim of the Constitution.

But, Mr. President, would that purpose be met, if in the name of an alleged state religion, which does not exist, as I have just demonstrated, we were to corrupt these other high principles: freedom to practice a religion, freedom of conscience?

No, Mr. President, it would not.

The immigrant will come to our shores: he will come, attracted by the beauty of our sky, the mildness of our climate, the liberality of our customs. The immigrant will come to consolidate our greatness.

But, Mr. President, let us not begin by placing obstacles, we ourselves, to such a coveted outcome. We need, as the member for Entre Ríos has said, to open our doors to the civilized element that Europe sends us, just as the one hundred doors of ancient Thebes were opened. We need to summon all men, whatever their country, whatever their creed, and instill in them, through the display and the reality of our liberties, a love for this land, which they will grow to consider their own, taking an interest in and contributing effectively to its prosperity and greatness.

Your bill, Gentlemen of the committee, runs counter to those noble purposes. The immigrant would be alienated from us were we to begin by saying to him: we are going to force your children to profess the Catholic Apostolic Roman religion; or, at least, we are going to oblige your children to be educated in a religious atmosphere, dangerous for the faith you might teach them, were you at full liberty to do so.

We cannot do this in the name of the well-understood interests of the Republic. We shall not thus ensure the benefits of freedom for all those born on our soil or for all those who come to it trusting in the beautiful promise of our Constitution.

The basis of freedom is equality, and there is no equality where there is no respect for the rights of all, not only of the majorities, but also of the minorities, the minorities who, as one of our great publicists said a few days ago, even when they are made up of a single individual have the same prerogatives as the largest majorities when it comes to defending a right.

I shall go further. I shall demonstrate that this bill, as the committee submits it, would undermine one of the most liberal principles of our fundamental law.

Our Constitution reads: "All the inhabitants of the land are admissible to public employment without any other requirement than their ability." Will it, therefore, be possible to apply this principle if the committee's bill is passed? The committee tells us: The Catholic Apostolic Roman religion will be taught compulsorily; and, as I demonstrated earlier, the Catholic religion could only be taught by a Catholic.

I suppose that the committee does not intend to suggest that the schoolmaster could hypocritically renounce his beliefs to teach a religion that is not his own, to become a propagandist for it. I declare that any schoolmaster who did such a thing should have the doors of education closed to him in this country!

Therefore, we can only impose this condition of religious teaching on those schoolmasters who are Roman Catholic. And I believe that the Chamber will agree with me that it would be necessary to modify the article of the Constitution establishing, in addition to the condition of suitability, the condition of being Roman Catholic for the job of schoolteacher, and, if we follow that path, every other post. I will even go so far as to say that this bill, as it stands, attacks the preamble of the Constitution and attacks also some of its highest principles.

But it attacks something else. It attacks freedom of conscience, which is above all the constitutions of the world because it is an inalienable right of man. Allow me to demonstrate.

It is said: We save freedom of conscience because we leave the dissident free to prevent his children being taught religion. There is no violence in our bill; the Catholics will learn their religion, and the dissidents none. That is, as Representative Lagos noted, that the propagandists for religious schools proclaim the atheist school for the dissidents, who will precisely need more than that teaching, having been born in error.

But not even this is accurate, and in making these claims, the committee forgets all the natural laws that bear on the building of a child's intelligence. The child learns not so much from the lessons of his schoolmasters as by contagion or by example. Hence, if the Catholic doctrine is taught at school, inevitably the children of dissidents, immersed in that atmosphere, would not be able to escape from the dominant influence. Everything around them will speak of Catholicism; their classmates, the style of their lessons, everything will attract them with invincible force, and they will end up being Catholics, against the will of their parents.

And this is so much more dangerous and unconstitutional, inasmuch as mandatory schooling is established and the dissident is told: you have no choice but to send your children to this school, even though you may not wish to, and even though they will be taught doctrines that are not your own.

. . . Sir: the mission of the state, inasmuch as it is a supplementary mission, goes only as far as the true needs of the state itself. The true need, the primary purpose of the state, is to educate citizens capable of continuing the work of civilization, in which all human societies are involved. But once this objective is fulfilled, its right disappears, as does its duty. And because, in order to make citizens civilized and free, there is no need for special teaching of revealed dogma, and because in society there are more than enough elements for this teaching to be done without need for official intervention, there is no place for state intervention in accordance with the very principles upheld by Representative Goyena; and if this is the case, the right disappears, as does the duty.

Upholding the doctrine of freedom of education, which, as I said at the start, is now the banner raised in France, the official school, the state school, was attacked, and it was said: If all teaching were surrendered to the state, we would run the risk of seeing tyrannies grow up.

I have stated already that I do not wish at present to go into this great question of freedom of education.

. . . No! Mr. President. Let us not put such power in the hands of the state.

The state is there to fulfill temporal needs in the world. It is there to ensure benefits that are related to man only as a social being. For spiritual needs, there is the Church. May the Church undertake its mission as the shepherd of souls. May it teach religion. Let us leave the state to teach only temporal things, limiting itself, as I said earlier, in religious matters, to what is indispensable for the fulfillment of its mission, that is, those where reason may rise up by itself, without need to resort to revelation.

. . . In the common schools in the United States, they teach what we wish for: morals, based in God and the immortality of the soul; but it is left to the Sunday schools, entirely independent of the others, to teach the religions of different faiths. It is in these diverse Sunday schools where the Catholic teaches people to be good Catholics, the Protestant to be good Protestants.

And it is this system that rests on human nature, which reconciles all liberties, one that by taking the same path as the Republican institutions founded by Washington and Franklin, Hamilton and Jefferson, must obtain the ultimate victory.

Do you want the schools of the United States in our midst?

We will receive them with veneration and pride. But before that, consider and see how what we propose, which is a transaction, just as the article of our Constitution on religion is a transaction, goes much further than the prevailing doctrine in that nation.

But I digress from my purpose, to which I now return.

I have, in making this brief incursion into the state of the question in the world, only sought to establish this fact: the United States, Holland, Canada, Australia, Belgium, even Ireland, they all have neutral schools. And they are surely not peoples whose religious sentiment is any less developed. No. Nowhere has religious sentiment been so high, so splendid, as in the United States.

6

ROQUE SÁENZ PEÑA
Speech on the American "Zollverein"[1] (1889) (Conference of the Pan-American Union)

... I would like to begin by stating that I do not hold the key to Argentine markets, perhaps because they have no such key, since they lack any instrument of closure or any machinery of monopoly or prohibition. We have lived with our customs open to world trade, our rivers free for all flags, our industries free, inviting the labor of man with their benefits, and above all, free the man himself, who joins in our national life, his person protected under the guarantee of habeas corpus, respected in his conscience by the broadest religious tolerance, and protected in his rights by the principle of civil equality for nationals and foreigners alike. Yet neither the declarations we advanced in the past, when we had only just rid ourselves of the Spanish Crown and were publicly announcing, in 1813, that there were no slaves on Argentine soil, nor the liberties we proclaim in the present, with the conscience of our national individuality, pose a threat to the security of the states. The history of our autonomies bears witness to it and it will be proven by the times to come, saluting in the plenitude of their rights the same nations that have come to discuss their material interests, undoubtedly because their political fates were well fixed by the sword of three great men, who ...[2] and share the dominion of immortality.

The mutual exchange of inert products and the human tides constituted by beneficial waves of immigration, which have been encouraged rather than restricted by our governments, can hardly be considered cause for concern to the firmly consolidated sovereignties. Products

Original title: "Discurso sobre el 'Zollverein' americano." Source: Roque Sáenz Peña, *Escritos y discursos* [The writings and speeches of Roque Sáenz Peña], vol. 1 (Buenos Aires: J. Peuser, 1914).

1. German Customs Union, a coalition of German states formed in 1818 to manage customs and economic policies within their territories. [E.N.]

2. Some words are missing in the original text. [E.N.]

seek consumers without concerning themselves with hegemonies or supremacies, just as immigrants seek well-being and fortune without aspiring to the leading action of political government. Thus we greet immigrants with hospitality and without distrust, providing them not only with the tools for work, but also with ownership of the land that will form their property and allow them to mix with our nationals in the government of the municipalities, where they represent interests carved out by the abundant wealth of our own soil.

As immigrants are our friends, as their children are our fellow citizens, international trade is our ally in the transfer of wealth: *friendship, trade, wealth, citizenship* are terms that exclude those fanciful dangers that would unhappily have arrested the development of the peoples of America. And were we to need reassuring examples for our practices, we would once again find them in the nation that receives us with such benevolence. Immigration was for this nation an element of greatness, and naturalization, a strong play of advantageous avulsions. We proceed with a certain deliberation: we summon the immigrant with his own nationality and without urging him to change it through acts restricting his legal status; we expect citizenship to develop by the natural laws of generation. The assimilated whole is less dense, but the ties of the soil are no less vigorous, nor is the sense of nationality perceived to be weaker. So it is that we preserve the unity of our people, without destructive localisms, without selfish rivalries or any other emulations than those born of the cult of their independence and sovereignty, of those generous ideals that reject the language of disbelief and of protest about thoughtless auguries closer to anathema than to prophecy.

. . . Unfortunately, Honorable Delegates, feelings may upset our decisions in this case. Trade is inspired by interest and maintained by profits. It ends where generosity begins, and lives disconcerted under the action of the affections. It is not enough, then, that we greet each other as friends and embrace each other as brothers to divert or connect tides that it is not in our power to direct. We may have signed friendly and cordial agreements, endorsed—I do not doubt—with sincerity, but disavowed in a not-so-distant future by the very action of those forces we tried to control by our actions. Human agreements will never be able to dominate the intensity or the direction of these tides formed by production and trade, fueled as they are by insuperable egotisms, persistent activity, and autonomous energies of their own. Trade being the work of necessity, convenience, and benefit, production obeys the decrees of nature. When state action has sought to violate the result of these forces, it has made itself felt generally as a symptom of disturbance, and the governments entering into alliances to avert it have been no luckier in their means and successes. As old as the original forms of trade and as primitive as the barter of yore, the laws of supply and demand shall continue to govern the exchange of surpluses between peoples, and if reform and evolution are to occur, they will be born of the choice of consumption imposed by civilization and culture, which make societies exacting, producers industrious, and the land twice as fertile and fruitful.

. . . It is no mystery to anyone that the nations of America maintain and develop their trade from their relationships with Europe. The economic phenomenon has an effortlessly natural explanation: our riches are formed by the products of the soil, and if there is a market on that continent which in turn produces manufactured goods, it must deserve our special consideration, which I shall be pleased to give it. But it is logical, necessary, and inevitable that countries producing natural fruits or raw materials should seek to procure manufacturing markets, especially those that receive them freely.

. . . I find that the inalterability of tariffs is an insurmountable barrier for our trade, and, even if the league should wish to make exceptions that looked to the autonomy of the customs of the North in relation to Europe, forming a "Zollverein" with a giant's head, we should not succeed in increasing trade: this will be born strong and sturdy when protection has switched its tariffs for Gaurey's maxim of *laissez faire, laissez passer.*

When the political side of the "Zollverein" is considered, it may be difficult to ignore the fact that it entails a substantial diminution of sovereignty, which would not be offset by any discernible advantage. An international assembly would replace the legislative bodies of the state to fix or impose customs revenues within the national territory. In Argentina, as in the United States, this power rests exclusively with the national Congress, the true representative of sovereignty delegated by the people. This precept is written into the Constitution and could not be repealed without a constituent assembly to exonerate national legislators from such an important power. Most American constitutions derive this power from their own legislative bodies, and we would then find ourselves faced with general political upheavals necessary to form eighteen constituent assemblies with the purpose of reforming each and every one of the constitutions that govern our peoples. Such upheaval would not be justified by utopian fantasies.

The complications would be no less serious at the international level. The effects of restricted leagues on the general movement of trade are middling to poor. We see, however, that differential duties have brought with them destructive antagonisms between nations. Proof of this in our own day and age is found in the tariff war between Austria and Romania, while a similar war between Italy and France has happily ended, not without the former seeking a closer relationship with the sovereign of Alsace and Lorraine. But we are a most important factor in trans-Atlantic trade relations, representing $2.7 billion, and it is easy to picture Europe's retaliation when it feels the effects of a continental blockade, maintained, true, not by warships, but by belligerent tariffs. It would not be peoples bound by political ties that reach agreements inspired by national feeling, it would be a war of one continent against another, eighteen sovereignties in alliance to exclude from trading activity the same Europe that holds out her hand to us, stretches her arms out to us, and complements our economic life, after sending us her civilization and her culture, her sciences and her arts, industries, and customs, which have completed our sociological evolution. We would have inserted an isolating membrane that time could render unbreakable, when we would have enclosed our fragmentary civilizations, which need to seek their complement in the free contact of mankind.

. . . The truth is that our trading with the United States suggests observations that could be presented in a spirit of equity and friendship. Our wools, which are the most substantial item in Argentina's output, are at a disadvantage in relation to those of other wool-producing markets.

. . . It is odd that the opinion expressed by the commission, advising the principle of reciprocity, should run perfectly contrary to the trade relations it was commissioned to study. The commission advises the adoption of this principle through trade agreements. But the principle may arise both from such agreements and from autonomous tariffs, in which case it would become counterproductive. If the Argentine government were to levy a 60 percent tax on American pine, machinery, and oil, as Argentine products are taxed in the United States, would this not be the principle of reciprocity recommended by the commission? If the MacKinley [*sic*] Bill were to take up citizenship under our laws, would not that too be reciprocity in the practices of international trade?

My honorable colleagues will answer that they recommend reciprocity through agreements. But treaties are the *modus faciendi;* they do not attack or transform the principle when it is imposed through the free tariffs set by each nation.

There is something else. If my information is correct, the Ways and Means Committee is discussing heavier new duties on our products at the request of livestock breeders. Will the commission insist on advising us to follow its opinion? If the former duties were differential — and I regard them as prohibitive for the Argentine Republic — what would the result of strict reciprocity be? The commission recommends a principle that may lead us inexorably to retaliation, which we would not wish to hear or feel in our trading practices.

I deplore having expatiated over such thorny issues, but the opinion of the majority leads us to this territory and we cannot avoid it.

The response from the United States has been categorical for the Argentine government: they will continue to favor imports from Oceania and southern Africa, despite the liberality of our laws, which have allowed them to double their trade in relation to our own. The delegation, in whose name I have the honor of speaking, is justified, then, in not opening doors that have been firmly closed to it. It merely declares that its customs shall remain inalterable and free for this continent, and for the rest of the world, adding, in compliance with its instructions, that it does not reject the possibility of striking agreements, though it does refrain from recommending this, since advice is not what trade is in need of.

I have completed my official duties.

Allow me now to make a highly personal statement. Do not look on what I have spoken about as anything but considerations of brotherly affection for all the peoples and governments of this continent. If anyone believes he has seen those feelings weakened in my spirit, he must persuade himself otherwise: I am not lacking in affection or love for America; I am lacking in distrust and ingratitude toward Europe. I do not forget that Spain, our mother country, is there, watching with open delight the development of its old dominions under the actions of generous, virile peoples who inherited her blood. Nor that our friend Italy is there, and our sister France, who lights the waters of New York with her effigy of a goddess, the free continent par excellence shimmering with the free part of democratic Europe, which has just brought together the world on the Champ de Mars, to spread the example of liberty to the future republics of the New World.

I believe that sociological law leads peoples to representative government in the same way that contemporary economy steers societies to freedom of trading. The nineteenth century has given us possession of our political rights, consolidating those our elder sister brought after struggles worthy of her sovereignty. May the American Century, as the twentieth century has been dubbed, look on our open trading with all the peoples of the Earth and testify to the noble duel of free work, in which God has rightly been said to measure the ground, level the souls, and spread the light.

America for the human race!

7

LEANDRO N. ALEM
Speech at the National Senate (1891)

. . . I shall be as brief as possible and try to find a way through this thorny political matter.

It has rightly been said there is unease in our country and, it has been added, revolution is rife.

There is indeed great unease in our country and revolution is indeed rife. What remains to be seen is the cause of this unease and who the real revolutionaries are.

To my mind, the revolutionaries are those who break the law, who try to subvert our system, who subjugate public freedoms, and who subsequently thrust our country into an abnormal, unconstitutional situation, which must of necessity bring about this state of restlessness and agitation—this unease that we are feeling.

Those of us who fight against this still-prevailing system are not really the revolutionaries: we are the conservatives. We can say of our revolution what Macaulay said of the English Revolution when comparing it to the French.

The French Revolution shook society to its core, bringing about profound innovation in the political, social, and economic order; the English Revolution did nothing more than defend itself from the usurpation and despotism of the Crown: namely, it sought to reestablish its freedoms and institutions. It sought a return to the normal situation from which Charles II's blind obstinacy, poor counseling, and all the usurpation in Parliament had torn it away.

It is possible that, when there is no free exercise of the right to normal development of individual and collective activities, when the guarantees accorded by the Constitution, when the most sacred right, the

Original title: "Discurso sobre el senado nacional." Source: Leandro N. Alem, *Obra parlamentaria de Leandro N. Alem* [Parliamentary works of Leandro N. Alem], vol. 6 (La Plata: Camara de Diputados, 1949).

basis of our republican system, which is the right of suffrage, is ignored and subjugated, is it possible for there to be well-being in our country, or for the peace that is sought to be attained? True peace will not be attained, beneficial and fruitful peace will not be attained, the peace that comes from a normal situation, from the free exercise of law; an enforced quietism may be attained, somber silence may be attained, the silence and peace of graves.

And it is because of this, Mr. President, that this unease is being felt, because of this that all those in government, as I have said, in open war against the people, are, like criminals, at every step and every moment and in every way seeing the shadow of the agent of justice. Because of this they dream of conspiracies and great plots; because of this they make up so many fables, and because of this they impart such tall stories to the national executive.

I am a revolutionary, I must frankly confess, I am a revolutionary in the highest sense of the word. I do not pay lip service to revolution; I know perfectly well that it is an extreme resource and a supreme right of the people: it is the natural law: *Lex non inscripta, lex nata est,* as Cicero said. It is the legitimate defense that is made by the people as it is by individuals; and this right is recognized by all constitutionalists, because when a government oversteps its functions, when it shatters the foundations of the political system that governs the people, a system that they have given themselves in order to guarantee their rights and their freedoms, that power has lost its authority, gone beyond the source of the law, and, consequently, placed itself in the position of a genuine aggressor.

Therein lies an undeniable fact. The people's party is the most powerful party, the only organized force that exists in all the Republic. There is, Mr. President, no other political organization before it in such conditions; there is no such thing as a government party. If so, where is its base? Where are those powerful expressions of opinion? Nowhere do I see them.

How much time and how much effort is being spent in reestablishing, or rather, in elaborating, perhaps, if I may use the phrase, in manufacturing a special party ad hoc, for specific political ends!

The people's party is the only one that exists in the whole Republic. And why has the people's party been able to develop freely until now? Why has the people's party been unable to triumph in any state in the

Republic at any of its electoral acts? Might it have come down to the cowardice of the people? Might it have come down to negligence or abandonment? We are seeing what is happening day by day, and nobody thinks of that. It is fighting fiercely; yet the fact remains, Mr. President, that it is fighting the immense power of the nation.

The senator for Santa Fe wished to bring a charge against me, saying that I excused the people of Mendoza for not having the necessary pride or energy to withstand two hundred regular soldiers. There were not two hundred soldiers in Mendoza; there were not fifty soldiers in Catamarca; there were not two hundred soldiers in Córdoba; there were not twenty soldiers in any other such province. The fact is that behind those two hundred soldiers was the entire army of the nation. The fact is that there was all the authority of the nation against that party, and when the people know and are fully conscious that two hundred men are at the disposal of the governor, who wishes to win an election and form a legislature, or wishes to leave a successor in his post, it is futile, Mr. President, to demand that they go forth into useless sacrifice, for if at first they do succeed in overcoming those forces, more or less weak in their numbers, they know that the committed national authority, which is unthinkingly committed, will immediately take action and overwhelm them completely.

But today patriotism advises, it was said, acceptance of this situation, albeit de facto, and the national executive's conduct is wise and patriotic in distributing the nation's forces everywhere to support those agents who, as I have said, are engaged in open war against the people. The fait accompli, the force, to then obtain the results that suit certain policies.

I do not see patriotism that way. I do not believe that compromising with situations of that nature, compromising with those who break the law, compromising with political immorality, can ever result in a common good for our country.

It may suit and be the politics of the clever men, the practical men who are wont to call themselves statesmen and who I might say are fishing in troubled waters.

Such practical men, such wise politicians, always appear in situations such as the one we are going through, accepting the accomplished facts, accepting established situations, regardless of their origin and regardless of the principles that are compromised.

... I support the politics of principles and always will: whether I stand or fall, I will never negotiate with a fait accompli, I will never negotiate with force, I will never negotiate with immorality, I will never negotiate with those who violate institutions and public freedoms. I will never stand back and see how certain situations play out before entering into them; I must also fight as a strong man and a good man, regardless of the results, because for me the moral idea is the only one that can regenerate society.

Yes, I agree with the senator for Santa Fe: these people were badly downcast. There were undoubtedly elements for unconditional compliance, compliance that is not of this or of any other year, but which has been germinating ever since the administration that was born in 1880, which was what started all these attacks on our institutions, and all the attacks on political morality and administrative morality, an administration of which the senator for Santa Fe was once a part. Yes, these people were prepared, as I have said on one solemn occasion, for oppression. Corruption was rife, and the worst kind of corruption, for it descended from the upper reaches of government and penetrated and filtered down, so to speak, through all social classes. That fatal corruption that disconcerts and annihilates all, that lacerates all hearts, that breaks down all characters, that infects all intelligence. That fatal corruption that leaves men with no notion of what is fair, what is honest, what is lawful, and which, making personal interests and material wealth the only goal in life, drags people like corpses at the feet of all ambitions and all tyrannies.

To attack this evil there came the reaction of April 13 and the revolutionary movement of July 26, closely linked, for, say what you will, the July revolution is no more than the product of the popular meeting of April 13 in the *frontón* of Basque *pelota* in Buenos Aires.

I agree with the senator that once public opinion has been stirred and this resurrection of the civic spirit has occurred, we must encourage it in every way. But we must do so not with his propaganda and doctrines, but with our doctrine, so that it may remain firm in supporting their rights, denouncing and condemning lawbreakers, pursuing all degenerates and prevaricators, all those, indeed, who might undermine our institutions and bring about the disrepute of the nation before the consideration of our own people and foreigners. Yes, Mr. President, it is necessary to educate the people, and to do so what is most needed, unquestionably, is character in the ruling classes, in those of us who believe we are capable of ruling the people and leading them on the path of good. Of what use is intelligence without character? None. And what the people of the Republic suffered at certain moments was precisely that, the breakdown of character.

In this people, favored with intelligence and valor, in this people in whom one can see the stuff and cut of a hero on the battlefield in every last officer of our army, in every student in our schools the echoes of a powerful talent, there was, however, a lack of character.

Character is strength, character is the true potential of the human personality; intelligence is no more than clarity, no more than light. It is a focus that sheds light, I repeat, but which in itself raises not so much as a clump of grass. The steam engine gives no light but it runs, it drags, it overcomes all obstacles, triumphs over all problems: that is character.

All reformers, all religious leaders, all leaders of sects, as the senator for Santa Fe has said, have stood out and placed themselves in that condition not because of their talent, but because of their character: Moses, Jesus, Mohammed, Buddha, were not, Mr. President, great intelligences; they were great characters.

8

UNIÓN CÍVICA [CIVIC UNION]
Declaration of Principles (1891)

In view of the extraordinary gravity of the political, financial, and economic situation, which forces all inhabitants of this land to be aware of the causes that have brought us to this distressing state, the National Committee feels that the time has come to speak to the Republic, for, bent as it is on the fight to renew national powers, it believes that, for the sake of the greater understanding of the righteousness and sincerity of its purposes, the Committee must frankly reveal the causes of the trouble and propose the unique and proper means of combating it, hereby expanding and commenting on the principles of the Civic Union in the current political struggle.

The Argentine Republic had reached an era of exceptional prosperity. Capital and men from the civilized nations came to seek profitable employment, coupling to their own advantage social and scientific progress, and the development of the nation's productive potential. These goods were not the work of our efforts: they have been prepared by the illustrious men who founded independence and by those who, inspired by high feelings of patriotism, gave us the national Constitution, a charter of freedom and justice.

This inheritance is therefore doubly sacred: on the one hand, the tradition of patriotism and honor, which we must preserve intact as a solid foundation of institutional life; on the other, the solemn pledge to provide a perfect guarantee to the rights of all men who should come to inhabit this soil. To our shame, when we should have been writing the most brilliant page of our history, in which, at the time that marks human fates, this land is the most privileged place on the planet, bad governments have placed us in danger of appearing to the world as a society of men without conscience, without justice, and without free-

Original title: "Declaración de principios." Source: Hipólito Yrigoyen, *Pueblo y go-bierno* [People and government], vol. 2 (Buenos Aires: Editorial Raigal, 1956).

dom. Today, the Argentine Republic, it pains us to say, is deeply compromised, and some European newspapers have dared suggest something that the Republic and the Americas will nevertheless indignantly reject, namely, the formation of international committees to intervene in its finances, as in Turkey and Egypt.

. . . Such an alarming situation imposes serious duties on citizens, and out of concern for them the National Committee of the Civic Union has resolved to publish this manifesto of the Republic, in order to expose frankly the dangers surrounding it, so that all well-intentioned patriotic men may join in the work of common salvation. The National Committee has already expressed in other manifestos its main principles and the disinterestedness of its cause, and now proceeds to establish these noble ideals more positively, recording in concrete formulas the bases of the reforms it initiates and will strive to see prevail in government.

It is axiomatic to the Argentine mind that this sickness has been produced by an excess of influence of the governing party and that the official banks have been the active agent of the ruin of public and private fortune, and of the depression of the national character. The official bank constitutes a permanent danger, because it will always be a political medium tied to the influence of partisan passions. Therefore, to work against this type of establishment is to work with sanity and patriotism. Citizens need to develop freely in the life of the state, but to do so the state must not take over all means of their individual action. If the state, taken in the restrictive sense of government, which manages the treasury, the army, the fleet, the civil service, already constituting an enormous force, also has the power to manage the private credit of citizens, they do not in fact exist as free men, being imprisoned in the sole terrain that should have been their bastion of defense, their home. Human history teaches us that men show heroism against the dominance of force, but that they are weak against influence in their feelings. This is perfectly logical. They group together as a people or nation to guarantee their individual action and the happiness of their homes. The official bank, then, is an element that disturbs the social order, and it will be a wise policy that tends to suppress it.

In support of this theory, an important historical precedent may be found in the Democratic Party of the United States, which in 1836 abolished the national privileges of the Bank of Philadelphia to save the North American nation from political corruption. President Jackson, in a solemn moment, told Congress: "The balance established in our Constitution will be broken if we keep on accepting the existence of associations invested with exclusive privileges. Those privileges soon provide them with the means of exercising a powerful influence over the political conduct of the people, or of availing themselves of the labor and earnings of the greater number. Wherever this spirit of monopoly becomes an ally of political power, tyranny and despotism are born."[1]

Whatever will happen, as is so often the case among us, if political power continues to absorb everything, that is, capital, privileges, and the management of the main state banks? The National Committee, which is decidedly inclined toward banking freedom but does not yet settle on a definitive system to be adopted by the Republic, as this depends a great deal on the circumstances and the means, states that it will favor the absolute suppression of any governmental interference in banking administration, regardless of the system that might predominate.

... Another topic worthy of public attention is that of setting a limit on fiduciary issues and insuring the country against inconvertible paper currency laws with a retroactive effect. Resorting to issuing currency is a vulgar means of resolving momentary difficulties, and one that does not resolve financial problems, unless it is used as a system component that embraces all extremes to be consulted. It shall, however, be necessary as long as credit is not exhausted, so that any such issue shall produce a beneficial effect, for if it were to come when there was no credit, it would have a depressing effect on the capital created. For it is a serious evil in collective life, because the formation of capital takes a great deal of time and effort. The theory of issue must be accepted only as an extension of capital, but not as a substitute for capital, which is what is presently being done in the country in establishing a bank with fifty million paper pesos and no effective backing. It is doubly necessary to

1. The quotation seems to be taken from a Spanish (or French) translation of President Jackson's seventh State of the Union Address (1835). The original text is as follows: "Lavish public disbursements and corporations with exclusive privileges would be its substitutes for the original and as yet sound checks and balances of the Constitution— the means by whose silent and secret operation a control would be exercised by the few over the political conduct of the many by first acquiring that control over the labor and earnings of the great body of the people. Wherever this spirit has effected an alliance with political power, tyranny and despotism have been the fruit." [E.N.]

incorporate these principles into the financial and economic policy of the Republic because of the considerable hindrances that constant, sharp alterations in currency value bring to immigration and the increase of wealth. This is the main reason why the arrival of men suitable for agriculture has been paralyzed, why many settlers emigrate, and why the movement of business and industry is in abeyance. Therefore, any unguaranteed issues must be avoided, as in addition to increasing the cost of living, they prevent the arrival of foreign capital and people, which are indispensable to Argentina's progress. And it must be affirmed that as an invariable rule of our government, in no case shall inconvertible paper currency rules be passed that alter the monetary obligations established in contracts, for they constitute a property, and property has been declared inviolable by the Constitution. The National Committee shall seek to limit issues within the ideas expressed and declares itself openly opposed to the inconvertible currency laws.

Under the system of liberties that the Civic Union shall uphold in government, the National Committee believes in the need to suppress governmental interference in the stock exchanges, as these institutions must be managed with complete independence, allowing any errors or abuses committed therein to have their own corrective via legal intervention, in the relevant cases, or via the clash of conflicting interests. Human experience has shown that the best vigilance is the kind exercised by those who have a stake in producing it and that interference by foreign authorities is futile, if not pernicious. For four years the public power has intervened in our stock exchange, and the result of this has been to disturb private business and further aggravate the ruinous state of the nation's finances.

... In our determination to pay preferential attention to the country's output, it becomes necessary to provide effective guarantees of population and labor to the sales of fiscal land. The general laws regarding public land state that sales carried out by the state be for different persons, in small lots, but this condition has often been violated, and a buyer may, via numerous applications, acquire larger areas of land than was permitted him. The community is most interested in correcting this abuse, for property should be placed within the reach of the greatest number and the large areas of land that pass into the hands of a single owner are intended not for work, but for speculation. It is therefore best for it to be determined in the law that public land shall be sold only in small lots, under the condition of population or labor, and that the buyer may not transfer it to another, under penalty of nullity and loss of the price of purchase, before duly fulfilling these conditions. If any major capitalist or colonizing enterprise should request a considerable area, it shall be a matter for a special law, but such a concession, if believed to be suitable, should be granted under the mandatory clause of the division of land, making the settler the owner, with absolute prohibition of any leasing contract.

. . . Everyone is concerned about the unsuitable distribution of the army in the territory of the provinces, and how the national government makes use of this means to restrict the electoral right of citizens or pressure the local authorities. The Constitution provides the president with the powers to use the military forces, distributing them according to the nation's needs, but such a power should not be seen as arbitrary.

How will the autonomous authority of a provincial governor be reconciled with the stationing of forces in his territory that do not belong to him? Any such forces shall have to be automatic, for otherwise any action they conduct will infringe national sovereignty. Without suggesting the idea of categorical prohibition, which would clash with the constitutional principle, the National Committee shall favor a law regulating this presidential power and adapting the stationing of federal forces in peacetime in the territories of the provinces to the true spirit of the Constitution.

The distribution of the army in the provinces constitutes a permanent and clandestine intervention, one that we have repeatedly seen used to alternatively overthrow or sustain governors.

It is necessary to put a stop to such abuse, for the autonomy of the States to be respected, and for our regular army to watch over the safety of our frontiers and only perform the national roles inherent to its post.

. . . One of the main factors of the deep unease afflicting the Republic is, beyond question, the absolute predominance of heads of state over parliaments, the judiciary, and public opinion. The excess of power concentrated in the hands of the president and governors, due to the absence of any prudent laws regulating certain constitutional faculties, which, out of malice or perhaps because those same faculties are exorbitant, they have abused, has enabled them to gradually suppress political rights, rule without controls in the legislative bodies, and even perniciously influence the judiciary. This systematic process, slow but sure, to undermine our institutions, to lead our country to ruination and govern it without the healthy checks and balances of a free people, demonstrates that not all the ills of the times are the fault of the rulers, but of the deficiency of our own legislation. The National Committee, which calmly analyzes the causes of general unease, shall put all its endeavors into undertaking serious legislative reforms to guarantee public opinion and the parliaments their legitimate influence in the acts of government, reduce to prudent limits the exercise of the powers of the executive power, and combine the independence of the judges with the effectiveness of their responsibilities.

. . . The fundamental question left for the Civic Union to resolve is that of the freedom to vote, the scandalous suppression of which has caused the ills afflicting the Republic. On this issue, official abuse has reached its climax: citizens are fined, persecuted, imprisoned, and even hunted down like wild animals so that they might not vote or assert their status as Argentines. Two thousand years ago, the Latins found shelter in the law by stating: "I am a Roman citizen!" Today, at the end of the nineteenth century, in the heyday of world civilization, men are being killed because they claim, "I am an Argentine citizen!" This infamy must end forever; all men must be made aware that when the law exercises the right of the citizen, and when anyone attacks this right in any form whatsoever, it is an abominable crime.

The Argentine citizen's electoral rights must be guaranteed: in registration, in the ballot, and in the count. The National Committee therefore declares that, considering the right of the citizen supreme, it shall promote the reform of the electoral law on the basis of a permanent electoral register, punishing with imprisonment and the temporary loss of political rights those public officials who, from the government or from the boards qualifying or receiving votes, fraudulently deprive Argentines of their electoral rights. It also believes it appropriate to seek a way to give representation to the minorities.

Since the foundation of the true republican system lies in the suitability of the citizens, in their aptitude to exercise public liberties and defend their rights when these are threatened, and as furthermore, large masses of our fellow citizens lack the necessary preparation to duly fulfill these political functions, the Civic Union shall promote, via the most suitable means, the civic and military education of the people, thus making them aware of their rights and preparing them for the defense of the nation and its institutions.

9

FRANCISCO BARROETAVEÑA
Speech in the Debate on a Mandatory
National Language for Schools (1896)

... As a first, general question, covering the matter in all
known nations, it would be best to give a brief overview to see whether
linguistic unity is an unequivocal and essential sign of national unity.

Language, Mr. President, does appear to be a sign of national unity,
but it is not, as I shall demonstrate to the honorable Chamber.

Those who support the ideas of the bill say that nothing separates
men as much as linguistic diversity: that language is not only a material
connection, but also an intellectual and a moral one that provides the
community with feelings and ideas.

Saint Augustine in this regard states: "There is no more connection
between two men speaking different languages, than between men and
animals."

When, in 1848, almost all of the nations of Europe were shaken by
revolutionary fervor, a council of Catholic bishops and archbishops,
princes of Christianity, met in Vienna. This council discussed the subject of the bill submitted for consideration to the honorable Chamber,
and the bishops voted for this formula: "Diversity of language is a consequence of sin; it is due to a rebellion against God and the depravity of
the human species."

Hence diversity of tongues is not only combated as a sentiment that
dissolves national unity, it is even presented as something repugnant to
Christian and religious sentiments.

Well, Mr. President: that is the doctrine, but the facts disprove it.

... In the quotations I have just presented to the Chamber, it can be
seen that the facts disprove the doctrine that presents linguistic unity —
the uniformity of language — as an essential element in nationality. I have

Original title: "Debate sobre la obligatoriedad del idioma nacional en las escuelas."
Source: Cámara de Diputados, Diario de Sesiones [Chamber of Deputies, Congressional
Record] (Buenos Aires, September 4 and 9, 1896).

cited at length numerous nationalities, Mr. President, to demonstrate to the Chamber, by universal experience, the negation of this theory — presented as something generally accepted — both by nations whose government is similar to our own and by those who have an entirely different one. I have cited hereditary monarchies, constitutional monarchies, federal countries, centralist countries, republics, and empires.

And so, Mr. President: all these nationalities, where there is diversity of tongues, have demonstrated to the world that their bonds of nationhood, whether centralist or federal, stand strong against great national dangers. In none of them has the character of nationality been weakened by the diverse tongues, for this diversity, far from conspiring against the existence of the state, helps to make it stronger; like all diversity in one nation it tends to satisfy regional demands, to make men calm, who are ever prone to joining close together when faced with a common danger.

If we open the treaties on international law, where publicists strive to distinguish the attributes of nationality after defining what it consists of, its typical traits, everyone says in unison: It is not language, for several languages are spoken in all nations. Nor is it religion, for everywhere men live in community with different religious ideas, and religious freedom and tolerance are the greatest conquests of this century. Nor is it racial unity, for races are mixed in all nations. Nor is it geographic boundaries. In a word, all internationalists stumble when they try to give a concrete definition of nationality, concluding by saying that it is indefinable, that it is something that can be formed only from a series of composite ideas, none of which is essential.

Very well, if observation of all peoples demonstrates that linguistic unity is not necessary for national unity, for in almost all organized nations there are diverse languages, without imperiling these nations, without slowing the progress of civilization; if international law does not present language as an element, an essential factor of nationhood, then what is left of the arrogant claim that linguistic unity is essential for consolidating national unity?

Furthermore, generally speaking, though not precisely for our country, the ideal of nationality is not the desideratum of the people.

The people who exercised and exercise the greatest intellectual and artistic influence did not constitute a homogeneous nationality. The Hellenic peoples never formed a united nation, never had a general government. And yet, in no other nation have the arts, letters, and sciences progressed so much. Here was a people made up of thinkers, philosophers, artists, men of letters, and, as I say, they extended their civilization eastward and westward, throughout the ancient world, and formed a people whose intellectual and artistic influence has endured the longest in time, to such an extent that in several sciences and arts their distinguished wisdom has yet to be surpassed.

Nationality is by no means the desideratum of the people. It is not an essential element in achieving fertile, civilizing, immortal works in the passing of the ages.

The speakers who support the bill, and especially the honorable member who reported for the committee, have told the Chamber there are foreign groups among our people who hinder and delay the resolution of the problem of our national unity, and the bill is submitted as a pressing and urgent demand to consolidate national unity.

Mr. President, in my opinion this is the fundamental flaw of the bill. And it is the fundamental flaw not only because of the philosophical ideas that it contains, but also because it goes against our fundamental form of rule, against the form of government that the Argentine Republic has adopted.

It is well known, Mr. President, and it is set out in the first article of the Constitution, that the Argentine nation has adopted the democratic, republican, and federal form. And not only is this written in the first article, but also the fifth article demands, as one of the indispensable requisites for protecting the provinces, that its constitutions ensure municipal government and elementary education, as social molecules, I would say, of our vast confederation. In short: our Constitution has established the most decentralized form of government known to the world.

And if such is our system of government, to seek unity now, to seek centralism and homogeneity through language, is to conspire most gravely and dangerously against this constitutional desideratum that the Argentine people attained after long years of struggle, after bloody civil wars, after tearing each other limb from limb.

It is well known that in all peoples there are elements of unity and elements of diversity. The elements of unity are required in a state only to maintain the union against foreign states and to fulfill the lofty and essential ends that are freely agreed on when the nation is formed.

The more advanced countries, the freer countries on the planet, do not strive so hard to consolidate and strengthen central government as they do to fully strengthen all the elements of diversity that exist in the country, to satisfy all regional and even social demands.

To come and tell us now that it is necessary to constitute national *unity,* to strengthen the national bond, wounding, jeopardizing, persecuting vital elements of diversity, I say that this amounts to conspiring against the republican, federal form of government, and against maximum decentralization, which is guaranteed by our fundamental institutions.

. . . However, Mr. President, in this debate, given the persistence with which the bill has been put forward and the great intellectual endeavors to maintain it, the question arises: are there symptoms contrary to national union in the Republic? To the *union,* I ask, not to unity, for our government is not one of unity but of *federation.* Are there any such symptoms? Are there Argentines, are there inhabitants in any region of the Republic, within our borders, who conspire against national union? Absolutely not, Mr. President! In order to honor the patriotism of our people, to honor the farsightedness and liberality of our laws, to honor progress and our country's culture, we must state: there is no citizen, no inhabitant, within our borders, who conspires against the national union, or against the Argentine confederation!

But are there perhaps those who conspire against the centralizing tendency that is taking shape in our country? There are not, Mr. President. There is yet to be noted a tangible resistance, an effective resistance to certain manifestations of centralization which, twisting the text and spirit of our fundamental law, attribute to the nation many powers that belong to the provinces.

I shall not speak of the political influences that act in a centralizing manner, for I fear a militant political stance will be attributed to my vote and to this part of my speech tht it does not have. I shall not speak of centralizing politics, but everyone knows that in our legislation, in numerous manifestations of ordinary life, particularly in our administrative and financial life, there is a growing centralizing tendency. It has been demonstrated, in a most interesting debate held in this Chamber, that a whole branch of major taxes, which appear to be national, belong not to the nation but to the provinces!

One need only glance at the budget to realize, Mr. President, that enormous sums of the national treasury and numerous items of that law are allocated exclusively to fulfilling provincial needs, municipal needs, plus the particular needs of private associations. It is almost a fashion in our country when establishing any private organization in the most faraway regions, when founding a library or associations of more or less general interest, that the first decision taken is to apply for a subsidy from the national executive power or from Congress. . . . And there goes the golden tentacle of central government, which, in multiplying, forms a network of invisible threads: it provides the money and with it the life of those private associations, in exchange for their connection to the federative government.

In finance it is a similar story, and I need not remind you of the laws that make exclusively provincial debts the burden of the nation. The national army battalions even defend local order, the jails of the provinces. They even watch over the slumber of some governors!

It can, then, be claimed that if any reactionary tendency conspires against the constitutional form of government of the Argentine Republic, it is the centralizing tendency, the unitary tendency.

But [no one] fights to decentralize the government, not even against this administrative corruption, which embezzles huge sums from the national treasury.

So what danger is there to nationality? None.

To centralization? None. Quite the contrary, what is becoming stronger is the centralist tendency!

So the bill, in this context, is not the answer to any burning interest, nor does it seek to prevent any institutional danger.

The subject of the bill under debate does not correspond to the nation, in my view. It corresponds, in the case it were constitutional, to the provinces.

The member for the capital city, Dr. Gouchón, has demonstrated with abundant erudition and quotations from authorities on the matter, that the power to impose teaching in a given language, in an Argentine province, corresponds to the confederated provinces, not to the nation. As said demonstration was conclusive, I shall not insist on it. I share the opinion.

Let us look at another constitutional side of the bill. It attacks the freedom of teaching and learning guaranteed by Article 14 of the Constitution to all inhabitants of the nation, whether Argentine or foreign. I maintain that it damages the freedom to teach, Mr. President, and to demonstrate this I need only present some specific cases, which are evident to the mind.

It is contrary to teaching and the freedom to teach, because this freedom is an absolute right guaranteed by the Constitution for all inhabitants, and it is also an equally guaranteed profession.

In both cases, no foreigner who possesses only his language may teach. He may instruct nobody who speaks a different language. He may not exercise the profession of teaching to his fellow man: a German who does not know another language may only teach in his language. And the same would be true of an Italian, a Frenchman, or any man of any nationality. He would be forbidden to teach, if the law dictated that he teach in a language unknown to him.

The member for Entre Ríos, Dr. Ayarragaray, in responding to the argument Dr. Gouchón merely touched on, maintained that there was no attack on the Constitution contained in the bill, because the Constitution itself authorizes the regulation of absolute freedoms that it recognizes and guarantees the inhabitants of the country.

But my distinguished colleague forgot that Article 28 of the Constitution forbids Congress from altering, limiting, or restricting absolute recognized and guaranteed freedoms; and as I have just demonstrated, the bill would not only restrict, it would suppress the freedom to teach and the profession of teaching in the Republic for all those foreigners who wished to practice their profession.

. . . This bill attacks the freedom to learn guaranteed to all inhabitants by Article 14 of the Constitution. And I say that it attacks the freedom to learn, because I will demonstrate later that this bill will, pedagogically speaking, lead us to one of these extremes: to the closure of numerous schools, to obstructing or preventing teaching in them.

I imagine a group of children who possess only a foreign language, the language of their parents, in those fortunately few regions in our country where foreign immigration from a single origin is isolated from the rest of the nation.

Those children will not be able to learn if the bill under debate is passed, because it is pointless to strive to show that one can teach in our language those children who have absolutely no knowledge of it.

Hence those children who know only a foreign language would be deprived of teaching; they would be deprived of the right to learn, and one of the absolute freedoms guaranteed by the Constitution would be attacked.

. . . I maintain that the bill under debate would exceed the role of the state in terms of teaching, that it goes beyond what our fundamental laws permit, that it goes beyond the well-understood convenience for the Republic.

It is useful to define, Mr. President, the educational mission of the state vis-à-vis society and the action of individuals.

. . . For Laboulaye "it is the supreme goal of politics to give to every citizen the free use of their strength, because this free use is, as much for the individual as for the state, a condition for well-being and progress. The state must be no more than a guarantee of freedom."

Stuart Mill refutes Canning's theory that democracy, the sovereignty of the people, be a safeguard of freedom. He maintains that it is not; that despotism can just as easily arise from a majority, from a democracy, as from a minority, from an oligarchy, from a despot, or from a tyrant, and in this he is right. And after defining with near mathematical precision the state's responsibilities to society, the educational roles of the state according to the people's rights, he maintains that the most secure means of safeguarding individual freedoms, the absolute rights of a people, is by defining them precisely in the fundamental laws as absolute rights recognized by the Constitution and the state so that they may not be modified in the slightest by the law, by the majority, or even by a unanimous vote.

. . . Language teaching is demanded by our law, but what is arbitrary, what does not fit the Constitution and the role of the state within its faculties, is that that teaching be done in a specific language.

What the national laws and convenience demand is that the people be taught, but in what language? Well, Mr. President, that is unimportant. Arithmetic is taught the same in English as in French as in German. The sciences, the arts, everything is taught the same.

So the state, in seeking through the bill under debate to rule that teaching in schools be done in a national language, goes beyond the tolerable role of its powers, exceeds its faculties, attacks absolute freedoms guaranteed to all inhabitants.

. . . But, Mr. President, if this bill were to become law it would be the first dangerous step; it would be the vanguard of obscurantism, of a reactionary legislation, because after linguistic unity they will call for religious unity, racial unity, other centralist unities, which in addition to conspiring against the Constitution, and the freedoms it guarantees, would conspire against the prosperity and civilization of the Republic.

If it is established that teaching in schools should be in the national language, why not then prohibit that a foreign language be used in theaters? Is the theater not a school where, in addition to the moralizing influences of the plays that are performed, one also learns the language in which it is spoken? Are there not thousands of Argentines who have learned the language of Dante by attending the performances of Italian artists who have come to our country? Is this not the case also in the French theater? Why not close down the theaters in which the performance is not in the national language? It would be the same patriotic foresight, the purpose of liberating us from the contamination of foreign languages. Why not forbid foreign languages from being spoken in the home, if this is the first school?

I believe the state should limit its educational mission to demanding that the minimum of teaching marked in the laws now in force be fulfilled. I believe that it should require that the national language be taught well, and go no further. Anything else would be tantamount to exceeding its role, and would offend communities of foreigners who have come under the guarantees of our Constitution. It would mean stopping the stream of immigration to our country and considerably increasing the number of illiterate children, thrusting anarchy and disorder upon the families of foreign residents, who would not know what to abide by if the foundations of our Constitution are eroded by organic laws.

Basing my ideas on these considerations, I shall vote against the bill submitted to the Chamber by the honorable member for Salta.—I have spoken.

10

FRANCISCO BARROETAVEÑA
Speech on the Customs Act (1894)

... Is it constitutional to turn import duties into a vehicle for protectionism, and elevated levels of protection at that? Does our Constitution, in its chief guidelines for revenue and the economy, enshrine any of the schools of thought or principles that govern production in the world? Does it contain provisions in favor of free trade or protectionism? And once these initial questions have been answered, where does the benefit for Argentina lie?

For, aside from the overarching principles contained in the Constitution, the fiscal interest, and the interests of consumers, I cannot comprehend what national benefit justifies the survival of elevated tariffs that, if, as the honorable informing member said, having caused alarm in the country's two great industries—agriculture and livestock—they have also caused serious harm to an extremely numerous class in our country, namely, the consumer class, which has suffered their consequences in the raising of prices on essential items owing to the excessive protection of certain industries developing here. This protection has excluded similar foreign items from our commerce and enabled Argentina's national industry to raise its prices while keeping all competition at bay.

After studying the Constitution and the economic principles set out in the Constitutional Assembly on the sanctioning of our charter, and reading Dr. Alberdi's fundamental work, I have reached the following conclusion: that the Argentine Republic must base its tariff system, its system of revenue laws on the principles of industrial freedom, on free trade, and the commercial freedom provided and guaranteed in more than one of the articles of that Constitution, which together form a desideratum for the increased economic stature of our country.

Original title: "Discurso sobre la Ley de Aduana." Source: Cámara de Diputados, Diario de Sesiones [Chamber of Deputies, Congressional Record] (Buenos Aires, November 9, 1894).

These momentous views of Dr. Alberdi's display a clear vision of the future and of the development of the Argentine nation. And so, Mr. President, because we have forgotten these essential principles of our charter, because we have forgotten our country's historical precedents, we have arrived at an exorbitant, prohibitionist tariff rate on certain articles, seriously harming consumers and the major livestock and agricultural industries, and exposing us — as everyone knows and the honorable treasury minister has reminded us — to a tariff war and international hostility toward our livestock and agricultural products.

... I have no reason to hide from the Chamber which of the two great economic systems I sympathize with.

I openly declare my sympathy for the system of free trade. Yet, given the development of protected industries in our country, I understand that one cannot abruptly switch from such excessive protectionism to total free trade, but must set off gradually but unswervingly on such a course.

I also wish to state for the record that, like everyone, my national sentiment is satisfied when I see industries developing in our country that make products and manufactured goods that, until a short time ago, one could not even dream of producing. But above this I must put my duties as a member of the Congress to adjust the tariff system to the principles of the Constitution and the benefit of consumers in order not to encumber the country with high taxation to protect industries that do not, at this particular moment of our history, have the economic means to cope.

Instead of boasting about fictitious industries, let us wait for our population to grow denser, for savings to become fortunes, for larger capital to be accumulated and made more affordable, and for a gradual development of industries better suited to our economic background.

In a word, in spite of my sympathy for the school of free trade, given our country's tariff system and the degree of industrial development it has attained, I am in favor of a serious reduction in tariffs, greater than the one proposed by the committee appointed by the executive power and by the Chamber's budget committee.

I will say it loud and clear: I am a supporter of viable industry, of manufacturing that does not demand painful sacrifices to the country, for these mark the degree of civilization and the progress of a people. But just as systems of government cannot be improvised in an institutional regime, so the economic forces of the people must not be forcibly persuaded to produce at any given time what the economic means and the age do not permit.

Thus I believe that levying a tariff of 60 percent on a series of foreign items in order to protect industries that survive only with the aid of such high, almost prohibitive duties is ruinous for our country, not only because it encourages, to the detriment of the consumer, the artificial development of industries that we are not economically mature enough to produce, but because it exposes us to tariff wars with nations that produce similar items. Such hostility causes serious harm to our true, great industries.

I also believe that, with a sharper reduction in tariffs than the one proposed, we would ultimately be encouraging our national production on a grand scale, for an increase in imports means similar growth in our products.

We must not become infatuated with our country's aspiration to produce all consumer items, even if it is with the help of such prohibitively elevated duties, for our economic happiness will not consist in producing everything, but in consuming inexpensive, high-quality goods.

Agriculture and livestock breeding have, without protection of any kind, achieved the astonishing levels of development that we are all familiar with. And it would jeopardize this sturdy and buoyant growth — nay, it would be unjust and contrary to the Constitution, to provoke international attacks on those great industries in order to encourage others that, I repeat, do not yet have the economic wherewithal, that do not have sufficient capital, that do not have a cheap, skilled labor force, that do not have the accessory machinery and factories to make the most of every last scrap the way Europe does, and that would not, for many years, be able to compete with comparable manufacturing from the nations of the old continent. . . .

11

PEDRO CORONADO
Speech on the Residence Act (1904)

... But it is sufficient to open the preambles to the constitutions of the United States and the Argentine Republic, and place them side by side to see they have one fundamental difference. They are both intended to safeguard liberty. What liberty can they be referring to when both constitutions refer to it? Might it be political freedom or civil freedom? There is not one North American, English, or South American writer who does not say that the preambles of the constitutions I am alluding to refer solely and exclusively to civil liberty.

And it cannot be otherwise. Political organizations are designed to maintain civil liberty. And the Argentine nationality, in organizing itself, has had necessarily to refer to this civil liberty.

Mr. Gutiérrez, speaking as a reporting member of the Convention of '53, stated perfectly the Argentine Constitution's uniformity of ideas with those of the North American Constitution. If there were any doubt, the solution ought, then, to have been sought in the source, namely, the American Constitution, which states clearly and incontrovertibly that the liberty enshrined in the Constitution is civil liberty.

Mr. Sarmiento, whose authority has been brought to this Chamber, says on the subject, referring to the declarations I have mentioned, the following:

> Such a declaration amounts to an invitation to all the men in the world to come and share in the liberties that are assured them, a promise to make those freedoms effective, and an indication that there is land available for those who wish to join the Argentine family of the future. In a word, the Argentine Republic declares

Original title: "Discurso sobre la Ley de Residencia." Source: Cámara de Diputados, Diario de Sesiones [Chamber of Deputies, Congressional Record] (Buenos Aires, July 25, 1904).

itself to be in a state of colonization and incorporates in its institutions the expression of this feeling, the desire to see it satisfied, and the sure means of verifying it.

Spain closed its colonies to all men of a stock, a language, or a belief different to her own, whence there resulted an exclusive and prohibitive system of institutions that violated all the principles of freedom of action and thought, without which the population of the territory is impossible and government becomes tutelage or a tyranny.

As the honorable deputies can see, I have made every effort to provide the evidence that the liberty enshrined in our Constitution is civil liberty.

. . . Political rights change, Mr. President, with the spirit and regulations of each nation. But what nobody has been able to change is this generally accepted and uniformly acknowledged principle that the right to residence is a civil right, just as the freedom to reside is a freedom that emerges from this civil right, and freedom of residence is expressly enshrined in the National Constitution.

If the right to reside were not a civil right, there would be people within the territory of the Republic who, not having political rights, would not be able to reside in our country. Women who are Argentine, who are of age, who are unmarried and do not therefore have to follow their husbands in their abode, without political rights would not have the right to reside. Can we deny Argentine women without political rights the right to reside in any part of the Republic's territory? Clearly not. Therefore, the right to reside is not a political right. To have the right to reside, then, it is necessary to be able to enjoy such rights, and to maintain them, all individual guarantees must be maintained, and it is wholly unacceptable for the Argentine Constitution to establish differences between nationals and foreigners in this matter.

I enumerate all this because I understand that, if the right to reside is a civil right and is enshrined in civil liberty, acknowledged by all the inhabitants wishing to come to our land, any foreigners given this civil status have the right to reside in our country wherever and however they like without anyone having to expel them, save by means we shall see later on. But if by establishing coercive laws we were to abolish civil freedom, if by establishing these laws we were to cease to acknowledge that the right to reside is a civil right, we would have created an empty wordplay that would end in the abolition of these liberties.

I think it advisable, on this occasion, to recount Alberdi's view. I have deliberately tried not to get embroiled in expounding this man's opinions, for, by and large, they are extremely well known; I shall simply keep to quoting some words of his regarding this freedom:

"You are all aware that the time has come when our talk of freedom is worth no more than our freedom of speech, and that any act of tolerance, of respect for this antagonism of conscience, this dissidence, is worth more in terms of practical liberties than all the Tartuffism of politicians." Mr. Alberdi was a supporter of practical liberty at the time. But there can be no practical liberty without the absolute maintenance of individual rights.

Mention has been made of England, that traditional land of freedom, from which foreigners are not expelled. A book of Napoleon III's memoirs was published in 1854. After Orsini's assassination attempt, Napoleon had the suspects law enacted in France, and he wrote, in 1854, saying that foreigners in England cannot be expelled without a trial.

Moreover, it is a well-known fact that Pitt established what he called the Bible of the English constitution. The maintenance of the principles established by this Bible lies behind the greatness of this eminent minister. There are three of them: first, every man's home is his castle; second, general arrest warrants are prohibited; and third, habeas corpus.

To see how the feeling of freedom pervades that country I shall tell you what is done with a boy entering school for the first time. The schoolteacher approaches him and says to him, "Every man's home is his castle." The boy asks him, "Is it surrounded by a moat or a wall?" "No," the teacher answers: "The wind may blow through it, the rain may penetrate it, but not the king."

How different to what happens in our country!

The house may be a great mansion of stone, the rain unable to penetrate it and soak the carpets, or the wind to waft the tapestries, but the president of the Republic may, by this law, penetrate freely and seize the man accused of holding socialist or anarchist ideas, and frogmarch him to the border!

12

JUAN BAUTISTA JUSTO
Signor Lorini's[1] Monetary
Theory (1904)

. . . The Argentine Monetary Act of 1899 has had the practical consequences that were foreseen and sought thereby: the agio on gold has not fallen below 127.27 percent, the ceiling value represented by one peso m/n[2] being reduced to 44 gold cents. What this means for the class of salaried workers and, consequently, for the country's general development has already been demonstrated, and there would be no point in going back over this law unless to discuss the opportunity to repeal it. Such opportunity recedes with the passing of time, for, on the one hand, the paralyzation of immigration and the workers' political and trade union action tend to offset, albeit slowly, the depressing action of bad currency on salaries; and on the other, year after year there is a growing mass of collective and individual interests intent on shoring up the current value of the paper peso.

But if the practical consequences of the 1899 act have been bad, worse are the theoretical ones: the lucubrations of Professor Lorini of the University of Pavia about the Argentine currency, a doctrine whose flimsiness it is necessary to demonstrate, not so much concerning the terms of that law as regarding the general principles he is attempting to establish, under which South American leaders receive an approval of great scientific appearance for their blind and disastrous work in matters of currency.

Signor Lorini presents his imposing volume on the Argentine cur-

Original title: "La teoria monetaria del Señor Lorini." Source: *La Internacional,* Buenos Aires, July–October 1904, in Juan B. Justo, *La moneda* [Currency] (Buenos Aires: Editorial "La Vanguardia," 1937).

1. Eteocle Lorini (1865–1919), Italian economist, visited Argentina at the beginning of the twentieth century, later published *La Repubblica Argentina e i suoi problemi di economia e finanza,* 3 vols., 1902–10. [E.N.]

2. "Peso moneda nacional," the currency unit in use at the time. [E.N.]

rency as an "inductive analysis," and boasts of "having maintained, in the midst of lively competition between opposing local opinions, that objective spirit, directed at the purest scientific research that has guided him in his earlier volumes," on currency in general, and the monetary question in Austria-Hungary, Italy, Russia, Persia, India, and, in particular, Japan.

A great pity that there is no truth in so much beauty! Rather than a study of the Argentine currency, what Signor Lorini offers us is an argument for the law known as the Conversion Act, of which he declares himself an ardent supporter in the first pages, to the extent of denying all reason and authority to the strong national opposition provoked by said law. According to Signor Lorini (p. 4), "from the Buenos Aires Stock Market" irradiated a "potent and seditious" violent agitation against the famous bill; "the most damning allegations were issued; the darkest threats were heard; facile slanders filtered everywhere, and opposing newspapers attacked men and their opinions with remarkable virulence. Even University chairs . . . became the focus of propaganda and systematic opposition." "It was not the newspapers most beloved of the masses that argued so violently," but those "read by agitators and others with a vested interest." And, in the Parliament, "it was those who legally, but not in fact, represented working people's rights, that had given themselves such toil," namely, to fight the bill, without Signor Lorini telling us in what capacity the deputies and senators who voted in the new law represented the people.

. . . How far can a doctrinaire obsession blind the intelligence! Having spent time in Argentina, Signor Lorini has not understood what he should have supposed before his arrival and what everyone here, even the lowliest country grocer, knows. Argentine prices are in gold, being regulated in the world market, both for imported and exported products. Gold is our measure of values, and although we do not see it, although it is virtual gold, it is calculated yearly that the yield from agriculture and stock breeding comes to so many millions of gold pesos. Wool and wheat are gold for the businessman, the producer, so much so that, in contracts, many breeders and farmers have chosen to set the amount of their lease in gold in order to be free of the fluctuations of the agio. Fabrics, metal goods, and other imported items are valued in gold to reduce them in each case to paper pesos, according to the agio of the hour. Even prices of domestic produce for internal consumption are in gold. Meat prices are never higher than when young steers are sold for export at one hundred gold pesos. And the Argentine Union, a cooperative society for butter production, regulates the price of said item for local consumption according to the price of a *quintal* of butter in shillings in London. Argentine paper money, like any other paper a simple means of circulation without any intrinsic value, could never have been nor has ever been a measure of values. As a sign of value, the paper peso has, in different periods, been a symbol of widely differing amounts of gold, according to the nominal amount of paper in circulation and the real monetary needs of the moment. Paper prices have varied, then, with the amount of gold represented by each paper peso, but not simply according to the amount of paper in circulation. The real prices of things have depended on the state of the world market: apparent prices, in paper money, have depended on the agio on gold, and this speculation that speaks so ill of Argentine monetary administration means, furthermore, that the world's gold is to be exchanged, in one proportion or another, for our little scraps of paper. Are these as void of meaning as those fabricated by Signor Lorini for the use of Primus, Secundus, and Tertius?

. . . What are we, politically speaking? "In our experience," says Signor Lorini, "between the tsar of Russia, and even between a monarch of any Asian khanate and a president of the South American states, we could not say where more absolute power is held, nor where the politics of government could be more personal" (p. 105). And, economically speaking, this "people of giants" is no more advanced. We have only recently left bartering behind, thanks to our empirical invention of the paper peso, which has finally found a worthy theoretician in the professor from Pavia; and we continue with our "monetary sign" in an isolation of barbarians. "Thus as there are still individual economic hermits and tribes of a barter economy, there can exist a country (Argentina) with a '*valuta a numerario*' regime" (p. 98), which then develops as a "*mercato chiuso*" (p. 134).

A closed market? This country of coastlines and great rivers, which has not even managed to close the narrow, despotic colonial policy. Closed market, a country that produces raw materials, consumes only a small proportion of them, and is only now learning how to manufacture them! Closed market, a country whose per capita foreign trade is higher than that of the United States and Canada! This nonsense from

Professor Lorini can be explained by the barely lucid inebriation of his discovery; but also because only with materials of this type has he been able to erect his flimsy construction.

According to Signor Lorini, this country has spent the nineteenth century facing the tough dilemma of "either isolating itself with its paper currency, enjoying the advantages of this primitive economy, or taking part in international exchanges . . . suffering from the effort of re-supplying itself (*rifornirsi*) with a sound currency" (p. 155).

The truth is that our paper money dates from the time when the entire Río de la Plata was opened to foreign trade; that despite the abuse of this paper money and its devaluation, the country has been increasingly integrated in the universal market; and that its close trade ties with the world's main markets have been favored, where exports are concerned, by the devaluation of paper money, which, depressing salaries and thus reducing production costs, has allowed exporters to pocket a part of the amount of this reduction as extraordinary earnings. The drop in salaries and subsequent reduction on consumption in general and of foreign items in particular has been, it is true, an obstacle to development of the import trade. But how could Signor Lorini admit this, according to whom the paper peso has scattered the cornucopia of abundance for everyone in this country?

. . . If someone were to tell us they had discovered on the city streets vast numbers of large and strange beings never before seen, we would receive the news with the greatest incredulity; but if he claimed to have found them on some desert island or in some dark cavern, his assertion would appear more credible to us. Thus, the discovery of the "monetary sign," made in this country by Signor Lorini, will have found more acceptance among those ignorant of commercial geography when they have learned via the same source that the broad Río de la Plata is a closed market. This crass inaccuracy plays, at the same time, another no less important role in this "imbroglio" of Signor Lorini's, according to whom our isolation and the desire to, at some stage, enter the economic order of the world are the only reason for our monetary concerns, for in terms of our internal relations a more perfect instrument than our paper peso would be inconceivable.

According to Signor Lorini, everything here inside Argentina worked as in the best of all possible worlds, not in spite of the repeated issuing of paper money, but thanks to it in virtue of a law of balance discovered

by the monetary Candide himself. "To whose advantage was this prolonged printing of money? Everyone's, and not just the government's,"
answers Signor Lorini (p. 166), adding: "Is there much yerba mate . . . ?
Everyone knows: it is passed around and everyone sips twice his share
from the straw. . . . Thus, is there a great deal of monetary sign raining
from the bosom of the good father government? We all know this too,
and so much more is asked and so much more is given, things remaining as they were. . . . The successive monetary sign increases, instantly
introducing new positions of stable equilibrium, do not impinge on the
equations between existing assets . . . and permit no pillaging by equally
raising, ceteris paribus, the common and general measure of the value"
(!?) (pp. 99–101). And then the highest and clearest note in such a harmonious concert: "By the virtue of the monetary sign spreading quickly
and reaching all budgets—even the most modest—private individuals
become accustomed to closely shadow the inflations of the circulating
mass, and its respective consequences on the movement of prices and
salaries" (p. 101).

This supposed law of "instant and stable" balance and of the subsequent harmlessness of issuing paper pesos is the most dangerous
of Signor Lorini's errors, and the part of his doctrines that will most
hastily be accepted and applied by the Juárez Celmans, the Pachecos, the
Pelligrinis, and other accomplices of South American monetary chaos.
And it is also the most unforgivable of his false assertions, a blatant lack
of observation of facts subject to the methods of number.

Do I have to demonstrate for Argentine readers that the issuing of
paper pesos has not been to everyone's advantage? Do the workers in
general know anything of the amount of paper in circulation? And, even
if they did, did the official banks print that paper for the workers or
for the favorites who squandered the greater part of it in unproductive
spending? How could contracts have been adapted to the "instant and
stable balance" that, in the midst of the maelstrom of printing, Signor
Lorini discovered? Is it not evident that paper creditors have lost with
the debasement of the peso, as too have debtors since it began to gain in
value? Is it not clear that the rise of gold benefits tenants as the fall benefits proprietors who had signed leases in paper pesos?

And if the prices in paper have fluctuated, not of course according to
the amount of paper, but rather according to the agio on gold, has it not
occurred here, as always and everywhere in similar cases that, ceteris

paribus, the price that rose most slowly was that of wages, the price of the labor force? For Signor Lorini, who occasionally permits himself to speak of the *"grande anima lavoratrice,"* there has been the most exact parallelism in this country between the rise of gold and the rise of nominal paper salaries. As proof of this he presents a diagram created with data provided for him by the architect Victorio Meano about salaries in the construction industry during the years 1895 to 1900: the diagram shows that the paper salaries of masons, carpenters, blacksmiths, marble craftsmen, and laborers fell over those years along with gold, but not that they rose along with gold in the preceding years, for which Mr. Meano did not have sufficient data. Of the salaries during the rise of gold and in the most important jobs Signor Lorini knows nothing or has found out nothing, and it is with such paltry information that he dares to establish new laws as he goes along, denying what all the world knows: that the degradation of the paper peso has been a cause of ruin and misery for working people. It is because Signor Lorini cannot admit "dynamic sufferings" due to the issuing of his "monetary sign" for fear of us mistaking it for a vulgar paper currency of the state, issued in excess, which would detract from the brilliance and importance of his discovery.

13

JOSÉ NICOLÁS MATIENZO
Representative Federal Government
in the Argentine Republic (1910)

. . . The electoral power of the Republic, in actual fact, lies in the hands of the president of the nation and the governors of the provinces, with each of these state officials receiving a share proportional to the political influence they have managed to attain. The governor of Buenos Aires exercises the greatest electoral power, because, as well as having a higher number of elective offices at his disposal, he almost always enjoys greater independence from the president.

If one were to draw a line between the prerogatives of the president and those of the governors, in electoral matters, I believe it would be accurate to say that, as a general rule, each of these officials appoints his successor: the president is appointed by his immediate predecessor in the same way that each province's governor is appointed by the governor he replaces. Also as a general rule, the governors behave like absolute and exclusive lords and masters in filling provincial elective offices, which results in provincial legislative chambers being governors' puppets, save for some very rare exceptions.

As for federal elective offices (deputies and senators in Congress and presidential electors), governors act as administrators of a business in which they are the main stockholders, but in which they acknowledge a fairly important share for the president, depending on political expedience, that is, depending on how much the governor needs the president's support to remain in power.

These common rules for exercising electoral power are not so rigid as to exclude exceptions from time to time due to the action of divers causes, which can be grouped into three main types: the temporary growth of public desire for the Constitution to be fulfilled in terms of

Original title: "El gobierno representativo federal en la República Argentina." Source: *El gobierno representativo federal en la República Argentina* (Buenos Aires: Coni Hnos., 1910).

popular suffrage, an extraordinary increase of the president's personal authority, and abnormal weakening of such authority.

As a result of these causes, it often happens that one or more provincial governors temporarily increase or decrease their electoral powers, in relation to either provincial or national offices, or both. Thus, national deputies or senators can be elected without any intervention from the president, which is tantamount to giving the governors complete freedom to appoint the candidates themselves. On other occasions, the president limits himself to recommending a small number of candidates, for example, one, two, or three in the provinces that elect five, ten, or fifteen. On other occasions, the president is happy to give his *exequatur* to the candidates proposed by the governor. I also know of the case of a governor who, having to provide a single vacancy for a deputy, sent a short list of three candidates to the president so that he would appoint the one he favored, which he did without delay.

The exercise of this overwhelming electoral power is not limited by customary rules or civic morals about the qualities required in candidates anointed by official grace. Electors' and candidates' scruples have diminished little by little, especially in the more populous provinces, and Congress is, in consequence, increasingly home to persons lacking in intellectual and moral merit. Often a deputy's post is a reward for personal services of a private nature, or alms tossed into the hands of some friend who has fallen on hard times and has no hope of economic improvement in his private work. It also tends to be the recompense for illicitly proffered political aid, which has accounted for the presence in Congress of citizens known for their ability for all kinds of fraud and forgeries of electoral documents. Men renowned for their knowledge or their virtues almost never feature in the list of candidates drawn up by governors. The predominant tendency appears to be to systematically exclude from legislative bodies all those persons who take the written Constitution seriously or who habitually observe austere conduct. They are dubbed troublemakers and ignored, permitting them, at most, to use their mental capacities in the universities, out of reach of militant political interests and from which such interests cannot be disturbed.

The usual recruitment of candidates to members of Congress occurs among the governor's friends and relatives. Their ministers consider themselves to have better rights than any other candidate, as they are closer to the governor and able to serve him more usefully. Even subordinate employees, whose functions allow them to be in continuous contact with the governor and tamely provide him with services, find in these circumstances plenty of grounds to aspire to office, and it tends to be the case that they fulfill these aspirations.

Using these prerogatives, one of the higher-profile governors of Buenos Aires Province had no hesitation in placing one of his friends who had permanently lost his voice in Congress and who, as the same governor declared in private, was unable to participate in a deliberative assembly.

As for the post of national senator that happens to become vacant, the outgoing governor has first choice and tends to use all the means his position affords him to make the election safe. As the elective body is the provincial legislature, all the governor's efforts are directed at filling this body with faithful friends who will vote for him whenever the opportunity arises. On some occasions, the vacancy becomes available during the governor's mandate, and he will then usually resign from his present post to have himself named senator, unless he chooses to postpone the election until the end of his mandate. At other times the post is given to the candidate for the next period so that his vacancy in the Senate can be filled by the outgoing governor, giving way to a veritable carousel of political posts.

When the governor cannot gain control of the legislature through peaceful means, there begins a struggle in which both entities use all means possible to win. The legislature then seeks to overthrow the governor via impeachment, while the governor seeks to take advantage of the elections to the legislature to modify his majority by introducing staunch supporters. A large number of interventions by the federal government in provincial rule have been motivated by conflicts arising between governors and legislatures as a consequence of the type of struggle mentioned here. I believe that the political life of the provinces and of the nation would be more orderly and pure if provincial governors could not be elected members of Congress for three years after completing their mandate.

The governors of the most important provinces are sometimes not content with retiring to a senator's post: they have the presidency or vice presidency of the Republic in their sights. The governors of Buenos Aires are generally candidates for the presidency; but with the exception of General Mitre, none has achieved this. However, two have obtained the vice presidency: Governor Alsina in the Sarmiento administration, and Governor Acosta in the Avellaneda administration. One governor for Córdoba, Dr. Juárez Celman, attained the presidency in 1886.

Naturally, as ambitions grow, so too do efforts to control the electoral machine, and scruples are cast aside. Everything possible is done to keep up appearances, but ultimately most governors sacrifice this.

One of the authors of the Constitution, Don Salustiano Zavalía, senator for Tucumán during General Mitre's presidency, said at the session of July 2, 1868, that the greatest benefit Congress could give to the people of the Republic that year was to guarantee its freedom to name its representatives, and added: "I shall provide a shameful but truthful recollection of what has happened in Tucumán Province in the space of six years. In this period of time, one obscure man has been the only elector of Tucumán Province. Citizens were led to public polls not out of their willingness to vote for their preferred candidate, but to vote for the government candidate, driven like a flock of sheep, Mr. President, under the whip of commanders and officers of militias."

Local officials who, due to the nature of their powers, are in closer contact with the people and can dispense favors or cause grievances to particular interests, are usually the governor's assistants. These officials' titles vary from province to province, according to the respective administrative organization. In Buenos Aires Province, they are the police chief, the tax appraiser, the justice of the peace, and the mayor (*alcalde* as the Spanish say, or *maire* as the French have it). The first two are appointed by the governor, the third is appointed by the same governor from a short list proposed by the municipality, and the last one is elected by the municipality. If these four local authorities are in agreement in any given electoral campaign, there is nothing to be done: their favored cause will inevitably triumph. The practice is that the governor gives what is called the *position,* that is, the right to appoint or control these four officials, to a single person, popularly called the *caudillo* of the locality. The main duty of this caudillo, or chieftain, is to take any due measures needed to ensure the victory of the governor's friends or recommended candidates in all the elections held during his tenure, and, to this end, he exercises constant vigilance over the conduct of local authorities. The caudillo is frequently the mayor or justice of the peace, although this is not necessary, nor is it necessary for him to reside in the district that he controls politically. Sometimes the caudillo is genuinely popular, having gained the affections of locals through acts of generosity, justice, or comradeship. Physicians, especially, when they have a generous and humanitarian spirit, tend to acquire numerous political friends. The opposition parties seek them out, and governors wishing to conciliate public opinion also seek to use these elements as electoral agents. But more often than not, those in control of such *positions* are obscure, ignorant men with no moral fiber, accustomed to twisting the law in favor of their political cronies and against their adversaries. Petty thieves and occasionally major felons can rely on the police to turn a blind eye, if they are useful contacts for winning elections on account of their aptitude for fraud or intimidation. The appraiser estimates the value of the property of political adversaries more highly than that of his friends. Legal procedures move more smoothly for litigants in the justice of the peace's party. The mayor concerns himself more with fixing the streets and roads used by his fellow party members than other roads. And so life goes, with few exceptions.

This exploitation of administrative powers for electoral ends is so deeply rooted in the customs of local officials that, when the governor disregards it, they do it themselves or for more or less influential citizens. That is why the governor's abstention in the electoral contest means only that subordinate employees are left with the ability to abuse their authority for their respective interests or individual tastes, a consequence that can be avoided only through vigorous action from the governor to impose effective impartiality on them. I do not recall any chief executive of an Argentine province ever setting such an example of political morals.

The fact is that every governor promises to guarantee electoral freedom on entering office, but when the polls come, events occur, mutatis mutandis, as they have in the past and as they may continue to do for a very long time. The best governors are those who exert their influence to raise the level of legislative staff, taking learned and honest men to parliament. But even this can be difficult. The local caudillos aspire to sit in the provincial legislature, and from these seats they aspire to the national Congress. Governors temporize with these aspirations inasmuch as they consider them suitable to preserve the electoral mechanism I have just described. It is necessary to avoid certain discontent in the electoral agents, and to ensure their faithfulness and activity with the appropriate stimuli. In this model, one of the most intelligent citizens to have occupied the Buenos Aires governorship, examining his adversaries' criticisms, told me: "If I want to be of use to my country, I have to make use of the only elements of political action that exist at present. The contrary would be to claim that bronze tools were used in the Stone Age. I work with the materials and tools of my day."

According to the Constitution and the law, the verdict of the elections is down to the legislative bodies whose vacancies are to be filled. Each body, at both national and provincial levels, is the sole judge of the election of its members: but it is impossible to state that it always proceeds with the impartiality implied in the concept of judge.

Legislative chambers are all too frequently inclined to accept pretenders they sympathize with in the event of disputed elections.

It is also often the case that polls in which opposition candidates win are declared null and void. The conduct of the chambers as judges of elections has not yet resulted in political practices being purified, nor has it led to the role of popular suffrage being dignified. The vices condemned are the adversary's, and the polls annulled are those that bring victory to persons whose presence in parliament is undesirable.

One circumstance that has contributed to corrupting judgment in elections is that national and provincial legislatures are only partially replaced at election time, thus leaving half or more than half of the former members to judge the new elections, who then rule on which of their new colleagues to admit and which to reject. In the national Congress, half of the deputies are renewed every two years, and one-third of the Senate every three years. In the province of Buenos Aires, half of the Senate is renewed every two years, and a third of the lower chamber every year. Another disadvantage of this partial renewal in the two chambers is that when public opinion manages to triumph in an electoral campaign—which seldom occurs—it manages to take control of only a fraction of the chamber, if indeed the election is not annulled or altered by the fraction that is not renewed. The opposition parties are discouraged by this prospect and prefer to abstain and seek via revolutionary means a wholesale renewal of the existing legislature. It would be a different matter if, as is the case in England, the USA, France, Italy, Germany, and other countries with representative government, the lower chamber were entirely renewed. This way, the people would have the opportunity to be fully represented and to impose their opinion on the more numerous chamber, while the newly elected would not have to pass through the *exequatur* of those already in office. Partial renewal can only be accounted for in the Senate, in order to give this chamber a more conservative nature than the other. But it is vital in a republican country that the people be able to regularly renew the body that is supposed to represent it, as a legal means of effectively expressing its current opinion or will.

Before elections can be approved, the counting of votes is vital for the proclamation of elected candidates or presumed representatives. This part of the electoral procedure in the Argentine Republic leaves much to be desired. In national elections for deputies and electors of the president, in every province the central vote-counting board is a committee made up of the federal judge, the president of the highest court of the province, and the president of the province's legislature. In the nation's capital, the vote-counting board is formed by the federal judge, the president of the Court of Appeal of the capital, and the president of the municipality's deliberating council.

These boards collect the records, add up the results, and declare which citizens have been elected, subsequently issuing them with the titles or powers with which they must present themselves in the Chamber of Deputies or the electoral college of the president, as appropriate.

However, for the provincial elections, some provinces entrust the mission of counting the votes to the chambers themselves. The first result of this is that there are no presumed deputies before the election is approved, and therefore the possibility for the elected citizen to defend his title in the event of disputed elections, as happens in the national Congress, disappears. Another practical result is that, in counting the votes, the chamber makes the deputy, because, its procedure not being subject to review, it computes or does not compute the records as it sees fit, or adjusts them as it pleases, without the candidate in question having a voice to oppose any of it. There have been cases of persons declared elected without receiving votes in the elections, but a good many votes when they were counted in the chamber.

Buenos Aires Province, which, as the most important in the Republic, is generally taken up as an example by all the others, has maintained in its laws this vicious confusion between vote counting and the verdict of the election for many years. In 1896, with participation by the author of this work, who at the time was a senator of that province, a law was passed to entrust general vote counting to a board made up of the president of the Supreme Court of Justice, the auditor general, and the attorney general.

The first counts carried out by this board were not to the liking of the dominant groups in the chambers, who altered the votes quite substantially. The board ultimately abandoned its duties, and the chambers have in fact recovered the arbitrary power they exercised before 1896. It has often been the case of a conspiracy of the members of all the parties represented in the province's Chamber of Deputies to reelect, through *vote counting*, almost all the outgoing deputies to the exclusion of the other candidates proclaimed by the committees or conventions and regardless of the number of real votes obtained by them. To facilitate such dealings records are fabricated of elections that have not been held in order to submit them in conflict with the records of real elections and admit them in the count, while rejecting those that go against them.

In the 1889 conflict between Governor Irigoyen and the Buenos Aires Province Chamber of Deputies, Irigoyen refused to recognize as deputies the citizens whom the legislative body declared elected, arguing that some deputies had approved their own reelection by feigning elections that had not taken place. The national government intervened and called a new election.

This form of vote counting not only corrupts the composition of parliamentary bodies, but also has a serious influence on the formation of the executive power, since provincial legislatures practice the general vote counting in elections for electors of governor, and therefore are able to include, exclude, and rectify records in accordance with their political sympathies or interests. The college that names the governor is therefore, with the exception of very rare cases, a puppet of the legislative bodies, which via such indirect vote counting have recovered the power to elect the governor the legislatures had before 1853 and during the first part of the constitutional period inaugurated at that time.

This does not mean that the legislature exerts its will spontaneously and independently in such cases. Generally speaking, it is a mere instrument in the hands of the outgoing governor. Rarely does a legislature show the resolve to free itself of this submission, and, when it does, the governor uses all means available to reestablish his own predominance.

These precedents are indispensable for an understanding of Argentine political life. It is subject to a periodic rhythm that corresponds to the periods for the presidential elections in the Republic. Shortly after the new president is installed, governors' opinions are examined on the likely candidates for the coming presidency. The president's close friends play an important role in this assessment. Little by little, the presidential influence begins to be felt, in favor of the governors whose electoral opinions flatter, and against those who demonstrate or are suspected of opposing ideas. The accommodating political intriguers take great pains to consult the smallest indications, to discover which way the president's intent will go regarding the citizen who is to succeed him. Among these political intriguers there are some really cunning men, who know how to work their way successfully around a tangle of conjectures in which others lose themselves. One of the most influential men of the Republic has labeled them "pathfinders." Once they have found the path, the arrangement is easy. When I was very young, I happened to be in Mendoza when I met one of these pathfinders, whom we shall call Dr. Q, who later attained the highest authority. I was supposed at the time to be very close to one of the presidential candidates, Dr. Bernardo de Irigoyen. Dr. Q, who had been away from public posting for some time, sought me out and asked me to report on the state of my candidate's work. I gave him those reports I thought prudent. He then said to me, and I quote: "I have come to Mendoza because I know that, here, the president's opinion on the candidates to succeed him will be known. I would like to accompany your candidate, who seems to me the best. But I am tired of lyricism and must adhere to the candidacy supported by the president." President Roca had just inaugurated the railway to Mendoza and was in town.

Shortly after that, my interlocutor sat on the executive committee of Dr. Juárez Celman's supporters. Juárez Celman was elected president and has continued to hold high political posts ever since.

The calculation of the odds in favor of the candidates is based on the governors' attitudes. Each province appears in the electoral assessment with the opinion of its governor, the rule being that presidential electors from one province vote for the candidate backed by their governor. According to the 1895 census, the total number of presidential electors is 300, of which 44 are from the capital, 60 from Buenos Aires Province, from Santa Fe 28, Entre Ríos 22, Corrientes 18, Córdoba 26, San Luis 10, Santiago del Estero 14, Tucumán 18, Salta 12, Jujuy 8, Catamarca 10, La Rioja 8, San Juan 10, and Mendoza 12. The governors' electoral importance is measured by the number of electors in their province. When it is said that candidate X has the support of Córdoba, Mendoza, and La Rioja, it means that he has the support of those provinces' governors. The president of the Republic, who is the governor of the capital, almost always has the votes of this district, which is nevertheless the district that enjoys the most electoral freedom.

The presidential campaign consists of a series of maneuvers with the aim of forming, by argument or by force, a group of governors with a majority of votes at their disposal, computed by province in the said proportion.

The president, or the party leader whom the president allows to maneuver, has had a manifest advantage over all competitors in this campaign since 1880. Until then, the governor of Buenos Aires Province was a political rival of the president, who resided without jurisdiction in the capital city of that province, as the nation still had no capital. So it was that Governor Alsina could decide the presidential campaign of 1868 in favor of Sarmiento, having himself appointed vice president and obtaining posts for his ministers Avellaneda and Varela in the new president's cabinet. In 1880, Governor Tejedor stood for president, clashing with General Roca, then war minister under Avellaneda. Defeated in the election of electors, he staged a rebellion. He was also defeated on this terrain, and the national government took advantage of the circumstances to establish the Republic's capital in the city of Buenos Aires, separating it from the province of the same name, previously following constitutional procedures, thus completing the organization of the country begun in 1853. Since then, the president is really the supreme head of the nation, and makes this felt when he exerts his electoral influence.

Thus, when the number of governors supporting the candidate backed by the president is not enough to ensure victory, conflicts or insurrections are prepared against opposing or indifferent governors it is thought expedient to change. This provides a pretext for the national government to intervene and preside over the election of a new governor. Sometimes federal intervention is unnecessary, because the insurrection triumphs immediately and order is restored, with no greater innovation than the replacement of the governor with the vice governor or official who is to replace him under the provincial constitution.

Impeachment is frequently used against governors who hinder presidential policy, when the president has a majority in the provincial legislature. In such cases, if the chambers' majorities do not reach two-thirds of the votes required by the constitutions to accuse and condemn, all kinds of ruses tend to be used to attain this proportion, even the unfounded removal of members of the minority.

It is not uncommon for impeachment and insurrection to combine, as was the case in Santiago del Estero in 1884. A riot expelled the governor from government headquarters and the legislature removed him immediately after staging a sham impeachment, handing executive power to the vice governor, who was a supporter of the citizen elected president of the Republic shortly after. The deposed governor had not wanted to commit himself to any one candidate.

What does the people do while these official elements operate as described here? The people are ordinarily divided into three parts, namely: *situationists,* or friends of the governor in the province or of the president in the capital; *opponents,* or adversaries of the governor or president; and *neutrals,* including all those who, out of indifference, disenchantment, or for any other reason, do not play an active part in electoral movements. This third group has grown a great deal in the last thirty years. Neither situationists nor opponents generally adopt clearly defined policy or administration programs. They are content with vague, abstract declarations that compromise no one, and with promises to respect the freedom and purity of suffrage that they never keep. They are usually organized into political clubs or committees under local denominations, which allow them to pass from one side to the other on questions of national importance without difficulty. The terms *provincial party, popular union, united parties, electoral coalition,* and other meaningless names circulate constantly around the provinces, used as names for transitory collections of citizens grouped together to shore up or undermine a given government.

Unlike in the United States, there are no large organized national parties that contest both central and regional governments. Attempts to set them up have failed. In each province, local matters prevail over national matters, and local matters are nothing but personal controversy: they consist of being for or against the governor or the right candidate to succeed him.

Only with presidential elections approaching do local parties group together or splinter according to their interests and affinities. They enter the realm of national politics and form large disorganized, disparate electoral masses, which remain cohesive because of the influence a presidential candidate holds over the respective local leaders. But these groups soon disintegrate and separate once the enthusiasm for the national campaign has passed, and local interests once more prevail.

As all governors, with rare exceptions, tend to monopolize all the advantages of government for a small group of friends, they must necessarily raise justified resistance, and there is hardly any opposition that cannot make use of effective arguments in their electoral campaigns. The part of Argentina that is a mere onlooker during elections tends to support this opposition, but unfortunately when they manage to win, via direct or indirect collaboration from the president, they quickly fall into the same or similar vices as the defeated opponent, with the result that unbelief concerning the aims with which militant politicians solicit public opinion becomes general.

Often, the opposition groups limit themselves to propaganda in the press and in conversation. They abstain from taking part in elections, considering the fight against the governor and his official agents uneven. Seldom are they willing to make sacrifices to gain victory, but it is fair to say that there is no province that has not at some time witnessed a truly democratic contest, in which two opposing parties have expended an extraordinary amount of energy, perseverance, and activity. There has even been the case of the opposition winning through endeavor alone. But these are exceptional cases, in which the input of new men or some other singular circumstance has led to a brief awakening of civic enthusiasm. We Argentines are still not convinced that the price of freedom is eternal vigilance.

. . . Protests in favor of the free vote and against undue interference from state officials have no moral scope and lead to no sanctions that might jeopardize the reputation of the governor or employee censured. The official who breaks his promise to abstain in the election, and even the one who commits electoral fraud, does not lose the regard of society as a result, and continues to enjoy the friendship of the persons whom public opinion labels honorable.

Another case of political ethics is the high esteem in which the personal qualities of boldness and comradeship are held. The bold politician, who sweeps away everything in his path, who gives little or no consideration to principles and forms, who aims for success via the fastest route, even if it is the most reprehensible, is assured of the admiration and support of many, and the tolerance of many others.

Comradeship, or rather, close friendship between the public official and his personal or political friends, is generally held to be a virtue, though it may be taken to the extreme of sacrificing public for private interests. "A very good friend of his friends" is a much used and much coveted epithet in the Republic, whose highly sensitive people are very forgiving of those who love a lot. A thousand improper acts, a thousand undue concessions, a thousand unfair favoritisms, and a thousand ex-travagances or embezzlements are protected under the friendly flag of the love of one's friends.

Truthfulness leaves much to be desired in political and social life. Debate, which, according to Bagehot, characterizes a stage in human progress, in the Argentine Republic stumbles against election candidates' frequent lack of sincerity. Dr. Vélez Sarsfield, author of the Civil Code and a minister in the Mitre and Sarmiento governments, and oftentimes a member of the national and Buenos Aires Province parliaments, was famous for his habit of quoting inaccurately. When corrected, he would say: "Well, if that author doesn't say it, I say it."

In the press, where articles are usually anonymous, the opponent's opinions and arguments are often adulterated in order to refute them more easily, and any requests for correction are ignored. When a public official is the target of an attack from the press, the official may be totally in the right, but the newspapers that attack him will not acknowledge this, and will refuse to reproduce documents and evidence of facts they do not recognize. It is just as true the other way around: victims or critics of officials defended by the press will find no refuge or sincerity in the press. It is understood that these bad habits seriously hinder the formation of healthy and effective public opinion.

I have sometimes thought, in view of the state of public morals in my country, that, before founding reformist parties, a far more pressing need is to educate citizens' judgment, raise their ethical level, and even form leagues responsible for defending the principles of common morals, which all parties should profess as a sine qua non for all institutional progress.

The imperfection of social ethics means there is little development of the aptitude for collective action. This can be observed wherever a group of Argentines meets for a common purpose, be they jurisconsults or traders, capitalists or workers, politicians or students, erudite or ignorant. The majority are always erratic and inconstant, and if they show consistency in something, it is in their repugnance to subject their conduct to impersonal norms. Individual indulgences, private interests, and personal antipathy are the everyday ills of these majorities, who, to satisfy their tastes and inclinations, more or less openly disregard the laws, statutes, and regulations. The virtue of obeying the law is not a social custom in the Argentine Republic, although the story of Mary Magdalene and the Pharisees is frequently replicated, especially in political matters. This explains why the dictatorship or autocracy that corporate or group leaders lean toward can always be plausibly justified and can, on occasion, provide an important service for the common good, imposing order on behavior and the way particular cases are dealt with. Those who suffer the action of these groups and their leaders, or examine and then judge it, must hesitate long before deciding between collective or individual action. Out of the frying pan, into the fire, as the saying goes. Militant politicians who resolutely attack an authoritarian president or governor do not generally take the time to examine what would happen if those officials gave the majorities in the legislatures absolute freedom to do as they like.

. . . The only feasible reform at present, it seems to me, is to remove the powers that have been harmful to the people from provincial governments, since to preserve them is good for nothing but hindering the protection owed by the national government to the rights of all citizens.

And for that, the only thing to be done is to return to the national government the powers it had under the 1853 Constitution, lost with the 1860 Reform, under the influence of the political interests then prevalent in Buenos Aires Province.

The delegates of 1860 removed from the federal authority its immediate jurisdiction over the city of Buenos Aires, which was supposed to lend it vigor and prestige. This delayed the consolidation of Argentine nationality for another twenty years, prolonging the life of the caudillo system and encouraging a localist spirit until the painful upheavals of 1880 restored, on this matter, the 1853 Constitution.

They removed the national Senate's right to impeach provincial governors, when this was at once a safeguard for the people and for impeachable officials. That amendment has given us irresponsible governors constantly abusing public freedoms, or impeachments carried out by biased and partisan legislatures.

They took away from the federal Supreme Court the powers to settle disputes occurring between the public powers of the provinces, resulting in such conflicts having no practical legal solution, because they are resolved by the wielder of force, namely the governor.

They also eliminated from the Supreme Court's powers the power to judge cases between a province and its neighbors, and this amendment has made governors and legislatures the arbiters of civil rights of the people they govern, who consider these are guaranteed only when they find a way of taking their claims to the federal jurisdiction.

They abolished the obligation of the provinces to submit their constitutions for approval by the national Congress, and thus suppressed the only practical way of preventing the provinces from having institutions contrary to the common interests of the Argentine people.

I believe all these powers should be returned to the national government so that, in exercising them, it squarely assumes the responsibility it avoids today in its clandestine interventions, and can genuinely guarantee that the people of the provinces benefit from republican institutions both formally and essentially. Otherwise, it will continue to be what it is now: the bodyguard of all obliging governors, willing to defend them against any attack, even if provoked by violation of the most sacred rights.

Because the present Constitution, as the 1860 liberals left it, does not give the people guarantees against governments, but guarantees governments against the people. With its former obligation to impeach bad governors now removed, Congress today merely has the obligation to support or replace them when they are threatened or deposed by insurrection. Therefore, it can legitimately wash its hands of any complaints it receives regarding attacks on freedom in the provinces of the Republic whose sovereignty it represents.

And the national government must not only recover the powers reduced by the 1860 Reform, but also take advantage of its own and other experiences since then, and adopt further powers, which in the hands of the provinces are dangerous for freedom and national progress.

For example, in economic terms, the facts have already eloquently shown that the ambiguous use of external credit by the nation and provinces alike seriously jeopardizes the nation, which appears to foreign

creditors as morally responsible for all the loans and financial procedures of the provinces. And the provinces clearly have no business outside Argentina's borders, for, to make contact with foreign peoples, it
has the nation and its indivisible external sovereignty. Nothing would be
more logical, then, than prohibiting provinces from taking out foreign
loans, as Minister López suggested.

Another set of powers that could easily be passed from provincial to
national governments concerns indeterminate powers.

Dilke, the author of *Problems of Greater Britain,* has observed that our
political age is characterized by the tendency to create federal governments and fortify existing ones. The reconstruction seen in the USA
from 1865 to 1871 has strengthened national at the expense of local government. The colonies from British North America, once isolated, have
become consolidated since 1867 in the federal nation that takes the name
of the Dominion of Canada. The unstable German confederation was
transformed in 1871 into a powerful empire, tightening federal ties. The
prosperous colonies of Australia, abandoning their earlier isolation,
have united under the federal model and, with the approval of the English Parliament, passed their first national constitution.

In this great federal movement, Canada has inverted the power distribution method established a century ago by the USA. While the latter
confers on the states or provinces all the powers not delegated in the
national government, Canada confers on the federal government all the
powers not delegated to the provinces. It has thus ensured effective and
farsighted action by its central authority, blocked the source of many
power conflicts, and prevented fresh needs, whose uniform fulfillment
is in the interests of the country as a whole, from falling under the diverse legislation of different provinces, which are oftentimes incapable
of fulfilling them.

Herein lies a principle I consider reasonable to adopt in the Argentine
Republic, whose provinces, almost always afflicted by budget deficits,
usually have a pointless surplus of sovereignty, like those poor noblemen who, for want of money, display titles and lineage that serve no
purpose for their needs in their struggle for existence.

Such constitutional reforms, legalizing and channeling the centralist
tendency seen in current events, would meet with no serious resistance
in the governing classes, whose national sentiment is far stronger now
than in 1860. The only difficulty might lie in making militant parties

agree on the advisability of participating patriotically with their most distinguished men in the reviewing convention to be convened. But this difficulty is far from insurmountable in a country that has already averted it on other occasions.

The expediency of strengthening the national government's licit action and increasing its responsibility as a means of consolidating justice, order, and liberty can be fulfilled without resorting to the centralist system, as seen in the evolution of Anglo-Saxon and German federal systems. The concentration of power in the hands of national government has a natural limit in the incapacity of effectively attending to the growing number of ventures of all kinds that demand the intervention of authority in any civilized country, and in each of its regions and towns. Federalism is, without any doubt, the model that best allows governmental duties to be shared out so that all society's legitimate interests and the interests of territorial groups can be sufficiently satisfied.

Having studied the practices of Argentine institutions with an unprejudiced mind, I have become convinced that the substantial vices that disturb them do not depend on the federal structure established by the Constitution, but on causes deeper than the simple distribution of political power between central and local authorities. What above all becomes evident in my research is the people's incapacity as demonstrated thus far to practice the representative system, an incapacity that cannot be perpetual and must gradually be corrected; but this has led to an electoral system unknown by the constitutional theory, although generally accepted by the citizens, a system that distributes the power to vote among Argentina's ruling national, provincial, and municipal authorities. The truth is that the country, on putting Spanish rule behind it and becoming organized in 1853, was better prepared for the federal than the representative system.

Unlike the British colonies, the Spanish colonies freed themselves from the mother country without first trying out the representative model, and this lack of preparation for popular rule very largely accounts for the setbacks suffered by the Spanish American republics in their independent constitutional life.

It is no surprise that the whole of the nineteenth century was used by the Argentine Republic in learning popular suffrage, when its former mother country, Spain, did the same with no great success.

If one were to attribute the failure to the territorial distribution of authority, regardless of other factors of political evolution, it should be noted that the centralist model failed in Spain. However, this may be an unfounded inference. What is frustrated in Spain, as in the Argentine Republic, is not the centralist or federal system, but the representative system, popular government, the rule of the country by the country. Race, no doubt, has a large part in this result, as do the habits acquired and passed on from generation to generation over many centuries of despotism. Popular government requires its citizens to have a permanent aptitude for collective action and to steer it in the direction of the common good. It is not enough for laws to follow ideal principles if there are no ideal citizens to obey them and enforce them. Political progress depends on successive and opportune transactions between the ideal and the real. The best constitutional reforms are those that implement such transactions with foresight and patriotism. The Argentine Republic owes this great lesson in politics to its Constituent Congress of 1853.

There is no need to despair if time brings no improvement in the institutions with the desired speed. What is important, above all, is that the country should know itself, so that it can consciously improve itself, strengthening its weak organs and making their respective functions more effective. In this regard, half a century on, Alberdi's words are still relevant: The Argentine Republic needs population and education. These are the great assets that must be acquired at all cost.

In the meantime, let us acknowledge that federalism is deeply rooted in our nation and, alongside it and like all things, it is still evolving, adapting to new needs, with all the imperfections that appear in any adaptation in which human will and interests are involved.

Let us also acknowledge that institutional deficiencies have not prevented the Argentine Republic from progressing in terms of population, wealth, culture, and civil liberties, more so than any other Latin American country. Before its first centenary, it has earned the right for all the world's free nations sincerely to repeat the last verse of the 1813 national anthem: Greetings to the great Argentine people!

5 | Liberalism on the Defensive (1912–1940)

1

ROQUE SÁENZ PEÑA
Message on the Electoral Reform
(Buenos Aires, February 29, 1912)

The political moment that it is my honor to preside over is one that I regard as significant for the future of our institutions insomuch as the electoral reform heralds an evolution in representative government, and in the environment and customs in which Argentine democracy is to develop. And so crucial do I consider the new state that the new practices will generate that I have deemed it necessary to speak to public reason and national sentiment in order to establish by an act of persuasion the responsibilities that will rest on the popular masses and, with a serious preference, on the thinking classes of society.

The present manifesto is an exceptional act, but this makes it no less democratic, for, if it behooves the head of the executive to suggest ways ahead for the general politics of the country, I also feel obliged to outwardly express my thoughts and live in healthy contact with the collective soul of the nation. Only this way can so many noble desires be given a course. They are born and remain dispersed till patriotism condenses them and the leader guides them to their definitive formula. Hence the need to interpenetrate, People and Government, endeavoring for my part to bring to your intimate selves my vision and desires. In the simple language of confessed intentions, I want to persuade and at the same time convince myself, controlling my natural leanings. The statement I had the honor of making when I told the honorable Congress that between the Argentine people and their elected leader there is a communion of ideals will thus be put to the test of events. It is for the sake of this mutuality that we must set out on the road of reform with faith in the country, the institutions, and mankind.

I promised a government of freedom, dialogue, and scrutiny. I am delivering. I do not, however, perceive the activity of the parties making

Original title: "Mensaje sobre la reforma electoral." Source: Roque Sáenz Peña, *Escritos y discursos* [Writings and speeches] (Buenos Aires: Peuser, 1915).

my labors effective, committed as I am in the fight against routine and the interests that are defended. I am confident, nonetheless, that I was not wrong to undertake the policy I am carrying through, yet I must repeat once again that it is not the work of my inspiration, but the demands of the times that give to each government its own mission.

The intention is far from my mind to file charges against the causes that have held up our political progress. It would not be fair, of course, to personalize errors that I have deemed collective, or to attribute them to certain governments, who living in their time and making their history have broken down powerful obstacles while maintaining the principle of authority, which must take precedence over improvements. I have, on other occasions, said that defensive governments cannot be reformist. This accounts for the delays. In the present period, when I am exercising my mandate without convulsions or threats, it would be unfair to attack my predecessors or dismiss their patriotism because it fell to their lot to lead in times of agitation that called for drastic measures imposed by the incipient nature of our democracy. They have all been factors in our greatness and have brought their intensive contributions to national development. Let us reap the benefits of so much effort and use the experiences attained for the good, without rashness or reproach.

The transformation of a country is not the result of chance, but of many joint causes that bring closer, prepare, and establish solutions. Once *caudillismo*[1] had disappeared, the Republic began to take shape and, through profound upheavals, the law prevailed over men, and the national concept emerged from the defeated anarchic ferment. The struggle was no less harsh for that: blood ceased to be spilled in the fields of rebellion, but it flowed in the cities, and elections witnessed bloody contests between the impassioned people and supporters of the ruling party. The absence of weapons was certainly a breakthrough, but it is not a final sign of victory for democracy. It is not enough. We need to destroy the surrogate agents of force: the crafty arts that make the vote and the effective rule of majorities an illusion. When they disappear, then we will have arrived.

Before undertaking the reform, I asked myself with foresight and caution whether the political period we are going through was really ripe to carry it through. The answer was categorical.

---

1. Domination by local strongmen (caudillos). [E.N.]

External peace has clearly been secured within international harmony and the power of the nation itself. The principle of authority is seen as unalterable through free struggles that respect order. A lawful government maintains the harmony of the powers of the state within their independence and will not accept interference in its own, or attempt it in others. Influential men of all parties patriotically associate themselves with the true and prosperous course of the Republic, lending it their moral or effective cooperation. Revolution has become a memory, disarmed by liberty, which ensures enduring harmony and peace. Education multiplies the number of its schools and constantly improves its systems. The army methodically instructs itself and is in turn a civilizing agent, both when preparing a conscript and returning him to the community to teach what he has learned, and when expanding effective possession of this vast territory as far as the northern border. The navy increases its power by acquiring ships and by the skill of its personnel, the discipline of both institutions strengthened by the certainty that they do not live in the realms of the arbitrary and that no right lacks a judge.

Having broadly sketched out the political outlines of the present, I must return to education in order to dismiss, on the basis of its progress, a specious argument: namely, the people's lack of preparation. We have grown accustomed to repeating it and thus to justifying an inadmissible tutelage. Those intense developments, defeating darkness and opening up horizons, that have been taking place by means of conscription and schooling are not taken into account. Let us show our loyalty. Let us verify the state of the process, and the capacity of our people will appear with the native wisdom of their race and temperament. Let us recognize it *sui juris*.

Having demonstrated the country's favorable position regarding its most crucial problems, one must ask: How many decades will have to elapse for a similar situation to arise, without a partisan government, or overwhelming passions, or high-handed caudillos? Could we be sure that future governments, if or when this effort fails, would attempt it once again equally tenaciously? Would they feel inclined to divest themselves of militant action and that personal influence, which, for all its humanity, remains harmful to the freedom of parties and the character of citizens? I am not claiming this will not be attempted, yet I doubt it will be done, for the same reason that history repeats itself in its successes as in its setbacks.

Sharing these criteria, the honorable Congress has given the country electoral legislation; and before recommending to my fellow citizens the obligations that this creates, allow me to do justice to the Parliament that has debated its bases with such enlightenment and patriotism. I have respected the different criteria in which their opinion has been divided, though I have discussed them openly, not only as a proponent of the law, but fulfilling my duties as co-legislator in the use of my own powers. My government has tortured no conscience nor stung any pride in the honorable Congress. No selfish interests on one side or the other have prevailed there, nor has the vote been split between supporters or opponents of the government. The executive, of course, has no enemies and recognizes none among the representatives or in the parties. I aspire to be, as I have said on occasion, the guarantor of all opinions and the president of all Argentines.

The new law provides two substantial innovations to our positive law: the incomplete list and the compulsory vote. In the wake of the debates, I regard it as superfluous to explain its aims. I will only say that the system, breaking unanimity and monopoly, recognizes the minorities, giving reason and existence to the permanent parties. From here on, there will, of course, be winners, but there will no longer be losers, because the majority and the minority will share in the governmental function. Compulsory voting is a reaction to abstention. The secret ballot eliminates venality, and as mercenaries disappear, citizens will reach positions through the concourse of free wills. Candidates will become such through reputation and merit, not by anyone's grant, but through the decision of all. And there will be political sanctions, for in place of the ruler's favor, public opinion will be what is required: praise that does not depress, because it translates into services and virtues.

Let us make no mistake, however. Neither the law nor the system it creates is an end in itself: it is merely a means to carry out a living work helped by the warm encouragement of the citizens. If they were to remain impassive and act as foreigners in their own home, the country would have to return to the familiar regime, a reversal that would not be without its complications. I shall not consider the moral disappointment of the leader before the clear relinquishment of the right he upholds by the active subjects. I disregard it, for, although I do not derive satisfaction from authority, I am inspired by the passion for good: I owe myself to my country and I must exhaust my last efforts in order to see its material greatness matched by its political probity—signs of harmony that signal the stature of each civil society. Peoples achieve respectability by virtue of their efforts and the harmony of features that shape their character. And they are called upon to prevail through a living sense of their rights.

I need not repeat that, in my exercise of the law, I shall meet my commitments to the nation, yet I do believe that the time is ripe to say how the president understands this law that he has just enacted and what kind of life he wishes to breathe into it.

With the precise concept of my powers, I understand that the formation of the honorable Congress is not a set of fragmentary actions, nor a local or regional matter. It is the unit-people that elects, it is the whole Republic that decides, exercising a national function, as the elector too is national, and national the law that protects or punishes him, as is ultimately the power it constitutes.

With this precise criterion of doctrine and law, I unflinchingly face the responsibility of my duty, attending to the requirements of the times. I shall fulfill. Neither the will of the president nor that of the members of the executive need favor or veto any personal or collective aspiration. The executive is concerned for the Congress to be the expression of the ballot and nothing else. The actions of provincial governments, I hope, will fall within the framework of this same healthy rule. I hold indispensable the preservation of autonomies, entailed by the regular ballot as a condition and essence of the republican regime.

The Ministry of the Interior must remain alert to all movements. Wherever civic struggles recommend it or a responsible group requires it or the constitutional situation advises it, the federal power shall be present. Wherever citizens wish to vote and governments make ready to prevent it, the warning of the head of state must first be expected, and, if that were not enough, the authority of the nation. Faced with the subversion of the Republican form, Congress or the executive as the case requires shall proceed to act on it. And I do not doubt the attitude of the honorable Congress given the law it has just enacted. If it is a criminal act not to vote, so too must be the obstruction of this duty by local authorities. And above these guarantees are those that behoove the honorable Congress, the high judge of its members' election. Nor do I doubt at this time its moralizing determination or the severity of its sanctions. The rejection of impure diplomas and the impossibility of acts of nepotism, perpetuity, schism, and barter shall be imposed through the same spirit of the law and the times.

Having promised the efficacy of the ballot so categorically, it remains for me to define the motivation of its effective guarantee. If the national government is obliged to protect liberty, it needs the reason for that protection, because just as in law there is no obligation without cause, there are no repressive actions in the political order for only the suspicion of oppression. If the parties do not organize or act, how could they claim a lack of security, when what is omitted is votes lost to abstention? What legal basis can justify my intervention where there is but one party that exercises such respectable rights as those I propose to guarantee to the others? For the central government to intervene where there is no voting because there is no will to vote, one would have to proceed on the hypothesis, which means repressing conjectures or intentions. I do not suppose one would wish to entrust me with destroying or vanquishing certain parties. The former would be an attack on the very liberty I intend to consolidate; the latter would make me a party in the strife, and in the place of guaranteeing rights, I would exercise militant, oppressive actions. This is precisely the power I have declined, aspiring to govern and not to command.

I consider governmental groups to be as legitimate as opposition groups. The failing does not lie in parties supporting the government, but in the governments defeating the parties with the vast means of the administration. This influence must not weigh heavily. Parties of opinion must deem it to be unnecessary. Parties of principle must feel it to be incompatible. Governments must calculate the intensity of its complications. But what is the dividing line between the lawful and the unlawful in the expansion of the executives? The dividing line is hard to pin down, but a line there undoubtedly is. Neither must the government be the party's headquarters, nor must the party fill out the administration. I expect of the governors not merely the fulfillment of the law, but also the moral influence that will place me with them in the same patriotic communion. I have confidence in their declarations and I do not think that my word has lacked communicative force or convincing virtues, inasmuch as it is inspired by a real selflessness. National representation cannot be the expression of the governors, but that of the parties freely expressed.

I have, according to my beliefs, avoided the formation of presidential circles that, dear to the affection of the leader, limit the wide outline of his vision, and more than once, in the warmth of friendship, deform the feeling of the general interest. I am well aware that such groups are pleasing to the head of state and that, by lightening the burden of his normal administration, they are an estimable support in times of difficulty. But these advantages weigh less on my spirit than the certainty of knowing the impossibility for other groups defeated and discouraged in advance, if they are to find before them the parties in power with the president at their head. It is not that I lack ties or friendships: I preserve them intensely and I devote to them all my integrity, yet I do not believe that I deserve reproach for loving my country collectively more than my friends individually.

On accepting my candidacy, I said publicly and on no few occasions to its initiators that my name was at the service of collective aspirations. And because I long for great and stable organizations, I regard myself as necessarily removed from party campaigns. The general concept does not escape me and I do not believe I will be accused of ignorance about the political activity of high-ranking officials in nations whose perfection we are far from achieving. In this precisely resides the painful reason that imposes on the Argentine leaders of the hour the resignation of their influence. The deficiency and inferiority of our habits, the scant interest aroused by the public sphere in populations whose nationalism is weakened by cosmopolitan growth, the indifference of citizens in new countries, where efforts are focused on the rapid advancement of wealth; these operative factors and the traditions of the regimes are what characterize and differentiate the current context. In order for all citizens to feel guaranteed and for no flag to desert the struggle, being attributed a disadvantageous position, it is necessary for governments to stay away from party strife.

My fellow citizens have shown me their trust and do not doubt my impartiality. It is, and shall always be, the invariable conduct that shall inspire members of the national executive, obliged by their convictions and their public adherence to my program. The national government shall not interfere, but I call on my fellow citizens to ponder the new situation. It is not fitting in the political order to eliminate forces without immediately creating their substitutes. Anticipating such a void, the reform of the electoral law makes the vote compulsory, and the abstention of the Executives encourages and makes party discipline possible.

May possibility be a foretaste of consummation. May the forthcoming elections and all Argentine elections be the stage for frank and free struggles, for ideals, and for parties. May both individual indifference and eventual groups, joined by transitory pacts, be things of the past, impossible to be revisited. Lastly, may the elections be the instruments for ideas.

I have told my country all my thoughts, convictions, and hopes. May my country hear the voice and the advice of its head of state. May the people vote.

2

JUAN BAUTISTA JUSTO
The Protectionist Fallacy (1916)

War brews superstition, fuels hatred between peoples, and creates antisocial interests. It is quite unremarkable, then, that in the heat of the conflagration in Europe, the protectionist fallacy should once again rear its ugly head and find new supporters.

Nations today are separated by the blockade, the submarines, and lines of forts and trenches. Among some of the wealthiest and most populous nations there is no trade, except for rifle and cannon fire, and the occasional convoy of wounded prisoners. And this picture of relations painstakingly established—sometimes by war—now ruptured, seduces certain politicians and publicists who dream of prolonging the peoples' isolation, even once the war is over. They may perhaps agree to dismantling and razing to the ground the fortresses on the borders, but only to replace them with customhouses.

This topic of conversation is found mainly among the enemies of Germany, which they loathe the more because, before the war, it supplied other peoples with certain useful products that they lack today.

And there is patriotic talk of locking it away behind a defensive customs wall, particularly in England, which owes the high standard of living of its people to free trade, and becomes rich by acting as a carrier and transit market to all peoples.

This replay of the old sophisms that make up the doctrine of customs protectionism comes as no great surprise. Our very own country lives in total peace under a regime of the rawest mercantilism, which has made a money box of the Republic, where gold comes in but cannot get out, building national prosperity on the expensive, sterile, impoverishing accumulation of the noble metal.

Protectionist paradoxes are nothing but a watered-down version of such mercantilism. We are supposed to buy as little as possible from the

Original title: "La falacia proteccionista." Source: *La Vanguardia,* May 8, 1916.

foreigner and at the same time try to saturate him with our own products.

Let us not allow him to freely introduce his, as that would impoverish us, especially if they are cheap and well made.

Let us manage on our own and take our products to other countries, albeit at a loss.

Let us, however, be wary of imports, for how could we ever afford them? A matter that importers, in their unrepentant altruism, are not to bring up.

These frivolities, underlying the so-called protectionist theory, cannot be taken seriously. Yet protectionist political forces are too alive and well for us to believe they are driven or guided by them.

What we find is destructive hatred and fury, and newly created interests that, instead, reinforce the interests of businessmen either in difficulty or simply limited in their profits by international competition.

Inept businessmen, hungry for monopolies and thirsty for profits torn away from their own people, are always the ones who fly the flag of customs protectionism and seek to impose it as a national ensign. By interrupting and disrupting international trade, the war has been responsible for the ubiquitous appearance of new industries, determined to secure their survival through the customhouses. This accounts for certain articles in the well-heeled press about "the death throes of free trade," when, for the first time in history, the entry of America's agricultural products to the European countries is free.

Protectionism is one gigantic lie that may, for a time, reconcile the interests of businessmen and workers in certain branches of production, but always at the expense of the country's entire population.

And if the so-called doctrine of customs protectionism did indeed have some real foundation, it would never be as superfluous as it is now, in times of war. Does it not isolate us from the world? Has it not raised ocean freightage to fifteen times its former cost? Does it not prevent raw materials from leaving the country? Does it not stop foreign products from reaching us? If these are the foundations for the future of our industry, may the war be praised! Meantime, the German submarines ensure their presence among us, and may do so for a long time to come.

3

ANTONIO BERMEJO
Dissenting Opinion in *Ercolano, Agustín v. Lanteri Renshaw, Julieta* (1922)

Buenos Aires, April 28, 1922

Whereas:

1. The judgment appealed in the last instance applying Article 1 of Law Number 11,157 is contrary to the right that the appellant has founded in Articles 14, 17, and 28 of the national Constitution, and consequently an extraordinary appeal has been rightly granted by this Court according to Article 14 of the Law of Jurisdiction and Competence, number 48, and Article 6, of Law 4055.

2. Under the contested article: "For two years from the enactment of the present law, the rental price of houses, rooms, and apartments intended for habitation, commerce, or industry in the territory of the Republic must be no higher than the price paid for these on January 1, 1920."

3. The appellee and the acting attorney general uphold the constitutionality of the law, contending: that it is in response to the scarcity of rooms due to the paralyzation of construction during the World War; that Congress may establish regulations for the aforementioned constitutional rights; that it is an emergency measure intended to be valid for two years only; and that the honorable Congress has exercised its regulatory powers by putting the general interest before personal interest.

4. The importance of interests involved, due less to the pecuniary value of the differences in the rents stipulated than to the broad swathe of persons affected by them; the orientation that this law reveals in the appreciation of the limits of state action in the economic development of the country and the imperative mandates of the national Constitution, which are the prime concern and priority, demand thorough consideration in these proceedings.

Original title: "Voto en disidencia en la Corte Suprema de la Nación." Source: Fallos de la Corte Suprema de Justicia de la Nación [Cases adjudged in the Supreme Court of the nation], 1922, vol. 136, pp. 180–95.

5. Even dispensing with other points of view foreign to the constitutional provisions invoked, it cannot be ignored that Article 1 of Law 11,157 is not in accordance with the guarantees that our Constitution sets out for the property and civil liberty of all inhabitants, inspired by the goal of promoting individual initiative and activity, or as its preamble emphatically states: to promote the general welfare and secure the blessings of liberty to ourselves, to our posterity, and to all men of the world who wish to dwell on Argentine soil.

6. Under Article 14, All the inhabitants of the nation are entitled to the following rights, in accordance with the laws that regulate their exercise, namely: to work and perform any lawful industry; . . . to make use and dispose of their property, etc.; and pursuant to Article 17 "Property may not be violated, and no inhabitant of the nation can be deprived of it except by virtue of a sentence based on law. Expropriation for reasons of public interest must be authorized by law and previously compensated." Article 28 adds the following safeguard: "The principles, guarantees, and rights recognized in the preceding articles shall not be modified by the laws that regulate their enforcement."

7. Fixing the scope of these provisions, the publicist Alberdi, who in his *Bases* and his *Project* had suggested them to the constituent members of '53 and whose authority is rightly recognized in constitutional and economic matters, said the following: "The freedom to use and dispose of one's property is complementary to the freedom to work and the right to own property; an additional guarantee of great usefulness against the socialist economic trend of the times, which under the pretext of organizing these rights, intends to restrict the use and availability of property," etc., and, in reference to Article 17:

> Property is the motive and stimulus of production, the incentive to work, and a fitting reward for the efforts of industry. Property has no value nor attraction: it is not wealth, properly speaking, when it is not inviolable by law and in fact. But it was not enough to recognize property as an inviolable right. It can be respected in principle, but attacked in its most precious aspect: the use and availability of its advantages. . . . Keeping this in view and the fact that property without unlimited use is a right only in name, the Argentine Constitution has, under Article 14, established the full right to *use and dispose of one's property* with which it has bolted the door on the

errors of socialism forever. (*Organización política y económica de la Confederación Argentina* [The political and economic organization of the Argentine Confederation] — official edition of 1856, pp. 379, 381, 384, and 385.)

8. It has rightly been said that property is one of the cardinal bases of civil organization of peoples in the current state of culture and civilization, and that, without it, the concepts of freedom, fatherland, government, family are disturbed, and after noting the failure of attempts at social organization that have ignored it, it has been affirmed that "we must consider it as the starting point of contemporary social orderings" (Montes de Oca, *Der. Const.* I, ch. XII; Estrada, *Obras completas* VI, 183 and 334; González Calderón, *Der. Const. Arg.* I, 364, II, 170ff.).[1] The national Constitution contains a series of provisions to ensure its inviolability according to our ancient common laws and to those of a political nature that have included it in the rights of man, such as the regulations of 1815 and 1817 in chapter 1, Article 109, of the Constitution of 1819 and Article 159 of the Constitution of 1826, which served as a model for the single chapter of the first part of the 1853 Constitution.

9. And in accord with that doctrine can be remembered the declarations of the American Supreme Court, at various times and circumstances, and in terms that might be considered prophetic: "Our social system rests largely upon the sanctity of private property; and that state or community which seeks to invade it will soon discover the error in the disaster which follows" (212 U.S. 1, 18). "There can be no concept of property divested of the faculty to dispose of it and of its use, as its value depends on such use"[2] (154 U.S. 440, 445).

10. The dearth of rooms is said to be the *raison d'état* that authorizes the imposition of reductions in rents. But this dearth at any given moment may become overabundance at another and the same *raison d'état*

1. Manuel A. Montes de Oca, *Lecciones de derecho constitucional,* 2 vols., 1902–1903; José Manuel Estrada, *Obras completas,* 1897; Juan A. González Calderón, *Derecho constitucional argentino: Historia, teoría y jurisprudencia de la constitución,* 3 vols., 1917–1923. [E.N.]

2. The Spanish translation in the text differs from the English original, which is as follows: "But the value of property results from the use to which it is put, and varies with the profitableness of that use, present and prospective, actual and anticipated. There is no pecuniary value outside of that which results from such use." [E.N.]

would lead to the authoritarian imposition of increased rents, which would ultimately mean the disappearance of landlords and tenants, replaced by the state, which would in turn have become the manager of an immense phalanstery. This dearth cannot be the source of civil obligations for owners, and as our constitutionalist, Estrada, used to observe, pointing out the dangers entailed by sovereignty that subjects individuals to the observation of those duties that are not enforceable because their neglect causes no direct damage to others, "demolishes property in order to favor the poor or the idlers, that is to say, it becomes the Guaraní constitution (*Obras* VII, 336), and as Alberdi used to say: "Jeopardize, wrest away property, that is to say, the exclusive right of every man to use and dispose fully of his work, his capital, and his land in order to produce what fits his needs or pleasures, and you do no more than wrest the tools of production away, that is, paralyze their fertile functions, make wealth impossible" (*Organización,* etc., cited, p. 384).

11. As to the varying duration assigned to the validity of a law (two years to number 11,157) its constitutionality cannot be decided upon notwithstanding the importance attributed to it by the majority of the American Court in the case *Block v. Hirsh,* settled on April 18, 1921, which stated that such a limitation would justify a law *that could not be upheld as a permanent change,* as it is not a question of extending the exercise of power, but of not recognizing the power to supersede the owner and dispose of the use of his property for another's benefit.

12. The value of all things, or the value of the use and enjoyment of them, as well as the value of work in its various manifestations, depends on many factors outside the authority of governments and of the powers that constitute them, and well within his rights is the man who demands the current market price for his work or for the control or the use of property, which is the one true and legitimate price, and therefore his right and in no way an abuse, because, as the codifier observes in reference to the absolute nature of the right to property: "any preventive restriction would have more dangers than advantages. If the government sets itself up as the judge of abuse, a philosopher once said, it would soon become the judge of use, and all true ideas of property and freedom would be lost" (note to Article 2513, Civil Code).

13. Nothing authorizes public powers, be they legislative, executive, or judicial, to act outside the Constitution, since, in all circumstances

and at all times, its authority persists and even in extraordinary cases that lead to a state of siege, the Constitution itself sets out the powers it confers on the government (Article 23). Its terminology is quite broad in order to adapt to the ways peculiar to the times and the advances of civilization, always in harmony with the spirit of its provisions, since the national government has a number of powers that have to be exercised within the limitations set out by the Constitution. Under no circumstances is any deviation authorized, because its meaning remains unaltered. What the Constitution meant when it was adopted it means now and will continue to mean so long as it is not reformed with the formalities prescribed under Article 30. As Chief Justice Taney stated in a famous ruling: "any other rule of construction would abrogate the judicial character of this Court, and make it the mere reflex of the popular opinion or passion of the day" (19 How 393, 426).[3]

14. The government of the Argentine nation is ruled by a written constitution that has recognized the individual rights preexistent to it as inherent in the human personality. It has organized the various different powers and laid out their functions by placing limits on their exercise and establishing the means to prevent those limits being exceeded. Right or wrong, we need only comply with it by bowing to the sovereignty of the people expressed in it in the most solemn and imperative way, as one of the reporting members said at the session of April 20, 1853: "The Constitution is the people, it is the Argentine nation made law." And the guarantee of the inviolability of property, as well as that of personal safety against the advances of governments, is the essence of civil liberty, which can be considered the soul of the institutional body of the nation.

15. But it is observed that the rights recognized by Article 14 are not absolute and that, according to that article and Article 67, paragraph 28, they will be enjoyed "in accordance with the laws that regulate their exercise." Precisely. The laws regulate the exercise of individual rights recognized by the Constitution, and the decrees of the executive branch, in turn, regulate the implementation of the laws, under paragraph 2 of Article 86. Hence the legal problem is this: What are the constitutional limits of that regulatory capacity? For, if there are none, if it is a discretional capacity or power, our Constitution would then feature among

---

3. The correct citation is 60 U.S. 393, 426. [E.N.]

those that have been mentioned as "models of the tactics of political fascination and mystification" and would be open to the reproach of "absurd" inflicted on it by the publicist Lastarria, as refuted by Alcorta (*Las garantías constitucionales*, ch. II).[4]

16. It is not only Article 28 of the Constitution that restricts this power by stipulating that these rights "shall not be modified by the laws that regulate their enforcement," but also Article 19, under which "The private actions of men that in no way offend public order or morality, nor injure a third party, are reserved only to God and are exempted from the authority of judges." This Article 28 was suggested to the constituent members of 1853 by Article 20 and other articles in the bill proposed by Alberdi, who dedicated several paragraphs in his *Bases* to recommending this precept, observing that "like all loyal and prudent constitutions, it must declare that the Congress shall pass no law limiting or distorting the guarantees of progress and public law on the occasion of organizing or governing its exercise" (*Organización*, etc., pp. 54, 146, and 148).

17. The very same thinker who in his *Bases* had laid the foundations for Argentina's constitutional structure intended the work entitled "Sistema económico y rentístico de la Confederación Argentina según su Constitución de 1853" (The economic and revenue system of the Argentine Confederation according to its Constitution of 1853) to highlight the freedoms and rights that it establishes and, with remarkable insistence, records the opposition of its provisions to what has come to be called new spirit, whereby the providential direction of economic activity of the nation's inhabitants is attributed to the state, justifying this as regulation, police power, the promotion of general welfare, or *raison d'état*. But, he says, the Constitution took precautionary measures against the danger that the power to enforce it should degenerate into its abolition and sketched out in his "First Part" the principles that should serve as a check on those powers. He built first the limits, and then the power. In doing so his aim was to limit not one but all three branches of power. And in providing forthwith that the scope of the regulatory laws of agriculture, trade, and manufacturing be limited to preventing damage to the rights of others, he summarizes his statement, saying: "There is only one system for governing freedom; and it is that the freedom of some should not impair the freedom of others; to go any further is not

---

4. Amancio Alcorta, *Las garantías constitucionales,* 1881. [E.N.]

to regulate the freedom to work, but to suppress it" (*Organización,* etc., cited p. 421).

18. And this Court, declaring in 1903 the unconstitutionality of the Tucumán Law of June 2, 1902, which reduced the amount of sugar each refinery could produce and taxed the surplus at a higher rate than the current market price, stated: "It is clear that, if a regulatory law cannot and must not constitutionally alter the right that it is made to govern, this is because it must preserve intact and in its integrity that right, that is, that it must not and cannot diminish it, much less extinguish it, in whole or in part; etc. (Fallos, vol. 98, p. 20; item 8, p. 37; vol. 128, p. 435; item 11, p. 453; and opinion by the attorney general, p. 435).[5]

19. If the property is inviolable and no person can be deprived of it, save by virtue of a sentence based on law (Article 17), that is, without due process of law, as in Amendments 5 and 14 of the American Constitution, nor can property be expropriated without a declaration of public use and prior compensation, and if the law includes the use and possession of property according to the will of the owner (Article 14 of the Constitution and 2513 of the Civil Code), because "property without unlimited use is a nominal right," those constitutional guarantees are undoubtedly altered in fixing the price of its use by law, without the will of the owner and for the benefit of another, depriving him of an essential element of the property with no court sentence to authorize it and no prior compensation.

20. It is quite inconceivable to say that all the inhabitants of the nation have the right "to use and dispose of their property"—which enjoys no franchise or privilege, nor harms third parties—if it is admitted that, via regulations or otherwise, another inhabitant, who is not the owner, may fix of their own free will the price of this use or that provision. As one of the members of the general legislation committee, a learned professor of public law, observed in reference to Article 6 of the bill, which declared invalid any increases in rents after January 1, 1920: "that provision of a general and absolute nature, which means instituting the regime of the arbitrary by attributing to Congress the power to fix the value and price of things on its own terms, regardless of the indisputable and categorical provisions in our fundamental charter and of all the laws and principles

5. Fallos alludes to "Cases Adjudged in the Supreme Court" (see source of text). [E.N.]

governing values, besides being a perfectly ineffectual provision, since there would be no court that would not declare its unconstitutional nature, it would, to my mind, affect the purpose of its authors, since on the day that Congress institutes such a policy of fixing the value of the things on its own terms, without any rule or criterion whatsoever, nobody will dare invest his money or savings in buildings and so deliver it into the hands of chance" (Diputados [Congressional Records, Chamber of Deputies], 1920, III, 688).

21. Finally, to justify the legislative capacity of fixing by its own authority the rent to be produced by private property, so-called police power is cited in order to ensure the predominance of the general interest or welfare over private interest. But this power has no basis outside the rule of Roman jurisprudence, a guarantee also of social coexistence, according to which each person must exercise his right in a way that does not damage others; *sic utere tuo ut alienum non ledas.* Nor can there be any suspicion that, by renting out his property, the landlord impinges on the right of others, unless it is alleged that those others are his co-owners, which would imply a community of property that did not fall within the intentions of the authors of the Constitution. Preventing harm to others' rights is what legitimizes restrictions to the right of property, as noted by the codifier in his note to Article 2611 and as recognized by this Court, of which Dr. Gorostiaga, the reporting member of the 1853 Constitution, was part in the trial against the province of Buenos Aires on the occasion of the law to remove industries processing salted meat from the Riachuelo. That measure was required by public health and did not attack the right of property "for no one has it in order to use his property to the detriment of others" (Fallos, vol. 31, p. 273).

22. Given the evident increase that, in recent times, state interference has taken in view of "general welfare" with regard to the exercise of private rights and activities, it is necessary to insist on the constitutional limitations of this power, noting that the treatise writer, Tiedeman, who has examined it in relation to each of the individual rights, provides the key to its solutions in the aforementioned rule of civil law and the principles of abstract justice as they have been developed under the system of republican institutions, stating that "no one has a natural right to the enjoyment of another's property or services upon the payment of reasonable compensation; for we have already recognized the right of one man to refuse to have dealings with another on any terms, whatever

may be the motive for his refusal" (Tiedeman, *State and Federal Control of Persons and Property,* I, pp. 4, 5, 302ff.).[6]

23. This police power "is an attribute of government fundamentally necessary to the public safety, but so easily perverted as to be extremely dangerous to the rights and the liberty of the citizen,"[7] according to Campbell Black. This power, which, as Justice Brewer observes, "has become the refuge of every grievous wrong upon private property. Whenever any unjust burden is cast upon the owner of private property which cannot be supported under the power of eminent domain or that of taxation" (200 U.S. 600), has been defined by the above-mentioned author as follows: "[In constitutional law] its scope is limited to the making of laws which are necessary for the preservation of the state itself, and to secure the uninterrupted discharge of its legitimate functions, for the prevention and punishment of crime, the preservation of peace and public order, for the preservation and promotion of the public safety, the public morals, and the public health, and for the protection of all the citizens of the state in the enjoyment of their just rights against fraud and oppression" (*Handbook of Am. Const. Law.,* p. 390;[8] Blackstone 4 Com. 162;[9] Cooley Const. Lim.,[10] 7th ed., pp. 829 and 839).

24. This very Court, shortly after its organization, had occasion to appreciate this police power—which Story did not deal with in his famous commentary and which Marshall mentioned only incidentally in his famous rulings (Const. Dec., p. 537)[11]—and on the occasion of the challenge made to the law of the province of Buenos Aires banning bullfights, stated that: "the police power of the province is in the hands of local governments and is understood to be included in the powers

6. Christopher G. Tiedeman, *A Treatise on State and Federal Control of Persons and Property,* 1900. [E.N.]

7. Henry C. Black, *Handbook of American Constitutional Law,* 4th ed. (St. Paul, Minn., 1927), p. 366. [E.N.]

8. English version is from the second edition (1897), 338; page number differs, probably Bermejo had another edition. The online version is: http://www.archive.org/details /handbookamerica03blacgoog. [E.N.]

9. Sir William Blackstone, *Commentaries on the Laws of England,* 4 vols., 1753. [E.N.]

10. Thomas M. Cooley, *A Treatise on the Constitutional Limitations which Rest upon the Legislative Power of the States of the American Union* (Boston: Little, Brown, 1868). [E.N.]

11. *The Constitutional Decisions of John Marshall* (New York: G. P. Putnam's Sons, 1905). [E.N.]

384 : ANTONIO BERMEJO

they have reserved for themselves such as providing what is convenient for the safety, health, and morality of their inhabitants" (Fallos, vol. 7, p. 150; vol. 101, p. 126; item 3, p. 143; vol. 134, p. 401; item 11, p. 412).

25. And in relation to this regulatory legislation of property and industry, in the case *Nougués Hnos. v. Tucumán,* this Court asserted that the legislative restriction of rights to prevent damages to third parties in the enjoyment of other rights prior to the Constitution, or arising from it and from the laws, must not be confused with the restriction intended to provide for the general public or for certain social classes some advantage or benefit: in the first case, the legislative action is absolutely necessary for the very existence of society, which requires the reciprocal limitation of human activities; in the second, no one can be deprived of his property, restricted or inhibited in his use of it, without previous compensation, as expressly set forth in Article 17 of the fundamental law, etc. (Fallos, vol. 98, p. 52, item 8).

26. It is not a question in the case *sub judice* of the property of things allocated for public use or in which public health, morals, or safety are compromised; or as the codifier says, of restrictions imposed on ownership solely out of public interest, for the health or safety of the people or in consideration of religion; nor of those private actions of men that in some way offend public order or morals, or injure a third party. It is simply a matter of the "rental of houses, rooms, and apartments intended for habitation, trade or industry," that is, private uses, in the exercise of the freedom of trading by means of the use and disposition of property. Renting a house, room, or apartment constitutes for the landlord and the tenant a private contract, which does not become an act of public interest simply by injunction of the law, and the interference of the state in issuing police regulations, but only if the interests of the general public and not those of a particular class require it, "because it is a rule that police power may not be invoked to protect a class of citizens against another class, unless such interference is for the sake of the real protection of society in general" (152 U.S. 133; Ruling Case Law. VI, para. 194). Hence the codifier limited the exclusivity of ownership in "the prevalence *for the greater good of each and every one,* of the general and collective interest, over individual interest."

27. The simple alternatives of supply and demand, common to all businesses, do not constitute a de facto privilege that subjects them to the imposition of prices by the government. And the doctrine of "virtual

monopoly" of the majority of the American Court in the well-known case of Chicago elevators (*Munn v. Illinois,* 94 U.S. 113), which left all property and businesses in the state at the mercy of a majority of its legislature, does not fit in our Constitution, which has expressly prohibited rights that it recognizes being altered, and it has rightly been observed "that modern constitutions were a limitation placed on popular sovereignty itself, while the Constitution requires the legislator not to alter what it establishes, the executor of the law to be limited by what it prescribes, and even the judge who must judge the very law he applies, insofar as it may exceed the limits to the power of legislating indicated by the Constitution" (El Redactor de la Comisión, etc., of 1860, no. 6).[12]

28. Any law can, in general, be considered of public interest because it is enacted taking into account the common good. But if, in obtaining this result, it should deprive the owner of his property, it must previously compensate him, in accordance with paragraph 2 of Article 17 of the Constitution. If it merely restricts or limits an inherent right to property, such as use or possession—*jus fruendi*—there is no real expropriation in the strict sense of the word ("taking," say the Americans). In this case, regarding compensation, it must be distinguished: (a) whether the restriction is demanded for the preservation of public health, morals, or safety, when the use of one thing is irreconcilable with those inescapable demands of the community, no compensation is required because no one may have rights irrevocably acquired against public order, and it is an implicit condition that these must cease when they enter into opposition with it; (b) whether the restriction on the right to property corresponds simply to the benefit of some to the detriment of others, or rather the benefit of the greater number (in the hypothesis that the state should have the power to impose it) the compensation of the damages caused would be appropriate, as according to the first paragraph of Article 17 "property is inviolable" and would cease to be so if it were diminished without compensation in order to satisfy the convenience of others. Constitutional doctrine and national jurisprudence in this matter could be summarized in such terms.

29. Our Constitution, which in its preamble intended to ensure the

---

12. Convención de Buenos Aires: El Redactor de la Comisión Examinadora de la Constitución Federal, 1860 [Buenos Aires Convention: The Editor of the Committee Examining the Federal Constitution]. [E.N.]

benefits of civil freedom and in its Article 33 explicitly affirms the rights and guarantees deriving from the principle of sovereignty of the people and the republican form of government, does not admit the absolute subordination of the individual to society and rejects the idea of general welfare acquired at the expense of the individual right and freedom, which will ultimately no doubt lead to more perfect social welfare — temporary disturbances notwithstanding.

30. Lastly, it would not be too difficult to foresee that if the faculty of public powers to fix rents — that is, the price the owner must charge for the use of his property — is accepted, even in the case of private use free of any franchise or privilege, either voluntarily or involuntarily, "it falls into the Guaraní constitution," as Estrada used to say, since it would be necessary to accept also the power of fixing the price of labor and of all things that are the object of trade among men, or as expressed by this Court in 1903: the economic life of the nation and the freedoms that encourage it would be confiscated by legislatures or congresses who would, with artful regulations, usurp all individual rights until they fell into a kind of state communism, in which governments would rule manufacturing and trade, and be the arbiters of capital and private industry (Fallos, vol. 98, p. 20; item 24, p. 50).

On these grounds, after hearing the acting attorney general, it is hereby declared that Article 1 of Law number 11,157 is in violation of Articles 14, 17, and 28 of the Constitution, and consequently the ruling challenged is revoked in the part that has been the subject of the appeal. After payment of Court stamp taxes, it is ordered to return the docket according to the instructions set out in the first part of Article 16 of Law number 48.

A. Bermejo

4

MARCELO TORCUATO DE ALVEAR
and JOSÉ NICOLÁS MATIENZO
Message and Bill of the Executive Declaring the Need to Amend Articles 42, 46, 67, Section 7, and 75 and 87 of the National Constitution (1923)

Buenos Aires, August 16, 1923

To the Honorable Congress of the Nation

The executive submits the attached bill for the honorable gentlemen's consideration, declaring the need to amend certain provisions of the national Constitution.

As it stated at the opening of the current legislative sessions, the executive believes our fundamental law has gradually to be perfected by means of partial amendments, as advised by experience. The executive believes the amendments indicated in the attached bill to be of such a nature.

Of course, the election of senators by the provincial legislatures has paved the way for a good many political disturbances, which have frequently been the motive for national intervention in order to return the enjoyment and exercise of republican institutions to the disturbed provinces. The United States, which we have imitated in this form of election, has already abolished it, handing to the people the right to choose members of the Senate directly, just as it does members of the other chamber. There is no reason for us to keep a system that has brought us worse results than in its country of origin.

The form of renewal of the Chamber of Deputies also requires change. The present system—renewing half the chamber every two years—does not respond to the need to consult the opinion of the entire nation periodically and simultaneously, as it is done in the world's great democracies. The lower chamber is entirely renewed at certain times in Great Britain, the United States, France, Germany, Switzerland, Italy, Spain, Canada, Australia, Brazil, Chile, and many other countries. This

Original title: "Mensaje y proyecto del poder ejecutivo, declarando necessaria la reforma de la Constitución Nacional." Source: Cámara de Senadores, Diario de Sesiones [Senate, Congressional Records], August 28, 1923.

is the only way to give periodic access in parliament to the predominant opinion in the nation as a whole.

The Chamber of Deputies in our constitutional regime is meant to collectively represent the people of the nation, considered as a single state (Arts. 36 and 37), unlike the Senate, which represents the provinces and the capital as separate entities (Arts. 36 and 46). If, then, it is understandable that the form of renewal of the Senate not take into account the need to simultaneously consult the opinion of the nation as a whole, this need cannot be overlooked where the chamber in which the Argentine people has to be represented as a united whole is concerned.

Having established this, it seems advisable that the general elections for the renewal of both chambers take place at the same time and periodically coincide with the elections for the president of the Republic. To this end, the deputies' mandates need only be set at three years so that, upon their termination, a third of the Senate also terminates, and every two triennia this event also coincides with the renewal of the nation's presidency. Such a reform would lend the national government a broader democratic base and ensure harmony among the political powers wherever possible.

As for the organization of the executive, experience has shown that it is appropriate to introduce two amendments into the Constitution. One of them, the more important, mentions the impediments that bring about the delegation of the executive in the legal replacement.

The first clause of Article 75 mentions sickness and absence from the capital as being among the causes that render the president unable to exercise executive power. The second clause in the same article, anticipating that the vice president may also be impeded, replaces those two grounds with the general term of inability, which implicitly establishes that sickness and absence from the capital need only be taken into account when they do truly render the president unable to exercise executive power. This is how presidents have understood it in practical terms. But the fact cannot be ignored that the article is worded with an ambiguity that leaves room for doubts and may indeed be the source of more or less serious conflicts. Moreover, when the president absents himself from the capital in order to carry out official duties in any part of the national territory, there is no reason whatsoever to justify the delegation of executive power. There cannot be two presidents within the nation:

one inaugurating a public work or reviewing the army outside the capital and another in government house signing decrees, among which there may well figure an order of suspension of those acts. The article needs, then, to be amended, eliminating from the first part the terms *sickness* and *absence from the capital* in order to adopt the concept of inability contained in the second.

The other amendment, proposed with regard to the organization of the executive, is that of authorizing Congress to increase the number of ministers, set at eight by Article 87. The continuous increase of public services as the country develops will soon make it indispensable to alleviate the growing burden on some ministries by subdividing them or forming new departments to attend to special and related matters, at present dispersed or confused with others of a different kind.

Lastly, experience has shown that the clause of Article 67 prescribing the annual assignment of the budget has not foreseen one frequent case, namely, the fiscal year ending without the budget for the following year having been voted in by the Congress. The negative consequences of this lack of foresight are well known: it places the executive in the dilemma of ordering spending without prior legal authorization or paralyzing the administration. Several provincial constitutions have been more far-sighted, and the executive feels it is advisable to imitate them, providing in the national Constitution for the contingency that, once the fiscal year has ended without the new budget of expenditure having been approved, the last effective budget is deemed to be extended until another is sanctioned.

The executive holds that if the reforms it has proposed were to be sanctioned, it would have effectively contributed to the improvement of our political and administrative institutions.

God save the honorable gentlemen.

M. T. de Alvear
José Nicolás Matienzo

The Senate and Chamber of Deputies, et cetera,

BILL

Article 1: The reform of the Constitution is declared necessary with regard to the duration and renewal of the Chamber of Deputies (Art. 42), the manner of election of senators (Art. 46), the annual approval of the budget of expenditure (Art. 67, paragraph 7), the delegation of executive power in the event of the president absenting himself from the capital (Art. 75), and the number of ministers (Art. 87).

Art. 2: The following amendments to the articles of the Constitution are to be submitted to the consideration of the reforming convention:

a. Art. 42: Deputies shall last three years in the exercise of their mandate, after which time the chamber shall be renewed entirely.

b. Art. 46: The Senate shall be made up of two senators from each province and two from the capital, all elected in the form prescribed for the election of the nation's deputies. Each senator shall have one vote.

c. Art. 67, para. 7: To annually set the budget of the nation's administrative expenditure, and to approve or reject the investment account. Should the fiscal year expire without the new budget having been fixed, the one currently effective shall be extended until such time as another is sanctioned.

d. Art. 75: In the event of the death, resignation, removal, or inability of the nation's president, the executive power shall be wielded by the vice president, and in the event of the absence or inability of both, by the government official appointed by law, until such time as the impediment has ceased or a new president is elected.

e. Art. 87, to be added: The Congress may increase, but not decrease, the number of ministers.

Art. 3: A convention is convened for the purposes of this law that shall meet in the nation's capital and shall be made up of the same number of members as the Chamber of Deputies, elected in the same manner and proportion by the provinces and the capital.

Art. 4: The convention shall be elected on the last Sunday of the month following that of the promulgation of this law and shall be instituted thirty days later.

Art. 5: In order to be a member of the convention the qualities required to be a deputy are needed.

Art. 6: Convention members shall receive compensation at the end of their work amounting to one thousand pesos and shall enjoy the same immunities as members of the Congress.

Art. 7: The convention shall complete its assignment within two months of its institution.

Art. 8: The executive is authorized to make any spending necessary from general revenues for the pursuance of this law, to which they will be ascribed.

Art. 9: Notify the executive.

Matienzo

5

MARCELO TORCUATO DE ALVEAR
and VÍCTOR MOLINA
Internal Taxation (1924)

To the Honorable Congress of the Nation:
In my opening speech of the previous legislative term, I set out to this honorable chamber the need to reform taxation laws along the following bases: burden of taxation more in tune with the economic wherewithal of the taxpayer; coordination of the taxation systems of the nation, provinces, and communes; determination of the limits of the country's tax-paying capacity; participation of the provinces in national internal taxation, and establishment of a nationwide general taxation.

The bill I submit today for the honorable gentlemen's consideration is the result of my government's concern to find a remedy to the need noted here.

I

While internal taxes on articles of general consumption were introduced, in circumstances known to all, as a provisional financial resource, they then went on to become a permanent feature of the nation's financial system.

The revenues from this taxation, restricted in the early years of its application, grew along with the national system, so much so they now constitute the largest tax resource after customs revenues.

The annual growth of internal revenues occurred with no serious detriment to taxed productive, commercial, and manufacturing industries, which have performed without major hindrance within the legal norms and regulatory measures required by strict tax collection and imposed by the properly understood defense of industry.

The productivity of this source of revenues later led certain provinces

Original title: "Impuestos internos." Source: Cámara de Diputados, Diario de Sesiones [Chamber of Deputies, Congressional Record], June 20, 1924.

to adopt it to cover budget expenditure. Thus, imperceptibly, the problem of double taxation was born, which, while limited to the nation and two or three isolated provinces, did not have the repercussions or the complexity it has today, when all the federal states have fixed taxes on items already taxed under national law.

Determined to confront decisively the solution to a problem capable of compromising institutional, economic, and financial principles, the executive power has studied the question meticulously with a view to finding a way to reconcile the various interests in conflict.

The executive power believes that such a state of affairs goes against the Constitution and the harmonious development of the federal system: against the Constitution because although the sphere of influence of the nation and the provinces has not been precisely established with regard to taxation, it seems clear that the resources deriving from direct taxation are allocated to the provinces in principle, and only exceptionally to the nation. However, contributions proportionately equal to the population are allocated especially to the federal state, as mentioned in Article 4. Into this category fall customs duties and internal taxation on certain items of consumer goods.

I have said that the present state of affairs also goes against the harmonious development of the federal system. If a province can pass laws that tax the introduction and consumption of national products or those of other provinces, there is the possibility of an internal tax war that would mean the death of federalism and the weakening of national ties, which it is of such concern to strengthen. Between two or more provinces that produce sugar, wine, alcoholic beverages, etc., or between them and those that do not have such produce, rivalries would grow up that would result in struggles about competence in some cases and duties in others that would end up in mere fiscal profit or in inhibiting the development of other secondary industries.

Allowing the provinces to have recourse to internal taxation would be tantamount to permitting them to set up internal customs, taxes on dispatch forms, or any other tax on traffic.

The investigations ordered by the treasury that have drawn attention to the extreme taxation anarchy disrupting the national economy are another angle of the problem. It is well known how disastrous tax anarchy is, as it fundamentally affects tax revenues; the normal development of output, industry, and trade; as well as the free movement of products, the essential basis of wealth, which flees from the uncertainties and the abrupt changes—not always foreseeable—that such anarchy inevitably entails.

A summary examination of tax laws in the provinces reveals their most outstanding features. These are: disparity—one might say confusion— in the bases for taxation; diversity of forms, modalities, denominations, and descriptions of taxes; basic equality of ad valorem internal provincial duties with national taxes of the same kind, an equality entailing the falsification of the basic unit of national taxation and consequently leading to the transformation of the provincial tax into a genuine tax on the nation's fiscal revenues; differential treatment of products, whether domestic or foreign, local or extraprovincial, that is, the creation of internal and external customs; recognition of three taxable matters, namely provincial, extraprovincial, and national or imported articles; and overlap of local penalties and supervision with analogous national ones.

When one descends from the examination of the general characters of such laws to the particularities and details, the confusion grows: some provinces tax three times the same output that constitutes their main source of wealth, in the form of a license duty on the raw material and of two taxes, principal and supplementary or additional, on the finished product. Such triple local taxation gives some idea of the existing state of affairs and the degree of danger that threatens the future of thriving industries.

Evidently, this is no longer a question of taxation duality, but a complex plurality of taxes, which jeopardizes the vitality of the economy as a whole. This local ill, repeated in fourteen provinces, translates into collective damage, an eminently national problem, affecting the economic health of the country in terms of its productive sources and taxation bases.

Before the matter took on its present dimensions, farsighted legislators attempted to seek a remedy, and found it in the distribution of internal revenues between the nation and the provinces according to population, on the condition that the federal states abolished the relevant legal taxation. On June 13, 1910, the national deputy Sr. Luis Leguizamón presented a bill that stipulated the payment of 20 percent of internal revenues to the provinces. Two years later, in the August 21 session of the honorable Chamber of Deputies, Dr. Miguel Laurencena presented a similar bill that stipulated the distribution of 20 percent according to each province's population with a view to improving rural highways. The following year, in the August 22 session, the national deputies Luis Agote, Jerónimo del Barco, Manuel Mora y Araujo, Faustino M. Parera, Carlos Conforti, Rodolfo Freire, Eduardo Sobral, Miguel B. Pastor, Ramón A. Parera, and A. Cabanillas proposed a similar measure, raising the percentage to 33 percent. Subsequently, on March 15, 1917, Dr. Félix T. Garzón reproduced an identical initiative before the honorable Chamber of Deputies, of which he was a member, fixing at 30 percent the amount of revenues to be distributed among the provinces. Recently, at the July 6 session last year, National Deputy Dr. Juan A. González Calderón breathed new life into the idea, founding it on reasons of an institutional, economic, and financial nature.

All prior initiatives agree in acknowledging:

1. The importance of the problem;
2. The urgent need for a solution; and
3. The advisability of proceeding with the distribution of a given portion of internal revenues among the provinces according to the number of inhabitants in each of them.

In the presence of such legislative precedents, it should be pointed out that for some time there has been a school of thought favorable to the solution of the problem through the application of an almost invariable formula. This school of thought is currently shared unanimously by the representative forces of output, industry, and trade, who are effectively hindered in the full performance of their functions by the obstacles and restrictions of the plurality of taxes.

There is therefore nothing left but to give legal expression to the national movement of opinion created in relation to the matter, for it has already been widely debated and studied.

II

The executive power, certain as it is of the good reasons that might form the basis of a bill to prohibit the provinces from establishing these taxes, being inasmuch constitutionally unentitled, has chosen instead to propose a law of conciliation that would consult the provinces' financial needs, as well as a principle of fairness, helping them with a part equivalent to what their inhabitants pay on consumer goods in relation to the services provided by those entities.

The present bill is a response to such ends. Inspired by similar projects submitted for the consideration of the honorable Chamber of Deputies, it differs, however, from them on three substantial points:

1. Article 2 endows the provinces with a full right, with its correlative obligation.
2. Article 3 completes the basis of the distribution of revenues—the population—with another essential one: output, either of raw materials or of products manufactured with them.
3. Article 5 authorizes the reduction of customs duties in proportion to the taxes that any provinces should persist in maintaining on products for national consumption, favoring with a fair compensation those industries in the provinces where these taxes have not been established.

In regard to the first point, it has been deemed more advisable and suitable to establish as a right of the provinces their share of the distribution of 25 percent of internal revenues, because the federal states possess their own legal status and make up the nation as a whole.

As a correlative obligation, the provinces are obliged not to impose the same taxes levied under national laws.

The population is the basis for the proportional distribution of 25 percent of internal national revenues. In view of the material impossibility of establishing for certain the real contribution of each province to the product of internal taxation, a contribution that would have provided the exact criterion of the share, the number of inhabitants was taken as the closest basis to reality and truth. This is, furthermore, the predominant norm in other bills.

Twenty-five percent of the total amount of internal taxation is the portion to be distributed proportionately among the provinces according to their population. This portion is not a fixed sum but a variable, no doubt growing, amount. Today it might represent 40 million pesos; tomorrow, 50 or 60 million, according to progressive increases in revenues. Taking as a basis for calculation that 160 million pesos will be raised annually in taxes, this 25 percent would represent the sum of 40 million pesos, to be distributed as follows among the provinces according to their population as fixed by the last national census:

Buenos Aires	$13,822,643
Santa Fe	$6,018,591
Entre Ríos	$2,845,745
Corrientes	$2,321,797
Córdoba	$4,921,307
Santiago del Estero	$1,750,635
Tucumán	$2,227,321
Salta	$942,801
Jujuy	$512,661
Mendoza	$1,856,709
San Juan	$797,795
La Rioja	$533,554
Catamarca	$671,615
San Luis	$777,819
Total	$39,999,993

From careful calculations made by the treasury, the only provinces that might momentarily be jeopardized would be: Buenos Aires, Tucumán, Mendoza, and Jujuy.

But, with the purpose of preventing any possible disadvantage, a certain percentage of the yield of taxes on sugar, wine, alcoholic beverages, beer, and tobacco will also be distributed to the provinces that produce them.

The table below shows how this distribution would work, according to each province's output for the year 1922:

Buenos Aires	$186,111
Santa Fe	$399,328
Entre Ríos	$56,930
Corrientes	$25,754
Córdoba	$162,864
San Luis	$4,366
Tucumán	$3,077,942
Santiago del Estero	$1,432
Salta	$113,316
Jujuy	$380,139
Mendoza	$3,754,400

San Juan	$1,006,628
La Rioja	$28,317
Catamarca	$8,115
Total	$9,205,696

Adding the above amounts to what the provinces would receive per capita, we get the following result:

Province	By Population	By Production	Total
Buenos Aires	13,822,643	186,111	14,008,754
Santa Fe	6,018,591	399,328	6,417,919
Entre Ríos	2,845,745	56,930	2,902,675
Corrientes	2,321,797	25,754	2,347,551
Córdoba	4,920,307	162,864	5,083,171
Tucumán	2,227,321	3,077,942	5,305,263
Salta	942,801	113,316	1,056,117
Jujuy	512,661	380,139	892,800
Mendoza	1,856,709	3,754,400	5,611,109
San Juan	797,795	1,006,628	1,804,423
La Rioja	533,554	28,371	561,925
Catamarca	671,615	8,115	679,730
San Luis	777,819	4,366	782,185
S. del Estero	1,750,635	1,432	1,752,067
Total	39,999,993	9,205,696	49,205,689

or 49 million pesos in round numbers. Hence the part of internal revenues to be shared would be higher than 25 percent due to the addition of the other portion, which, under Article 3, would be distributed proportionately among the productive provinces. In actual fact, the full amount to be distributed would be no lower than 36.7 percent of the overall total of internal taxation.

However, if we compare the total amounts to be distributed among the provinces with the respective internal revenues calculated in their respective budget laws, we get the following table:

Provinces	Apportioned Share	Calculated Internal Revenue	Differences	
			Plus	Minus
Bs. Aires	14,008,754	11,406,910*	2,601,844	—
Santa Fe	6,417,919	6,000,000	417,919	—
Entre Ríos	2,902,675	1,962,000	940,675	—
Corrientes	2,347,551	300,000	2,047,551	—
Córdoba	5,083,171	3,043,854	2,039,317	—
Tucumán	5,305,263	3,510,000	1,795,263	—
Salta	1,056,117	220,000	836,117	—
Jujuy	892,800	826,691	66,109	—
Mendoza	5,611,109	13,750,000	—	8,138,891
San Juan	1,804,423	550,000	1,254,423	—
La Rioja	561,925	37,000	524,925	—
Catamarca	679,730	34,900	644,830	—
San Luis	782,185	260,000	522,185	—
S. del Estero	1,752,067	800,000	952,067	—
Total	49,205,689	42,701,355	11,648,222	8,138,891

*For six months.

As for the second point, in which the bill of the executive power differs from the other bills, it is worth mentioning that it was considered necessary to have a complementary element for the proportional distribution of revenues among the provinces. What might such a basis be? It could be none other than output, as consumption is impossible to determine precisely, and, as mentioned earlier, this was ruled out. While it is true that all the inhabitants of the provinces are consumers—that is, contributors to internal revenues—it is also clear that productive states participate with taxable matter, as the source of those revenues. There is nothing fairer, therefore, than to return to these provinces a part of the yield of the tax on raw materials or manufactured items with which they contribute to the formation of tax revenues, aside from their own consumption.

In order to fix the percentage to be distributed according to each province's volume of production, we took as a means of estimation both the industrial and tax values, and especially the economic circumstances of the sugar, wine, alcohol, beer, and tobacco industries, as this is another right recognized for federal states.

On the basis of the taxes planned, 25 percent of the tax on the provinces' wine production would be $4,881,887; 10 percent of the tax on beer, $169,401; 2½ percent of the tax on alcohol, $654,651; 10 percent of the tax on tobacco, $421,310; and 50 percent of the tax on sugar, $3,075,447, making a total of $9,205,696.

Regarding the third point in which the executive power's bill differs from previous parliamentary initiatives, the reduction of protectionist customs duties is authorized proportionally to the internal taxation applied by the provinces to products of general consumption in the country.

This is a precautionary measure. Although all the provinces will certainly benefit from the distribution of internal revenues, it is not impossible that there will be some that will waive the rights afforded to them by law. Under this hypothesis, the executive power must ensure the integrity of its economic and tax policies, annulling through customs duty any attempts to upset the established balance.

There being no reason for the industries of the provinces that have abolished internal taxation to suffer for the survival of such taxes in others, Article 4 provides for the return to those provinces' producers of a part equivalent to the amount calculated on the highest internal provincial tax, multiplied by the amount of each industry's output released for consumption.

Let us suppose, for example, that Mendoza maintained its tax on wine of $2 per hectoliter and that San Juan abolished its own tax on the same product. The executive power, under Article 4 of the bill, would lower the customs duty on wine by $0.02, a reduction that would stimulate imports of this item, and with the amount collected, the wine producers of San Juan would be refunded a sum equivalent to their individual output volumes, multiplied by the highest internal provincial tax, which in this case would be $0.02 per liter.

This reduction of customs duties under such hypothetical circumstances is nothing new in our tax legislation. It is established by Laws 8,877 and 11,002, under which, when the market price of sugar reaches its highest ceiling price, or when provinces tax these products, the executive power is authorized to immediately lower the specific duty on foreign sugar in order to regulate the market, neutralizing the effects of speculation or monopoly in the first case, and the consequences of over-lapping taxation in the second.

The measure included in Article 5 of the bill is taken from the one submitted by National Deputy Dr. González Calderón, aiming effectively to strengthen the previous temporary provision.

In conclusion, the solution offered by the executive power's bill for the serious issue of double taxation is in line with the procedure followed in other federal countries, and even certain centralist countries. It does, however, have one original aspect: the complementary basis of production that, as mentioned above, was adopted for the share of productive states in the portion of the yield of a group of taxes that are levied on national industries.

This originality is due to the specific characteristics of this problem in our country. It has rightly been observed that there are no universal financial regulations but only national ones limited in their application. Indeed, if the population were taken as the sole basis for the distribution of revenues, as laid down in other bills, one would have made the mistake of putting productive and nonproductive states on an equal footing, considering only their capacity as consumers. Furthermore, there would have been a risk of harming the group of prosperous provinces and rewarding those that lack industries and resources.

After close study of the national economic situation and of the particular characteristics of our production, the conclusion was reached that it was necessary to complete the principal base chosen with a further accessory base that would consult the needs of regional industries and avoid harming the states of greatest industrial prosperity and highest tax capacity. Production was therefore included in the structure of the bill. Without such a complementary base, it would not have been possible to achieve the ideal of justice pursued in the reform, or to satisfy the reform's overarching purpose of economic development.

III

For the honorable gentlemen's reference, the taxation bill is included separately, with rates modified to obtain the annual revenues of 160 million pesos budgeted to make this distribution effective without impairing the national resources arising from these taxes.

The executive power acknowledges that the cooperation of the Republic's industry, production, and trade is needed in order to put into practice the government's project. In this respect, it has received expressions of opinion from various points of the country. It is welcome to note the fact as proof of the patriotic spirit encouraging the nation's economic forces, which are aware of the significance of the national problem we are attempting to resolve satisfactorily.

The favorable disposition of the trade unions affected by tax reform has facilitated the drafting of the executive power's financial plan. The new tax organization shall not in any area exceed the normal limits that production, industry, trade, and consumption can withstand.

IV

It is common knowledge that in the United States this type of tax (known there as *Internal Revenue*) belongs to the general state and its creation by individual states is banned. Here at home, the Supreme Court of Justice has found in favor of this doctrine, as can be seen in its rulings, volume 3, page 131, and volume 10, page 308, coinciding with the principle established by the Supreme Court of the United States in the cases *Lane County v. Oregon,* 7 Wall, 77; and *Railroad Company v. Peniston,* 18, Wall, 31.

The interpretation of Article 108 of the Constitution, which states that the provinces cannot exercise the power delegated to the nation, complementary to Article 104, by virtue of which the provinces maintain all the power not delegated to the federal government, lends weight to the healthy fiscal principle sacred to the North American Constitution and which has been violated in Argentina.

As it is not the purpose of the national government to discuss its constitutional powers with the federal states, confronted by an ever-worsening factual situation, it adopts a conciliatory policy designed to establish the uniform nationwide introduction of general taxes and eliminate today's fiscal multiplicity.

Corroborating this theory, Professor Gaston Jèze,[1] one of the few writers to have studied our tax system, has this to say:

> There are also very broad-based consumer taxes: these are taxes on items for everyday consumption, such as beverages, sugar, or tobacco.

---

1. Gaston Jèze (1869–1953), French jurist, wrote several treatises on public law, among them *Les principes généraux du droit administratif* (1904, 1925), and *Las finanzas públicas en la República Argentina* (1924). [E.N.]

These are consumed by the whole population. The fact that their consumption is general leads to the immediate consequence that taxation on items for general consumption has to be reserved for the nation. There must be no provincial tax on products of general consumption. Indeed, in every federal state, the Constitution formulates the rule of taxation equality for individuals and of the uniformity of taxes throughout the territory. Were each province to establish taxes on items of general consumption, the rule of taxation equality and uniformity would be violated. This is so self-evident that the federal Constitution of the United States of North America has expressly declared that consumer taxes have to be uniform throughout the country. There are other arguments: taxes on general consumer goods tend almost inevitably to be used not only as fiscal instruments, but as a means to protect local industry. In effect, the consumer tax is added to the price of the merchandise. Producers of taxed items then find themselves in an unfavorable situation in the market, as compared to producers of untaxed items. Let us suppose provincial taxes on general consumer goods, such as tobaccos, alcohol, or sugar. It will inevitably occur that one province will attempt to set differential tariffs according to the origin of the products. Merchandise produced in the province will be free of taxation to the detriment of products from neighboring provinces. This is a total and manifest violation of numerous constitutional principles in Argentina:

1. The abolition of internal customs duties;
2. The ban on provinces waging tariff wars;
3. National unity and solidarity.

In favor of this principle of national solidarity, and as long as a reform does not establish more precisely what tax the nation is exclusively entitled to and what tax originally belongs to the provinces, it is desirable, as a patriotic solution, to reach an agreement by virtue of which double taxation will be eliminated from the national territory, provided that both levies are concurrent and fall on one single taxable item.

The bill is a response to these aims and it is my honor to submit it to the honorable gentlemen.

God save the honorable gentlemen.

M. T. de Alvear
Víctor M. Molina

BILL

The Senate and House of Deputies, etc.

Article 1: From the enactment of the present law, internal taxes affecting general consumption will be collected exclusively by the nation.

Art. 2: Provinces not levying taxes in any form or designation on the same tax effects levied by national legislation shall be entitled to receive the part due to them of 25 percent of the total revenues from the existing national internal taxation and any created in the future, according to their population as established by the last national census.

Art. 3: Provinces producing raw materials or manufactured products made from them, within their territory and taxed solely under internal national taxation, shall be entitled to receive the following proportions of the rates of internal taxation raised, according to their output: 50 percent of the tax on sugar; 25 percent of that on wine; 10 percent of that on beer; 10 percent of that on processed tobacco; and 2½ percent of that on alcohol.

Art. 4: The executive power is authorized to lower customs duties proportionately to internal taxation applied by the provinces to products for general consumption within the Republic.

When the product is common to several provinces, the executive power, with the amount of customs revenues received under similar headings, shall return to the manufacturers of those provinces that have not established a duty a part equivalent to the amount represented by the highest internal tax set in another province or provinces, multiplied by each manufacturer's volume of output released for consumption.

Art. 5: Notwithstanding the provisions of the previous article, the executive power shall proceed to withdraw any subsidy that, for whatever reason, is received from the nation by those provinces maintaining local internal taxation, with the exception of subsidies intended to promote public education.

Art. 6: Report to the executive power.

Victor M. Molina

6

JOSÉ NICOLÁS MATIENZO
Civilization Is the Work of the People,
Not of the Rulers (1932) (Excerpts)

The subject I will deal briefly with tonight was suggested to me by unfair criticisms that, during the dictatorship that has just elapsed, have frequently been made regarding the ability of the people to manage their own life. They have been accused of natural ineptitude, which, according to their critics, must be made good by the wisdom of a dictator, be it a Mussolini, a Primo de Rivera, or a Porfirio Díaz.

These critics are silent about the way the dictator is elected, no doubt because they want him to appoint himself by sheer force or force preceded by guile. Nor can they envisage a way of putting an end to a dictatorship that is misguided or detrimental, perhaps because they cannot conceive of a dictator who commits mistakes or wrongs, or because they are predisposed to applaud unconditionally any of the dictator's acts without prior examination and whatever their consequences.

I have since my youth been against all dictatorship and any institution that impedes or obstructs the development of individual and social life in peace and freedom.

In 1880, in my student days, I attended a dissertation at the Faculty of Law in Buenos Aires by the most distinguished of our fellow Tucumanos, Juan Bautista Alberdi, then a representative for Tucumán Province, the only parliamentary post he held in his life, conferred on him at the time of his long exile begun in 1835 during the tyranny of Rosas and interrupted in 1879 under the presidency of Avellaneda. The dissertation was entitled "La omnipotencia del estado es la negación de la libertad."[1] Although I was already familiar with the *Bases,* his *Sistema económico y*

Original title: *La civilización es obra del pueblo y no de los gobernantes.* Source: *La civilización es obra del pueblo y no de los gobernantes* [Civilization is the work of the people, not of the rulers] (Buenos Aires: Anaconda, 1932).

1. [The omnipotence of the state is the negation of freedom]. See pp. 284–89. [E.N.]

rentístico,[2] *and Peregrinación de Luz del Día,*[3] works in which Alberdi expresses his radical liberalism and opposition to any government action that might obliterate or debilitate private initiative, his dissertation impressed me by the clarity and energy with which it showed the error of those who attribute to governments tutelary functions in social life to the detriment of freedom.

In particular, two quotations by British authors caught my attention: one by the great philosopher Herbert Spencer, the other by the father of political economy, Adam Smith.

I quote here the words of the former, which, as I subsequently found out, belonged to an article published in 1853:

> Private enterprise has cleared, drained, and fertilized the country, and built the towns — has excavated mines, laid out roads, dug canals, and embanked railways — has invented, and brought to perfection, ploughs, looms, steam-engines, printing-presses, and machines innumerable — has built our ships, our vast manufactories, our docks — has established banks, insurance societies, and the newspaper press — has covered the sea with lines of steam-vessels, and the land with electric telegraphs. Private enterprise has brought agriculture, manufactures, and commerce to their present height, and is now developing them with increasing rapidity.[4]

In the lengthier quotation by Adam Smith, he transcribes the following words taken from the *Wealth of Nations,* a work published in 1776.

> The uniform, constant, and uninterrupted effort of every man to better his condition, the principle from which public and national, as well as private opulence is originally derived, is frequently powerful enough to maintain the natural progress of things towards improvement, in spite both of the extravagance of government, and of the greatest errors of administration. Like the unknown principle

2. [The economic and revenue system of the Argentine Confederation according to its Constitution of 1853]. See pp. 177–215 in this volume. [E.N.]

3. [Daylight's pilgrimage]. Juan Bautista Alberdi, *Peregrinaje de Luz del Día, o viajes y aventuras de la verdad en el Nuevo Mundo,* 1871. [E.N.]

4. Herbert Spencer, "Over-Legislation," in *Essays: Scientific, Political and Speculative,* vol. 3, p. 234 (1891). [E.N.]

of animal life, it frequently restores health and vigour to the constitution, in spite not only of the disease, but of the absurd prescriptions of the doctor.[5]

Given this background, you will not be surprised if, in the lawsuit submitted to the court of history over the paternity of civilization, I take the side of the people against the government; that is to say that I contend that civilization is the work of private initiative among the members of the people, not of the official action of government agents.

Let us quickly look back at the genesis and development of civilization.

Man's dominion over nature began to be established in remote antiquity. Minerals, plants, animals gradually came under the power of primitive man, who made them serve his need for food and shelter. First, he enjoyed them in the state he found them: he drank water from springs, rivers, rain; ate the spontaneous fruit of plants; covered his nakedness with leaves; and protected himself against the weather in caves or beneath trees. Then, moving gradually through the prehistoric ages, which scholars term "stone," "bronze," and "iron," he learned in succession to use stones, horns, bones, branches, wood, and metal as tools. He began to domesticate animals: the dog, the goat, the chicken, etc., and used meat and milk as food, with which he invented butter- and cheese-making. He invented a way of making fire, and this invention — a marvel in savage peoples — had incalculable consequences for human progress thanks to its numerous applications in individual and collective life, the most ancient of which were the stove, the hearth, and the oven. No government intervened in these discoveries and inventions, or in any subsequent ones.

Primitive men also invented procedures to help nature produce the fruits they needed: they plowed and they planted.

They discovered the textile fibers of cotton, flax, and wool, and invented spinning and weaving, producing fabrics to clothe themselves and keep themselves warm.

They excavated mines and extracted copper, tin, and iron from them,

5. Adam Smith, "Of the Accumulation of Capital, or of Productive and Unproductive Labour," in *An Inquiry into the Nature and Causes of the Wealth of Nations,* vol. 1, ed. E. Cannan (London, 1904), book II, chap. III, p. 325. [E.N.]

and they alloyed the two first of these metals to make bronze. And moving a little further on in civilization, they built homes, first with branches, then with stones and wood.

Likewise, they laid up their observations of the phenomena of nature, forming a rudimentary science to be applied to the needs of life. Thus they gathered the first notions of astronomy, enabling them to predict the return of the right seasons for sowing and reaping.

But the most admirable creation in human evolution is, in my view, language. This means of communication between members of the same social group enables anyone to discover and use other people's experience and opinions, and, since being complemented by the invention of writing, has ensured the transmission of the thought of man up to the furthest posterity.

Language, from its primitive form as simple exclamation to its current form of sets of words capable of expressing the most complex ideas, has developed and continues to do so as a social product subject to the natural law of evolution and not to any precepts by the rulers of nations.

"That human language ever consisted solely of exclamations, and so was strictly homogeneous in respect of its parts of speech, we have no evidence," says Herbert Spencer.

> But that language can be traced down to a form in which nouns and verbs are its only elements, is an established fact. In the gradual multiplication of parts of speech out of these primary ones—in the differentiation of verbs into active and passive, of nouns into abstract and concrete—in the rise of distinctions of mood, tense, person, of number and case—in the formation of auxiliary verbs, of adjectives, adverbs, pronouns, prepositions, articles—in the divergence of those orders, genera, species, and varieties of parts of speech by which civilized races express minute modifications of meaning—we see a change from the homogeneous to the heterogeneous. And it may be remarked, in passing, that it is more especially in virtue of having carried this subdivision of function to a greater extent and completeness, that the English language is superior to all others.[6]

6. Herbert Spencer, "The Law of Evolution Continued," in *First Principles,* 2d ed. (London, 1867), part II, chap. XV, p. 1867. [E.N.]

The great American linguist, William Whitney, has pointed out that all language and all change within it are the work of the community of speakers, for all that this community cannot act unless by accepting or rejecting the initiative of its individual members. The work of each individual is done unpremeditatedly, for he alone set about using the common language in his own interests, serving his own purposes. But each is thus an actor in the great work of perpetuating and shaping common speech.

Every shift of vocabulary or grammatical form initiated by an individual needs to enter circulation and obtain general assent, which is earned only slowly, overcoming any resistance offered by previous usage or surprise caused by novelty.

"The speakers of language," said Whitney, "thus constitute a republic, or rather, a democracy, in which authority is conferred only by general suffrage and for due cause, and is exercised under constant supervision and control. Individuals are abundantly permitted to make additions to the common speech, if there be reason for it, and if, in their work, they respect the sense of the community."[7]

To these sage remarks of the American philologist I shall add that linguistic democracy admits of no dictatorships, oligarchies, or personal government of any kind. The most absolute of monarchs cannot impose on a people words or grammatical constructions it does not consent to. Nor can the most eminent orator or skilled speaker. The so-called language academies in Spain and France have never attempted to alter the grammatical rules established by usage or inserted words in their dictionaries that have not acquired the right of citizenship in common speech. The French Academy has not ventured to make a grammar. The Spanish Academy has, but has limited itself to methodically setting out the result of its researches into the actual way the Spanish language is spoken. England and the United States, proprietors of the most perfect language according to Spencer, have no language academy, no doubt because, being the most developed democracies on Earth, these two nations wish to leave the people free to exercise their linguistic sovereignty.

The grammar of a language is like a traditional constitution, gradu-

7. Cf. William D. Whitney, *Language and the Study of Language. Twelve Lectures on the Principles of Linguistic Science,* 5th ed. (New York, 1867). [E.N.]

ally amending itself according to how the conditions and circumstances of social life alter.

This is why no one can tell the precise moment a word or phrase stops being used and is replaced by other equivalents. We in America still use expressions no longer used in Spain, their country of origin. Terms that are still heard in the interior have ceased to be used in the Argentine coastal provinces. Such verbal differences reveal differences of opinion or taste, a diversity that promotes a feeling of social or political autonomy.

The action of the state never intervenes in these accidents in the life of language. There is no known law, decree, or ordinance that has determined or altered the parts of speech or the construction of the sentence, or that has regulated the agreement of adjectives and nouns or the conjugation of verbs. All this has been done by the linguistic democracy of which Whitney speaks. It is what has fashioned new languages out of the words of others. It is what has formed the group of Indo-European languages, which are used by the Earth's most civilized nations to express their ideas, knowledge, emotions, doubts, and acts of volition.

7

EMILIO A. CONI
Letter to a Martian (1933)

What is going on on Earth? This is the question the Martians are asking themselves about the strange rumors reaching them from our planet. Their powerful telescopes have revealed nothing new. Save for an uncommon screaming, there is nothing abnormal to be observed. No seismic catastrophe has convulsed the surface of the globe. The Sun still shines as it always does, transmitting its cosmic force to terrestrial life. No epidemic has decimated the population. Men seem no less intelligent than before. On the contrary, their dominion over the natural forces is more marked with each day that passes. So, what is going on on Earth?

From the screaming, the Martians have only been able to clearly make out the occasional word, half smothered by the hum of the masses: "poverty," "unemployment," as well as other words quite unknown to them, like "minimum wage" . . . "Saturday half holiday" . . . "planned economy" . . . "foreign exchange control" . . . "quotas" . . .

To satisfy my Martian friends' curiosity I shall explain to them in my capacity as an eyewitness just what is happening on Earth.

There are men on our planet whom we call "politicians" and to whom we alternately entrust the government, invariably giving them full power to deal with us as they please. Latterly, things had not been going exactly well, so some politicians, smarter than the others, invented a system they claim to be highly original, which they called "planned economy" and which, according to them, ought, in just a short time span, to bring happiness to all.

What is all this about "planned economy"? Quite straightforward, in fact: it means that the state—or rather the politicians—controls, regulates, establishes compulsory rules for all economic relations between

Original title: "Carta a un Marciano." Source: Emilio A. Coni, *El estado contra la nación* (Buenos Aires: Espasa-Calpe, 1939).

men, from the most important to the most trivial. To help the Martians better understand, I shall give them some national and international examples of planned economy.

If in one country wheat is worth very little because it is surplus to needs, then the government buys it at, say, five pesos, stores it for a year or two, and then sells it at three pesos. As is plain to see, the procedure could not be simpler or more practical, no matter how much farmers—eternal malcontents—claim that after application of the system they are worse off than before.

In other countries, there is, for example, a shortage of work opportunities because certain repulsive beings called "capitalists" refuse to work at a loss for the benefit of Humanity. So, what does the government do? Well, it sets a minimum wage, obliges people to sit idle on Saturdays after one in the afternoon, forces stores to close at eight in the evening, etc. "What?" I hear my Martian friend say. "If there is a shortage of work, how come the hands of those who provide it are tied?" This is precisely the formula's secret: the business of understanding this paradox is within reach only of the superior minds of politicians. Under this system the number of unemployed rises every day, of course, but the procedure must clearly be slow to produce results—a remedy in installments—and there is not the smallest doubt that we shall very soon see the final result.

In other nations, the state says that we individuals are useless wasters incapable of managing our own economy, and so it has invented certain organizations called "monopolies," in which the hateful profit of the capitalist is abolished. Sometimes the costs of these monopolies greatly outweigh the one-time capitalists' profits. But what does that matter if it benefits the community? Monopolies of gasoline, meatpacking, Portland cement, cereals, etc., are created, and the state sees to everything in order to keep down the price of consumer goods. This procedure must also be in installments, as no reductions have yet been seen, but they are sure not to be long in coming. Some wicked tongues who are never happy with what the state does say the procedure is older than walking upright, as, even at the time of the Ptolemies (300 B.C.), there were salt, wine, oil, and other monopolies.

We have certain parasites in our midst that are called "middlemen," on whom we have declared war with no quarter, no matter how hard they try to sweet-talk us, bringing milk, bread, meat, and other items to the doors of our houses. The better to deceive us, they even offer us credit facilities. When, from simple oversight, we omit to pay their bills for a month or two, or three, they play the generous soul and wait for us as long as it takes until . . . we move to another neighborhood, in which case they are still waiting. As it is easy to appreciate, all this is just sheer hypocrisy on the part of these middlemen.

So, the state, watching over us poor, defenseless little beings in the clutches of capitalists, intermediaries, etc., firmly intends to do away with them, an intention it trumpets at every turn in public statements, each more vigorous and promising than the last. Also, the state frets a great deal about prices: minimum prices to help producers; maximum prices to favor consumers. In spite of certain minor drawbacks, there is not the smallest doubt that the state will forge an agreement between producers and consumers, especially if it appeals to the supreme argument, the one that has so far proven truly to work magic whenever it has been used: human solidarity.

People's basic needs have the state's special attention. For instance, it has been observed that a carcass worth no more than seventy pesos at the slaughterhouse retails at more than two hundred at the butcher's. Of course, the intermediaries snap up the difference and endeavor to make us think that taxes, wages, rents, etc., put up the final price and they are earning less and less by the day. They also want us to believe that the public is extremely fussy and will accept only the choicest parts of the animal and that the mediocre parts must be lost or end up as tallow. But as there is nothing that withstands the power of "planned economy," a distinguished politician has had a brilliant idea: he is to present a bill whereby, from now on, all cows must have eight loins instead of the two they have had to date.

A great country, the same one that had that famous revolution for freedom, has discovered that there were sixty million farmers in Central Europe still living in the Middle Ages and that it sufficed to increase their buying power to save Western European manufacturing from rack and ruin. And it has set about the task of helping them, lending them money, revaluing their cereals, etc. And to help them it has closed the door on our own cereals and meat.

This, if truth be told, has somewhat annoyed us, for we Argentines used to spend a good deal of money in that country's great capital when we went there on vacation. And of course, as they were no longer buying our products from us, our compatriots had to return to their homeland

and stopped spending money on hotels, couturiers, and beaches. Wicked tongues say it would have been simpler to revalue our own rather than the Balkans' cereals, as that way we would go on spending our money over there—for, indeed, the hotels and couturiers of Lutetia have so far not seen any Balkan passengers; and neither have the beaches.

Other wagging tongues say this Balkan policy is due to the desire to isolate yet another Mediterranean power. But this cannot be true, as that country's politicians are of the first water in their wisdom and are descended from those who proclaimed freedom of trade more than a century ago.

In another country, vaster than all of Europe, the planned economy has been perfected to a tee and is said to be paradise on Earth. And that must be just what it is, because, to prevent others swiping their secret of happiness, this country has cut itself off utterly from the rest of the world and lets no one enter or leave. This somewhat oversteps the bounds of caution, since, to prevent having their formula stolen, this nation's government takes excessive measures with some of its inhabitants, who, tired of so much well-being, make a break for the border. It dissuades them from this with certain automatic equipment that rattles out three hundred arguments a minute.

Here in Argentina, we too are entering the system of planned economy. For instance, wages will no longer be paid according to work output—an antiquated procedure of the capitalist economy—but according to individual needs. We are to appoint a few officials to assess the value of every man's work in relation to his needs. If, for example, Pérez needs hot chocolate and toast instead of the commonplace breakfast, an official will set a wage for him so that he can afford it. And if Rodríguez, asking for the same exemption, is not entitled to it according to the official inspectors, he will have to lump it. The system could not be simpler to apply, even if we will have to appoint a few superofficials to set the wages of the subofficials. Anyhow, this will only serve to hasten our arrival to the port of happiness, for in the genuine planned economy we must all be state officials.

Everything is going just dandy over here, as everybody understands perfectly what the politicians are about with their planned economy, excepting a few unpleasant beings who call themselves "economists" and who, by means of History, which they call "the experience of the past," a few lined-up numbers, which they call "statistics," and a science they claim to be "psychology," try to convince us that the politicians are deceiving us. They come along with their stories about political economy being "the science of freedom" and tell us that, under the present system, which dates from 1789, Humanity has progressed more in one century than in the previous twenty. Happily, no one pays economists any heed, and the resounding bugling of social claims heralds for us the magnificent dawning of a Humanity governed not by the vile spirit of personal gain, but by the solidarity of all men working with an enthusiasm multiplied a hundredfold by love of their neighbors.

So, my Martian friend's legitimate curiosity is satisfied. Here on Earth, nothing is wrong. Everything is fine. The politicians are directing the economy.

8

MARCELO TORCUATO DE ALVEAR
Speech Delivered as Guest of Honor
of the British Chamber of Commerce
in the Argentine Republic at Lunch
in the Plaza Hotel, July 11, 1940

Mr. Ambassador, Mr. Minister, Mr. President of the British Chamber of Commerce,

Gentlemen:

I greatly appreciate the kind invitation extended to me to attend this meeting, affording me direct contact with the most representative personalities of the British community in my country, a community that has always been remarkable for its activities promoting the progress of our Republic and its steadfast, unrelenting action toward the consolidation of ever closer relations between the empire and Argentina.

The occasion also affords me an opportunity to express my feelings—not recent, but long-standing—of warmth and admiration for that empire, whose connections with Argentina date back to the early hours of our existence as a nation. Minister Rivadavia, with his pioneering spirit and a statesman's vision, realized that the European nation that might, in those days, feel most inclined to recognize the Argentine Republic was England. He accordingly sent a confidential envoy to the great foreign minister, George Canning, and chose a young general for the mission on whom victory had already smiled in the continent's war of emancipation. The meeting of Rivadavia's agent with Canning paved the way for the recognition of Argentine independence, which Canning, in reference to other American nations, later defined in these prophetic terms: "The New World has been called into existence, competing with the Old, which in time it will surpass."[1]

Original title: "Discurso en el Cámara de Comercio Británica en la República Argentina." Source: Marcelo T. de Alvear, *Argentinos! Acción cívica* (Buenos Aires: M. Gleizer, 1940).

1. Cf. George Canning, "Speech on the Affairs of Portugal in the House of Commons, 12 December 1826": "I called the New World into existence, to redress the balance of the Old." In Anthony Jay, ed., *The Oxford Dictionary of Political Quotations* (Oxford and

When one rereads the confidential agent's report to his government, describing his conversations with the foreign minister, the English statesman's knowledge about the development of events in this part of the continent, and of the personalities of its most distinguished men, is already apparent, and also the interest and sympathy with which he viewed the resurgence of America's new sovereign nations.

ENGLAND, OUR FIRST FRIEND

This was in the year 1824. Observe then, Gentlemen, the long standing of our Anglo-Argentine friendship and this never-recanted mutual cordiality; also that I have personal reasons to recall with special feelings these first steps to establish it. Even though it is well known, it is never amiss to repeat the fact that England was the first country, in the uncertain hours of our nationhood, when we were but a promise, to put her faith in our destiny and make available ample credit from the London banks for us to steady our first teetering steps on the march toward our ultimate organization. This steadying and recollection hold special meaning in these times. For, though luckily few, there are Argentines here—and I do not wish to speak about foreigners—who, mistaken or swayed by the wrong kind, speak passionately against England, guided—I am certain of it—not only by their inclination toward totalitarian countries, but by their manifest hostility to democracy, so vigorously entrenched in the English spirit that it created its splendid liberal institutions over long centuries of uninterrupted development toward the noblest forms of political civilization.

I still retain the clear impression that England and, above all, London made on me when I had the opportunity to visit them. A great city that gives the impression of an immense machine working away constantly and steadily without gathering speed or lurching suddenly; a machine that runs like a powerful engine, or rather, an immense heart whose throbbing is heard even in the farthest corner of that great empire that spans all the latitudes of the Earth. In that capital city even the smallest vibrations from the empire reverberate and from it spring the directives, guidelines, and ideals of England toward all its component regions.

New York: Oxford University Press, 1996), p. 75. Translated in the text as Alvear quoted it. [E.N.]

WHERE MAN'S RESPECT FOR HIS
FELLOW MAN IS A WAY OF LIFE

Could anyone possessing a liberal spirit, loving freedom and human individuality, not admire your country? There, the principle of man's respect for his fellow man has been taken to its highest point. Human beings are sacred in their integrity, their conscience, their thought; the laws guarantee individual personality. And that is why this great organism that brings together in its bosom men of such different races and mentalities, such diverse religions, has a spiritual and moral unity that nothing can destroy. At times of danger, when England calls on the citizens of its empire, they all respond with a solidarity not prompted by violence or despotism or force, but by the conviction and voluntary collaboration of free men paying homage to a free nation to which they feel bound and of which they are subjects by their own decision.

THIS IS ENGLAND

If a deeper, more precise vision of the unique structure of this great political, economic, and social organization that is the British Empire were needed, and in order to grasp the extraordinary spirit of that assemblage of peoples grouped under one roof in all its intensity, it would be enough to follow closely the debates of its representatives in its Parliament. It would be enough to see how sincerely and freely those representatives, even in the dramatic times of our present, do not hesitate to express their thoughts and opinions categorically and unreservedly, rebuking the government when they honestly deem it necessary, or expressing their confidence in it when they consider it right. This trait, this spiritual vigor in the English character, this pride in its political conscience make it abundantly clear how great the soul of this people is, which has left its mark on millions of men living in all climates of the Earth, and is, moreover, admirable proof of political and moral health, which cannot be conceived without the kind of freedom that is practiced in England.

And we need not recall England's eminence in the fields of pure science, thought, and art. Her great geniuses, even those born in times convulsed by hatred under harsh political circumstances, provide a wondrous example of her masterly creations, reflecting complex and definitive types from the world of feeling and passion. Nor need we mention her admirable perseverance and indomitable energy, which have brought her days of imperishable glory, to which she is adding the glory of these hours when she is performing the extraordinary feat of standing alone to defend world freedom and civilization.

This is England. I still recall when I paraded through the streets of London as president-elect. The public applauded the Argentine Republic in the person of its leader. I recall the welcome afforded me at the palace of the Lord Mayor, head of the Municipality whose autonomy can be cited as a paragon of communal liberties. And the warm words of welcome and affection for my country from this Lord Mayor still echo in my ears, and also those of the head of government, Mr. Lloyd George, an energetic politician who still today, after such a long career, fights on through good times or hard times for England with all his characteristic determination and fervor.

THE FIRST TRADE AGREEMENT WITH ARGENTINA

"Great Britain," said the Lord Mayor in his welcome speech, "was the first power to sign a trade agreement with the young Republic. British capital was the first to grasp Argentina's potential and to demonstrate confidence in its future." And speaking for the government, the prime minister, Mr. Lloyd George, said, in reference to my time as ambassador in France: "He found himself in Europe . . . and he saw something of the tempest, destruction, and devastation, and so, when he returns to Argentina, he will, deep in his heart, take with him a knowledge of and affection for this continent that has suffered so much damage and has been turned into a wreck. We can then be certain that he will judge our hardships leniently, in full knowledge of the facts. We welcome him because he has been called on to be president of a great country destined to become greater still." "We depend on Argentina," he added, "as she gives us our daily bread, and so we feel great affection for her and bless her at every meal."

AMERICA CANNOT LOOK ON UNMOVED

The wreck that the great minister referred to and of which I still retain a deep impression after all these years managed to restore its rigging in times of peace and continue on its happy voyage toward the broad horizons of culture and progress. But today the tempest again unleashes its fury on its sails. And therefore America cannot look on at this danger unmoved, for, from the very sources now being threatened, it has received and still receives many material goods, and the moral and intellectual lifeblood that animates its being and enables it to cultivate the ideals that secure its destiny.

IT IS OUR DUTY TO THINK FREELY

I am aware that speaking up vehemently in this day and age for the cause defended by Great Britain may appear to run counter to the neutral stance many Argentines have adopted. But I must say here, as I have on several occasions in the past, that, while I understand the neutral position officially adopted by my country's government, it is the duty of us citizens, who are not responsible for it, to think freely and voice our thoughts openly.

In this case, the silence of men who have weight in public opinion is worse than indifference: it is a culpable weakness. Fundamental precepts are at stake in the world—superior ideals, norms of civilization established only after a millennium of struggle against barbarism. And what we are, in fact, witnessing at this hour is the struggle of the spirit and the ideal of humanity, defending themselves against the dark, dread, primitive forces that are striving to subdue them. It is democracy itself that is in danger, not just in its political or economic dimensions, which are perhaps its least lofty and perfect expressions, but the entire democracy inspired by the humanist view of man placed within individual life and in his relations with his fellow men and the state.

OLD NATIONS AS VICTIMS OF PERSECUTION
AND MARTYRDOM

How then, while we have, in the essence of our lives, been constantly nourished on the higher emotions of the spirit and the soul, can we close our eyes and ears to this terrible struggle unleashed like a whirlwind of fire and blood on Europe? A struggle sparked not by mere territorial questions, nor by so-called *Lebensraum,* conjured up to justify aggression, but by a will to dominate in order to create a worldwide empire and, above all, to impose a new doctrine that will stop at nothing. We need only look at the example of those old nations victims now of persecution and martyrdom, like Austria, where the greatest musical geniuses of all time lived, worked, and died; Czechoslovakia, where the energy and industriousness of its sons and daughters, and the fierce pride of its highlanders mean that, when the eagerly awaited time for their vindication comes, they will find their faith intact to represent once again the sovereignty of their soil; Poland, for centuries the prey of its neighbors' ravenousness, a land of geniuses and admirable poets who have preserved the national features of their people against the odds, even when their political sovereignty was fading; and Norway and Denmark, the great Scandinavian democracies, paragons of civilization and welfare, whose sages and thinkers have incorporated discoveries and formulas to the cultural and scientific heritage of humanity that have earned unanimous admiration; then there is quiet Holland, a tireless worker also leading the onward march of world science with its laboratories, a beautiful corner of humanity pervaded by the memory of its wondrous artists, whose brushes have illuminated the world's most famed canvases; Belgium, which the industriousness, the spirit of initiative, and the heroism of its children have turned into a great nation in spite of its limited population and the small scale of its territory; and France the glorious, France the admirable, which gave its ancient homeland and the bodies of its children to the devastating swords of its implacable foes, and which, with Britain's heroic soldiers, is defending the most highly prized treasures of Christian and human civilization. On that wondrous land subjugated by the invader's sword stands Paris, a shining beacon of intelligence and the cradle of contemporary thought. But it matters not at all that a foreign flag flies over her buildings and monuments: it merely casts a temporary veil across the light from that immense torch of thought and art, whose radiance has left such deep and abiding traces on the world.

THE FATE OF THE WORLD IS AT STAKE
No matter what tragic predicament this people is subjected to, no matter if their territory is occupied and dismembered, they shall reemerge revitalized from their distress and misfortune, for the spirit and thought that breathe life into their sublime and eternal soul cannot perish. How can we remain indifferent when the fate of such great things is being attacked and put in jeopardy? Let us not imagine that, by remaining morally aloof from the conflict, we or the whole of America will not be affected by the consequences of the tragedy we are witnessing; to believe so would be worse than mental blindness; it would be sheer irresponsibility. How can we remain indifferent when, on reflecting on the potential consequences of the triumph of force over law, all we see is chaos in

the world, a civilization destroying itself, and can discern nothing that will replace it?

CREATORS OF DESTRUCTION AND MISERY

The oft-mentioned order and discipline within the borders of those totalitarian countries have so far served only to disqualify thought, to destroy creative geniuses, to banish the loftiest intelligences from their bosom. The only things that order has created are the powerful instruments of war that are the scourge of the world today and lay waste the treasures of culture, even in countries that have endeavored to remain aloof from the conflict. In other words, the only thing this order has so far created, seeing the misery and servitude of the peoples over which it reigns, is worldwide disorder.

Thus we see how the great geniuses of the sciences and the arts who emerged in those countries have left their borders behind to seek an environment where they can think and work in freedom, and they change nationality, rejecting that of their origins, in spite of the brilliance and renown their works have brought the country they are now leaving.

But let us remember, gentlemen, that when, as has happened on so many other occasions in the course of history, the name of today's conquerors, like so many in the past, has been wiped from human memory, the name of the great talents and benefactors who struggled and suffered to bring men a little more beauty, an instant of noble emotion, a moment of happiness, a day of peace, shall still fly with a renewed light over the bastions raised by the undying spirit. This has often been the only way an entire culture has been saved from oblivion and an entire epoch of human history has been lit up with the glow of eternity.

SOONER OR LATER JUSTICE AND RIGHT WILL PREVAIL

As a fervent admirer of what contemporary civilization holds to be noble and human, I feel the need to say here and now, in these dark days for the world, that I hope and passionately desire that the rule of freedom and of the high principles of culture, which are in danger of disappearing, should be successfully established once and for all through the courage and sacrifice of the great peoples fighting alongside your own. I desire it not only for you, but for my own country and the entire world.

History, besides, shows us that force cannot prevail over justice and law indefinitely. The nations fighting for freedom in this hour have with them the sympathy of all men on Earth. And upon the ideals they embody, the opinion they lead, the human energy these nations stand for, shall founder all the tactics of evil.

A DEFENDER OF AMERICAN IDEALS ON EUROPEAN SOIL
A great American president who speaks your language, President Roosevelt, despite being the leader of one of the world's greatest democracies that has kept neutral in this conflict, never omits, however, to draw attention—passionately and anxiously, every time he raises his voice from the platform bestowed on him by his function, and the vigor and radiance of his extraordinary personality—to the principles that form the essential basis of American ideals, which are the very ones your own country is now defending on European soil.

As for us Americans, our governments may be neutral. These countries may not be belligerent and may adopt an equidistant stance from the warring parties. But we citizens of America cannot be indifferent. For, if we were, we would be deserting this continent's purest, most beautiful tradition. And, were we Argentines to behave like this, we would have abandoned the postulates of freedom and justice that have guided our country in its international relations, and that have led it, in every case, to uphold those higher rules as cornerstones of our nationality.

WE MUST NOT BE CARELESS
The present tragedy in Europe, some results of which we are already seeing, shows us that, in the happiness of liberty, democracies sometimes neglect the measures needed to defend their regimes against the ever-watchful enemies lurking within their borders or clearly visible outside them, enemies who act without the restraints implied by the respect for human rights and justice enforced by the principles of political morality.

When history judges serenely the events of the present, it will determine responsibilities and pass the final judgment. Caught up as we are in the tempest, our sight clouded by the deep emotions stirred by its consequences, we cannot properly establish responsibility, nor could we do so impartially. But this must not prevent us profiting from this lesson to keep a vigilant eye on ourselves so as to reject the vices that may weaken our faith and our liberal, democratic system. For only under such a system can America and Argentina continue to fulfill their grand destinies and prevent prejudice, hatred, the desire for predominance, and disdain for the formulas of peaceful coexistence from taking hold in this conti-nent—evils that have led to the conflict in the old continent.

AMERICA: A HAVEN OF THOUGHT AND CIVILIZATION
United by one and the same American ideal, upholding the same laws and endeavoring, where possible, to find substitutes for the markets on the old continent that will be closed to our output, we can usher in a new era, one in which America will be a haven of thought and civilization to which the men of other countries will turn when persecuted in their own by the misery and despotism occasioned for its inhabitants by the situation in Europe.

And when I say "America," I also mean "the British Empire," ever since its most extensive Dominion,[2] which is now a great state, is a part of this continent and will therefore be subjected to the same contingen-cies as all the other nations in this hemisphere.

Nonetheless, our Argentine ideals will not give way. We must look after them zealously and defend them against attacks from abroad or those hatched in our own country. It will not be enough to add to our military defenses if they do not first and foremost serve to guarantee that, in the very heart of our country, the germs threatening our politi-cal and institutional organization shall not prosper.

WE ARE UNITED BY UNBREAKABLE BONDS OF FRIENDSHIP
In conclusion, I want to tell you what a pleasure it is to find myself at this meeting of free citizens from a free country, assembled here in my own, also free, country and keeping alive common desires that will make the bond of friendship with Argentina as unbreakable in the future as it has been in the past and is in the present.

Whatever difficulties there may be with your country, whatever issues may arise between Argentines and yourselves, I am sure we will solve them on a footing of absolute equality, always within the rules of international law, which are sacred for civilized countries and under which the given word and the respect originating from relations be-tween peoples are a solemn matter of national honor.

I have no intention of explaining you: the British character is too well

2. Canada. [E.N.]

known and easily recognizable. I am, therefore, familiar with your admirable spirit and I know that you are able to take the knocks serenely and recover from critical or adverse circumstances, whatever they may be. But I am not deceived by your attitude, apparently always phlegmatic and impassive, as I have also seen you on a day of victory and know what you are like deep in your heart. On that day I saw all classes of society come together as one in a collective delirium, women and children alike, old folk, stern-looking magistrates and lowly laborers, intellectuals and rough workers. Pouring onto the streets and squares of your metropolis, they cheered the empire and the great victory, and total strangers embraced.

ENGLAND'S VICTORY IS A VICTORY FOR HUMANKIND

As you will observe, I have my reasons for claiming not to be duped by your outward coldness. And I sincerely hope you will have further reason to abandon it and again experience those hours of elation, cheering a fresh victory—one not just for England, but for all humankind in its noblest aspect.

I would like, on this opportunity that you have offered me, to raise my glass in respectful homage to your great monarch and express my sincere wishes for his personal happiness, for the glory and prosperity of your empire, and for you citizens of England who dwell on Argentine soil to find in our laws and institutions, and the cordial manner of my fellow Argentines, a home fit for your lives and those of your children, under the protection of democracy and freedom.

Short Biographies

Juan Bautista Alberdi (1810–1884)
Born in Tucumán, Alberdi was a lawyer, writer, and jurisconsult, and a member of the May Association (1836–1837). He was exiled during the Rosas government. His economic, constitutional, and political writings were the main source for the drafters of the 1853 national Constitution. He was a diplomatic representative of the Argentine Confederation's government to Europe between 1854 and 1860, and subsequently lived in France until his death.

Leandro N. Alem (1842–1896)
Alem was born in Buenos Aires. He fought in the Confederation army at Cepeda (1859) and Pavón (1861), and performed outstandingly in the Paraguayan War (1865–1870). He was a legislator at both national and provincial levels. In 1880 he contested the federalization of Buenos Aires and led the armed uprisings of 1890 and 1893. He founded the Civic Union and later the Radical Civic Union.

Marcelo Torcuato de Alvear (1868–1942)
Alvear, a lawyer, was born in Buenos Aires. He was a national representative between 1912 and 1917, and ambassador to France and the League of Nations. He was president of the Republic between 1922 and 1928, and led the Radical Civic Union from 1931.

Nicolás Avellaneda (1837–1885)
A lawyer and writer, Avellaneda was born in Tucumán. He was a minister and legislator, and president of the Argentine Republic between 1874 and 1880. During his presidency, immigration and agriculture were encouraged and the first public land law opening the way for the settlement of farmers was approved.

Francisco Antonio Barroetaveña (1856–1933)
The lawyer and journalist Barroetaveña was born in Gualeguay in the province of Entre Ríos. He took part in the founding of the Civic Youth Union (1889) and the Civic Union (1890), and in the 1890 uprising, and was a national representative for the Radical Civic Union (1891).

Antonio Bermejo (1852–1929)
Bermejo, a jurisconsult, was born in Chivilcoy, Buenos Aires. He was a provincial representative, national senator, and minister. He took part in the 1890 up-

rising and, in 1903, was appointed to the Supreme Court of Justice, over which he presided until his death.

Emilio Angel Coni (1886–1943)

Born in Buenos Aires, Coni was an agronomist, historian, economist, writer, and university lecturer. He was also a consultant for the economic committee of the League of Nations.

Pedro Coronado (1830–1911)

Coronado was born in Buenos Aires Province and settled in Entre Ríos Province. He was a journalist, writer, provincial legislator, and national representative.

Esteban Echeverría (1805–1851)

A poet, essayist, and journalist, Echeverría was born in Buenos Aires. He was the intellectual leader of the "Generation of '37" and one of the founders of the May Association. He was exiled in Montevideo during the Rosas dictatorship.

Delfín Gallo (1845–1889)

Gallo, a lawyer and journalist, was born in Tucumán and was a national representative on several occasions. In the parliamentary debate on the education act, he championed the cause of secularism.

Pedro Goyena (1843–1892)

Goyena was born in Buenos Aires. A Catholic leader, legislator, law professor, journalist, and literary critic, he was a member of the provincial legislature and the national Congress. He led the opposition to secular legislation.

Juan Bautista Justo (1865–1928)

Born in Buenos Aires, Justo was a medical doctor, writer, economist, and university lecturer. He was a national representative and senator, and was the founder of the Socialist Party (1896).

José Nicolás Matienzo (1860–1936)

A jurist, political scientist, and historian, Matienzo was born in Tucumán. He was a professor and dean at the Faculty of Philosophy and Arts in Buenos Aires, and took part in the revolutionary activities of 1890 and 1893. He was a national and provincial senator, director of the Department of Labor (1907), and interior minister in the Alvear administration.

Bartolomé Mitre (1821–1906)

Mitre was born in Buenos Aires. After the Battle of Caseros (1852), he became governor of Buenos Aires Province (1860–1862). He led the armies of Buenos Aires to victory in the Battle of Pavón (1861), and was elected president of the Argentine Republic, a post he held from 1862 through 1868. After his term as president he became a diplomat and national legislator. He was a historian and founder of the newspaper *La Nación*. He was one of the leaders of the Civic Union and National Civic Union, and he took part in the revolution of 1890.

Víctor Molina (1861–1933)

Molina, a doctor of jurisprudence, was born in Buenos Aires. He was a national representative for the Radical Civic Union on several occasions. He was also treasury minister.

Julio Argentino Roca (1843–1914)

Roca was born in Tucumán. A career soldier, he took part in all the military conflicts of the day. He was a national minister, national legislator, and, on two occasions, president of the Republic (1880–1886 and 1898–1904). During his term of office, trade and immigration grew, there was a vast program of public works (railroads, ports, etc.), and public education was secularized.

Roque Sáenz Peña (1851–1914)

A lawyer, diplomat, and journalist, Sáenz Peña was born in Buenos Aires. Son of President Luis Sáenz Peña, he was president of the Republic from 1910 through 1914. The Electoral Act of 1912 establishing the mandatory, secret, male ballot was passed under his mandate.

Domingo Faustino Sarmiento (1811–1888)

Sarmiento was born in San Juan. A man of letters, essayist, historian, educator, and diplomat, he was exiled during the Rosas years. He was a national and provincial legislator, a delegate to the Constitutional Assembly, interior minister, governor of San Juan Province, and, from 1868 through 1874, President of the Argentine Republic. He fostered education and immigration throughout his public career.

Chronology

1776	Creation of the viceroyalty of the River Plate
1806–1807	English invasions
1808	Spanish Empire in dynastic crisis
1810	May Revolution; formation of the first autonomous governments (*gobiernos patrios*) in Buenos Aires
1813	Assembly of the Year XIII
1816	Proclamation of independence
1819	1819 Constitution
1820	Dissolution of central government
1824	Constituent Congress
1825–1828	War with Brazil
1826	Presidency of Bernardino Rivadavia
1827	Dissolution of the Constituent Congress
1829–1832	First governorship of Juan Manuel de Rosas in Buenos Aires
1831	The Federal Pact is signed
1835–1852	Second governorship of Juan Manuel de Rosas
1852	Battle of Caseros; fall of Rosas; the San Nicolás Agreement is signed
1853	Sanction of the national Constitution; Buenos Aires rejects it and separates from the Argentine Confederation
1854–1860	Presidency of Justo José de Urquiza
1859	Battle of Cepeda; victory of the Argentine Confederation over Buenos Aires
1861	Battle of Pavón; victory of Buenos Aires over the Argentine Confederation
1862–1868	Presidency of Bartolomé Mitre
1865–1870	War of the Triple Alliance
1868–1874	Presidency of Domingo Faustino Sarmiento
1874–1880	Presidency of Nicolás Avellaneda
1879–1880	Conquest of the desert
1880	Federalization of Buenos Aires
1880–1886	First presidency of Julio Argentino Roca
1886–1890	Presidency of Miguel Juárez Celman

WARS OF INDEPENDENCE;
CIVIL AND BORDER WARS

CIVIL AND BORDER WARS

NATIONAL
ORGANIZATION

SOCIAL AND
ECONOMIC
EXPANSION,
AND MASS
IMMIGRATION

1890	July Revolution; foundation of the Civic Union
1890–1892	Resignation of Miguel Juárez Celman and presidency of Carlos Pellegrini
1891	Foundation of the Radical Civic Union
1892–1895	Presidency of Luis Sáenz Peña
1895–1898	Resignation of Luis Sáenz Peña and presidency of José Evaristo Uriburu
1898–1904	Second presidency of Julio Argentino Roca
1904–1906	Presidency of Manuel Quintana
1906–1910	Death of Manuel Quintana and presidency of José Figueroa Alcorta
1910–1914	Presidency of Roque Sáenz Peña
1912	Electoral law reform (mandatory, male, secret ballot)
1914–1916	Death of Roque Sáenz Peña and presidency of Victorino de la Plaza
1916–1922	First presidency of Hipólito Yrigoyen (UCR)
1922–1928	Presidency of Marcelo T. de Alvear (UCR)
1928–1930	Second presidency of Hipólito Yrigoyen
1930	Coup d'état
1930–1932	De facto government of José Félix Uriburu
1932–1938	Presidency of Agustín P. Justo
1938–1940	Presidency of Roberto M. Ortiz
1940–1943	Death of R. Ortiz and presidency of Ramón S. Castillo
1943	Coup d'état

SOCIAL AND
ECONOMIC
EXPANSION,
AND MASS
IMMIGRATIO

Index

agriculture, xx, 200–201, 225–30, 236–44

Agüero, Julián Segundo de, 10–11, 260, 260n3

Alberdi, Juan Bautista: biographical information about, 427; centralization and, 155, 156–57; economics and, 179nn1–2, 179–81, 180nn3–4, 181n6; government omnipotence versus liberty and, xxiii–xxiv, 284–89; industrial school of economics and, 180n4, 180–81, 181n6; liberty and, xxiii–xxiv, 284–89, 338; mercantile school of political economics and, 179, 179nn1–2, 180; physiocratic school of economics and, 180, 180n3; on Rosas dictatorship compared with constitutionalism and liberty, x–xi, 3–26; socialist economics school and, 179–80

Alberdi, Juan Bautista, and Constitution of Argentina: agricultural production principles and guarantees, 200–201; basic needs and spirit of Constitution, 120–21; California constitution as model, 121–24, 123n3, 166; Chilean Constitution comparisons, 172–76; civic legislation, 149–53, 151n27, 160–63, 164–65; commercial production, 149–53, 150n26, 162–64, 201–4, 203n8; constitutional law in historical context, 116–19; constitutional principles, 153n28, 153–59; consumption in relation to economy, 177, 184–85, 190, 205, 209; economic production, xxx, 177, 183–215; education, 127–31, 198–99, 205–6, 362; emigrants from Europe as means of progress, 139–40, 142–47, 144n23, 148n25, 160–61, 362; equality in relation to economic production, 192–94; European civilization, 131n12, 131–37, 132n13, 133nn15–16; executive branch, 171–76; exemptions privileges for immigrants, 145; federalism, xvii–xix, 157–59; foreign policy, 139–40, 203, 203n8; immigration plans, 140; industrial economy, 207–9; inland immigration, 142–47, 144n23, 148n25; inland navigation, 146; intellectual property in relation to industrial production, 196, 199, 208; liberty, 160–61, 183, 188–92, 209–10, 210–15, 212; manufacturing industry, 204n9, 204–7; monarchy as interim government, 124–27; national unity, 167n30, 167–71; political organization, xv–xix, 115–76; property in relation to industrial production, 194–96, 213; railroads, 143–45; religious tolerance, xvi–xvii, 159–61; safety for individuals in relation to production, 196–98; suffrage and, 150, 183; unity, xvii–xix, 155, 156–57; U.S. Constitution as model, xviii–xix, 130–31, 131nn10–11; wealth distribution in relation to economy, 177–80, 182–85, 192; women, 130–31, 131nn10–11. *See also* Alberdi, Juan Bautista; Constitution of Argentina

Alem, Leandro N.: biographical information about, 427; education as important in Argentina and, xxii, 264–70; on federalism, xxii, 279–83; liberalism in relation to government opposition to liberalism and, xxv–xxvi, 314–18

Alvear, Marcelo Torcuato de: biographical information about, 15, 16n25, 427, 432; independence versus liberty and, 287–88; liberalism versus government and, 416; on reforms through amendments to Constitution of Argentina, xxix–xxx, 387–91; taxation laws reform and, xxx, 392–404

This book is set in Espinosa for the text type, with Klavika
Medium and Regular for the display. Klavika was designed by
Eric Olson in 2004. Espinosa was designed by Cristóbal Henestrosa
in 2010. The face is based on type used by Anonio de Espinosa,
a sixteenth-century Mexican printer. He is thought to have been
the first punch cutter in the Americas.

This book is printed on paper that is acid-free and meets the
requirements of the American National Standard for Permanence
of Paper for Printed Library Materials, z39.48-1992. ∞

Book design by Richard Hendel,
Chapel Hill, North Carolina

Typography by Tseng Information Systems, Inc.,
Durham, North Carolina

Printed and bound by Worzalla Publishing Company,
Stevens Point, Wisconsin